Evolving Principles of International Law

Queen Mary Studies in International Law

Edited by

Malgosia Fitzmaurice
Panos Merkouris
Phoebe Okowa

VOLUME 5

Evolving Principles of International Law

Studies in Honour of Karel C. Wellens

Edited by

Eva Rieter
Henri de Waele

MARTINUS NIJHOFF PUBLISHERS

LEIDEN • BOSTON
2012

This book is printed on acid-free paper.

Library of Congress Cataloging-in-Publication Data

Evolving principles of international law : studies in honour of Karel C.
Wellens / edited by Eva Rieter and Henri de Waele.
p. cm. -- (Queen Mary studies in international law, 1877-4822 ;
v. 5)
Includes bibliographical references and index.
ISBN 978-90-04-19226-3 (hardback : alk. paper)
1. International law. I. Wellens, Karel. II. Rieter, E. R. (Eva R.)
III. Waele, Henri Clemens Ferdinand Jozef Alexander de, 1979-
KZ3410.E93 2012
341--dc23

2011034627

ISSN 1877-4822
ISBN 978 90 04 19226 3

PRINTED BY DRUKKERIJ WILCO B.V. - AMERSFOORT, THE NETHERLANDS

CONTENTS

FOREWORD FROM THE GENERAL EDITOR OF THE SERIES

It is my great pleasure to be able to contribute to this celebration of the work of Professor Karel Wellens. Professor Wellens has had an illustrious and outstanding career, as a scholar and teacher of international law.

His expertise in international law places him in the ranks of the most highly regarded lawyers. His research and publications are characterised by an unusual breadth of topics. They include the law of international organisations, the theory of international law, and environmental law. His standing among international lawyers was confirmed by numerous invitations to speak and several memberships in learned societies, such as most notably his appointment as a Co-Rapporteur (with Professor Malcolm Shaw) of the International Law Association Committee on Accountability of International Organisations. He also served as a Chairman and a Member of the Advisory Committee on Public International Law to the Netherlands Minister of Foreign Affairs.

His research on accountability of international organisations gave rise to the publication of his outstanding monograph *Remedies Against International Organisations*.[1] This book includes in its chapters a thought-provoking analysis of several issues concerning remedies against international organisations. Wellens discussed a multitude of aspects of this issue in his study, such as the forms of potentially available remedies and who has access to them. He deals with several complex procedural aspects of remedial action against international organisations, i.e. issues such as the various types of potential claimants (states, staff members, private claimants, and NGOs asserting representing the interests of particular groups). Interestingly, Wellens also analyses the role of the International Court of Justice in a largely defunct review system. Further, he deals with the substantive outcome of remedial action against international organisations, He investigates the different available remedies, such as declaratory and pecuniary judgments, *ex gratia* payments, non-pecuniary remedies, punitive damages and legal costs (including costs and attorney's fees). Wellens submits certain proposals for alternative remedial action, i.e. pre-remedial action, non-legal alternative remedial action and amendment of existing legal remedies. In this context as well, he explicitly assesses the role of the International Court of Justice.

One of the reviews of his book fully evidences the notable contribution it made to a better understanding and development of international law. The author of the review states as follows: "Wellens is to be commended for his

[1] Cambridge: Cambridge University Press 2002.

original and thought-provoking rearrangement of traditional categories. Too rigid an intellectual system may sometimes become a straightjacket for analysis; Wellens manages to avoid this problem by presenting new combinations and cross-references between the questions that he addresses in his study (…). Wellens deserves particular credit for bringing into concrete focus the often very abstract debate on the accountability of international organisations. He squarely addresses jurisdictional immunity, lack of standing before the ICJ, and the far-reaching absence of internal judicial review within international organisations in general. It is to be hoped that this book will contribute to making international lawyers and policy makers aware of existing deficits with regard to the accountability of international organisations."[2]

An example of another study of Wellens that made a considerable impact on the expansion of knowledge of international law is *Resolutions and Statements of the United Nations Security Council (1946–1989) – A Thematic Guide.*[3] As one reviewer observed, with this book, Wellens "has provided international lawyers with a unique and extremely useful tool to comprehend the way the Security Council has handled the international conflicts and threats to peace".[4] Professor Wellens provided introductory notes for resolutions, including historic explanation of the situation that triggered the Security Council's action. The book also offers the registered number of the Council's meetings, which enables identification of minutes and reports of those meetings. There are other very useful details provided such as, e.g., how each and every resolution was adopted. This led the reviewer to remark that "Professor Wellens should be highly praised for this classification of all of the Security Council's resolutions and statements in such as skilful and systematic manner. The international lawyer's job has become a lot easier after the appearance of this book".[5]

His continuing research interest in the Security Council and general international law, can also be found in the essay 'The Practice of the United Nations Security Council with regard to Treaties and (Other) Agreements Governed by International Law'.[6] In this essay, Wellens made a profound study of various Security Council practices regarding treaties and other agreements. He concluded as follows: "The above picture of Security Council practice with regard to treaties illustrates the wide range of Council involvement. The Council has called for and monitored negotiations. Appeals to conclude a treaty have been accompanied by the (potential) imposition of coercive measures. The Council

---

[2] August Reinisch, (2003) 97 *The American Journal of International Law*, p. 466.
[3] The Hague: T.M.C. Asser Institute / Martinus Nijhoff Publishers 1990.
[4] Frederik Harhoff, 59 (1990) *Nordic Journal of International Law*, p. 329.
[5] Ibid., p. 330.
[6] In: Matthew Craven and Malgosia Fitzmaurice (eds.), *Interrogating the Treaty. Essays in the Contemporary Law of Treaties*, Nijmegen: Wolf Legal Publishers 2005, p. 139–175.

has, admittedly to varying degrees, actively determined the substantive content of treaties to be concluded. Sometimes treaties were subject to Council approval. In monitoring treaty implementation the Council has not hesitated to set aside the *res inter alios acta* rule" (p. 172). He added: "The overall Council approach towards treaties and agreements, although reflecting a rich palette of modalities, has maintained its instrumental character, as it is necessarily incidental and subordinated to the exercise of its primary responsibility and restore international peace and security." (p. 173)

Another remarkable book is his *Economic Conflicts and Disputes before the World Court (1922–1995), A Functional Analysis.*[7] According to the editor of the series in which it was published Professor Wellens offered "remarkable new insights" in this volume, and his analysis also supported "the general observation that the differences between adjudication and arbitration, the distinction of which was relatively clear in the past, are in fact diminishing, as can be noted for example, by the rise of the use of the Chamber procedure of the International Court of Justice (…)".[8]

Recently, with the essay 'Revisiting Solidarity as a (Re-)Emerging Constitutional Principle: Some Further reflections', Wellens made an important contribution to the development of the theory of international law.[9] This essay deals with many complex issues, such as: the rediscovery of the ethical and religious foundations of public international law; the distinction between the international society and the international community; and the constitutional role of the principle of solidarity in the international legal order. Another outstanding publication in the realm of the theory of international law that has to be singled out is the monograph, co-written with Professor Teruo Komori, *Public Interest Rules in International Law: Towards Effective Implementation.*[10]

Professor Wellens served for many years as a member of the Editorial Board and the Editor in Chief of the *Netherlands Yearbook of International Law*. It was under his Editorship that the *Yearbook* published a seminal volume (co-edited with L.A. Barnhoorn) on *Diversity in Secondary Rules and the Utility of International Law* in 1995. The essays published in this Yearbook still feature in many publications and the *Yearbook* itself triggered many comments and proved to be one of the most challenging and thought-provoking issues.[11]

---

[7] The Hague: Kluwer Law International 1996.

[8] Peter Malanczuk, 'Note by the Series Editor', ibid.

[9] In: Rüdiger Wolfrum and Chie Koijma (eds.), *Solidarity: A Structural Principle of International Law*, Heidelberg-Berlin-New York: Springer 2010, p. 3–38.

[10] Farnham: Ashgate 2009.

[11] See e.g. Axel Marschik 'Too Much Order? The Impact of Special Secondary Norms on the Unity and the Efficacy of the International Legal System', (1998) 9 *European Journal of International Law*, p. 212–239.

Wellens wrote an introductory essay in this volume, in which, apart from a description of the method adopted in the *Yearbook*, he presented many very innovative thoughts on the effect of subsystems on the unity and efficacy of international law, including their possible detrimental effects on international law. The *Yearbook*, although in fact very controversial, gained many positive reviews. One of these featured a substantive discussion (and also criticism) of the presentation of certain issues contained in this volume, with the reviewer stating that "[a]ny evaluation of the book under review must first stress that the authors' investigation of the diversity of secondary norms is a singular achievement in the debate on the relationship between subsystems of international law and the general legal systems. Legal literature knows no other study of secondary norms that covers such a broad range of subsystems (...). This book demonstrates the importance of studying a variety of secondary norms and analyses a multitude of subsystems".[12]

The issues of diversity in secondary rules, unity of international law and fragmentation of international law have occupied an important role in Professor Wellens' research, also in relation to international organisations, as documented by e.g. his article 'Fragmentation of International Law and Establishing of accountability Regime for International Organisations: the Role of the Judiciary in Closing the Gap'.[13] In this contribution, he advocated an amendment of Article 34 of the ICJ's Statute in order to allow international organisations to become the parties before the Court, which "would undoubtedly constitute a major step towards the envisaged role for the international judiciary".[14] He also supported the more extensive involvement of domestic courts, which "would also enhance the role of the judiciary in closing the 'accountability gap' of international organisations".[15]

The breadth of the interests of Professor Wellens is well documented by his essay 'The Court's Judgment in the Case Concerning the Gabcikovo-Nagymaros Project (Hungary/Slovakia): Some Preliminary Reflections'.[16] Despite the fairly modest title of the essay it is an in-depth analysis of the legal questions in the *Gabčíkovo-Nagymaros* case, such as the law of treaties, the law of state responsibility, and international environmental law. Wellens was very correct in noting that the "[International Court of Justice] did not take the opportunity to present its integrated view on the different branches of international law and thus failed to make a substantial contribution to the conceptual structure of the system of international law",[17] and that "[t]he rigid separation

[12] Ibid., p. 236.
[13] (2004) 25 *Michigan Journal of International Law*, p. 1–23.
[14] Ibid., p. 23.
[15] Ibid.
[16] In: Karel Wellens (ed.), *International Law: Theory and Practice. Essays in Honour of Eric Suy*, The Hague: Martinus Nijhoff 1998, p. 765–799.
[17] Ibid., p. 797.

of the different branches followed by the Court could raise the question of whether the fairness of the overall result of the Court's findings had become jeopardized".[18] The incisive legal reasoning of Professor Wellens is also visible in his essay on 'Transboundary Environmental Impact Disputes before the International Court. The Case Concerning Pulp Mills on the River Uruguay (Argentina v. Uruguay): Some Preliminary Remarks'.[19] Wellens presents an in-depth analysis of the relevant documents, as well as observations on the environmental aspects of the case and its general international law issues. For instance, he comments on the argument of *fumus boni juris*, an issue that is not frequently raised, but is of enormous importance, as particularly evident from the judgment of the International Court of Justice in *LaGrand*.[20]

Professor Karel Wellens has greatly contributed to the clarification and development of many complex issues of international law. He is one of the true intellectuals who have dealt with the most challenging problems. In his research, Professor Wellens has been a real generalist, exhibiting an outstanding knowledge of classical international law, such as state responsibility, international courts and tribunals and the law of international organisations. He has always striven for perfection in his writings, and as one of the very few managed to achieve it. It has been my great privilege to have been his friend for many years, and to have profited from his excellent and ever-lasting input in international law.

Malgosia Fitzmaurice

[18] Ibid.

[19] In: Roger Brakelé et al. (eds.), *Een Kwestie van Grensoverschrijding, Liber Amicorum P.E.L. Jansen,* Nijmegen: Wolf Legal Publishers 2009, p. 369–396.

[20] *Germany v. United States,* ICJ Reports 2001, p. 466.

BIOGRAPHY OF KAREL WELLENS

Born in Antwerp, 20 January 1947

Legal Education and Degrees

July 1973	Licentiate in Law, Law Faculty, Catholic University of Leuven, Belgium (*summa cum laude*)
January 1977	Dr. iur., Law Faculty, University of Antwerp, Belgium (*magna cum laude*) • Dissertation title: *Handvest van Economische Rechten en Plichten van Staten: Resolutie 3281 (XXIX) [The Charter of Economic Rights and Duties of States: UN General Assembly Resolution 3281 (XXIX)]* (mimeographed version 1123 pages)

Academic Career

1973–1976	Junior Lecturer in Administrative Law, Law Faculty, University of Antwerp, Belgium
1976–1979	Junior Lecturer in International Law, Law Faculty, University of Antwerp, Belgium
1980–1982	Senior Lecturer in European Law, Law Faculty, Catholic University of Nijmegen, The Netherlands
1982–2011	Professor of International Law and the Law of International Organisations, Law Faculty, University of Nijmegen, The Netherlands
1988–1990	Visiting Professor of International Development Law, Law Faculty, University of Antwerp, Belgium
1997–1998	Professeur invité at the Faculty of Law, Political and Social Sciences of the University of Paris XIII (France)
Since 2000	Life Member of Clare Hall, University of Cambridge

Guest lecturer at various universities and academic institutions in the Netherlands, the United Kingdom, Spain, Sweden, Croatia, Poland, Greece and Japan.

Contributions to various international conferences in Belgium, the Netherlands, the United Kingdom, Norway, Spain, the United States and Japan.

Co-organisor of various international conferences in The Netherlands, Belgium, Spain and Japan.

Editorships

1988–1998	Member of the Editorial Board of the Netherlands Yearbook of International Law
1990–1998	General Editor of the Netherlands Yearbook of International Law
1996–1999	Member of the Board of Recommendation of the Leiden Journal of International Law
1997–2002	Editor of the International Encyclopaedia of Laws, Intergovernmental Organisations (with M. Eyskens)
2001–Present	Member of the Advisory Board of Non-State Actors and International Law (now The International Community Law Review)

Advisory Services

1986–1997	Member of the Advisory Committee on Public International Law to the Dutch Minister of Foreign Affairs
1999	Member of the Dutch Preparatory Committee for the Centennial of the first International Peace Conference held in The Hague
1998–2006	Member and Chairman of the Advisory Committee on Public International Law to the Dutch Minister of Foreign Affairs

Membership of Learned Societies

- Co-Rapporteur of the International Law Association Committee on Accountability of and towards International Organisations (with Malcolm Shaw, until August 2004)
- Member of the International Law Association
- Member of the French Society of International Law
- Member of the Dutch Society of International Law
- Member of the British Institute of International and Comparative Law
- Member of the Dutch Association for the United Nations
- Member of the Dutch Society of European Law (until 2000)
- Member of the Belgian Society of International Law (until 1999)

Other Functions

1980–1984	Coordinator Junior Researchers Training Programme in International Law, T.M.C. Asser Institute, The Hague
1980–1984	Member of the European Law Commission, T.M.C. Asser Institute, The Hague
1986–1987	Coordinator Junior Researchers Training Programme in International Law, T.M.C. Asser Institute, The Hague
1983–Present	Member of the Scientific Council and of the Public International Law Commission, T.M.C. Asser Instititute, The Hague

BIBLIOGRAPHY OF KAREL WELLENS

Monographs

- *Internationale reglementering van transnationale ondernemingen* [*International Regulation of Transnational Corporations*], CED Samson, Brussels, 1979, 333 pp.
- *Volkenrecht '83* [*International Law '83*], Kluwer, Deventer, 1983, 24 pp. (inaugural address)
- *Enige volkenrechtelijke vragen rond de Nederlandse Taalunie* [*Some International Legal Problems Surrounding the Dutch Language Union*], Stichting Bibliographia Neerlandica, Den Haag, 1987, 317 pp. (with N. Sybesma-Knol)
- *De Nederlandse Taalunie en de spelling: enige juridische beschouwingen* [*Some International Law Issues Regarding the Dutch Language Union and Spelling*], Stichting Bibliographia Neerlandia, Den Haag, 1989, 85 pp.
- *Resolutions and Statements of the United Nations Security Council (1946–1989). A Thematic Guide*, Martinus Nijhoff Publishers, The Hague, London, Boston, 1990, 691 pp.
- *Resolutions and Statements of the United Nations Security Council (1946–1992). A Thematic Guide*, Martinus Nijhoff Publishers, The Hague, London, Boston, Second enlarged edition, 1993, 963 pp.
- *Résolutions et Déclarations du Conseil de Sécurité (1946–1992) Recueil thématique*, Centre de Droit International de l'Université de Paris XIII, Bruylant Bruxelles, 1993, 991 pp.
- *Economic Conflicts and Disputes before the World Court (1922–1995). A Functional Analysis*, Kluwer Law International, The Hague, London, Boston, 1996, 318 pp
- *Resolutions and Statements of the United Nations Security Council (1946–2000). A Thematic Guide*, Kluwer Law International, The Hague, London, Boston, Third Edition, 2002, 193 pp.
- *Remedies against International Organisations*, Cambridge University Press, Cambridge, 2002, 295 pp.

Edited Volumes

- *Peace and Security, Justice and Development. Report of a Congress held on the Occasion of 40 years United Nations*, The Hague, 1985, 99 pp.
- *Diversity in Secondary Rules and the Unity of International Law*, Martinus Nijhoff Publishers, The Hague, London, Boston, 1995, 365 pp. (with L. Barnhoorn)

- *International Law: Theory and Practice. Essays in Honour of Eric Suy*, Kluwer Law International, The Hague, London, Boston, 1998, 800 pp.
- *L'influence des sources sur l'unité et la fragmentation du droit international, Travaux du sémonaire tenu à Palma, les 20–21 mai 2005*, Bruylant, Bruxelles, 2006, 300 pp. (with R. Huesa Vinaixa).
- *Public Interest Rules of International Law: Towards Effective Implementation*, Ashgate, Farnham, 2010, 510 pages (with T. Komori)

Book Chapters

- 'International Law and the New International Economic Order', in *Xth Congress of Comparative Law*, Budapest, 1978, Bruylant, Bruxelles, 1978, pp. 349–375 (with B. De Schutter)
- 'The United Nations: 40 Years On', in K. Wellens, (Ed.), *Peace and Security: Justice and Development. Report of a Congress held on the Occasion of 40 Years United Nations*, The Hague, 1985, pp. 81–99
- 'Apartheid, an International Crime', in L. Heydte et al. (Eds.), *Begrensde Vrij-heid. Opstellen over mensenrechten aangeboden aan Professor D. Scheltens*, Tjeenk Willink, Zwolle, 1989, pp. 288–311
- 'La jurisprudence de la Cour Internationale de Justice et la Protection des Droits de l'Homme', Colloque de Poitiers, *L'incidence de la jurisprudence sur la protection des droits de l' homme*, Presses Universitaires de France, 1992, pp. 42–82
- 'Reflections on Some Recent Incidental Proceedings before the International Court of Justice', in N. Schrijver and E. Denters (Eds.), *Reflections on International Law from the Low Countries in Honour of Paul de Waart*, Kluwer Law International, The Hague, Boston, London, 1998, pp. 417–441
- 'The Court's Judgment in the Case concerning the Gabcikovo-Nagymaros Project (Hungary/Slovakia): Some Preliminary Reflections', in K. Wellens (Ed.), *International Law: Theory and Practice. Essays in Honour of Eric Suy*, Kluwer Law International, The Hague, Boston, London, 1998, pp. 765–799
- 'The Primary Model Rules of Accountability of International Organisations: the Principles and Rules governing their Conduct or the Yardsticks for their Accountability', in N. Blokker and H. Schermers (Eds.), *Proliferation of International Organisations*, Kluwer Law International, The Hague, Boston, London, 2001, pp. 433–470.
- 'Visits by Security Council Missions to Conflict Areas: a Legal Postcard', in A. Giardina and F. Lattanzi (Eds.), *Essays in Honour of Gaetano Arangio-Ruiz*, Editoriale Scientifica, Napoli, 2004, pp. 1793–1816
- 'Final Report on Accountability of International Organisations' (with Malcolm Shaw), in International Law Association, *Report of the 71st Conference held in Berlin*, London, 2004, pp. 164–234

- 'Solidarity as a Constitutional Principle: its Expanding Role and Inherent Limitations', in R.St.J. Macdonald and D.M. Johnston (Eds.), *Towards World Constitutionalism. Issues in the Legal Order of the World Community*, Martinus Nijhoff Publishers, Leiden, Boston, 2005, pp. 775–807
- 'The Practice of the United Nations Security Council with Regard to Treaties and (Other) Agreements Governed by International Law', in M. Craven and M. Fitzmaurice (Eds.), *Interrogating the Treaty: Essays in the Contemporary Law of Treaties*, Wolf Legal Publishers, Nijmegen, 2005, pp. 134–152
- 'Quelques réflexions d'introduction', in R. Huesa Vinaixa and K. Wellens (Eds.), *L'influence des sources sur l'unité et la fragmentation du droit international. Travaux du séminaire tenu à Palma les 20–21 mai 2005*, Bruylant, Bruxelles, 2006, pp. 1–21
- 'Observations finales', in R. Huesa Vinaixa and K. Wellens (Eds.), *L'influence des sources sur l'unité et la fragmentation du droit international. Travaux du séminaire tenu à Palma les 20–21 mai 2005*, Bruylant, Bruxelles, 2006, pp. 277–282
- 'L'autorité des prononcés de la Cour Internationale de Justice', in Nicolas Angelet et al. (Eds.), *Droit du pouvoir, pouvoir du droit. Mélanges offerts à Jean Salmon*, Bruylant, Bruxelles, 2007, pp. 729–781
- 'General Observations', in T. Komori and K.C. Wellens (Eds.), *Public Interest Rules of International Law. Towards Effective Implementation*, Ashgate, Farnham, pp. 15–52
- 'Concluding Remarks', in T. Komori and K.C. Wellens (Eds.), *Public Interest Rules of International Law. Towards Effective Implementation*, Ashgate, Farnham, pp. 459–479
- 'Transboundary Environmental Impact Disputes before the International Court of Justice: the Case concerning Pulp Mills on the River Uruguay (Argentina v. Uruguay); Some Preliminary Remarks', in Roger Brakelé et al. (Eds.), *Een Kwestie van Grensoverschrijding. Liber Amicorum P.E.L. Jansen*, Wolf Legal Publishers, Nijmegen, 2009, pp. 369–396.
- 'Revisiting Solidarity as a (Re-)Emerging Constitutional Principle: Some Further Reflections', in R. Wolfrum and C. Kojima (Eds.), *Solidarity: A Structural Principle of International Law*, Springer, Heidelberg-Berlin-New York, 2010, pp. 3–14

Articles in International Law Journals

- 'Enige problemen in verband met de uitoefening van het recht op nationalisatie' [Some Problems in Connection with the Exercise of the Right to Nationalisation], *Belgian Review of International Law*, 1977, pp. 30–110
- 'Transnational Corporations: UN Involvement Towards a Code of Conduct', *German Yearbook of International Law*, 1978, pp. 442–461

- 'Codificatie en voortschrijdende ontwikkeling van internationaal economisch recht' [Codification and Progressive Development of International Economic Law], *Studia Diplomatica* 1978, pp. 401–435
- 'Les Sociétés Transnationales et les Pratiques de corruption', *Revue de Droit International, des Sciences Diplomatiques et Politiques*, 1979, pp. 1–44
- 'Recent Developments Towards a UN Code of Conduct', *Studia Diplomatica*, 1981, pp. 685–708
- 'The Second Lomé Convention: Some Aspects of its First Year of Application', *European Law Review*, 1982, pp. 255–280, pp. 369–389, pp. 477–491
- 'Towards a Review of the Multilateral Treaty-Making Process', *Revue de Droit International, des Sciences Diplomatiques et Politiques*, 1984, pp. 50–74, pp. 141–167
- 'Deployment of Cruise Missiles in Europe: The Legal Battle in the Federal Republic of Germany, Belgium and the Netherlands', *The Netherlands Yearbook of International Law*, 1987, pp. 145–228 (with P.J. Kuijper)
- 'Soft Law in European Community Law', *European Law Review*, 1989, pp. 267–321 (with G. Borchardt)
- 'Diversity in Secondary Rules and the Unity of International Law: Some Reflections on Current Trends', *Netherlands Yearbook of International Law*, 1994, pp. 3–37
- 'ILA Committee on Accountability of International Organisations', *International Law Forum*, 1999, pp. 107–109
- 'Accountability of International Organizations: Some Salient Features', *American Society of International Law, Proceedings of the 97th Annual Meeting*, 2003, pp. 241–245
- 'The UN Security Council and New Threats to the Peace: Back to the Future', *Journal of Conflict and Security Law*, 2003, pp. 15–70
- 'The Practice of the UN Security Council with Regard to Treaties and (other) Agreements governed by International Law', *Colombian Journal of International Law*, 2003, pp. 11–70
- 'Fragmentation of International Law and Establishing an Accountability Regime for International Organisations: The Role of the Judiciary in Closing the Gap', *Michigan Journal of International Law*, 2004, pp. 1159–1181.

Articles in Other Law Journals

- 'Bouwstenen voor een nieuwe internationale economische orde?' [Building Blocks for a New International Economic Order?], *Jura Falconis*, 1974–1975, pp. 479–507 (in Dutch)
- 'Het Handvest van Economische Rechten en Plichten van Staten. Enkele algemene aspecten van zijn totstandkomingsgeschiedenis' [The Charter of Economic Rights and Duties of States. Some Main Features of its Drafting History], *Rechtskundig Weekblad*, 1977–1978, p. 801–826 (in Dutch)

- 'Enige juridische gedachten over de gebeurtenissen in Shaba (Zaïre)' [Some Legal Thoughts on the Events in Shaba (Zaire)], *Rechtskundig Weekblad*, 1977–1978, p. 2735–2744 (in Dutch)
- 'Het Handvest van Economische Rechten en Plichten van Staten: juridische aard en reikwijdte' [The Charter of Economic Rights and Duties of States: Its Legal Nature and Scope], *Jura Falconis*, 1977–1978, pp. 277–291
- 'Enige opmerkingen over titel IV van de Tweede Lomé Conventie' [Some Remarks on Title IV of the Second Lomé Convention], *Nederlands Juristenblad*, 1981, pp. 85–98
- 'Soft Law in het Europees Gemeenschapsrecht' [Soft Law in European Community Law], *Sociaal-Economische Wetgeving*, 1987, pp. 663–727 (with G. Borchardt)
- 'Humanitaire hulp aan oorlogsslachtoffers: enige juridische beschouwingen' [Humanitarian Assistance to Victims of War: Some Legal Thoughts], *Rechtskundig Weekblad*, 1993–1994, pp. 417–429, pp. 449–458
- 'Internationale organisaties: verantwoordelijk voor (on)verantwoordelijk gedrag?' [International Organisations: Reponsible for (Ir)responsible Conduct?], *VN Forum*, 1997, pp. 36–41
- 'Internationale organisaties: verantwoordelijk voor (on)verantwoordelijk gedrag?' [International Organisations: Reponsible for (Ir)responsible Conduct?], *VN-Berichten*, 1997, pp. 59–68
- 'Is het water tussen België en Nederland niet diep genoeg? Volkenrechtelijke aspecten van de verdieping van de Schelde' [Is the Water between Belgium and The Netherlands Not Deep Enough? International Legal Aspects of the Deepening of the River Scheldt], *Rechtskundig Weekblad*, 1999, pp. 553–559 (with E. Suy)
- 'Het Advies van het Internationaal Gerechtshof over de onafhankelijkheidsverklaring van Kosovo' [The Advisory Opinion of the International Court of Justice on Kosovo's Declaration of Independence], *Rechtskundig Weekblad*, 2010, pp. 556–559 (with E. Suy)

Book Reviews

- *Liber Amicorum Elie Van Bogaert*, Kluwer Rechtswetenschappen, Antwerpen, 1986, 340 pp., in *Rechtskundig Weekblad*, 1986–1987, pp. 1113–1119
- R. Siekmann, *Basic documents on United Nations and Related Peace-Keeping Forces*, Martinus Nijhoff, Dordrecht, 1985, 273 pp., in *Netherlands International Law Review*, 1987, pp. 410–411
- M. Bedjaoui, *The New World Order and The Security Council, Testing of legality of its acts*, Kluwer Law International, 531 pp., in *Leiden Journal of International Law*, 1996, pp. 507–512
- A. Reinisch, *International Organisations before National Courts*, Cambridge University Press, Cambridge, 2000, 449 pp., in *Leiden Journal of International Law*, 2001, pp. 258–266

- P.H. Kooijmans, *Public International Law in a Nutshell*, Tjeenk Willink, Kluwer Deventer, 8th Edtion, 2000, 369 pp., in *Leiden Journal of International Law*, 2001, pp. 946–948
- Ph. Sands and P. Klein, *Bowett's Law of international Institutions*, 5th Edition 2001, Sweet and Maxwell, London, 610 pp., in *International and Comparative Law Quarterly*, 2003, pp. 264–265

LIST OF CONTRIBUTORS

Mariano Aznar-Gómez is Professor of Public International Law at the Universitat Jaume I, Castellón de la Plana

Laurence Boisson de Chazournes is Professor of International Law at the University of Geneva

André de Hoogh is Senior Lecturer in International Law at the University of Groningen

Henri de Waele is Senior Lecturer in European Law at the Radboud University Nijmegen and Guest Professor of European Institutional Law at the University of Antwerp

Pierre Michel Eisemann is Professor of Law at the Université Panthéon-Sorbonne (Paris I)

Malgosia Fitzmaurice is Professor of Public International Law at Queen Mary, University of London

Teruo Komori is Emeritus Professor of Public International Law at Chiba University

Pieter Jan Kuijper is Professor in the Law of International Organisations at the University of Amsterdam

Rein Müllerson is President of the Academy of Law of Tallinn University and Member of the Institut de Droit International

Eric Myjer is Professor of Conflict and Security Law at the University of Utrecht

Frans Nelissen is General Director of the T.M.C. Asser Institute for International Law, The Hague, and Professor of International Environmental Law at the University of Groningen

André Nollkaemper is Professor of Public International Law at the University of Amsterdam

Photini Pazartzis is Senior Lecturer in International Law at the National and Capodistrian University of Athens

Eva Rieter is Lecturer in Public International Law at the Radboud University Nijmegen

Malcolm Shaw is Sir Robert Jennings Professor of International Law, University of Leicester, and Senior Fellow of the Lauterpacht Centre for International Law, University of Cambridge

Eric Suy is Emeritus Professor of International Law, K.U. Leuven, Former Under-Secretary-General for Legal Affairs and Legal Counsel of the United Nations, and Member of the Institut de Droit International

Theo van Boven is Emeritus Professor of Public International Law at Maastricht University

ABBREVIATIONS

ACHR	American Convention on Human Rights
ACHPR	African Commission on Human and Peoples' Rights
ACtHPR	African Court on Human and Peoples' Rights
ACP	African, Caribbean and Pacific countries
AMISOM	African Union Mission for Somalia
AI	Amnesty International
ASEAN	Association of South East Asian Nations
ASIL	American Society of International Law
BSP	Biosafety Protocol
C	Communications series of the Official Journal of the European Union
CACAS	Civil Aviation Caretaker Authority for Somalia
CFI	Court of First Instance of the European Union
CFSP	Common Foreign and Security Policy
CHG	Civilian Headline Goal
CITES	Convention on International Trade in Endangered Species of Wild Fauna and Flora
CoE	Council of Europe
CSDP	Common Security and Defence Policy
DG	Director General / Directorate General
doc.	document
DSB	Dispute Settlement Body
DSU	Dispute Settlement Understanding
EC	(Treaty establishing the) European Community
ECJ	European Court of Justice
ECHR	European Convention on Human Rights and Fundamental Freedoms
ECOSOC	Economic and Social Council
ECR	European Court Reports
ECtHR	European Court of Human Rights
EEAS	European External Action Service
EEC	European Economic Community
EFTA	European Free Trade Association
EIDHR	European Initiative for Democracy and Human Rights
ESIL	European Society of International Law
ESS	European Security Strategy
ETS	Emissions Trading System
EU	European Union

FAO	Food and Agriculture Organization
GAOR	General Assembly Official Records
GATS	General Agreement on Trade in Services
GATT	General Agreement on Tariffs and Trade
GC	General Court of the European Union
GSP	Generalised System of Preferences
HDI	Human Development Index
HR	High Representative of the EU for Foreign Affairs and Security Policy
HRC	Human Rights Committee
IACHR	Inter-American Court of Human Rights
IAEA	International Atomic Energy Agency
IAT	international administration of territories
ICAO	International Civil Aviation Organisation
ICC	International Criminal Court
ICCPR	International Covenant on Civil and Political Rights
ICISS	International Commission on Intervention and State Sovereignty
ICJ	International Court of Justice
ICTR	International Criminal Tribunal for Rwanda
ICTY	International Criminal Tribunal for the Former Yugoslavia
IDI	Institut de Droit International
ILA	International Law Association
ILC	International Law Commission
ILO	International Labour Organization
IMF	International Monetary Fund
IO	international organisation
ISAF	International Security Assistance Force
KFOR	Kosovo Force
L	Legislation series of the Official Journal of the European Union
LCBC	Lake Chad Basin Commission
LJN	Landelijk Jurisprudentie Nummer
MFN	Most Favoured Nation
MPI	Multidimensional Poverty Index
NATO	North Atlantic Treaty Organization
NGO	non-governmental organisation
OAS	Organization of American States
OECD	Organisation for Economic Co-operation and Development
OEF	Operation Enduring Freedom
OJ	Official Journal of the European Union
OSCE	Organisation for Security and Co-operation in Europe
PCIJ	Permanent Court of International Justice
PSC	Political and Security Committee

QMV	qualified majority voting
res.	resolution
RtoP	Responsibility to Protect
SPS	Agreement on the Application of Sanitary and Phytosanitary Measures
TBT	Agreement on Technical Barriers to Trade
TEU	Treaty on European Union
TFEU	Treaty on the Functioning of the European Union
TFG	Transitional Federal Government
TRIPs	Agreement on Trade Related Aspects of Intellectual Property Rights
UN	United Nations
UNCIO	United Nations Conference on International Organization
UNCLOS	United Nations Convention on the Law of the Sea
UNCTAD	United Nations Conference on Trade and Development
UNDP	United Nations Development Programme
UNESCO	United Nations Educational, Scientific and Cultural Organisation
UNFCC	United Nations Framework Convention on Climate Change
UNGA	United Nations General Assembly
UNHCR	United Nations High Commissioner for Refugees
UNICEF	United Nations Children's Fund
UNITAF	Unified Task Force
UNMIK	United Nations Mission in Kosovo
UNOSOM	United Nations Operation in Somalia
UNSC	United Nations Security Council
UNSG	United Nations Secretary General
UNTLOS	United Nations Tribunal for the Law of the Sea
VCCR	Vienna Convention on Consular Relations
VCLT	Vienna Convention on the Law of Treaties
WEU	Western European Union
WHO	World Health Organization
WTO	World Trade Organization

CHAPTER ONE

INTRODUCTION: EVOLVING PRINCIPLES OF INTERNATIONAL LAW – THE QUEST FOR DEMARCATION

Henri de Waele and Eva Rieter

1. *Aims of this Chapter*

This volume contains studies that reflect on 'evolving principles of international law' – a terrifyingly rich phrase. The sentence instantly prompts several questions, inter alia: which principles of international law are discussed? Did the authors deliberately opt for an indefinite indication, or have 'the' principles of international law been singled out? In the latter case, which may be qualified as 'the' (main) principles of international law? What period of evolution are we focusing on exactly? And how can one assess whether an international legal principle is truly 'evolving' or not?

The aim of this introductory chapter is to shed some light on these questions, as the title of this book would otherwise remain excessively enigmatic.[1] By way of prelude to the studies that comprise the heart of this volume, but also with the intention of proffering some building blocks for future scholarship, an attempt is made to delineate our subject of enquiry as clearly as possible. For that purpose, we will also elaborate on the merits of the approach that has been adopted, outline the results it aims to deliver, and indicate what inferences might be drawn from the evolutionary process we seek to portray.

2. *Principles of Law* – Quid?

To begin with, let us first muse for a short moment on the more general notion of a 'legal principle'. What are its determining characteristics, in other words, what makes a 'principle of law' truly a 'principle of law'? This is essentially a question of semantics and terminology. Usually, one means to indicate those basic precepts underpinning and defining a legal system. If something is qualified as a 'legal principle', one may assume it to have a certain normative quality; for cases of non-observance of and non-compliance with a legal principle immediately call for a condemnatory statement. Principles of law would seem to constitute the inner sanctum of any legal order, delivering guidance to, and preferably steering the conduct of, lawyers, judges, politicians, even the

[1] To be sure, there are other works explicitly devoted to 'principles of international law', but these commonly tend to be textbooks discussing the general aspects of the field.

public-at-large. Yet, the normative element need perhaps not necessarily be present: for a principle may equally function as a source of inspiration, outlining only a possible course of action, whereas another (possibly conflicting) principle may just as well lead to the satisfactory resolution of an issue. Therefore, the status of principles can be relatively soft, with the definite coercive force depending on the context.[2] At the same time though, it is rather difficult to confer the edifying qualification of 'legal principle' when one considers it totally unimportant whether it is ever being adhered to or not.

A further characteristic of a principle of law appears to concern the extent to which its 'principal' status is recognised. Evidently, an individual opinion will not suffice. There would need to be more widespread acceptance within the international judicial community, preferably proof of a broad consensus, before one can proceed to award the qualification of 'a principle of law'.[3] While for some, the recognition of a legal principle does not have to be universal, in our view, at least a certain level of generality should surely be present. This facet may pertain to either a protracted period of time, or a significant geographical area.[4] Admittedly, there is thus little room to distinguish between 'principles of law' and 'general principles of law'. However, as will be elaborated in greater detail below, the studies in the present volume are not confined to the 'general principles of international law' indicated by article 38 of the Statute of the International Court of Justice.[5]

It is comparatively easier to distinguish between 'principles' on the one hand and 'concepts' on the other. 'Concepts' are standard and predominantly practical notions, a category which in public international law encompasses e.g. 'state', 'territory', 'treaty' and 'use of force'.[6] Consequently, if the current volume would have been devoted to 'evolving concepts' instead of 'evolving principles of international law', its scope would have been unpalatably broad. Concepts are amply discussed in encyclopaedic works, alongside a plethora of other basic terms and expressions contained in the international lawyer's toolbox.[7]

---

[2] Besides, if the capacity to excite obedience is considered crucial, one would be reverting to John Austin's outmoded 'command theory of law'.

[3] To the mind of the authors though, one should not proceed to presume there exists a direct parallel with (the formation of) international customary law.

[4] Although a principle can develop and be recognised in only a few years' time (a point to which we will return below). This is akin, but not identical to the emergence of 'instant custom' in public international law.

[5] Matters are similarly blurred in the EU legal order, where the European Court of Justice established the official general principles of Union law as well as numerous other basic principles, taking its cue from the provision that instructs it to "ensure that in the interpretation and application of the Treaties the law is observed".

[6] Cf. Jan Klabbers, *The Concept of Treaty in International Law*, The Hague: Kluwer Law International 1996.

[7] Cf. Malcolm Shaw's contribution to this volume, referring to 'continental shelf' as one of the 'expressions' of international law, and the chapter by Eric Myjer, pointing to the interrelationship between values, rules and principles.

As remarked above, one should not immediately equate a legal principle with a binding rule.[8] Comity is but one illustration of this point. Conversely, a binding rule may well reflect a principle, as is the case for example with *bona fides* in contractual relations, enshrined in countless national and international legal codes. It is, however, hard to draw sharp lines here, since not all rules have to be binding, meaning that the latter can occasionally be just as 'soft' as principles. In the same vein, 'principles', 'concepts' and 'rules' share the trait that they need not be codified, as in virtually every legal system, unwritten rules, concepts and rules are known to exist.

3. *Principles of International Law* – Quae?

Now that we have sketched some contours of legal principles *sensu lato*, let us take a more specific doctrinal approach and outline which principles of international law will be highlighted in this volume. For starters, the studies included in this book are not directed at *the* principles of international law, since that would presume that there exists an official (and exhaustive) canon. Instead, there is no common agreement on the notions that may be designated as *the* principles of international law. At most, one can point to article 38 (1) of the Statute of the ICJ, but there is still no absolute unanimity as to the precise meaning and scope of the phrase "the general principles of law recognised by civilised nations".[9]

One might suggest confining the inquiries to the 'most important' principles of international law, but this too remains easier said than done. Whereas it could be tempting to focus only on the paramount norms, i.e. *ius cogens* or *erga omnes* obligations, we would first have to surmount classic and rather tiresome problems of definition. Moreover, countless publications have been devoted to these themes already. Suffice to say that some of the international legal principles discussed here can (also) be categorised as *ius cogens* or obligations *erga omnes*, but that this did not constitute a precondition for their inclusion.

At the other end of the spectrum, if an extremely liberal approach were to be adopted in which the weight or hierarchical position is considered totally irrelevant, the list of (supposed) international legal principles to be included

---

[8] We consciously deviate here from the approach of the ICJ, which has often referred to 'principles' and 'rules' interchangeably. In its judgment in the *Gulf of Maine* case (ICJ Reports 1984, p. 246, at p. 288–90), the Chamber of the Court noted that, in the context of the question put before it, 'rules' and 'principles' conveyed the same idea, since the term 'principles' clearly referred to principles of law, which also included rules of law. Yet in this respect, it did note the "more general and more fundamental character of general principles" (par. 79).

[9] See e.g. Bela Vitányi, 'Les Positions Doctrinales Concernant le Sens de la Notion de "Principes Généraux de Droit Reconnus par les Nations Civilisées"', (1982) 86 *Revue Générale de Droit International Public*, p. 48.

would grow infinitely long – albeit that such an approach does render it unnecessary to pronounce on their exact order of priority.

Something that is patently clear anyhow is that, for a principle of international law to be labelled as such, it does not need to have originated in that legal order. On the contrary, as is the case for the "general principles" referred to in article 38 (1) of the ICJ's Statute, first and foremost, notions that originate in municipal law have been recognised as international legal norms, a point underscored by a vast jurisprudence. This e.g. holds true for desuetude, acquiescence, *res judicata*, estoppel, and even for a principle as colloquial as that of proportionality. To this batch, one may add those principles derived exclusively from international legal practise and invariably identified as such in legal doctrine, *inter alia*: self-determination, non-intervention, self-defence, good faith and *uti possidetis*.

In all then, this book treads a middle ground. The reader will not find analyses of *the* principles of international law, in the absence of a sufficiently compact and coherent set of norms that could be qualified as such. At the same time, it contains no exhaustive treatment of every notion that might be tagged as *a* principle of international law, reflecting instead on a limited selection. Admittedly then, this amounts to an undertaking that is more modest than the title may have led one to believe. Yet, as will be further detailed below, it is one that does carry broader significance nevertheless.

4. *Ordering Principles of International Law*

Before elaborating further on the selection of international legal principles, it is useful to make a few observations on methods of classification. For sure, some principles are more ubiquitous than others, meaning that they are relevant to, and crop up in, virtually all different branches of international law (e.g. the principle of proportionality). Conversely, certain sub-domains contain specific principles that are never or only rarely applied elsewhere (e.g. the principle of equidistance in the law of the sea). More problematic are those principles that signify secondary rules of international law. Consider for example three principles with regard to the law of treaties. One of them, *pacta sunt servanda*, is the central tenet of the law of treaties, which may at the same time be labelled as a cornerstone of the international legal order as a whole; a treaty rule originating in a general principle, which is accepted as a rule of customary international law as well. In contrast, most authors agree that *rebus sic stantibus* and *exceptio non adimpleti contractus* are *lex generalis* rules of a less foundational character. A *lex specialis* can replace these general rules, while the principle of *pacta sunt servanda* is of a 'higher' level. Nevertheless all three principles are interconnected, and traditionally mentioned in the one and the same breath.

As already hinted at above, matters would have been comparatively easier if a definitive hierarchy of norms had been established. Of course, the classic distinction between *ius cogens* and *ius dispositivum* may still provide a valuable point of departure.[10] A number of international legal principles may be easily filed in the former or the latter category, for example the prohibition of torture, and certain norms regarding diplomatic and consular privileges.[11] Reliance on Article 38 (1) of the Statute of the ICJ does not resolve the issue either. It could tentatively be argued that principles that have been established exclusively in judicial decisions and scholarly writings ought to be placed in a subordinate position, and that there is no hierarchical relation between treaty law and customary law. In other words, the one principle need not be considered more weighty than the other simply on the mere basis of its source (being a principle reflected in customary law or one codified in a treaty). Overlaps render the issue more complex, as notions originally developed by the International Court of Justice may go on to form part of treaty law or custom, and many rules in the VCLT reflect norms of customary law. At most one could say that those principles reflected in all three sources mentioned in Article 38 have enhanced authority. Other than that, principles could only be ordered based on the norms they reflect, without any bearing on the formal sources, apart from the limited category of *ius cogens*.

Equity presents a further complication. When taken to mean "considerations of fairness, reasonableness and policy", it may in itself constitute a principle of international law that can be placed in one group or the other. It can however also denote "a set of principles constituting the values of the international legal system", thus constituting a league of its own.[12] The former sense does not facilitate much the drawing up of an overarching classification; the latter merely leads to the conclusion that some principles are part of equity while others are not. At most then, it serves as an indication of provenance, but a very crude one at that.

Lastly, principles of international law could be classified along the lines of the *lex generalis* – *lex specialis* distinction, as noted above. For example, in armed conflicts, international humanitarian law may serve as *lex specialis* of international human rights law. Of course, this classification is rather crude and facile, and would in the end only result in two tediously long lists of principles, assigned to either the first cluster or the second.

---

[10] But cf. Prosper Weil, 'Towards Relative Normativity in International Law', (1983) 77 *American Journal of International Law*, p. 413.

[11] Whereas in most national legal systems (and in the legal order of the European Union), general principles of law reside *eo ipso* at the top of the pyramid, thus being capable of overriding any clashing inferior norms.

[12] See respectively Ian Brownlie, *Principles of Public International Law*, Oxford: Oxford University Press 2003, p. 25; Malcolm Shaw, *International Law*, Cambridge: Cambridge University Press 2008, p. 106.

In sum, while not all international legal principles are equivalent, of the same pedigree or importance, there seems to be no fixed method to place them in separate (sub-)categories. Stubborn persistence here would run the risk of conveying a false sense of order, as the labels employed are easily too rigid, with the dividing lines proving much more murky in reality.

5. Evolving *Principles of International Law*

When staging an enquiry into the evolutionary trajectory of international legal principles, some careful thought should also be given to the question where to start. On the one hand, the focus could be placed on the recent past, and all the developments since then up to the present time. Yet, it is equally possible to go a much longer way back, or even attempt to span the entire history of international law, as principles are likely to be discernable in each different epoch. Of course, hereby we ought to take note of the fact that international law did not exist *eo nomine* before the 19th century, and that the profession of international lawyer was invented fairly recently.[13] This entails that, when assessing the more distant past, the sought after principles may be comparatively less visible, also due to the witting and unwitting application of domestic norms to interstate relations. The heuristic problems are compounded by the fact that, for several centuries, decisions of courts and actual state practise were seen as less determinative of the scope and content of the applicable rules than scholarly writings, whereas at present the contrary is true.

We furthermore share the view of those authors that consider the current state of the art with regard to the periodisation of the history of international law as rather unsatisfactory.[14] As a result, it is far from easy to ascertain which principles belong to which particular era – a problem that can only be sidestepped by not overrating the importance of dating them with complete precision. Still, it needs to be clear from the outset what period is referred to when one employs the epithets of a 'classic', 'medieval' or 'modern' principle of international law. Unfortunately, the precise ambit of these adjectives is still a subject of debate and controversy among historians.

Through the ages, certain principles have proven to be resilient and of an impressive longevity. These 'evergreens' usually receive greater attention than transient ones. Nonetheless, those of shorter duration did not necessarily have a lesser impact; they may just as well have defined their time, and determined the shape of the notions that subsequently took their place. Also, some of

[13] As magisterially recounted in Martti Koskenniemi's *The Gentle Civilizer of Nations* (Cambridge: Cambridge University Press 2002).

[14] See Randall Lesaffer, 'The Grotian Tradition Revisited: Change and Continuity in the History of International Law', *British Yearbook of International Law* 2002, p. 106.

them may re-emerge after a period of absence, possibly in a different guise.[15] This calls for a wider-ranging assessment, as the taking into account of the rise and demise of a principle provides valuable insight into the underlying process of evolution, and the underlying factors and variables that steer the course of events.

Of course, our analysis could be focused on principles that have been around equally long, but then the question remains what should be the preferred point of departure. Such a uniform set-up does benefit overall coherence, but there will always be a certain randomness in the choice of where to begin. Additionally, where a process of evolution stretches out through several different ages, proceeding on the basis of a strict temporal compartmentalisation requires making some hard choices, and may lead to rash exclusions that are not always scientifically tenable.

Ultimately, the studies in the present book are not symmetrical, in the sense of concentrating on one and the same timeframe. Taking a flexible approach with regard to the temporal dimension allows for a multi-faceted analysis, chiefly predicated on thematic foundations.[16] Therefore, the studies in the following chapters take a diachronic perspective, providing a chequered overview of principles of international law in varying stages of evolution.

6. *Tracing the Evolution of International Legal Principles*

In theory, it is not too difficult to pinpoint an evolutionary development: it seems acceptable to claim its existence whenever one stumbles upon consequential, but not overly radical signs of change. Appearances can be deceptive however: an established principle could appear to be morphing into a different shape, but may already become wholly unrecognisable at a very early stage. Consider for example the curtailing of the possibilities to lawfully resort to the use of force in the period between the First and the end of the Second World War. One might herein discern a process of sovereignty in transition, which eventually culminated in article 2 (4) of the UN Charter.[17] Yet, instead of a gradual evolution, it is possible to identify a 'hard break' with the past, as in the same short time span, the sovereign prerogative to start a war of aggression was already completely (albeit not effectively) forestalled.[18]

---

[15] Cf. Mariano Aznar-Gómez's contribution to this volume, discussing the extinction of states.

[16] Thus covering the "traditional themes of the modern international law project". Cf. Martti Koskenniemi, *From Apology to Utopia*, Cambridge: Cambridge University Press 2006, p. 5.

[17] Cf. the contribution of De Hoogh to this volume, referring to the first limitations on the sovereign right to wage war put in place at the Peace of Westphalia.

[18] See e.g. Antonio Cassese, *International Law*, Oxford: Oxford University Press 2001, pp. 30–1.

Conversely, not every mutation signals the dawn of an evolutionary trajectory, since the changes may only be slight, when there are only minor alterations in the general understanding, mode or scope of application of an international legal principle. So long as the 'hard core' remains intact, it can justifiably be regarded as 'static'. The same goes for principles that develop so as to remain in sync with changing times or circumstances: paradoxically, they do adapt, but merely in order to stay the same. Self-defence may serve as one example, reflecting a universal constant from ancient times up to the *Caroline* case, stretching out to the present article 51 of the UN Charter. By sifting out these 'static' principles, it becomes easier to isolate the evolving ones, but with the threshold between perceived and veritable evolution varying from case to case, this is no sinecure.

A related issue pertains to the question of when a new principle has emerged and superseded the previous one, and when it is still intrinsically the same, despite its evolution. Contemporary authors may deny that the established understanding, mode or scope of application has changed, until there are manifest and irrefutable indications to the contrary. Swift recognition of a complete novelty is even rarer. Consider the Responsibility to Protect (RtoP), which, although embraced by many, will not be accepted by everyone as already sufficiently 'mature' to qualify as a principle of international law. At the same time, one may argue that it represents the pinnacle of a development originating in the Roman *bellum iustum* doctrine, or, rather more narrowly, the outcome of decades of discussion on the defects of the UN Charter and the concept of humanitarian intervention.[19] For the moment though, RtoP cannot immediately be labelled as either an old or a new principle; it seems stranded somewhere between the past and the future.[20] The principle is evolving, rather than evolved and firmly established. At the end of the day, where a substantial change in bearing is required as proof of evolution, there needs to have been a substantial passage of time, apart from a more radical alteration, before a new principle will be recognised as such.

In sum, before one can contend that a principle has evolved, a meaningful shift should have taken place with regard to either its position, reach or content, without its essence being displaced. Where this is not the case, constancy appears to be its overriding characteristic. Even then however, the parameters are hardly fixed, and we should take heed of the subjective elements in appreciating the dimension of the change that has (or has not) occurred.

---

[19] In time, a possible analogy might be drawn with the 1930s authors who discounted the impact of the system of collective security installed by the Covenant of the League of Nations. Cf. Henri de Waele, 'Commemorating Robert Regout (1896–1942). A Chapter from the History of Public International Law Revisited', (2005) 7 *Journal of the History of International Law*, p. 87.

[20] But cf. the contribution of Van Boven to this volume, qualifying it as "a newly emerging principle of international law".

7. *The Significance of Studying Evolving Principles*

While almost every scholar in the field is – knowingly or unknowingly – engaged with (aspects of) the topic, the added value of taking a closer look at evolving principles of international law may not be readily evident.

To begin with, charting longitudinal changes to the theorems underpinning the public international legal order may shed new light on the broader patterns of change, and expose the key factors that are at play. Trends such as that of increasing humanisation and the emergence of international constitutional law can be better understood once it is clear which elements are in flux and which remain unaffected. Moreover, such developments have wider-ranging implications that are at present not yet fully known, but might be surmised once the underlying dynamics are uncovered. Trite as it may sound, here too, intense scrutiny of the past and present makes it possible to draw up a more accurate prognosis for the future.[21]

In addition, while to study the evolving principles is – quite agreeably – to study the evolution of international law itself, a full comprehension of the process enables us to better appreciate similar processes taking place elsewhere. Also, vice versa, the insights gained can be tested and compared with experiences acquired in other legal orders.[22] One example may illustrate this point. So far, it has been a general rule of thumb that principles are more necessary, more useful, and able to expand more vigorously in a new and pristine legal domain. As known, in comparison to municipal systems, international law has fewer courts, no central legislator and no uniformly structured rules. Consequently, there are gaps abundant, as most harrowingly exemplified by the ICJ's *Nuclear Weapons* opinion.[23] Nevertheless, one cannot automatically assume that general principles of law have been all-decisive in the shaping of international law, if only because this is hard to square with the order of preference stipulated in Article 38 of the Statute of the ICJ. While the rule of thumb might hold true for a sub-domain like international criminal law, thorough studies are needed to corroborate that inference as well. If such research were to validate the aforementioned rule of thumb, one may proceed to test the reverse hypothesis, and explore to what extent legal principles may induce the recasting of an overregulated field. This all goes to show how enquiries into evolving principles can contribute to the body of knowledge on international law.

---

[21] Which in passing could help subvert the excruciatingly bold assertion of Jack L. Goldsmith and Eric A. Posner in their *The Limits of International Law* (New York: Oxford University Press 2005) that, overall, states only pursue their own rational interests, and obey international norms only to the extent the latter serve those interests.

[22] For example the legal order of the European Union, where the general principles of law are of late steadily gaining in prominence – a process which, contrary to what one might expect, compounds problems of legitimacy instead of diminishing them.

[23] ICJ Reports 1996, p. 226.

8. *A Contextual Approach*

Contrary to what the title of this volume might suggest, in the following chapters, evolving principles are not portrayed individually. This is the result of a conscious choice, the very last point that needs to be clarified here.

Above all, if the studies were to discuss their topics completely severally, the book would risk to be permeated by a soporific repetitiveness. After all, the developments depicted have all taken place in the same field (public international law), and the timeframes of the evolutionary processes are bound to overlap.[24] A corollary drawback would be that the analyses proceed in an unsatisfactory staccato fashion. Interesting as it may be to observe the inevitable differences between the various contributions, especially as regards the accentuation or exclusion of specific details, this (potentially) positive aspect appears to be outweighed by the more negative ones.

The approach that has been preferred instead is one of enveloping movements, whereby principles of international law are studied within a broader context, or through a particular thematic lens. Thus, the analyses do not consist of (predictable) discussions to the background of the unfolding political, social or economic events – a story that is preferably not recounted more than once – but a more comprehensive survey of a field, theme or topic.[25] It is true that, in this set-up, international legal principles do not receive undivided attention, and do not play a starring role themselves. Yet, they are not pushed to the background either, but structurally – and arguably more effectively – weaved into the larger picture. This profoundly contextual approach enables a sound and natural elucidation of the factors contributing to their genesis and shaping, offering a richness and breadth that an assessment of isolated principles and their evolution is thought to lack. To this end, the authors of the studies were encouraged to make use of their expertise with regard to a specific field, theme or topic, and not to don any blinkers. This *modus operandi* also meant to ensure a bond with the intended readership, as this book was not intended to cater for an audience solely composed of specialists.

As such, the present volume evidently does not have the coherence of a dedicated monograph. On the other hand, it does constitute a treatise that is markedly different from the existing reference works, compendiums and textbooks. The upshot is an original series of reflections on international legal principles, highlighting their development over time from numerous different angles.

---

[24] For reasons provided above, a rigid chronological compartmentalisation has been deliberately shunned.

[25] But cf. the contribution of Teruo Komori, engaging in a scrutiny of the fragmented international public order in its entirety, while reviewing the available options for reassembling it.

PART I

THE EVOLUTION OF INTERNATIONAL ORGANISATIONS AND INTERNATIONAL GOVERNANCE

CHAPTER TWO

THE RELATIONSHIP BETWEEN INTERNATIONAL ORGANISATIONS AND THEIR MEMBER STATES – WHO PAYS THE CHECK?

*Frans A. Nelissen**

1. *Introduction*

Within the theme 'the evolution of international organisations and international governance' there are many issues worth exploring, both legal and non-legal. This chapter focuses on only a small portion of them, and concerns the relation between international organisations and their member states. The perspective is legal. Building *inter alia* on the so-called 'NATO cases' before the International Court of Justice[1] and the European Court of Human Rights,[2] two questions will be specifically addressed. These have in common that they are part of a broader study by the International Law Commission (ILC) on the topic of responsibility of international organisations,[3] which the ILC sought to complete at its session in the Spring and Summer of 2011.

The activities of international organisations[4] have been continuously broadening during the past decades. Accordingly, international organisations have been vested with an increasing amount of rights and duties. When realizing their purposes, they exert increasing influence on third parties.[5]

---

* The author would like to acknowledge the very valuable assistance in preparing earlier draft parts of this contribution provided by Mrs Mirja Peters (LLM) and Mr Steffen van der Velde (LLM), both research assistants at the T.M.C. Asser Institute.

[1] Legality of Use of Force (*Yugoslavia v. United States of America*); Legality of Use of Force (*Serbia and Montenegro v. United Kingdom*); Legality of Use of Force (*Yugoslavia v. Spain*); Legality of Use of Force (*Serbia and Montenegro v. Portugal*); Legality of Use of Force (*Serbia and Montenegro v. Netherlands*); Legality of Use of Force (*Serbia and Montenegro v. Italy*); Legality of Use of Force (*Serbia and Montenegro v. Germany*); Legality of Use of Force (*Serbia and Montenegro v. France*); Legality of Use of Force (*Serbia and Montenegro v. Canada*); Legality of Use of Force (*Serbia and Montenegro v. Belgium*), judgment of 15 December 2004 (preliminary objections).

[2] *Bankovic et al v. Belgium and 16 other states*, Application no. 52207/99, 12 December 2001 (GC) (inadm.).

[3] In support of the ILC elaborations on the Draft Articles on Responsibility of International Organisations, a study group of the International Law Association is currently engaged in studies on this matter. The present author is a member of this Study Group, under the chairmanship of ILC member Dr E. Valencia Ospina. This contribution is partly based on earlier works by the present author for the ILA Study Group.

[4] In the present chapter, *international organisations* refers exclusively to intergovernmental organisations.

[5] The term *third parties* encompass all entities other than Member States of the particular organisation (i.e. non-member states, individuals, companies etc.).

Consequently, there is a growing risk of causing damages. This growing risk of being injured by an international organisation has not been accompanied by a development of possibilities to hold international organisations liable for damages caused. There is essentially no forum for holding international organisations accountable for their acts because none of the international courts have jurisdiction over claims against entities other than states.[6] This legal vacuum is of particular relevance in non-contractual relations as contracts between international organisations and third parties may include an arbitration clause and hence provide for dispute settlement. As the 'NATO cases' before the International Court of Justice and the European Court of Human Rights demonstrate, the only possibility for third parties to receive any remedy is to bring claims against the member states. A problem additional to the lack of forum is that international organisations may simply be unable to provide adequate compensation because of their limited budget.[7] Furthermore there is the issue of the commissioning of acts by member states following orders or consent given by international organisations.

This small palette of examples of issues relevant in the relation between international organisations and their member states gives rise to many questions, two of which will be dealt with in this contribution.

2. *Who Pays the Check? Two Central Questions*

2.1. *Introduction*

One question is whether the members of an international organisation can be held liable for acts of the organisation for which they are not themselves responsible. The other is at what point does consent given by an international organisation to a state to commit a wrongful act, constitute a circumstance precluding wrongfulness for that state.

2.2. *Liability of Member States for Acts of the Organisation*

2.2.1. *The Issue at Stake*

Can the members of an international organisation be held liable for acts of the organisation for which they are not themselves responsible?[8] In the words of the ILC:

---

[6] Compare e.g. art. 34 (1) of the ICJ Statute and articles 33 and 34 of the ECHR.

[7] As the Tin Council Cases and the Westland Helicopter Cases demonstrate, the lack of own financial means of international organisations is relevant for both contractual and non-contractual relations.

[8] In the literature the terms responsibility and liability are often used interchangeably which may lead to the misconception that they mean the same. For instance, according to Leslie B. Curzon, *Dictionary of Law*, London: Pitman Publishing 1998, p. 327, *responsibility* can be defined as "[l]egal liability, i.e., accountability for some state of affairs to which one's conduct

> Do members of an international organisation that are not responsible for an internationally wrongful act of that organisation have an obligation to provide compensation to the injured party, should the organisation not be in a position to do so?[9]

One of the incentives for states to create international organisations is that such an organisation might be better suited than states to handle certain issues. Cruelly, another stimulation might be the lessened responsibility for that policy area for the state. Placing the major part of the responsibility on the member states will probably lead to the creation of less effective international organisations. As Klabbers observes, "the main point of restricting the liability of members of organisations is to make it possible for organisations to engage in activities in which the individual Member States would hesitate to participate".[10] Scrutiny in such organisations would be far more severe and powers more limited, as states will try to prevent the international organisations from causing damages or engage in activities entailing great risks. On the other hand, it is illogical to suppose that a group of states can create immunity from responsibility towards other states by simply creating an international organisation. Some authors believe that the correct analysis here is to treat an international organisation as one of the factual elements, which may lead to the responsibility of its member states, or some of them. The applicable law here would be that of state responsibility.[11] This scenario, however, would not be in the best interest of the development of well functioning, effective international organisations. For the reasons mentioned above, the allocation of responsibility for actions of international organisations in other ways is very relevant.

---

has contributed, together with an obligation to repair any injury caused". *Liability* is defined as "[l]egal obligation or duty" or "[a]mount owed" (Ibid., p. 222). For the term *legal liability* reference is made to *responsibility*. The given definitions indicate that overlaps between the two concepts do undoubtedly exist. However, the present author finds it necessary to make a distinction between the two: *Responsibility* of subjects of international law arises out of a breach of international law that is attributable to the subject concerned. Such a breach of international law can consist in either an action or an omission that amounts to non-compliance with an international obligation (see e.g. C.F. Amerasinghe, *Principles of the Institutional Law of International Organizations*, Cambridge: Cambridge University Press 1996, p. 224–225; and also the ILC Draft Articles on Responsibility of States for Internationally Wrongful Acts adopted by the International Law Commission at its fifty-third session (2001), November 2001). A violation of international law always causes injury, be it material damage or moral injury. Such injury requires reparation in form of restitution, compensation and/or satisfaction ("[R]eparation (…) shall take the form of restitution, compensation and satisfaction (…)." Art. 34 ILC Draft Articles on State Responsibility. Compare articles 34 and 35–37 ILC Draft Articles on State Responsibility). *Liability* thus means the obligation to pay compensation to the injured party (compare art. 31 ILC Draft Articles on State Responsibility: "1. The responsible State is under an obligation to make full reparation for the injury caused by the internationally wrongful act. (…)").

[9] ILC, 58th session (2006), 25 April 2007, chapter VII (a).

[10] Jan Klabbers, *An Introduction to International Institutional Law*, Cambridge: Cambridge University Press 2002, p. 314.

[11] Ian Brownlie, 'The Responsibility of States for the Acts of International Organizations', in: Maurizio Ragazzi (ed.), *International Responsibility Today*, Leiden-Boston: Martinus Nijhoff Publishers 2005, p. 360–362.

The question implies that an international organisation has committed an internationally wrongful act which has caused injury to a certain party. It also only refers to members of the organisation that are *not* responsible for this wrongful act, leaving aside other members that might in fact be responsible.[12] Generally speaking, a subject has the duty to provide compensation if it is responsible for the act from which the injury resulted. As provided in article 36 of the ILC Draft Articles on State Responsibility for Internationally Wrongful Acts, "[t]he state responsible for an internationally wrongful act is under an obligation to compensate for the damage caused thereby".[13] Furthermore, by way of reversing the provision of article 36 of the Draft Articles on State Responsibility, we might assume that a state *not* responsible for the internationally wrongful act is *not* under an obligation to compensate for the damage caused. This obligation *prima facie* remains with the international organisation that has committed the internationally wrongful act (and – as the case may be – member states that *are* responsible). However, as indicated in the question, the international organisation might not be in a position to provide compensation to the injured party.[14] If it is not capable of providing the compensation and if it was maintained that the member states not responsible do not have an obligation to pay compensation, the right to a remedy (here: the right to be compensated for damage caused by an internationally wrongful act) of the injured party would be prejudiced. It must thus be examined whether the members could have a subsidiary or indirect obligation to provide compensation.

The assessment of the matter is complicated by the large diversity of international organisations. It is very difficult to come up with a general body of rules applicable to the enormous variety of structure and area of activity

[12] Generally speaking, the responsibility of Member States is not excluded once the act is attributed to the organisation. As the Special Rapporteur points out, responsibility may lie with more than one subject of international law. The Draft Articles on the Responsibility of International Organisations provide that under certain circumstances states can be held responsible for acts committed by the international organisation. Compare art. 25–29 of the Draft Articles contained in the Report of the International Law Commission, Fifty-Eighth session, 1 May – 9 June and 3 July – 11 August 2006, UN Doc, A/61/10. Accordingly, states are internationally responsible if they aided or assisted the international organisation in the commission of the breach, or if they exerted control (or even coercion) of a certain level on the international organisation. As mentioned by the Special Rapporteur in his first report, states could also incur responsibility simply as being members of the international organisation, compare e.g. par. 38 of the First Report, UN Doc. A/CN.4/532). Depending on the circumstances of the case the responsibility could either be joint or joint and several. The responsibility of the State could be established by attribution of the act to the state or by mere membership. On shared responsibility, see also the contribution of Nollkaemper to this volume.

[13] Art. 36, Draft Articles on State Responsibility for Internationally Wrongful Acts. Compare also articles 31 and 34.

[14] According to the ILC commentary on article XV of the Draft Articles on the International Responsibility of International Organisations, an injured party "would in most cases be another State or another international organisation, [but] it could also be a subject of international law other than a State or international organisation" (commentary on draft article 29, paragraph 11, ILC Report 2006, p. 290).

of international organisations.[15] This problem does not occur in relation to states, of which there is only one internationally recognised legal structure. The fact that states posses a territory on which they are sovereign makes them an entity separate and definable like no other subject of international law. International organisations, with their multitude of different member states, of rules on their functioning and structure, and of the tasks they carry out, form a whole different section of the international playing field. However, considering every single institution would go beyond the scope of the present comments. Thus, as a general starting point, it is assumed that the greater the (financial) autonomy of the respective organisation, the less easily could an obligation of the members to contribute to the payment of compensation be established. Most organisations have a certain amount of own income, e.g. from sales of publications or stamps[16] but the majority still largely depends on the financial contributions of the member states. The Bretton Woods institutions and the European Union can be seen as notable exceptions to the rule. Even though to different extents, these institutions have considerable financial and political autonomy. In a considerable number of policy areas, their member states exert little or no control over the activities of the respective institutions, and an obligation of the member states to provide compensation for damage resulting from internationally wrongful acts of the organisation could thus arguably be denied. What is more, the Treaty on the Functioning of the European Union, specifically states that: "In the case of non-contractual liability, the Union shall, in accordance with the general principles common to the laws of the member states, make good any damage caused by its institutions or by its servants in the performance of their duties."[17] The case could be different for organisations where the members are more directly involved in the decision-making process. A parallel could possibly be drawn to the institution of a 'holding' in private/company law. A holding often provides common structures which saves costs by eliminating doubled structures among the participating companies. However, the latter cannot evade their financial obligations by 'hiding' behind the structure of the holding. While the parallel to holdings could be relevant when assessing the relationship between international organisations and their members in general, it seems to add little value to the discussion of the present question. Establishing that a state exerts power over the organisation would again raise the question of attribution of responsibility, which is explicitly not to be addressed in the present context.

[15] Niels Blokker, 'Comparing Apples and Oranges? Reinventing the Wheel? Schermers' Book and Challenges for the Future of International Institutional Law', (2008) 5 *International Organizations Law Review*, p. 203–204.

[16] Philippe Sands and Pierre Klein, *Bowett's Law of International Institutions*, London: Sweet & Maxwell 2001, p. 568.

[17] Article 340 of the Treaty on the Functioning of the EU.

We shall therefore return to the question whether the member states could have a subsidiary or indirect responsibility to provide compensation for damage caused by an internationally wrongful act committed by an organisation of which they are member. The (founding) members of an international organisation vest the international organisation with legal personality, i.e. provide it with rights and duties in the international sphere.[18] It would seem illogical to vest an international organisation with duties, but to not provide it with the necessary means to fulfil its obligations. Even though some institutions have an own income, the vast majority of institutions is largely dependent on the financial contributions of its members. Consequently, the respective constitutive instruments contain provisions that oblige the members of the organisation to contribute to the budget of the organisation, a budget that will in turn be used for the fulfilment of the latter's obligations. The United Nations can be taken as an example here: article 17 of the UN Charter provides, in paragraph 2, that "[t]he expenses of the Organization shall be borne by the Members (…)". The International Court of Justice in the 1962 *Certain Expenses* Advisory Opinion states that

> the amount of what are unquestionably 'expenses of the Organization' (…) is not in its entirety apportioned by the General Assembly and paid for by the contributions of Member States, since the Organisation has other sources of income. A Member State, accordingly, is under no obligation to pay more than the amount apportioned to it.[19]

This would lead to the assumption that member states do not have to provide any contribution that goes beyond the 'regular' budget. However, the Court further on adopts a rather broad approach to what can be regarded as 'expenses' of the organisation. It notes that the General Assembly had consistently included 'unforeseen and extraordinary expenses' arising in relation to the 'maintenance of peace and security' in its annual budget resolutions.[20] This could lead to the assumption that the payment of compensation for damage resulting from acts of the organisation would be included in expenses of the organisation. If this were the case, the members of the organisation would – according to article 17 (2) UN Charter – be obliged to provide a budget sufficient to cover all expenses of the organisation. However, the Court also held that in order for certain expenditures to be considered as expenses of the organisation in the sense of article 17 (2) UN Charter, the action taken must be appropriate for the fulfilment of one of the purposes of the UN as laid down in article 1 UN Charter. This gives rise to the question whether the

---

[18] Compare the ICJ's Advisory Opinion, *Reparations for injuries suffered in the service of the United Nations*, ICJ Reports 1949, p. 174.

[19] *Certain Expenses of the United Nations (Article 17, paragraph 2, of the Charter)*, ICJ Reports 1962, p. 158.

[20] Ibid., p. 160.

internationally wrongful act committed by the international organisation is appropriate for the fulfilment of the purposes of the organisation. While such assessment would certainly have to take into account the circumstances of the specific case, it seems rather likely that internationally wrongful acts would *not* be appropriate for the fulfilment of the purposes of the organisation. Compensations that would have to be provided for damage arising out of internationally wrongful acts, and thus presumably not appropriate for the fulfilment of the purposes of the organisation, would not fall within the meaning of the term 'expenses' of the organisation as understood by the Court in the *Expenses Opinion*. Therefore, the Member States not responsible for the act would not be obliged to provide for the compensation.

Nevertheless, it can be held that the situation in the present case is essentially different from the circumstances surrounding the *Certain Expenses* Opinion. The question explicitly refers to an injured party, thus the rights of a third party are involved and not merely the relationship between the organisation and the member states. It must be reiterated that the conclusion drawn above – that member states not responsible are not obliged to provide compensation – would prejudice the right to compensation of the injured parties. In order to protect this fundamental right, the members of the organisation should thus have the obligation to provide the appropriate compensation if the regular budget does not suffice. To support this point, it can be argued that in the case the budget of the organisation is sufficient to provide the compensation – presuming that it is largely made up by contributions – the member states are in fact providing this compensation *indirectly* by fulfilling their obligation to make their regular budgetary contributions to the organisation. In this situation, the matter of whether the member states are responsible for the act or not does not arise, but the budget is simply used for providing the compensation. If the regular budget does not suffice for the provision of certain compensation, it should be adapted to cover those expenses. Such additional budget would have to be borne by the member states. The respective amounts should be apportioned according to the distribution scheme set out by the competent organ. Keeping in mind the object and purpose of the international organisation is important in deciding on such a scheme. An organisation with powers that are more or less similar to those of states may behave itself more or less like a state. The UN administering Kosovo serves as an example, exercising a form of sovereignty over a territory which is normally the prerogative of states. Another example is the NATO bombing Belgrade, thereby using military force, again normally the exclusive power of states. Consequently, like a state, such an organisation bears a greater responsibility than an organisation providing, for example, school supplies in Africa. As Dominicé states, "when (…) the organisation is acting in the same way as States may act, it is reasonable to assert that it is bound by the rules of general international law (among them the rules of *jus cogens*) in the same way as

States are bound".[21] Another factor to take into account is the level of independence of the organisation from its members. The more independent an organisation operates the more responsibility it bears. A logical consequence thereof is the increased liability of this organisation for an internationally wrongful act.

2.2.2. *Conclusion*

To sum up, it can be stated that while the members not responsible for an internationally wrongful act of an organisation do not have a *primary* obligation to provide compensation to parties injured, the fact that they vested the international organisation with legal personality brings with it the obligation to provide the international organisation with the means sufficient for the latter to fulfil its obligations. Providing compensation for damages might belong to these obligations. The level of liability to be borne by the member state could, for example, be made dependent on the nature of the activities carried out by the international organisation and the risks they entail. As a corollary of the obligation to contribute to the budget of the organisation, the members can have an indirect obligation to provide compensation. This obligation would serve to ensure the right of the injured party to such compensation. To prevent further issues of member state liability international organisations should all have clauses in their constituent documents providing for a solution for damages incurred. The constituent documents should include a system of distribution which provides for sufficient means, provided by the member states to the international organisation, to handle its financial affairs independently. In this way, the effectiveness and independence of the international organisation are guaranteed. Indeed, the Institut de Droit International concluded that the development of a general rule of state responsibility for the actions of international organisations would undermine the credibility and independent functioning of international organisations and the establishment of new international organisations. Instead each international organisation should specify its position regarding liability in its rules and contracts; in communications to third parties prior to the action; and in response to any specific request by a third party.[22]

[21] Christian Dominicé, 'The International Responsibility of the United Nations for Injuries Resulting from Non-Military Enforcement Measures', in: Maurizio Ragazzi (ed.), *International Responsibility Today*, Leiden-Boston: Martinus Nijhoff Publishers 2005, p. 367.

[22] *The Legal Consequences for Member States of the Non-fulfilment by International Organisations of their Obligations Towards Third Parties*, Institut de Droit International, resolution of 1 September 1995, available at <http://www.idi-iil.org/idiF/resolutionsF/1995_lis_02_fr.pdf>.

2.3. *Consent by an International Organisation to the State's Commission of a Wrongful Act*

2.3.1. *Introduction*

The second question to be discussed here is: when can consent given by an international organisation to the commission of an act by a state be considered as a circumstance that precludes the wrongfulness of that state's conduct? Some preliminary remarks on this issue are in order.

With the widening and deepening of the tasks carried out by international organisations, their influence on the international playing field increases. Similarly, the actions of international organisations are capable of having greater impact on other actors. An important factor in assessing whether the international organisation or its member states bear responsibility, is whether or not valid consent is given by the international organisation to certain acts of its member states. The issue of 'consent' is dealt with in article 19 of the Draft Articles on Responsibility of International Organisations, which corresponds to article 20 of the ILC Articles on the Responsibility of States for Internationally Wrongful Acts:

> Valid consent by a State or an international organisation to the commission of a given act by another international organisation precludes the wrongfulness of that act in relation to that State or the former organisation to the extent that the act remains within the limits of that consent.

Consent, in relation to states, usually refers to allowing an international organisation to carry out certain tasks on their territory. Article 19 involves the issue of consent given to the commission of an act by an international organisation. Here, however, the reverse situation is at stake, namely consent given by an international organisation to a state to perform a certain act.

From the Commentaries to the Draft Articles on the Responsibility of States for Internationally Wrongful Acts we can deduce that article 20, concerning 'consent', reflects a basic principle of international law. Examples of when such 'consent' might be given could be: transit through the airspace; or location of facilities on (a) certain state's territory. During a session concerning the annual review of ILC-activities by the 6th Committee of the UN General Assembly, in October 2009, several commentators expressed their views on the issue of 'consent'. Horák said that a valid consent given by an international organisation to the performance of a certain act by the state precluded wrongfulness, provided that the consent was within the limits of the international organisation's authority, the state acted within the limits of the consent and the act did not conflict with 'higher law'. Popkov stated that 'consent' should be given explicitly and without coercion. Furthermore, the subsequent behaviour of the state should not result in serious injury.[23] The Commentaries to the ILC Articles on State Responsibility also hold that consent must be given freely and be clearly established. It must be expressed rather than presumed on the basis that a State would have consented if it had been asked. Furthermore, the Commentaries provide for grounds for invalid consent, being: error, fraud, corruption or coercion. The principles of consent to treaties might provide relevant guidance here.[24]

Hereafter, some scenario's will be discussed in which consent given by an international organisation to carry out a task by a state is considered a valid ground for the preclusion of the wrongfulness of the latter state's conduct. Furthermore, some elements required for such a finding will be dealt with.

2.3.2. *UN Security Council Resolutions*

One of the most influential entities in the international arena is without a doubt the United Nations Security Council (UNSC). Consent by the UNSC to carry out a certain action normally precludes the wrongfulness of that action. Thus, the execution of a UNSC resolution might amount to a result which, otherwise, would constitute internationally wrongful behaviour. A good example is the use of economic sanctions. Though frequently used by the UNSC, indirect victim of such measures is often the civilian population. Although the validity of UNSC resolutions is not a matter of debate, what is more problematic in the context of this contribution is the interpretation of their text and the actions taken subsequently. In other words, precisely to what kind of action did the UNSC consent? Occasionally, member states try to justify their behaviour on the basis of alleged consent given by UNSC decisions. For example, the UK tried to justify the invasion of Iraq in 2003 on the basis of UNSC resolution 678, which was one of the resolutions forming the basis for the first Gulf War. Hereby the UK placed the action under chapter VII of the UN Charter.[25] Here, the question whether consent is validly given or not is a matter of interpretation. For this, the rules on interpretation as enshrined in the Vienna Convention on the Law of Treaties might provide guidance. Could it be concluded that the act remained within the limits of the consent given when we apply the rule stated in article 19 of the Draft Articles and if we would accept the UK's argumentation? The United Nations should be known for its respect for the rule of law and the promotion of human rights. Nevertheless, in practice decisions of the UNSC are capable of violating rules

[23] Jaroslav Horák, Andrei Popkov, in: 64th General Assembly, 6th Committee, 15th meeting, document nr. GA/L/3374, annual review of the International Law Commission's activities.

[24] Report of the International Law Commission on the Work of its Fifty-Third Session, *Draft Articles on Responsibility of States for Internationally Wrongful Acts, with commentaries*, 2001, p. 72–73.

[25] Nigel D. White, 'Separate but Connected: Inter-Governmental Organisations and International Law', (2008) 5 *International Organizations Law Review*, p. 191.

of international law. Whereas customary international law is not covered by article 103 of the Charter,[26] it can be argued that a resolution of the UNSC prevails over an obligation under customary law, unless it violates rules of *ius cogens*. It can also be argued that the UNSC does not have the power to call upon States to take measures which would constitute a breach of rules of *ius cogens*.

To conclude, it is accepted under international institutional law that UNSC resolutions have the power to justify otherwise illegal behaviour by states. States, on the other hand, should be able to rely on the UNSC resolution as a preclusion of liability for eventual damages resulting from the execution of the resolution as long as they remain within their mandate.

2.3.3. *NATO Actions in Yugoslavia*

A controversial topic with regard to the responsibility of international organisations is the attack carried out by NATO on Yugoslavia. As is well established, NATO is an international legal personality capable of engaging in international relations. The military operation was carried out based on a decision of the North Atlantic Council, the political governing body of NATO. When it became clear that during the bombardments damages were inflicted on other than military targets on Yugoslavian territory, NATO paid compensation to individuals whose properties were damaged. Clearly, the member states did never consent to the execution of those failed missions. Nevertheless, Yugoslavia decided to bring claims against the NATO members separately, and not NATO itself, before the European Court of Human Rights (ECHR) and the International Court of Justice. NATO is neither a party to the ICJ Statute nor to the ECHR, so there was no other alternative. This implied that the NATO cover of the missions had to be lifted in order to effectively bring a complaint. During the proceedings, the NATO members surprisingly did not bring forth the argument that it was the NATO carrying out the attacks and not the member states, and that the member states could rely on the liability of the alliance. Therefore, neither the ICJ nor the ECHR had to deal with the issue during those proceedings. NATO has the capacity to carry out military attacks such as those in Yugoslavia, but was in casu not called upon to answer for the incurred damages. On the other hand, a decision of the North Atlantic Council is an authoritative instrument, and states should be able to rely on its legitimacy when carrying out the decision as long as they remain within the mandate given.[27]

---

[26] Article 103 UN Charter: "In the event of a conflict between the obligations of the Members of the United Nations under the present Charter and their obligations under any other international agreement, their obligations under the present Charter shall prevail."

[27] H.G. Schermers and N.M. Blokker, *International Institutional Law. Unity within Diversity*, The Hague: Martinus Nijhoff Publishers 2003, p. 1011.

2.3.4. *Conclusion*

The importance and strength of the organisation is an important factor in deciding whether a state may rely on consent given by an international organisation. For example, a hypothetical approval of a military mission of the Benelux in Africa will most certainly not preclude liability for its three member states. The Benelux, already long ago overshadowed by the EU, is of too little significance to be relied on in such an important context. When, on the other hand, a strong, widely recognised international organisation gives its consent to a certain action, the states carrying out the decision should be able to rely to a large extent on the validity of that decision as a justification for their actions. A UNSC resolution taken under chapter VII containing the words 'all means necessary' is generally seen as an exception to the prohibition on the use of force as enshrined in the Charter,[28] and a justification for the use of force by member states. It is often argued that a resolution of the UNSC could prevail over an obligation under customary international law as a *lex specialis*, unless it is contrary to rule of *ius cogens*.[29] Another factor of importance when assessing consent is the apportionment of influence on the decision-making process of the Member States within the international organisation. A decision of an international organisation which expresses only the will of one or a few member states should not be attributed solely to that international organisation. It might be that those member states threatened with the use of sanctions in order to persuade others. This would consequently amount to coercion and this could be, according to the ILC Commentaries, a factor which precludes the validity of the consent given. An example of a dominant state within an international organisation might be the United States within the Organization of American States (OAS). Studies have indicated that the USA more than once exerted its power to influence the policy outcome for its own benefit. For example, the ousting of Cuba from the OAS in 1962 and the subsequent sanctions imposed in 1964 were de facto US decisions, taken after pressure exerted by the United States on the other OAS member countries.[30] It could be argued that the legitimacy of such a decision by an international organisation should be questioned and hence its international acceptance. It is very difficult to speak of valid consent by an international organisation to a certain action in this context, whereas the other Member States would probably have acted otherwise without the US pressure. Still, to establish coercion is a difficult task before a tribunal.

---

[28] Art 2 (4) UN Charter.

[29] See e.g. Dominicé, supra n. 21, p. 366.

[30] Malcolm Shaw, *Cooperation, Conflict and Consensus in the Organization of American States*, New York: Palgrave Macmillan 2004, p. 101–102.

CHAPTER THREE

THE EXTINCTION OF STATES

*Mariano J. Aznar-Gómez**

1. *Introduction*

The state still is the *clef de voute* of the international system and of international law. Both social and legal layouts are based on the state. In several codification processes in the International Law Commission (ILC) – particularly with regards to the Declaration on the Rights and Duties of States, the Law of treaties or the Succession of States – attempts were made to clarify the legal meaning of the term 'state', but no definition was finally drafted. Actually, such a definition was qualified as controversial[1] or, even, non-useful.[2] A more recent definition, however, was given by the Badinter Commission: "The State is commonly defined as a community which consists of a territory and a population subject to an organised political authority; that such a State is characterised by sovereignty (…)".[3] Classical jurisprudence has also underlined these three core elements,[4] as it has been done by conventional practice of states[5] and doctrine.[6]

The state and the requisites for statehood – population, territory and government – have been interiorised as implied *terms of art* by tribunals, scholars

* The author would like to thank Carlos Jiménez Piernas for his most valuable comments on an earlier draft of this article, and Elena Pérez for her kind revision of the English text. The views expressed are solely those of the author, as are any errors. This contribution was prepared within the framework of the R+D Project DER 2009-13752-C03-03, of the Spanish Ministry of Science and Innovation.

[1] ILC Yearbook (1974), p. 19, par. 76.

[2] ILC Yearbook (1949), p. 259, par. 26.

[3] Opinion 1, 29 November 1991, (1991) 92 *International Law Reports*, p. 162.

[4] *Deutsche Continental Gesellschaft v. Polish State*, (1929) 5 *International Law Reports*, p. 11.

[5] See e.g. art. 1 of the 1933 Montevideo Convention, under which "[t]he state as a person of international law should possess the following qualifications: (a) a permanent population; (b) a defined territory; (c) government; and (d) capacity to enter into relations with the other states". Montevideo Convention on the Rights and Duties of States (adopted 26 December 1933, entered into force 26 December 1934) 165 *League of Nations Treaty Series*, p. 19.

[6] Jules Basdevant defined 'state' as "[le t]erme désignant, du point de vue du droit international, un groupement humain établi de manière permanente sur un territoire, ayant une organisation politique propre, dont l'existence politique dépend juridiquement de lui-même et relevant directement du droit international", in: *Dictionnaire de la terminologie du droit international*, Paris: Sirey 1960, p. 264. However, for Krystyna Marek, *Identity and Continuity in Public International Law*, Geneva: Droz 1955, p. 14,"[t]he identity of states is the identity of its international rights and obligations".

and, most evidently, by states themselves when recognising other states. Interestingly, most states before the International Court of Justice (ICJ) in the recent advisory proceedings regarding the *Accordance with International Law of the Unilateral Declaration of Independence by the Provisional Institutions of Self-Government of Kosovo*[7] – and some of the judges in their dissenting or separate opinions – have accepted those three elements, reducing the discussion to the assessment of the effectiveness of some of them (particularly an independent government) and the weight to be given to recognition of Kosovo by other states. Existence and recognition of states are thus interlinked terms, notwithstanding their different scope.[8]

The international community has witnessed (and still witnesses) situations in which some states might not deserve this legal qualification. The cases of the Congo around 1960 or Somalia since 1991 are paramount.[9] However, in no case has the international community derived from these situations the extinction of a state as a logical consequence. The 'pure' extinction of a state has been scholarly refused due to some terror of sovereignty vacuum,[10] hence labelling the state as 'failed'.[11] States have also preferred a somehow cynical *presumption of statehood* instead of admitting the disappearance of a state. Paradoxically, they use the same presumption for the admittance of 'new members to the club' barely fulfilling the criteria of statehood.[12] Legal order,

[7] Hereinafter: *Kosovo affair*.

[8] Recognition has been generally admitted as having a declaratory, non-constitutive character. See James Crawford, *The Creation of States in International Law*, Oxford: Oxford University Press 2006, passim. However, as a by-product of positivism, recognition used to be a constituent accepted criterion of statehood: see Oppenheim/Lauterpacht, *International Law: A Treatise*, London: Longman 1955, p. 125: "A state is, and becomes, an International Person through recognition only and exclusively."

[9] There are other cases that, in some moments of their recent history, could be equally labelled, like Afghanistan, Bosnia-Herzegovina in the first days of its independence, Haiti, Lebanon, Liberia, Rwanda during the days of genocide, Sudan or Sierra Leone, but also Cambodia after the 1991 Paris agreement, the Lebanon in the 1980s or, even, China during the 1930s.

[10] However, two decades ago, Koskeniemmi put it simply: "[S]tatehood has its reasons it is not a naturalistic *deus ex machina*. If and when those reasons do not exist, statehood can claim no particular protection"; see Martti Koskeniemmi, 'The Future of Statehood', (1991) 32 *Harvard International Law Journal*, p. 407–8. Some years earlier, Kristyna Marek expressed a quite similar opinion: "There is a beginning and an end to the state, as to everything else" (Marek, supra n. 6, p. 5). And even earlier, Kelsen opined that "a national legal order begins to be valid as soon as it has become – on the whole – efficacious; and it ceases to be valid as soon as it loses this efficacy" (Hans Kelsen, *General Theory of Law and State*, Cambridge (Mass.): Harvard University Press 1945, p. 220).

[11] See, however, the convincing arguments of Gérard Kreijen, *State Failure, Sovereignty and Effectiveness*, Leiden-Boston: Martinus Nijhoff Publishers 2004, particularly on p. 329–62. For older literature on this, see Thomas Baty, 'Can an Anarchy be a State?', (1934) 28 *American Journal of International Law*, p. 444; Arnold Raestad, 'La cessation des États d'après le droit des gens', (1939) 20 *Revue de droit international et de législation comparée*, p. 441.

[12] France recognising the United States in 1778 (protested by the UK), the United States recognising Panama in 1903 (protested by Colombia), more than 80 states recognising

stability, and continuity have been argued to deny the legal possibility of 'undoing' a state.[13] Furthermore, a state declaring the extinction of another state should be treated as a violator of the principle of non-intervention in internal affairs.

This chapter will not deal with the situations where a state might disappear in cases of succession of states: in these cases, a state is succeeded by other state.[14] It will not deal either with cases that could be labelled as 'dilution' of states, (i) in the sense of the progressive diminution and transfer of the exercise of their constitutional competences – due for example to the participation in an integration process such as the European Union –,[15] (ii) in the sense of the general interdependence due to economic process such as globalisation,[16] or (iii) in the general sense of diminution of sovereignty due precisely to the exercise of sovereignty.[17] The chapter will not deal with cases of (normally) transitory disappearance of a state by occupation or annexation.[18] It will not

(although some of them have suspended their public relations with) the Sahrawi Arab Democratic Republic since 1975 (continuously protested by Morocco). See for a recent appraisal Olivier Corten, 'Déclarations unilatérales d'indépendance et reconnaissances prématurées: du Kosovo à l'Ossétie du sud et à l'Abkhazie', (2008) 112 *Revue Générale de Droit International Public*, p. 721.

[13] Ian Browlie, *Principles of Public International Law*, Oxford: Oxford University Press 1990, p. 154.

[14] Somaliland in 1960, the Republic of Vietnam in 1976 or the GDR in 1990 disappeared and merged onto Somalia, the Socialist Republic of Vietnam or the Federal Republic of Germany, respectively. Tanganyika and Zanzibar disappeared in 1964 but were succeeded by Tanzania, and the two Yemens disappeared and merged onto the Republic of Yemen in 1990. The Socialist Federal Republic of Yugoslavia disappeared from 1991 onwards and was succeeded by several new states. The USSR also disappeared and 'was continued' by the Russian Federation (and the independence of 14 new states). Finally, Czechoslovakia disappeared in 1993 and was succeeded by the Czech and Slovak Federal Republics. There was *always* a successor state. As already said, "lorsqu'il y a entre prédécesseur(s) et successeur(s) une total communauté de substance, on peut se demander si l'on assiste vraiment à la disparition des uns et à la formation des autres et si le droit international n'aménage pas plutôt une formule particulière de continuité". Jean Combacau and Serge Sur, *Droit international public*, Paris: Montchrestien 1997, p. 298.

[15] See Alain Pellet, 'Les fondements juridiques internationaux du droit communautaire', in: *Collected Courses of the Academy of European Law V* (Book 2), Oxford: Oxford University Press 1997, p. 193.

[16] This process of 'obliged' economic system has diluted the classical principle upon which ""[e]very state possesses a fundamental right to choose and implement its own political, economic and social systems". *Military and Paramilitary Activities in and against Nicaragua (Nicaragua v. United States of America), Merits, Judgment*, ICJ Reports 1986, p. 131, par. 258. See L. Ali Khan, *The Extinction of Nation-States: A World Without Borders*, The Hague: Martinus Nijhoff Publishers 1996.

[17] Following the classical wording of the Permanent Court, "the right of entering into international engagements is an attribute of state sovereignty". *Case of the SS "Wimbledon" (UK, France, Italy, Japan v Poland)* PCIJ Reports, Series A, No 1, p. 25. For Dionisio Anzilotti, "[a]ccording to ordinary international law, every country is free to renounce its independence and even its existence". Individual Opinion, *Customs Régime Between Germany and Austria (Advisory Opinion)* PCIJ Reports, Series A/B, No 41, p. 59.

[18] From Ethiopia to Kuwait, not forgetting Czechoslovakia, Albania, Austria or the Baltic States.

deal, finally, with situations of dependence of States, regardless of the intensity of this dependence (such as the cases of Monaco, Marshall Islands, Liechtenstein or Puerto Rico).

This contribution – as a purely theoretical exercise – will try to assess a particular by-product of the so-called 'failed states' concept.[19] The latter comprises an amalgam of situations politically used to describe a situation of a non-functioning state[20] that, in some cases, could result in the simple extinction of a former state without the succession into a new or a pre-existing state. These cases deal with situations where one of the three elements of statehood simply disappears: the independent and effective government, taking effectiveness both as a sociological and as a normative principle.[21] Although, at least theoretically, the territory and the population of a State could completely evaporate,[22] in practice it is the disappearance of the third element – the government – that offers the possibility of this theoretical analysis.[23] The hypothesis of this paper is as follows:

---

[19] See generally Daniel Thürer, 'Failing States', in *Max Plank Encyclopedia of Public International Law*, available at <http://www.mpepil.com>; Oriol Casanovas y la Rosa, 'Los Estados fracasados' in: Caterina García and Angel Rodrigo (eds.), *La seguridad comprometida. Nuevos desafíos, amenazas y conflictos armados*, Madrid: Tecnos 2008, p. 83; and Robin Geiss, 'Failed States – Legal Aspects and Security Implications', (2004) 47 *German Yearbook of International Law*, p. 457. A 'Failed State Index' (FSI hereinafter) has been jointly created and electronically published since 2005 by *Foreign Policy* and the Fund for Peace. See its website at <http://www.foreignpolicy.com/failedStates>. Quite recently, in its 30 October 2010 issue, *Foreign Policy* re-published the seminal article written by Gerald H. Helman and Steven R. Ratner, 'Saving Failing States' (originally published in the Winter 1992–93 issue, 89 *Foreign Policy*, p. 16).

[20] Daniel Thürer, 'The "Failed State" and International Law', (1999) 81 *International Review of the Red Cross*, p. 732: "From a legal point of view, it could be said that the "failed state" is one which, though retaining legal capacity, has for all practical purposes lost the ability to exercise it. A key element in this respect is the fact that there is no body which can commit the state in an effective and legally binding way, for example, by concluding an agreement."

[21] These two approaches can be found, respectively, in Kreijen (supra n. 11) and in Enrico Milano, *Unlawful Territorial Situations in International Law – Reconciling Effectiveness, Legality and Legitimacy*, Leiden-Boston: Martinus Nijhoff Publishers 2006.

[22] At least theoretically, after a nuclear attack against a state, its entire population could perish and disappear. This has been a recurrent argument used, for example, by Israel in its policies against pre-nuclear regional neighbours, particularly Iran (now) and Iraq (two decades ago). Less theoretically, due to global warming, some Pacific Ocean island nations, such as Tuvalu, foresee the disappearance of their territory. Although the rumours about an *ad hoc* agreement between Tuvalu and New Zealand to allow the relocation of the population have been officially denied (see a New Zealand Press briefing of 4 August 2009 at <http://www.mfat.govt.nz/Foreign-Relations/Pacific/NZ-Tuvalu-immigration.php>), strong concerns are widespread in Tuvalu and other Pacific islands state about the subsistence of their territories. See for example the *Tuvalu's National Adaptation Programme of Action* of 2007 (available at <http://unfccc.int/resource/docs/napa/tuv01.pdf>).

[23] As argued by Marek, supra n. 6, p. 9, "[t]here exist no fixed criteria of state extinction". Current international law still lacks sufficient legal means to deal with this phenomenon. For Akpınarly, the solution to the absence of effective government can be found only in an economic and social approach and a true universalisation of international law: see Neyire Akpinarli, *The Fragility of the 'Failed States' Paradigm. A Different International Law Perception of the Absence of Effective Government*, Leiden-Boston: Martinus Nijhoff Publishers 2010.

(1) International law establishes as a customary principle that a state exists when the effective existence of a territory, a population and an independent government can be verified;
(2) International law does not properly foresee cases of extinction of states;
(3) Nothing precludes the idea of a *de facto* extinction of a state, and nothing necessarily impedes the *de iure* extinction of a state;
(4) The consequences of the extinction of a state are, however, still regulated by international law and, particularly, by the peremptory principles of self-determination, the prohibition of the use of force and of military occupation, and by the international law of human rights; and
(5) International administration of territories could be an effective and provisional tool in the hands of the international community to protect and secure the population and territory of an extinct state.

Keeping these ideas in mind, this chapter will try to address – as a theoretical exercise using the Somalia case[24] – different problems that the extinction of states might pose, namely (a) the *de facto* assessment of that situation; (b) the consequences that, *de iure*, the extinction of states poses to the international order and its core principles; and (c) the possible reaction of the international community when a state extinguishes.

2. *Government, Independence and Sovereignty*

In order to assess our hypothesis in the case of Somalia, we will try, first, to briefly revisit the general theoretical framework and, afterwards, to confront it with the particular Somali case in practice. As a preliminary assumption,[25] this contribution bases itself on the idea that a state, in international law, has plenary competence to perform in the international sphere, has exclusive competence with respect to its internal affairs, is not subject to compulsory adjudication without its consent, is formally equal to other states and, in principle, derogations to any of these components will not be presumed.

[24] Apart from the different UN reports made by its Secretary-General or by some of its agencies, some other sources are useful to assess the situation in Somalia as an 'extinct state'. In particular, together with the FSI data (see supra n. 19), the International Crisis Group's (ICG) reports have been used. See particularly its last report on Somalia: 'Somalia: To Move Beyond the Failed State', Crisis Group Africa Report no 147, 23 December 2008, available at the ICG website (<http:www.crisisgroup.org>). A recent and complete appraisal of the 'legal status' of Somalia as a failed state offers Carlos Jiménez Piernas, 'Los Estados fracasados y el Derecho internacional: el caso de Somalia', (2010), 62 *Revista Española de Derecho Internacional*, p. 17.

[25] Crawford, supra n. 8, p. 40–42.

A. *The Theoretical Approach*

Government, independence and sovereignty are interlinked terms.[26] Government means an independent exercise of power over the territory and population of the state. Government must be effective – not merely nominal – and independent from other states, giving a complete meaning to the term sovereignty.[27] In a classical arbitral award, Max Huber declared that "[s]overeignty in the relations between states signifies independence. Independence in regard to a portion of the globe is the right to exercise therein, to the exclusion of any other state, the functions of a state".[28] Charles Rousseau admitted that "[l]a perte de l'indépendence coincide nécessairement avec la disparition de l'État".[29] Daillier, Forteau and Pellet conclude that "[u]n territoire sans gouvernement dans l'acception moderne du terme ne peut être un État au sens du droit international".[30] Government has been defined "as the most important single criterion of statehood, since all the others depend upon it".[31]

An 'effective government' has thus been required by jurisprudence and doctrine. But doctrine has also modulated this effectiveness with regard to the continuity of a state already created. The requirement of effectiveness seems to be more strictly applied when it concerns the apparition of an entity whose statehood is opposed under title of international law.[32] However, it seems logical that effectiveness must also be equally and strictly assessed when it concerns the extinction of an existing state.[33]

To some extent, although provided for a secession situation (another extreme situation for a state), the strict test applied by the Commission of

---

[26] UNGA res. 2625 (XXV) (24 October 1970). *Nicaragua* (supra n. 16), p. 106, par. 202.

[27] A classical definition of this may be found in Anzilotti's individual opinion to the *Austro-German Custom Case*: "'[Independence] is really no more than the normal condition of states according to international law; it may also be described as sovereignty (*suprema potestas*), or external sovereignty, by which is meant that the state has over it no other authority than that of international law". For Anzilotti, "the legal conception of independence has nothing to do with a state's subordination to international law or with the numerous and constantly increasing states of *de facto* dependence which characterize the relation of one country to other countries". *Customs Régime* (supra n. 17) 57–8.

[28] *Island of Palmas case* (1928) 2 *Reports of International Arbitral Awards*, p. 838.

[29] Charles Rousseau, *Droit international public* (Vol. III), Paris: Sirey 1977, p. 330.

[30] Patrick Daillier, Mathias Forteau and Alain Pellet (Ngyuen Quoc Dinh), *Droit international public*, Paris: Bruylant 2009, p. 458.

[31] Crawford, supra n. 8, p. 56.

[32] Cf. Crawford, supra n. 8, p. 59, for whom "there is a distinction between the creation of a new state on the one hand and the subsistence or extinction of an established state on the other. In the former situation, the criterion of effective government may be applied more strictly" (footnotes ommitted).

[33] Not forgetting that (as applied in the Somalia case), "the process that culminated in the independence of sub-Saharan Africa essentially lacked the verifiable formation of a traditionally required ability for self-governent. (…) The post-colonial African state was thus primarily created by juridical means and as such it was emphatically not the affirmation of a process of empirical consolidation" '(Kreijen (supra n. 11), p. 330).

Jurists appointed by the League of Nations to assess the legal situation of the Åland Islands dispute could be useful and perfectly applicable to Somalia almost a century later. With minor changes of its wording, we could read that

> [the] situation was such that, for a considerable time, the conditions required for the formation of a sovereign State did not exist. (...) In the midst of revolution and anarchy, certain elements essential to the existence of a State, even some elements of fact, were lacking for a fairly considerable period. Political and social life was disorganised; the authorities were not strong enough to assert themselves; civil war was rife; further, the (authorities), the legality of which had been disputed by a large section of the people, had been dispersed by the revolutionary (parties), and the Government had been chased from the capital and forcibly prevented from carrying out its duties; the armed camps and the police were divided into two opposing forces, and (different tribal groups) took part in the civil war between the inhabitants.[34]

It is not a problem of a different pattern of government that could be applicable to Somalia. It is supposed that current international law still confirms the principle settled down by the ICJ in the *Western Sahara* case under which '[n]o rule of international law, in the view of the Court, requires the structure of a state to follow any particular pattern, as is evident from the diversity of the forms of state found in the world today.'[35] It is a problem of pure existence of a government given its incapacity to enter into relations with other states and to govern domestic affairs.[36]

B. *The Particular Situation of Somalia*

Initially faced as a humanitarian crisis, Somalia rapidly became the 'archetype' of a failed state.[37] As is well known, peacekeeping operations created by the UN Security Council needed to be reinforced and their mandates revisited several times until their withdrawal in 1996.[38] This derived from the UN Secretary-general appraisal that "[n]ational and regional Somali institutions

---

[34] *Åland Islands Case* (1920), League of Nations Official Journal, Special Supplement, p. 8–9, as adapted.

[35] *Western Sahara, Advisory Opinion*, ICJ Reports 1975, p. 43–4, par. 94. The last Court's 'evidence' seems to undermine the principle since, in the last thirty-five years, 'the diversity of the forms of state' has clearly diminished once the western model has been imposed *urbi et orbe*.

[36] Among the criteria used by the Failed State Index, the *delegitimisation of the state* supposes a "(w)idespread loss of popular confidence in state institutions and processes, e.g., widely boycotted or contested elections, mass public demonstrations, sustained civil disobedience, inability of the state to collect taxes, resistance to military conscription, rise of armed insurgencies". (source: FSI website, supra n. 19)

[37] See generally, for this first period, United Nations, *The United Nations and Somalia – 1992–1996* (Vol. VIII), New York: United Nations Blue Book Series); and Ioan Lewis and James Mayall, 'Somalia' in: James Mayall (ed.), *The New Interventionism 1991–1994*, Cambridge: Cambridge University Press 1996, p. 94.

[38] See generally Jorge Cardona Llorens, 'Las operaciones de mantenimiento de la paz de las Naciones Unidas: ¿hacia una revisión de sus principios fundamentales?' (2002) 6 *Cursos Euromediterráneos Bancaja de Derecho Internacional*, p. 759.

and civil administration [had] virtually ceased to exist".[39] Since then "all the efforts being undertaken by the United Nations in Somalia [were] directed towards one central goal: to assist the people of Somalia to create and maintain order and new institutions for their own governance".[40] Under its resolution 814 (1993), the Security Council mandated UNOSOM II with the reconstruction of Somali State, with the collaboration of civil society.[41] A 'Transitional National Council' (TNC) was created in 1993,[42] which was supposed to be the 'repository of Somali sovereignty' and 'the prime political authority having legislative functions' during the transitional period (until 27 March 1993). However, all the governance functions were exerted by UNOSOM II (backed by the Unified Task Force, UNITAF) and with a 'Somali Consultative Committee'. As said by Jarat Chopra, "in the absence of an existing infrastructure (…) the UN had effectively the power of a governor-in-trust".[43] Actually, Somalia seemed to be a neo-protectorate notwithstanding the cynicism of some states[44] and the self-constraint imposed by the UN Secretary-General.[45] However, since then, all the attempts to create a credible, fully supported government by the people of Somalia have failed notwithstanding the efforts of the international community through the UN, the League of Arab States, the African Union or, even, the European Union.[46] The 'Transitional Federal Government' (TFG) created in 2004 was non-functional.[47] Ethiopian military intervention of 2006 against Islamist

[39] UN doc. S/25354 (3 March 1993), p. 7, par. 27.

[40] Ibid., p. 9, par. 41.

[41] UNSC res. 814 (1993) (26 March 1993).

[42] Agreement of Addis Ababa of 27 March 1993, endorsed by UNSC res. 814 (26 March 1993). See a *résumé* in UNSG Report of 17 August 1993 (doc S/26317) 7–8, para 23–6.

[43] J Chopra, *Peace-maintenance: the evolution of international political authority* (Routledge, London 1999) 142.

[44] As remarked by Lewis and Mayal, "no government was prepared to support this view publicly, partly, no doubt, for fear of taking on an open-ended and costly commitment, far removed from their own vital interests, and partly out of respect for Third World sensitivities on the issue of colonialism" '(Lewis and Mayall (supra n. 37), p. 95).

[45] The SG held the "conviction that the political will to achieve security, reconciliation and peace must spring from the Somalis themselves" and that "UNOSOM II cannot and must not be expected to substitute itself for the Somali people". Further, under SG views, the mission "[n]or can or should it use its authority to impose one or another system of governmental organisation". UN doc. S/25354 (3 March 1993), p. 20, par. 92. For its part, UNSC has psalmodically reaffirmed in all its resolutions the "respect for the sovereignty, territorial integrity, political independence and unity of Somalia".

[46] For an overview of these attempts during the last 20 years of Somali history, see among others Maria Brons, *Society, Security, Sovereignty and the State in Somalia: From Statelessness to Statelessness?*, Utrecht: International Books 2001; I.M. Lewis, *Modern History of the Somali*, Athens (Georg.): Ohio University Press 2002; Kenneth Rutherford, *Humanitarian Under Fire: The US and UN Intervention in Somalia*, Sterling (Virgin.): Kumarian Press 2008; Abdullahi Osman and Issaka Souare (eds.), *Somalia at the Crossroads: Challenges and Perspectives in Reconstituting a Failed State*, London: Abbey Publishing 2007.

[47] However, for the UNSG, it was a "legally constituted and internationally recognised Government", UN doc. S/2009/373 (20 July 2009), p. 13, par. 63.

insurgency aggravated the scenario (including the surrounding states like Eritrea and Kenya), amid the Djibouti peace process. The most dramatic consequence, however, is the deterioration of the humanitarian situation, including the impossibility of delivery of humanitarian aid.[48] State cynicism has focused its preoccupation with the symptoms – the security of air traffic and the sea piracy, for example – instead of focusing on the main element of the Somali crisis: the absence of a government with a capacity to fulfil its sovereign faculties, rights and obligations. Paradoxically, those symptoms are also the evidence of the non-existence of an effective government in Somalia.

(i) The first symptom – the security of air traffic in Somalia airspace and in its surrounding air routes – moved the international community to interfere with "the complete and exclusive sovereignty over the airspace above (Somalia's) territory".[49] In March 1993, the International Civil Aviation Organisation (ICAO) and UNOSOM signed an agreement upon which "the force commander UNOSOM II is the airspace authority for Somalia airspace", based on a written communication between the UN Secretary-General and ICAO.[50] Operating from Mogadishu, the provisional aviation authority in Somalia could be understood as being derived from the mandate entrusted in UNSC resolution 794 (1992), first to UNITAF, then to UNOSOM II.[51] Once the latter withdrew, the management of Somalia's airspace was left in the hands of ICAO in collaboration with UNDP and created the 'Mogadishu Flight Information Region'. When the ICAO received

[48] Following Famine Early Warning System Network (FEWSNet), "about 27% of the total population (of Somalia) or an estimated 2 million people still remain in need of emergency humanitarian assistance and/or livelihood support until the end of 2010" (source: <http://www.fews.net>). The African Union peacekeeping mission in Somalia (AMISOM) – authorised by UNSC res. 1725 (2006) (6 December 2006), deployed since 19 January 2007 – has not alleviated this situation. In 2008, UNSC res. 1814 (2008) (15 May 2008) recommended a possible peacekeeping operation to succeed AMISOM in a new comprehensive UN strategic approach for peace and stability in Somalia designed by UN Secretary-General (UN doc. S/2008/178 (14 March 2008)).

[49] Art. 1, Convention on International Civil Aviation (Chicago Convention) (adopted 7 December 1944, entered into force 4 April 1947), 15 *United Nation Treaty Series* 295 (9th ed. 2006: Doc 7300/9).

[50] Text of the agreement on file with the author. Curiously, when the UN Development Programme (UNDP) was contacted on this question, from its office in Nairobi it was said that the information was not "for public consumption as this is covered by privileged communication".

[51] Under UNSC res. 794 (1992) (3 December 1992), the Council authorized the UNSG and Member States "to use all necessary means to establish as soon as possible a secure environment for humanitarian relief operations in Somalia". In its first report to the UNSC, UNITAF explicated that one of its first missions was "seizure of the airfield and port of Mogadishu". UN doc. S/24976 (17 December 1992) Annex. With regard UNOSOM II mandate, see UN doc. S/25354 (3 March 1993), p. 13, par. 57 (e): "to secure or maintain security at all ports, airport and lines of communications requires for the delivery of humanitarian assistance".

an authorisation from the UN Secretary-General,[52] in March 1996 ICAO and UNDP set up the 'Civil Aviation Caretaker Authority for Somalia' (CACAS), based in Nairobi, "to ensure safe air transport over Somali airspace in the absence of a functional central government."[53] In 2002, the UN Secretary-General recalled that

> [t]he United Nations is further engaged as caretaker in areas where the absence of an internationally recognised national authority could prevent operations. Due to the continued absence of a central Somali aviation authority with the capacity to provide essential aviation services, the International Civil Aviation Organisation (ICAO) Civil Aviation Caretaker Authority continues to perform the functions of a civil aviation authority for Somalia.[54]

To sum up, Somalia's airspace is not under its (complete) sovereignty. Two international organisations – ICAO and the UN – are vested with the responsibility to control air-traffic in extensive zones over the Somali territory (including sea spaces) up to the Seychelles. Apart from the legal basis of the authority self-vested by the UN Secretary-General,[55] this also poses the problems of international responsibility of an international organisation's conduct in a situation of absence or default of the official authorities of a state. Paradoxically, the ILC has neglected this possibility[56] and in the

---

[52] The UNSG had "agreed provisionally with the International Civil Aviation Organisation (ICAO) that it would continue to act in civil aviation matters with regard to Somalia, pending further guidance from the Council and/or the re-establishment of governmental authority in Somalia". UN doc. S/1995/231 (28 March 1995), p. 5, par. 19. The UNSC took note of this: UN doc. S/PRST1995/15 (6 April 1995).

[53] Some basic information can be gathered from the UNPD in Somalia website, at <http://mirror.undp.org/somalia/Themes/Governance/Aviation.htm>. CACAS was organised by the UNCP/ICAO Project SOM/96/002 from 1996 to 2003. Since then until 2009 has been organised by Project SOM/03/016/F. See the UNDP/ICAO last evaluation report of 24 July 2009, available at <http://erc.undp.org/evaluationadmin/manageevaluation/viewevaluationdetail.html?evalid=3789>.

[54] UN doc. S/2002/189 (21 February 2002), p. 7, par. 43. More than two years later, the 'Monitoring Group in Somalia' suggested that "[t]he new transitional government of Somalia that may emerge out of the current peace process should consider delegating its aeronautical responsibilities, such as licensing, the issuing of operating permits and certification, to a competent neighbouring country until such a time that the new transitional government is technically competent and capable of undertaking these responsibilities. This delegation of authority should be done in consultation with the International Civil Aviation Organisation (ICAO)". UN doc. S/2004/604 (11 August 2004), p. 44, par. 198.

[55] Are we moving again in the nebulous area of Article 41 of the UN Charter or in the 'general powers' vested on the UNSC by Chapter VII of the Charter, and then 'delegated' to the UNSG? On the powers of the UNSG derived from Article 99 of the Charter, see Jorge Cardona Llorens and Mariano Aznar-Gómez, 'Article 99', in: Jean-Pierre Cot, Alain Pellet and Mathias Forteau, *La Charte des Nations Unies. Commentaire article par article*, Paris: Economica 2005, p. 2051.

[56] In its report to UNGA of 2004, the ILC said: "Articles 4 to 7 of the present draft consider most issues that are dealt with in regard to states in Articles 4 to 11 of the Draft Articles on Responsibility of States for internationally wrongful acts. However, there is no text in the present Articles covering the issues addressed in Articles 9 and 10 on state responsibility.

current draft articles on the international responsibility of international organisations, no article foresees the legal consequences of that kind of situations.[57] It could be supposed that general rules of international responsibility not codified by the ILC[58] with regard to international organisations would govern those cases, attributing the conduct to the organisation in an analogous way to how Article 9 of the Articles on the Responsibility of States for internationally wrongful acts codifies these situations in the case of a state conduct and responsibility.[59]

(ii) With regard to piracy in Somalia, the history is better known,[60] mostly after the hijacking in September 2008 of the MV *Faina* – a Belize flag vessel carrying different heavy weapons allegedly destined to South Sudan. The bitter reaction of western states[61] (foreseeing new seizures, as

The latter Articles relate to conduct carried out in the absence or default of the official authorities and, respectively, to conduct of an insurrectional or other movement. These cases are unlikely to arise with regard to international organisations, because they presuppose that the entity to which conduct is attributed exercises control of territory. Although one may find a few examples of an international organisation administering territory, the likelihood of any of the above issues becoming relevant in that context appears too remote to warrant the presence of a specific provision. It is however understood that, should such an issue nevertheless arise in respect of an international organisation, one would have to apply the pertinent rule which is applicable to states by analogy to that organisation, either Article 9 or Article 10 of Draft Articles on Responsibility of State for internationally wrongful acts." *ILC Report of the International Law Commission on the Work of its 46th Session (3 May-4 June and 5 July-6 August 2004)* UN doc. A/59/10 (2004), p. 102–3 (footnotes omitted). For a critique on this option, see Mariano Aznar-Gómez, *La administración internacionalizada de territorios*, Barcelona: Atelier 2008, p. 293–301.

[57] *ILC Report of the International Law Commission on the Work of its 61st Session (4 May-5 June and 6 July-7 August 2009)*, UN doc. A/64/10 (2009), p. 13–178.

[58] To which Article 64 of the Draft Articles on Responsibility of International Organisations refers (ibid). "The applicable rules of international law continue to govern questions concerning the responsibility of an international organisation or a state for an internationally wrongful act to the extent that they are not regulated by these Articles". See also Article 56 of the Articles on Responsibility of States for Internationally Wrongful Acts. UNGA res. 56/83 (28 January 2002), Annex.

[59] This Article 9 says: "The conduct of a person or group of persons shall be considered an act of a state under international law if the person or group of persons is in fact exercising elements of the governmental authority in the absence or default of the official authorities and in circumstances such as to call for the exercise of those elements of authority."

[60] See among others José Manuel Sobrino, 'Piratería y terrorismo en el mar', in: *Cursos de Derecho internacional y Relaciones Internacionales de Vitoria-Gasteiz* 2008, p. 81; for the particular case of Somalia, see Antonello Tancredi, 'Di pirati e Stati "falliti": Il Consiglio di Sicurezza autorizza il ricorso alla forza nelle acque territoriali della Somalia', (2008) 4 *Rivista di Diritto Internazionale*, p. 937; Peter Pham, 'The Failed State and Regional Dimensions of Somali Piracy', in: Bibi van Ginkel and Frans-Paul van der Putten (eds.), *The International Response to Somali Piracy. Challenges and Opportunities*, Leiden-Boston: Martinus Nijhoff Publishers 2010, p. 31.

[61] As expressed by the International Crisis Group report, "'[T]he international pre-occupation with piracy may even appear hypocritical to many in view of the longstanding and rarely challenged practice of foreign entities to fish illegally and dump toxic waste on Somalia's coast". International Crisis Group, Africa Report No. 147 (supra n. 24), p. 22.

it happened)[62] was echoed in the UN Security Council, that began to adopt resolutions under chapter VII of the UN Charter. Once the Council took into account "the lack of capacity of the Transitional Federal Government (TFG) to interdict pirates or patrol and secure either the international sea lanes off the coast of Somalia or Somalia's territorial waters", it authorised states and regional organisations to

> (a) Enter into the territorial waters of Somalia for the purpose of repressing acts of piracy and armed robbery at sea, in a manner consistent with such action permitted on the high seas with respect to piracy under relevant international law; and
> (b) Use, within the territorial waters of Somalia, in a manner consistent with such action permitted on the high seas with respect to piracy under relevant international law, all necessary means to repress acts of piracy and armed robbery at sea.[63]

Two weeks later, in response to an invitation from the President of Somalia, and "[n]oting with concern (…) the lack of capacity, domestic legislation, and clarity about how to dispose of pirates after their capture", the Council further decided that

> States and regional organisations cooperating in the fight against piracy and armed robbery at sea off the coast of Somalia for which advance notification has been provided by the TFG to the Secretary-General may undertake all necessary measures that are appropriate in Somalia, for the purpose of suppressing acts of piracy and armed robbery at sea, pursuant to the request of the TFG, provided, however, that any measures undertaken pursuant to the authority of this paragraph shall be undertaken consistent with applicable international humanitarian and human rights law.[64]

It is true that the President of Somalia *invited* the Security Council to decide this, and that the TFG has repeated its invitation to operate in Somalia's spaces, both land and maritime. But it is also true that the representativeness and effectiveness – not to talk about transparency[65] – of current Somali

[62] In Spain, the question resulted in a national debate once pirates seized two Spanish tuna-fish vessels – the *Playa de Bakio* and and the *Alakrana* – and a rescue was paid. Spain, as one of the major maritime Powers, with a big fleet based in Seychelles Islands, is one the most conspicuous leaders of the reaction against piracy off Somalia coast. For an assessment from a Spanish perspective, see Jesús Bacas et al., *Crisis somalí, piratería e intervención internacional*, Madrid: IUGM/UNED, 2009, available at <http://iugm.es/uploads/tx_iugm/crisis_somali.pdf>.

[63] UNSC res. 1846 (2008) (2 December 2008), preamble and par. 10. See further UNSC res. 1897 (2009) (30 November 2009). The European Union (EU) launched on 8 December 2008 the *Operation Atalanta* (EUNAVFOR), decided within the Common Security and Defence Policy (CSDP). See Council Decision (CFSP) 2008/918 on the launch of a European Union military operation to contribute to the deterrence, prevention and repression of acts of piracy and armed robbery off the Somali coast (Atalanta), [2008] *Official Journal of the European Union* L 330/19.

[64] UNSC res. 1851 (2008) (16 December 2008), preamble and par. 6.

[65] In its last report, the 'global coalition against corruption' – Transparency International (TI) – has declared Somalia as the worst country out of 178 analysed in its Index. See *2010 Corruption Perception Index* at TI website (<http://www.transparency.org/>).

government is far from consolidated, amid the different and independent authorities in some autonomous regions of Somalia as 'Puntland' and 'Somaliland'.[66]

The UN Secretary-General has further underlined the sovereignty deficit of Somalia in some other aspects.[67] The Security Council had to repeatedly recall the general principle of "respect for the sovereignty, territorial integrity, political independence and unity of Somalia, including Somalia's rights with respect to offshore natural resources, including fisheries, in accordance with international law".[68] In 1999, the UN Secretary-General confirmed that "[l]ittle or no development (had) taken place in Somalia for 10 years".[69] The situation was defined as "unique":

> The functions that States perform, such as the provision of social services, including health and education, the regulation, for example, of the movement of goods and persons, control of the environment, airspace and coasts, and so on, as well as the representation of the Somali people in intergovernmental and international fora, are absent.[70]

After a new decade, apart from renewing the African Union Mission in Somalia (AMISOM) mandate for one more year[71] and from witnessing an amelioration of the situation, the UN Secretary-General reiterated that "[i]nsecurity remained widespread throughout Somalia"[72] and that "[t]he humanitarian situation in Somalia remains dire".[73] The UN-sponsored Djibouti negotiation initiated in May 2008 seems to have failed. Some of its rifts were the non-recognition of the TFG by insurgents, the neglect of clan elders and clan leadership councils, the increasing presence of radical islamist groups and the difficulties posed by the autonomous regions, on one hand, and the Ethiopian[74] (and Eritrea) presence, on the other. Actually, president Yusuf was also viewed as an obstacle to peace in Somalia, and he resigned on 29 December 2008.

---

[66] See further Jiménez Piernas, supra n. 24, p. 23–4.

[67] For the UNSG, "[a]ction could be taken by the international community to assist Somalia *to recover its sovereignty* in certain limited fields, for example the protection of offshore natural resources." UN doc. S/1999/882 (16 August 1999), p. 17, par. 77, emphasis added.

[68] See the last example in UNSC res. 1897 (2009) (30 November 2009), preamble.

[69] UN doc. S/1999/882 (16 August 1999), p. 14, par. 61.

[70] Ibid., par. 63.

[71] UNSC res. 1910 (2010) (28 January 2010).

[72] UN doc. S/2009/684 (8 January 2010), p. 4, par. 16.

[73] Ibid., p. 6, par. 24. For the Independent Expert on the Situation of Human Rights in Somalia, "[t]he human rights and humanitarian law violations in Somalia depict a grim picture indeed. The situation deteriorated further since the last report of the independent expert to the Human Rights Council". UN doc. A/HRC/15/48 (16 September 2010), p. 13, par. 51. For this, the report stressed the idea that "the United Nations and the international community to continue to back TFG and help it with greater vigour to grow into an *effective Government* which would not only be able to hold on to Mogadishu, albeit with the help of AMISOM, but also gradually extend its control through a combined military and political strategy". Ibid., p. 13, par. 54 (emphasis added).

[74] With the US support, in another chapter of the Bush Administration's 'war on terror'.

On 29 January 2010, a year after the moving of the TFG to Mogadishu, the situation seemed to worsen.[75] For the UN Monitoring Group on Somalia,

> [t]he current military stalemate in southern Somalia is less a reflection of opposition strength than of *the weakness of the Transitional Federal Government*. Since the nomination of Sheikh Sharif to the presidency and the withdrawal of Ethiopian forces from Somalia early in 2009, armed opposition groups – Al-Shabaab in particular – *have lost their popular support base and been gravely weakened*. (…) Despite infusions of foreign training and assistance, government security forces remain ineffective, disorganized and corrupt.[76]

As a provisional conclusion – that perhaps does not "overcome (the) formidable burden of proof" requested to ascertain the extinction of a state[77] –, it could be said that Somalia is still without effective government, thus lacking one of the main criteria of statehood. It is not a problem of the *exercise of independence* – formal or actual[78] – as a right of a state, but a problem of *existence of independence* as a criterion of statehood. Former UN Secretary-General Boutros Boutros-Ghali wrote when dealing with Somalia,

> A state that loses its Government (…) loses its place as a member of the international community (…) The Charter of the United Nations provides for the admission to the international community of a country which gains the attributes of sovereignty (…) It does not, however, provide for any mechanism through which the international community can respond when a sovereign state loses one of the attributes of statehood (…) Further reflection by the international community is required on this issue.[79]

It is not a theoretical game of 'undoing Somalia'; not a *delenda est Somalia*. It is just an assessment of facts: Somalia does not exist as a state.

---

[75] See the last report of the Independent Expert on the Situation of Human Rights in Somalia: "In Somalia there has been no sustained international effort. What the UN and others are doing can only be described as first aid. As a result the situation has gone from bad to worse. If it is allowed to fester, it can only get worse". UN doc. A/HRC/13/65 (8 March 2010), p. 26–7, par. 78.

[76] UN doc. S/2010/91 (10 March 2010) 79, par. 272–3, emphasis added. For the UNSG, however, in his last report on Somalia, "[r]ecent progress in key areas has rendered the (Somali) Government more confident and established it as a serious representative of the interests of the Somalis and a viable partner of the international community". UN doc. S/2010/234 (11 May 2010), p. 16–7, par. 77.

[77] "To establish such lack of independence, in the absence of foreign occupation or unlawful military intervention, is to overcome a formidable burden of proof", remarks Crawford (supra n. 8), p. 86. For the Cambridge professor, "it is important to distinguish independence as an initial qualification for statehood and as a condition for continued existence", and that "[t]here is a related distinction to be drawn between independence as a criterion for statehood and independence as a right of states" (ibid., p. 63).

[78] Crawford continues by saying that: "where formal independence masks the lack of any actual independence at all, the entity should be regarded as not independent for the purpose of statehood" (ibid, p. 88).

[79] *The United Nations and Somalia* (supra n. 37), p. 87.

3. *Consequences of the Extinction of States*

Once a state extinguishes, its territory and population remain. However, there is no government with the capacity to enter into relations with the other states with regard that territory and that population and to protect them both. Until the advent of contemporary international law, this situation might have led to the occupation and annexation of the territory and the subjection of the population to a new sovereign. The legality of that situation would be under no discussion given the 'inter-temporal' application of international law of each epoch.[80]

However, and using again this inter-temporal application of international law, today such a kind of occupation and annexation should suppose a violation of the current peremptory norms of international law, particularly those dealing with the prohibition of the use of force, the principle of self-determination and the respect for fundamental human rights. In a normative sense, international law hence becomes the *curator* of the territory and the population without state. In a social sense, the international community is bestowed with the faculty to administer the transition from a 'no-state' situation towards a final decision on that territory and population. In sum, the consequences of the extinction of states are (and must be) ruled by international law.

A. *Consequences for the Territory*

The territory of an extinct state, as any other territory, could only change its legal status through the classical modes of territorial transfer in international law:[81] occupation, conquest (*debellatio*), cession (conventional or unilateral, including *derelictio*), merger and prescription. Given that the main premise of an extinct state is the absence of a government with the capacity to enter into relations with the other states with regard that territory, both cession and merger are not legally possible nor politically legitimate given the lack of representativeness of any national leader. The other three possibilities – *debellatio*, prescription and occupation – also appear to be unsuitable for the case of an extinct state.[82]

---

[80] *Island of Palmas* (supra n. 28), p. 845; *Western Sahara* (supra n. 35), p. 38–39, par. 79; *Land and Maritime Boundary between Cameroon and Nigeria (Cameroon v. Nigeria: Equatorial Guinea intervening), Judgment*, ICJ Reports 2002, p. 405, par. 205. See also Institut de droit International, Resolution of 11 August 1975, Session of Wiesbaden (1975), available at <http://www.idi-iil.org/idiE/resolutionsE/1975_wies_01_en.pdf> (par. 1 of the Resolution: "Unless otherwise indicated, the temporal sphere of application of any norm of public international law shall be determined in accordance with the general principle of law by which any fact, action or situation must be assessed in the light of the rules of law that are contemporaneous with it.")

[81] See generally Marcelo Kohen, *Possession contestée et souveraineté territoriales*, Geneva: PUF 1997.

[82] We leave aside the case of accretion, not being applicable here.

From 1945 onwards, *debellatio* is expressly forbidden by international law. As is widely known, it is a principle of current legal order that "[n]o territorial acquisition resulting from the threat or use of force shall be recognised as legal".[83] This rule is one of the building blocks of the general principle prohibiting the use of force in international relations.[84] It has been said that "the independence of an existing State is protected by international law rules against unlawful invasion and annexation, so that the State may, even for a considerable time, continue to exist as a legal entity despite lack of effectiveness".[85]

Prescription supposes the acquisition of a territory through an effective, public, peaceful and uninterrupted possession *à titre de souverain*.[86] Prescription differs from occupation as to the legal status of the disputed territory: in the former a previous owner exists that relinquishes its title by acquiescence; yet, occupation needs a *terra nullius* to be operative. The genuine source of legitimacy in prescription seems to be the voluntary abandonment of rights by the previous sovereign[87] and the attitude of the new possessor.[88] The ICJ has used acquiescence either to reject prescription in absence of legal title[89] or to reject prescription against legal title.[90] In an extinct state legal title does exist; and, in absence of effective government, we have accepted *ex hypothesi* that acquiescence is not acceptable (either legally or politically).

---

[83] UNGA res. 2625 (XXV) (24 October 1970), which reflects customary international law. *Nicaragua* (supra n. 16), p. 101–3, par. 191–3.

[84] *Legal Consequences of the Construction of a Wall in the Occupied Palestinian Territory, Advisory Opinion*, ICJ Reports 2004, p. 171, par. 87. Principle that denies any 'effectiveness' to land occupation by force (*ex injuria non oritur ius*), as in the case of occupied Palestinian territories (see UNSC res. 242 (1967) (22 November 1967)) or in the case of the invasion of Kuwait by Iraq (see UNSC res. 662 (1990) (9 August 1990)). The violation of the prohibition of the use of force or some others compulsory principles of international law was also behind the reaction of the UN Security Council against the 'secession' of Southern Rhodesia in 1965, Northern Cyprus in 1983 or the Republika Srpska in 1992.

[85] Crawford (supra n. 8), p. 63.

[86] Although it has been pleaded in different case law, the ICJ has indicated that "for present purposes" it "need not concern itself with the status of acquisitive prescription in international law or with the conditions for acquiring title to territory by prescription": *Kasikili/Sedudu Island (Botswana/Namibia)*, ICJ Reports 1999, p. 1105, par. 97. For a complete review of these questions in current international law, see Kohen (supra n. 81), p. 17–34.

[87] And, as a matter of fact (and of law), it could be supposed that *pure* good faith is absent in prescription: the state invoking prescription *knows* that its claim is against the law. As remarked by Kohen, supra n. 81, p. 28: "Le problème ici n'est pas simplement celui de savoir si une attitude passive de l'État dépossedé est nécessaire pour qu'il y ait délaissement, mais encore quels sont les actes ou comportements de cet État susceptibles de constituer (ou d'empêcher) un acquiescement de sa part face à la nouvelle situation créée par la possession effective d'un territoire lui appartenant en souveraineté."

[88] In any case, "the intention to acquire sovereignty may appear from the conduct of the Parties" *Sovereignty over Pedra Branca/Pulau Batu Puteh, Middle Rocks and South Ledge (Malaysia/Singapore), Judgment* ICJ Reports 2008, p. 61, par. 149.

[89] *Kasikili/Sedudu* (supra n. 86) p. 1106, par. 98.

[90] *Land and Maritime Boundary* '(supra n. 81), p. 354, par. 70.

With regard the legal status of the territory of an extinct state, two main questions arise: (1) does the territory become *terra nullius* and, hence, subject to peaceful occupation by other state?; and (2) if not, what is the legal status of that territory? In the *Western Sahara* case, the ICJ proceeded from the idea that

> The expression '*terra nullius*' was a legal term of art employed in connection with 'occupation' as one of the accepted legal methods of acquiring sovereignty over territory. 'Occupation' being legally an original means of peaceably acquiring sovereignty over territory otherwise than by cession or succession, it was a cardinal condition of a valid "occupation" that the territory should be terra nullius – a territory belonging to no-one – at the time of the act alleged to constitute the 'occupation' (...).[91]

For the Court, therefore, a determination that a territory is a *terra nullius* would be possible only if it were established that the territory belongs to no-one "in the sense that it was then open to acquisition through the legal process of 'occupation'".[92] The reasoning, however, should be the contrary in current international law: if in the late 20th century, a territory was *terra nullius* because it could be occupied, in the beginning of 21th century a territory can only be occupied if it is *terra nullius*. Further, the Court does not assimilate *terra nullius* with 'non-state territory'.[93] The territory of an extinct state is not *terra nullius*. It is therefore not subject to occupation. In this sense, Somalis are the 'owners' of their land,[94] and no state could legally snatch their territory from them.

B. *Consequences for the Population*

Drawing a general panorama of the humanitarian situation in Somalia is both easy and dramatic. For Human Rights Watch (HRW),

> Somalia's people continue to endure one of the world's worst human rights catastrophes ... A humanitarian crisis of enormous proportions is unfolding, fuelled by years of drought and insecurity that has often prevented the effective delivery of aid. Some 3.75 million people —roughly half of Somalia's remaining population— are in urgent need of humanitarian assistance. More than a million people are displaced from their homes within Somalia and tens of thousands fled the country as refugees in 2009.[95]

---

[91] *Western Sahara* '(supra n. 35), p. 39, par. 79.

[92] Ibid.

[93] For the Court, "[w]hatever differences of opinion there may have been among jurists, the state practice of the relevant period indicates that territories inhabited by tribes or peoples having a social and political organisation were not regarded as *terrae nullius*"; ibid., par. 80.

[94] 'Ownership' here must be seen as equivalent to 'sovereignty'. See *Territorial Sovereignty and Scope of the Dispute* '(Eritrea/Yemen), (1998) 22 *Reports of International Arbitral Awards*, p. 219, par. 19, and p. 317–318, par. 474.

[95] Human Rights Watch, *Country Summary: Somalia* (January 2010) 1, available at <http://www.hrw.org/en/world-report-2010/somalia>.

Quite similar conclusions are given in the 2010 report of the Independent Expert on the Situation of Human Rights in Somalia:

> The medium to long-term perspective is based on the fact that almost twenty years of internecine warfare has caused so much of damage to Somalia – to its basic infrastructures, institutions, social structures, social values and norms and in the state itself – that it is not realistic to expect that they could be repaired in the short term. It would require a long process of steady rebuilding of the basic components of state-building, the foremost among which are trust and social cohesion, which have been key casualties of the conflict.[96]

The 'Multidimensional Measure of Poverty' (MPI) used by the last Human Development Index,[97] situates Somalia within the highest rates of deprivation: 81%.[98] In a somehow *couple diabolique*, the absence of effective state components lead to starvation of the Somali population, which became a structural component of the turmoil and impeded a political solution.

The Somali population has, first and foremost, the human right to survive. And the first duty for the international community is to afford every necessary means to permit that survival. When it was created, UNOSOM II had to be "in a position to press for the observance of United Nations standards of human rights and justice".[99] But, apart from this dramatic evidence with regard to the threats to survival, there is also a political right still bestowed on the Somali population: its right to self-determination protected by a *ius cogens* principle.[100] This right also implies to become again a sovereign and independent state, to associate or integrate with another independent state or to emerge into any other political status freely determined by its people, the three options foreseen in resolution 2625 (XVV) of the UN General Assembly;[101] but also the right to pursue its political, economic, social and cultural development,

---

[96] UN doc. A/HRC/15/48 (16 September 2010) 13, par. 57.

[97] MPI considers deprivation (and its overlapping) of the three basic components of Human Development Index (HDI): information on life expectancy, schooling and income, trying to show the number of people who are poor (suffering a given number of deprivations) and the number of deprivations with which poor households typically contend.

[98] UN Development Programme, *Human Development Report 2010* (available at <http://www.undp.org/publications/hdr2010/en/HDR_2010_EN_Complete.pdf>, p. 99.

[99] UN doc. S/25354 (3 March 1993), p. 20, par. 92.

[100] *Case concerning East Timor (Portugal v. Australia), Judgement*, ICJ Reports 1995, p. 102, par. 29 (self-determination "is one of the essential principles of contemporary international law"); *Consequences of the Wall* (supra n. 84), p. 171–2, par. 88. Common Article 1 of the two 1966 Covenants on Human Rights provides in its paragraph 1 that "[a]ll peoples have the right of self-determination. By virtue of that right they freely determine their political status and freely pursue their economic, social and cultural development". 999 *United Nations Treaty Series*, p. 171 (Civil and Political Rights), and 993 *United Nations Treaty Series*, p. 3 (Economic, Social and Cultural Rights). See generally Christian Tomuschat (ed.), *Modern Law of Self-Determination*, Dordrecht: Martinus Nijhoff Publishers 1993, and Antonio Cassese, *Self-Determination of Peoples. A Legal Reappraisal*, Cambridge: Cambridge University Press 1995.

[101] On self-determination outside decolonisation, see generally Théodore Christakis, *Le droit à l'autodétermination en dehors des situations de décolonisation*, Paris: Decitre 1999.

along with the complete respect of the human rights through democratic processes. Democracy here plays a pivotal role, giving its interlinked roots with human rights, development and self-determination. As adopted in the UN World Conference on Human Rights in 1993,

> Democracy, development and respect for human rights and fundamental freedoms are interdependent and mutually reinforcing. Democracy is based on the freely expressed will of the people to determine their own political, economic, social and cultural systems and their full participation in all aspects of their lives. In the context of the above, the promotion and protection of human rights and fundamental freedoms at the national and international levels should be universal and conducted without conditions attached. The international community should support the strengthening and promoting of democracy, development and respect for human rights and fundamental freedoms in the entire world.[102]

The population of extinct states can (and deserves) the aide of the international community in order to be protected and to ease a renewed *mise en œuvre* of its right to self-determination. Although drafted for the Namibia population confronted with the illegal presence of South Africa, the ICJ's words are fully accurate here when dealing with extinct states: "The injured entity is a people which must look to the international community for assistance (…)".[103] How this assistance can be provided will be briefly reviewed in the next section.

4. *The Role of the International Community*

As we have seen, the situation in Somalia is not unique, but quite representative of starvation and destruction of basic state structures. But it is also an opportunity for the international community vested in the UN:

> Of all the anthropogenic humanitarian crises that United Nations is presently dealing with, the crisis in Somalia is perhaps the most challenging. It also offers perhaps the most creative opportunities. If Somalia is the most 'failed' State in the world today, the United Nations has the unique opportunity to steer its revival. Such an opportunity does not exist for the United Nations in Afghanistan, Iraq or elsewhere, where there are other 'big' players to lead. The United Nations has thus a special responsibility for Somalia.[104]

As advanced in the introduction to this chapter, once a state extinguishes, the population of a territory remains. We have seen that both remaining elements of statehood are protected by peremptory rules of international law. But in

---

[102] Vienna Declaration and Programme of Action, 25 June 1993, UN doc. A/CONF.157/23 (12 July 1993).

[103] *Legal Consequences for States of the Continued Presence of South Africa in Namibia (South West Africa) notwithstanding Security Council Resolution 276, Advisory Opinion*, ICJ Reports 1971, p. 56, par. 127.

[104] UN doc. A/HRC/15/48 (16 September 2010), p. 17, par. 75.

order to foster a future for that piece of land and, overall, for human beings constituting a 'population' – the "most precious constitutive element of statehood", as described by Judge Cançado Trindade[105] – the international community has two possible and useful tools to manage the situation until a definitive solution be found: theoretically, the conceptual framework of the 'Responsibility to Protect'; and, instrumentally, the institution of international administration of territories.

A. *The Responsibility to Protect Extinct States*

As it is well known, the Responsibility to Protect (RtoP) concept was first presented by the Canadian-sponsored International Commission on Intervention and State Sovereignty (ICISS) in its report of December 2001.[106] The concept could be historically traced from *iustum bellum* to humanitarian intervention, revisited by the *devoir d'ingérence* and arriving at a new more fashionable label endorsed by the international community *atélier*,[107] not only by the United Nations[108] but by the European Union[109] and the African Union[110] as well. The concept, however, does not add any significant component to current international law,[111] apart from revisiting a rather interventionist approach. In sum,

[105] *Kosovo affair*, Separate Opinion by Judge Antonio A. Cançado Trindade, at p. 24, par. 77, among others.

[106] ICISS, *The Responsibility to Protect* (December 2001) 5.22, available at <http://iciss.ca/pdf/Commission-Report.pdf>, hereinafter RtoP Report. See further the documents and discussions in the website of 'The International Coalition for the Responsibility to Protect' at <http://www.responsibilitytoprotect.org/>. On the concept (and nuances) of the 'responsibility to protect', see Société Française pour le Droit International, *La responsabilité de protéger – Colloque de Nanterre*, Paris: Pedone 2008; Gareth Evans, *The Responsibility to Protect. Ending Mass Atrocity Crimes Once and for All*, Washington: Brookings Institute Press 2008; Richard H. Cooper and Juliette Voïnov Kohler (eds.), *The Responsibility to Protect: The Global Moral Compact for the 21st Century*, New York: Macmillan 2008. See also Rafael García Pérez, 'La "Responsabilidad de Proteger": Un nuevo papel para Naciones Unidas en la gestión de la seguridad internacional', (2006) 11 *Revista Española de Estudios Internacionales*, available at <http://www.reei.org>.

[107] See Jean-Marc Thouvenin, 'Genese de l'idée de responsabilité de protéger', in: Société Française pour le Droit International (supra n. 106), p. 21.

[108] *2005 World Summit Outcome*, UN doc. A/60/L.1 (15 September 2005) par. 138–40.

[109] *EU Council Conclusions on UN World Summit* (7 November 2005), text available electronically at <http://www.consilium.europa.eu/uedocs/cmsUpload/council_conclusions_on_un_world_summit-nov05.pdf>.

[110] Article 4 (h) of the 2002 *African Union Constitutive Act*, which stipulates "[t]he right of the Union to intervene in a Member State pursuant to a decision of the Assembly in respect of grave circumstances, namely war crimes, genocide and crimes against humanity". Constitutive Act of the African Union (11 July 2020) 2158 *United Nations Treaty Series*, p. 3. See also 'The Common African Position of the Proposed Reform of the United Nations: "The Ezulwini Consensus"', African Union Executive Council, 7th Extraordinary Sesion (Addis Ababa, 7–8 March 2005), AU doc Ext/EX.CL/2 (VII), available electronically at <http://www.responsibilitytoprotect.org/AU_Ezulwini%20Consensus.pdf>.

[111] Laurence Boisson de Chazournes and Luigi Condorelli, 'De la "responsabilité de protéger", ou de une nouvelle parure pour une notion déjà bien établie en droit international', (2006) 110 *Revue Générale de Droit International Public*, p. 2.

RtoP means that state sovereignty implies responsibility, and the primary responsibility for the protection of its people lies with the state itself. Where a population is suffering serious harm, as a result of internal war, insurgency, repression or state failure, and the state in question is unwilling or unable to halt or avert it, the principle of non-intervention yields to the international RtoP. Founded in the concept of sovereignty, in the UN Charter (particularly its chapter VII) and in human rights and humanitarian law principles, international practice has consolidated the subsidiary duty to intervene in those scenarios, including state failure.[112] In this last case, two of the RtoP components – responsibility to react and responsibility to rebuild – are particularly applicable.

In order to react, the RtoP concept establishes a 'threshold criterion' to intervene: the 'just cause', which includes halting or avert a failed state situation.[113] In order to rebuild, the RtoP concept recalls the basic principles of UN trusteeship enshrined in Chapter XII of the Charter:

> 5.22 Useful guidelines for the behaviour of intervening authorities during a military intervention in failed states, and in the follow-up period, might be found in a constructive adaptation of Chapter XII of the UN Charter. This would enable reconstruction and rehabilitation to take place in an orderly way across the full spectrum, with the support and assistance of the international community. The most relevant provision in this regard is Article 76 which notes that the aim of the system is to promote the political, economic, social and educational advancement of the people of the territory in question; to encourage respect for human rights; to ensure the equal treatment of all peoples in the UN in social, economic and commercial matters; and also to ensure equal treatment in the administration of justice.
>
> 5.23 A further element of Chapter XII which would often be of relevance to the populations of countries in which an intervention takes place relates to self-determination (Article 76.b). Protective enforcement usually indicates sustaining or restoring forms of territorial self-government and autonomy, and this in turn will usually mean elections being facilitated and possibly supervised, or at least monitored, by the intervening authorities. That said, the responsibility to protect is fundamentally a principle designed to respond to threats to human life, and not a tool for achieving political goals such as greater political autonomy, self-determination, or independence for particular groups within the country (though these underlying issues may well be related to the humanitarian

112 As explained in the report, RtoP embraces three specific responsibilities: to *prevent* (to address both the root causes and direct causes of internal conflict and other man-made crises putting populations at risk), to *react* (to respond to situations of compelling human need with appropriate measures, which may include coercive measures like sanctions and international prosecution, and in extreme cases military intervention) and to *rebuild* (to provide, particularly after a military intervention, full assistance with recovery, reconstruction and reconciliation, addressing the causes of the harm the intervention was designed to halt or avert). See RtoP Report, synopsis.

113 RtoP Report, par. 4.19. If the use of force is needed, previous authorisation by the UN Security Council must be adopted ex chapter VII of the UN Charter.

concerns that prompted the military intervention). The intervention itself should not become the basis for further separatist claims.

5.24 There is always likely in the UN to be a generalized resistance to any resurrection of the "trusteeship" concept, on the ground that it represents just another kind of intrusion into internal affairs. But "failed states" are quite likely to generate situations which the international community simply cannot ignore, as happened – although there the intervention was less than successful – *in Somalia*. [emphasis added, MA-G]. The strongest argument against the proposal is probably practical: the cost of such an operation for the necessarily long time it would take to recreate civil society and rehabilitate the infrastructure in such a state. There must be real doubts about the willingness of governments to provide those kinds of resources, other than on a very infrequent and ad hoc basis.

Again Somalia appears as the 'archetype' of a failed state; and a 'revisited trusteeship system' was proposed.[114] However, it must be said at the very outset that article 78 of the UN Charter should preclude the application of trusteeship to a failed state if member of the UN: "The trusteeship system shall not apply to territories which have become Members of the United Nations, relationship among which shall be based on respect for the principle of sovereign equality."[115] This should impose a legal limit that makes trusteeship unworkable.[116]

But, along with this formal limit, another obstacle also makes trusteeship unsuitable for extinct states: as it is well known, the UN General Assembly and the Secretary-General declared the Trusteeship Council useless, and both proposed its suppression,[117] leaving failed (and extinct) states without a

[114] "Revisiting trusteeship" could have been an option. In 1995, Malta submitted a proposal which included the transformation of the Trusteeship Council "from a guardian of dependent territories to a body that acts as guardian and trustee of the global commons and the common concerns in the interest of present and future generations", including among these the "safeguard of peoples in situations of complete breakdown of the states" (UN doc. A/50/142, Annex (16 June 1995), p. 3). The UNSG echoed this proposal in its document *Reviewing the United Nations. A Programme for Reform* (UN doc. A/51/950 (14 July 1997), p. 27, par. 85). However, states either rejected this new approch (the US or Japan) or postponed it *ad calendas graecas* (India, Norway, Russia, Korea and the EU) (UN doc. A/52/PV.83 (27 April 1998)). See Tom Parker, *The Ultimate Intervention: Revitalising the UN Trusteeship Council for the 21st Century*, a publication from the Centre for European and Asian Studies at Norwegian School of Management (April 2003), available at <http://www.bi.no/cccFiles/CEAS-Files/03-03The_Ultimate_Intervention.pdf>. See also Aznar-Gómez (supra n. 56), p. 338–40, and Kreijen (supra n. 11), p. 310–29.

[115] Somalia became a UN member on 20 September 1960. However, it could be argued that, as an extinct state, membership should decline since Somalia is unable to comply with the obligations contained in the UN Charter (Art. 4 (1) UN Charter).

[116] Cf. Kreijen (supra n. 11), p. 328.

[117] UNGA res. 60/1 (24 October 2005) par. 176. The previous proposal came from the UNSG in his *In Larger Freedom: Towards Development, Security and Human Rights for All*, Report of the Secretary-General, UN doc. A/59/2005 (21 March 2005), p. 52, par. 218: "The Trusteeship Council played a vital role in raising standards of administration in the trust territories and promoting the wider process of decolonisation. But its work is long since complete. *Chapter XIII, "The Trusteeship Council", should be deleted from the Charter*". (italics in original)

protective and proactive canvas of rules and institutions. As some sort of substitute for post-conflict tasks, the General Assembly and the Security Council jointly established the 'Peacebuilding Commission'.[118] For the moment, the Commission has dealt with peace building in Burundi, Sierra Leone, Guinea-Bissau and the Central African Republic.[119]

Now that the option of reviving the possibility of trusteeship is no longer available as a tool in the hands of the international community (vested in the UN), the other possibility is to use the device of international administration of territories.

B. *International Administration of Extinct States*

The institution of the international administration of territories (IAT) must not be understood in isolation, neither historically nor institutionally.[120] In 1992, UN Secretary-General Boutros Boutros-Ghali – within the conceptual framework of 'post-conflict peace building' – argued that, to successfully conclude peace-making and peace-keeping operations, they

> must come to include comprehensive efforts to identify and support structures which will tend to consolidate peace and advance a sense of confidence and well-being among people. Through agreements ending civil strife, these may include disarming the previously warring parties and the restoration of order, the custody and possible destruction of weapons, repatriating refugees, advisory and training support for security personnel, monitoring elections, advancing efforts to protect human rights, reforming or strengthening governmental institutions and promoting formal and informal processes of political participation.[121]

---

[118] UNGA res. 60/1, par. 97, and UNSC res. 1645 (2005) (20 December 2005), par. 1. In the preamble of its resolution the UNSC recalled "the primary responsibility of national and transitional Governments and authorities of countries emerging from conflict or at risk of relapsing into conflict, where they are established, in identifying their priorities and strategies for post-conflict peacebuilding, with a view to ensuring national ownership". On the Peacebuilding Commission, see generally Vincent Chapeaux, 'La réforme des Nations Unies et la consolidation de la paix: la céation de la Commission de consolidation de la paix', in: Jorge Cardona (ed.), *La ONU y el mantenimiento de la paz en el Siglo XII. Entre la adaptación y la reforma de la Carta*, Valencia: Tirant 2008, p. 245. The website of the Commission can be found at <http://www.un.org/peace/peacebuilding/index.shtml>.

[119] See the last report of the Commission in UN doc. A/64/341-S/2009/444 (8 September 2009).

[120] On the international administration of territories – along with my book referred to in n. 56 supra –, see generally Gregory H. Fox, *Humanitarian Occupation*, Cambridge: Cambridge University Press 2008; Bernhard Knoll, *The Legal Status of Territories Subject to Administration by International Organisations*, Cambridge: Cambridge University Press 2008; Carsten Stahn, *The Law and Practice of International Territorial Administration. Versailles to Iraq and Beyond*, Cambridge: Cambridge University Press 2008; Ralph Wilde, *International Territorial Administration: How Trusteeship and the Civilizing Mission Never Went Away*, Oxford: Oxford University Press 2008.

[121] Boutros Boutros-Ghali, *An Agenda for Peace. Preventive Diplomacy, Peacemaking and Peace-Keeping*, Report of the UNSG, UN doc. A/47/277 – S/24111 (17 June 1992), p. 16, par. 55.

One of his predecessors in the UN Secretariat – U Thant –, once the UN endorsed the 15 August 1962 bilateral agreement between Indonesia and the Netherlands on the Western New Guinea (Irian Jaya),[122] declared that "for the first time in its history the United Nations would have a temporary executive authority established by and under the jurisdiction of the Secretary-General over a vast territory (…)".[123] Almost forty years later, influenced by the East Timor and Kosovo international administrations, the Panel on UN Peace Operations reported that the Secretariat might "[anticipate] future transitional administrations as the rule rather than the exception, [and] then a dedicated and distinct responsibility centre for those tasks must be created somewhere within the United Nations system".[124] As we have already seen, the Peacebuilding Commission seems intended to fill in the gap left by the 'deletion' of the Trusteeship Council. However, it does not look well suited to manage the administration of a territory and population without government, as the Somalia case may be.

Despite this institutional weakness, which could be solved if so decided, IAT has its pros and cons that merit a brief analysis. Once determined to establish an IAT regime on Somalia by the UN, two previous, intertwined obstacles must be solved: the question of Somali sovereignty and the question of consent to the establishment of that IAT regime. On sovereignty, different discussions have been theoretically held since Lord McNair talked about sovereignty *in abeyance* referring to mandated territories in his separate opinion to the advisory opinion of the ICJ on the *Status of South*

---

[122] Text of the Agreement in 437 *United Nations Treaty Series* 274. Endorsed by UNGA res. 1752 (XVII) (21 September 1962).

[123] UN doc. S/PV.1127 (21 September 1962), p. 13. However, the UN had previously administered Libya (1949–1951). Since then it administered virtually Namibia (1966–1990) and effectively Cambodia (1992–1993), Eastern Slavonia, Baranja and Western Sirmium (1996–1998), East Timor (1999–2002) and Kosovo (1999-today). An IAT regime was also foreseen (but never applied) for Trieste and Jerusalem. Other IAT cases – like the City of Mostar, Bosnia-Herzegovina or the District of Brcko – were administered by the European Union (Mostar) or a 'group of states' (Bosnia and Brcko). See Aznar-Gómez (supra n. 56), p. 97–170.

[124] *Report of the Panel on United Nations Peace Operations* (the 'Brahimi Report'), UN doc. A/55/305 – S/2000/809 (21 August 2000), p. 14, par. 78. However, the International Commission on Intervention and State Sovereignty (ICISS), in its 2001 report *The Responsibility to Protect*, reminded that "[u]seful guidelines for the behaviour of intervening authorities during a military intervention in failed states, and in the follow-up period, might be found in a constructive adaptation of Chapter XII of the UN Charter. This would enable reconstruction and rehabilitation to take place in an orderly way across the full spectrum, with the support and assistance of the international community. The most relevant provision in this regard is Article 76 which notes that the aim of the system is to promote the political, economic, social and educational advancement of the people of the territory in question; to encourage respect for human rights; to ensure the equal treatment of all peoples in the UN in social, economic and commercial matters; and also to ensure equal treatment in the administration of justice". ICISS, *The Responsibility to Protect* (December 2001), par. 5.22, available at <http://iciss.ca/pdf/Commission-Report.pdf>.

West Africa.[125] As explained elsewhere,[126] this concept of 'suspended' sovereignty is particularly well suited for cases of IAT, but not for mandates or trusteeship territories. However, in the case of extinct states, the question of sovereignty could be responded in a short (and even sharp) way: no state, no sovereignty. Therefore, the question turns to who must (or can) give the consent to decide the establishment of an IAT regime over an extinct state.[127]

Apart from the dramatic consequences for its population, an extinct state is a danger for the international system, not only because of the destabilisation effects and the threats it could pose to international security,[128] but because of the dangerous consequences for the region created by human starvation (which drives to transboundary movements).[129] In addition, in an extinct state, the population cannot protect its environment nor manage its natural resources. From a more 'formal' and 'neutral' point of view, an extinct state is unable to enter into or abide by treaties (including human rights treaties and institutions), to participate in the dense network of international trade or to enforce contracts between its citizens and foreigners or protect settled property interests. Consequently, the reason to artificially maintain an extinct State – security, stability – clearly does not operate here: failed and extinct states are normally the cause of conflicts.

Given that an extinct state may be a 'threat to the peace' and given the widening of powers of the UN Security Council accepted by the international community in the last two decades, the Security Council, acting under chapter VII of the Charter, with the intense collaboration of the Peacebuilding Commission and in close contact with concerned regional organisations, should be the organ entrusted with the mission of deciding, monitoring and ending an IAT regime with regard to an extinct state. This decision must keep

---

125 *International Status of South West Africa, Advisory Opinion of 11 July 1950*, [1950] ICJ Reports 128, 150.

126 See on this question Mariano Aznar-Gómez, 'Soberanía y administración internacionalizada del territorio', in: *Studi in onore di Umberto Leanza*, Naples: Editoriale Scientifica 2008, p. 3.

127 Although we could also wonder, if there is no sovereignty, whether there is *anyone* to give that consent.

128 In its recent National Security Strategy, the US affirmed that "[f]ailing states breed conflict and endanger regional and global security. Global criminal networks foment insecurity abroad and bring people and goods across our own borders that threaten our people". *The National Security Strategy of the United States of America* (May 2010), p. 8, available at <http://www.whitehouse.gov/sites/default/files/rss_viewer/national_security_strategy.pdf>. A quite similar idea can be found in the European Security Strategy: "Collapse of the state can be associated with obvious threats, such as organised crime or terrorism. State failure is an alarming phenomenon, that undermines global governance, and adds to regional instability". *A Secure Europe in a Better World* (December 2003) p. 4, available at <http://www.consilium.europa.eu/uedocs/cmsUpload/78367.pdf>.

129 In the case of Somalia, the landmark development was perhaps resolution 794 (1992), of 3 December 1992, in which the Security Council held that "the magnitude of the human tragedy caused by the conflict" was sufficient in itself to constitute a threat to peace within the meaning of article 39 of the Charter.

in mind that current international law has included democracy and respect of human rights among the building blocks of IAT regimes.[130]

All those organs, acting on behalf of the international community, have the legal obligation to protect the population and preserve the territory (including its natural resources) and be proactive in order to offer a process of *new* self-determination. This process must be based on a full respect of human rights, both individual and collective. As a consequence, the UN should be accountable before the international community of the development, management and decisions adopted by the IAT, for example, in Somalia. As expressed by Karel Wellens – to whom I warmly dedicate my contribution to this well-deserved *Festschrift* –, "[i]n all circumstances in which an international organisation exercises some kind of governmental authority over a particular territory on a temporary basis there is obviously a direct personal jurisdiction".[131]

5. *A Conclusion?*

The state is a *carrefour* where law and politics, power and economics, identity and history conflict in a multilevel scenario. The state – a legal constituent fiction –[132] is a matter of fact. Without abandoning this theoretical realm and, therefore, without crediting recognition a constitutive, non-simply declarative nature, the extinction of states is also a matter of fact. Admittedly, recognition is no more than a subjective assessment of an empirical reality.[133] Recognition, however, *might* be based on effectiveness. Effectiveness here *solves* the legal fiction.[134] But effectiveness must also solve the legal presumption of the continuity of an (extinct) state.[135] And, perhaps, these are too many fictions and presumptions to be burdened on the shoulders of effectiveness.

---

130 Aznar-Gómez (supra n. 56), p. 190–205.

131 Karel Wellens, *Remedies against International Organisations*, Cambridge: Cambridge University Press 2002, p. 20.

132 Pierre-Marie Dupuy, 'L'unité de l'ordre juridique international', (2002) 297 *Recueil des Cours de l'Académie de Droit International*, p. 261.

133 See Institut de droit international (IDI), Resolution of 23 April 1936, Session of Brussels (1936), available at <http://www.idi-iil.org/idiF/resolutionsF/1936_brux_01_fr.pdf> (Art. 1 of the resolution: "La reconnaissance d'un Etat nouveau est l'acte libre par lequel un ou plusieurs Etats constatent l'existence sur un territoire déterminé d'une société humaine politiquement organisée, indépendante de tout autre Etat existant, capable d'observer les prescriptions du droit international et manifestent en conséquence leur volonté de la considérer comme membre de la Communauté internationale.")

134 As expressed some time ago in Monique Chemillier-Gendreau, 'Origine et rôle de la fiction en droit international public', (1987) 153 *Archives de philosophie du droit*, p. 162, "l'effectivité joue exactement le rôle inverse de la fiction ou plus exactement le recours à l'effectivité se fait utile lorsque la falsification opérée par la fiction est si grande qu'elle devient intolérable socialement (…) Elle joue le rôle inverse de la fiction. Elle démasque ce qu'on avait tenté de masquer par un procédé fictif: on réajuste la norme à une mesure exacte des réalités".

135 Crawford, supra n. 8, p. 34, holds that "[t]here is a strong presumption that the state continues to exist, with its rights and obligations, despite revolutionary changes in government, or despite a period in which there is no, or no effective, government".

Perhaps the main problem with some extinct states (and, even, with failed states) is that they arrived to the 'club of states'[136] with a mild exigency of statehood. The principle under which "[i]nadequacy of political, economic, social or educational preparedness should never serve as a pretext for delaying independence"[137] overruled effectiveness and forced recognition of entities barely arrived to its maturity as a state.[138] As Gerard Kreijen puts it, generally speaking for sub-Saharan African states, they were "the result, not of formation, but rather of *creation*. The term creation displays a distinctive element of proactive human interference. It is in a sense artificial. This is crucial: *what has been done artificially, can be undone in the same way*".[139] But this should imply giving recognition (in this case 'de-recognition') a rather constitutive character. "La reconnaissance a un effet déclaratif" said the IDI in its 1936 Brussels Resolution on *La reconnaissance des nouveaux Etats et des nouveaux gouvernements*.[140] Must 'de-recognition' have a constitutive character in order to undo a state? This and other questions are still open to new discussions.

Another question to be discussed is whether the 'deletion' of the trusteeship system virtually operating in the UN Charter was a correct decision or not. As a substitution (and perhaps better suited for the 'extinction of states' cases), IAT must be understood as an 'exceptional measure' for an exceptional situation:[141] an interim relief for the protection and preservation of the population and territory of a former state.

In any case, Somalia being the epitome of an extinct state, the rise of new cases should not be neglected, challenging the international community to imagine and put in motion its entire means and efforts to, mainly, protect a population without a state.

---

[136] Borrowing the words of Rosalyn Higgins in *Problems and Process: International Law and How We Use It*, Oxford: Oxford University Press 1994, p. 39.

[137] UNGA res. 1514 (XV) (14 December 1960). As an historical by-product, self-determination (in its external face) drove colonial peoples to independence, neglecting the internal face of self-determination: democracy and human rights. However, the original sin must be found not only in African states (and particularly in some of their brutal leaders) but in colonial powers as well, tracing artificial boundaries in Berlin 1885 and harvesting local resources during their subsequent presence until self-determination processess and afterwards.

[138] Actually, in the case of Ruanda-Urundi (currently again Rwanda and Burundi), the UNGA found itself obliged to authorize a $2 million "for the purpose of such emergencies measures as may be required to ensure the continuation of essential services in the two countries (…)" (UNGA res. 1746 (XVI) (27 June 1962), par. 5).

[139] Kreijen (supra n. 11), p. 330 (italics in original).

[140] Supra n. 130. In its Article 5, the 1936 IDI Resolution explicites that "[l]a reconnaissance *de iure* est irrévocable; elle ne cesse ses effets qu'en cas de disparition définitive de l'un des éléments essentiels don't la réunion se trouvait constatée au moment de la reconnaissance".

[141] When analysing UNSC res. 1244 (1999) which established the IAT regime over Kosovo, the ICJ said that "the establishment of civil and security presences in Kosovo deployed on the basis of Resolution 1244 (1999) must be understood as an exceptional measure relating to civil, political and security aspects and aimed at addressing the crisis existing in that territory in 1999" (*Kosovo affair*, par. 97).

CHAPTER FOUR

THE PRINCIPLE OF APPROXIMATE TREATY APPLICATION

ARTICLE 51 UN CHARTER AND THE 'NECESSARY MEASURES' BY THE SECURITY COUNCIL TO MAINTAIN INTERNATIONAL PEACE AND SECURITY

Eric Myjer

1. *Introduction*

A discussion of evolving principles in different areas of public international law is a most fitting tribute to Karel Wellens for he is not only an eminent international lawyer with an eye for its evolving dimension, but he is also a principled man willing to put his foot down when he is convinced that the right principles are not being applied in the interpretation of the law. As a member of the Dutch Government's Advisory Committee on Issues of Public International Law, I had the privilege of co-writing a dissenting opinion with Karel Wellens, the then chairman, in the Advisory Report on Humanitarian Intervention,[1] which was jointly produced with the Advisory Council on International Affairs (AIV). The issue was the following. The Joint Committees were asked by the Netherlands Government via the Minister of Foreign Affairs to outline under what circumstances humanitarian intervention would be allowed.[2]

---

[1] *Humanitarian Intervention*, Report by the Advisory Council on International Affairs (AIV) and the Advisory Committee on Issues of Public International Law, No. 13, April 2000. See <www.aiv-advice.nl>.

[2] In formulating its request for advice, amongst others, the Government stated: "Although humanitarian intervention can be justified on political and moral grounds, it has no clear and generally accepted legal foundation. If the law is not developed on this point, two dangers will arise. First, as long as humanitarian intervention has no clear and generally endorsed legal basis, it can be invoked as a cover for military operations of a different nature. Second, the position of international law may inadvertently be undermined if it does not provide for intervention in cases of flagrant violations of universally accepted human rights." The Minister therefore considered it crucial that the concept of humanitarian intervention be further developed: "This means on the one hand drawing up clear guidelines to which humanitarian intervention would have to adhere, and on the other hand establishing as broad a support base as possible for the more precise definition of this concept." In his letter, the Minister of Foreign Affairs requested the CAVV and the AIV to look both at what was necessary or desirable from a political and moral point of view and at what was possible from the point of view of international law.

It is important to note at this stage that in the course of its work it became clear that there was agreement within the Committees that when assessing unauthorised humanitarian intervention within a framework to be established, use would be made of the principle of 'approximate treaty application'. Thereby every effort should be made to approximate the procedures and mechanisms provided for in the UN system of collective security enshrined in the UN Charter:

> It is important that a framework for assessing unauthorised humanitarian intervention be established in order to appraise and adopt a justification on the subject. The possibility that such justification may eventually develop into a legal ground cannot be excluded. In this connection, too, an assessment framework can play an important part. The CAVV and the AIV consider that, when establishing and interpreting this framework, on the basis of the notion of 'approximate treaty application',[3] every effort should be made to approximate to the procedures and mechanisms provided for in the UN system of collective security enshrined in the UN Charter.[4]

The difference between the majority opinion and our opinion was that in our view in case no authorisation of the Security Council was forthcoming, no effort should be spared to obtain the necessary consent within the UN system. This is what, according to us, was the logical consequence of applying the principle of 'approximate treaty application', whereas for the majority it was the logical and preferable step to take, but not an absolute precondition. We therefore concluded:

> In pursuance of the principle of 'approximate treaty application' (…), and mindful of the aforementioned primacy of the UN system of collective security based on the Charter and the associated peremptory ban on the use of force, two members of the CAVV, Dr. E.P.J. Myjer and Prof. K.C. Wellens, consider that the use of force for humanitarian purposes (as referred to in the cases described) without the prior authorisation of the Security Council is only acceptable if no effort has been spared to obtain the necessary consent within the system of the Charter according to the rules of international law. These steps must be capable of being assessed. The Security Council must primarily pronounce on the admissibility of such use of force for humanitarian purposes by giving its opinion on a substantive

---

In the light of the relationship between political, moral and legal considerations, he asked the CAVV and the AIV to produce a joint report on the question of how the international community's ability to end large-scale violations of human rights in a particular country could be enhanced. The CAVV and the AIV might start, he wrote, by listing possible ways of increasing the Security Council's potential for action. This could include looking at the option of amending the right of veto. In addition, the Minister requested the two advisory bodies to consider the question of how the concept of humanitarian intervention could be given clearer shape under international law. Ibid., at 3.

[3] Referred to by Sir Hersch Lauterpacht in his separate opinion in the case of the *Admissibility of Hearings of Petitioners by the Committee on South-West Africa*, Separate opinion of Sir Hersch Lauterpacht, ICJ Reports 1956, p. 46, quoted in the *Gabčíkovo-Nagymaros* case, 25 September 1997, par. 75.

[4] Report, supra n. 1, p. 24.

> draft resolution. If such a resolution is vetoed, the General Assembly must – before use of force outside the UN (in the exceptional cases referred to) can be considered admissible – pronounce on it on the basis of its secondary (shared) responsibility for peace and security, given that the General Assembly is the only UN body apart from the Security Council that is competent to authorise such a deviation from the ban on force on the UN's behalf (see N. White, 'The legality of bombing in the name of humanity', in: Journal of Conflict and Security Law 5 (2000), pp. 27–43). In order to pronounce on the resolution, the General Assembly must be convened in emergency special session by means of a procedural resolution based on the Uniting for Peace resolution (see General Assembly Resolution 377 A(V) 'Uniting for Peace' (3 November 1950), UN Doc. A/1775), for which a majority of nine members of the Security Council is in practice sufficient (cf. Zieger/Rhode/Brokelmann/Khan in B. Simma, 'The Charter of the United Nations, a Commentary' (1994), p. 346: 'Hence there now appears to exist a rule that the convening of special sessions is a procedural matter not affected by the right of veto.'). In Wellens' and Myjer's view, the submission of the two resolutions referred to, and if possible a General Assembly resolution pronouncing thereon, are the very least that can be deemed a usable procedural and substantial criterion for the use of force other than under the terms of the Charter.[5]

We came to a different conclusion than the majority of the Committee Members in our application of what could be called a mega-principle of approximate treaty application, and the two central principles of the law of collective security, namely the primacy of the UN system of collective security and the principle of the ban on the use of force.

The principle of approximate treaty application is not only relevant when it concerns looking for the necessary consent within the Charter system for the use of force for humanitarian purposes, in case the Security Council is deadlocked. Another equally important instance would be the case when the Security Council is unable to make a determination that it has taken the necessary measures "to maintain international peace and security" under article 51 Charter, thereby incontestably ending a state's right to individual and collective self-defence. Such a determination is of crucial importance, for it concerns the only instance whereby a state is unilaterally allowed to use military force. In a broader sense it is also about the Security Council not fulfilling its general supervisory function following from its primary responsibility for the maintenance of international peace and security.[6] This is what I will look at in this contribution. After a brief sketch of article 51 UN Charter, it will be shown that the possibility of continuing self-defence in spite of the fact that the necessary measures have been taken is not a theoretical problem, for which I will use as an example the actual use of force in self-defence in Afghanistan. In conclusion, I will indicate why approximate treaty application may be a suitable solution to the problem and how this principle could be applied.

---

[5] Report, supra n. 1, p 27, footnote 55.

[6] Article 24 UN Charter

2. *Article 51 Charter and the Right of Self-Defence*

With regard to the use of force, the United Nations Charter is clear. Use of military force by a state is only allowed in case of self-defence against an armed attack, or when the Security Council so decides. Article 51 of the UN Charter concerns self-defence as an inherent right. It allows for individual or collective self-defence until the Security Council has taken "measures necessary to maintain international peace and security". These measures shall be reported to the Security Council immediately, but "shall not affect the authority and responsibility under the Charter of the Security Council to take at any time such action as it deems necessary in order to maintain or restore international peace and security".

When a state claims this right of self-defence, the institutional law of the United Nations is triggered. Crucial in this context is that it is the Security Council, not the individual state, which has the primary responsibility for the maintenance of peace and security and which to that effect has the power to take the necessary binding military and non-military measures in case of such an armed attack. It is therefore clear that self-defence by a state is by definition a temporary right until the Security Council has taken the necessary measures to maintain international peace and security. In case of (collective) self-defence after an armed attack, and ensuing Security Council measures, the question arises when exactly the moment has arrived that it is clear that the Security Council has taken the necessary measures. This is important for it means that from that moment onwards the right to self-defence stops. This means, in other words, that from then on there is no longer a legitimate basis for self-defence. How can it be established that this moment has arrived?

Given its primary role in the United Nations system of collective security, the logical organ that could irrefutably make such a determination is the Security Council itself. Although such decision by the Security Council would be practical (for there is no possibility of contesting it), it is however not mandatory; the *necessary measures* criterion is a material one.

Decision-making in the Security Council is a political process, whereby the Permanent Five (P5) have the power to veto any such decision that the Council has indeed taken the necessary measures. This means that when one of the P5 is itself taking the (collective) self-defence action, or a client state or an ally is involved, it is highly likely that the Security Council will be blocked by a veto by that particular state. In these cases it is even possible that no attempt will be made to get such a resolution adopted. Afghanistan and Operation Enduring Freedom appear to be a case in point.

Given that the necessary measures criterion is a material one, upon applying the relevant principles it is possible to establish on objective grounds whether the measures taken by the Security Council can be regarded as the necessary measures in the sense of Artikel 51 of the Charter. It will be clear that in order to make this determination the measures taken by the Security Council need to be tested against what can be regarded as a 'normal' legitimate self-defence operation. This means that they need to answer to the criteria of proportionality, necessity and immediacy,[7] as well as to the legitimate aim to be achieved by such self-defence operation. For this, one has to test against the armed attack that has given rise to the self-defence. Necessity is about the question whether the action in self-defence as a reaction really is necessary and whether there are no alternatives. Proportionality is about the question whether the actions in self-defence are comparable to, or proportional to, the attack, with regard to character, form and intensity. These principles are general principles of public international law, and are not just limited to the law of collective security. Related to these principles is the principle of immediacy,[8] which concerns the reaction time and duration of the self-defence operation, or in other words, the intrinsically temporal dimension of self-defence.

In applying these criteria and in the light of the Security Council's duty under article 51 of the UN Charter to take the measures necessary to maintain international peace and security, one may come to the conclusion that the Security Council has indeed taken the necessary measures. This at least may be the conclusion drawn by for example either a UN member state, an authoritative academic, or an NGO. However pertinent such a conclusion would be, it is likely that such assessment would have no effect. For given the way public international law operates as a consensual system, until the self-defending state itself decides that the Security Council has taken the necessary measures, or until the goal of its self-defence has been achieved and the state in question ends its military self-defence operations, the absence of a binding Security Council determination to the effect that it has now taken the necessary measures means that the self-defence operation may just continue.

This raises a dilemma with respect to the control of unilateral use of military force by a state when on all accounts it appears that there is no longer a legal basis for such use of military force. There is the clearly defined material criterion of article 51 of the UN Charter that is supposed to control such use of force. Yet there appears to be a void when the Security Council – as the primary body of the UN responsible for the maintenance of peace and security – does not explicitly establish that the necessary measures criterion has been fulfilled. This material criterion in article 51 therefore risks

---

[7] Compare Judith Gardam, *Necessity, Proportionality and the Use of Force by States*, Cambridge: Cambridge University Press 2004; Yoram Dinstein, *War, Aggression and Self-Defence*, Cambridge: Cambridge University Press 2005, p. 237–244.

[8] See Eric Myjer, 'Afghanistan, the Erosion of the Right to Self-Defence and the Case of the Missing Immediacy', in: Ineke Boerefijn and Jenny Goldschmidt (eds.), *Changing Perceptions of Sovereignty and Human Rights. Essays in Honour of Cees Flinterman*, Antwerp: Intersentia 2008, p. 529–550.

becoming obsolete. This leads to an erosion of the restrictions on the use of force following from article 51.

This author is not aware of any case in which the Security Council has made an official determination that in a case of self-defence it had taken the "measures necessary to maintain international peace and security" thereby establishing as a consequence that a state's right of individual or collective self-defence had ended. It could be said that this was due to the fact that "(..) since the Security Council has, for a long time, been far from performing its intended function, self-defence has become the regular course of action. Therefore, the restriction envisaged by the reporting duty, as well as the related duty to discontinue defensive measures, has so far been almost devoid of practical significance".[9] The situation, however, has changed. After the end of the Cold War the Security Council has on numerous occasions been active in the field of its primary responsibility for the maintenance of international peace and security.[10]

When discussing the role of the Security Council under article 51, the main focus of commentators has been on issues such as when in case of an armed attack the Security Council would be blocked from taking any necessary measures, or is even unable to decide whether the armed attack reaches the threshold of article 51 at all, and how that relates to a state's inherent right to self defence.[11] Kelsen raised the question: "[W]ho is competent to decide the question whether the Security Council has taken the measures 'necessary to maintain international peace and security?' The Security Council itself exclusively, or the state or states exercising the right of self-defence?".[12] He then asserted that it was probably not the intention of the original state parties to the UN Charter to "confer upon the attacked state the power to decide whether the measures taken by the Security Council are adequate", and he concluded on balance that the "idea was probably that a state is allowed to exercise its right of self-defence until the Security Council has taken the measures which the Security Council deems necessary to restore peace",[13] but adds "this idea is not unambiguously expressed in Article 51". That it is up to the Security Council to decide which measures it deems necessary in the specific situation of self-defence is not an issue any more, especially now that after the end of

---

[9] Albrecht Randelzhofer, 'Article 51', in: Bruno Simma (ed.), *The Charter of the United Nations, A Commentary*, Oxford: Oxford University Press 2002, p. 804. In their 1946 commentary on the Charter, Goodrich and Hambro in their treatment of article 51 only point at the possibility of a deadlock in the taking of concrete measures by the Security Council, allowing states to continue their independent action. They do not refer to the decision to conclude that these measures have been taken. See Leland Goodrich and Edvard Hambro (eds.), *Charter of the United Nations, Commentary and Documents*, Boston: World Peace Foundation 1946, p. 180–181.

[10] Article 24 UN Charter.

[11] Compare Hans Kelsen, *The Law of the United Nations*, New York: Praeger, p. 800–805.

[12] Ibid. p. 802

[13] Ibid., p. 803

the Cold War the Security Council has shown to actively take up its responsibility to maintain international peace and security. However, our assumption is that the Security Council might be blocked from considering the question whether it has taken the 'necessary measures' and taking a decision on it. Here we are faced with a dilemma, for given the primary role of the Security Council in the area of the maintenance of peace and security we would expect the Security Council to take such a decision, thereby unequivocally making clear whether or not the right to self-defence has ended. There is however no obligation for the Security Council to take such a decision. Dinstein is of the opinion that when there is no explicit decree by the Security Council to stop ("desist") the use of force, a state retains its right to continue to do so until the Security Council has taken measures "which have actually 'succeeded' in restoring international peace and security",[14] but that the defending state in doing so, acts at its own risk. This refers to the fact that the Security Council is the ultimate arbiter in deciding whether a state is rightly exercising self-defence.[15] One may wonder, however, how much risk there is for the state in question, unless at a later stage this is translated as an issue of state responsibility. The problem of unchecked use of force just might continue.

This raises the question whether there are no other possible ways within the UN system of supervision to authoritatively make such a determination. This brings to the fore the principle of approximate treaty application as applied in the aforementioned case of humanitarian intervention. Also in that example it concerned the authority to use military force, namely granting the power under article 42 of the UN Charter to do so in case of a humanitarian disaster. In our case here it is the reverse, namely putting a stop to unilateral use of force based on the inherent self-defence mandate of article 51.

That this is not a mere theoretical possibility is shown by the case of the use of force in Afghanistan in response to the terrorist attacks on the Twin Towers and the Pentagon, firstly in self-defence under Operation Enduring Freedom and subsequently by way of Security Council initiated operations, like the International Security Assistance Force (ISAF). Here the Security Council adopted a great number of binding resolutions under chapter VII of the UN Charter, resulting in large-scale actions. There has however not yet been a determination by the Security Council that these amounted to the necessary measures ending the right of individual or collective self-defence.

3. *The Case of Self-Defence in Afghanistan*

In reaction to the terrorist attacks against the Twin Towers and the Pentagon in the United States on 11 September 2001 the United States and the United

[14] Dinstein, supra n. 7, p. 215–216.
[15] Cf. Dinstein, ibid., p. 213 ff.

Kingdom, on 7 October 2001, undertook a military attack in self-defence against Afghanistan, basing themselves on article 51 UN Charter. This was 'Operation Enduring Freedom' (hereafter also: OEF). Although the passenger planes used in this suicide attack were different from classic weapons, it was argued that because of the impact and devastating effects (scale and effect), this use of force was equivalent to the armed attack envisioned in article 51. For this the US found support with their NATO allies, who regarded the 9/11 attacks as an armed attack under article 5 of their collective self-defence treaty.[16] This was the first time that such a decision was taken by NATO. This did not mean, however, that this self-defence operation did not raise questions.[17]

Immediately after the 9/11 events in 2001, the UN Security Council took measures under chapter VII of the UN Charter in response to these attacks. This was both in line with the Security Council's primary duty for the preservation of peace and security under article 24 Charter and more specifically under article 51, for when a state is being attacked and takes self-defence measures, the institutional law of the United Nations comes into focus.

Already on September 12, the Security Council adopted a first resolution.[18] Quickly thereafter it took binding measures to combat terrorism[19] by adopting Resolution 1373, which is of a special, legislative, character.[20] Shortly thereafter, on December 20, 2001, the Security Council adopted military measures by authorising the International Security Assistance Force (ISAF) with a mandate to use all necessary measures.[21] This resolution was adopted in reaction to the Bonn Agreement of December 5, 2001.[22] This agreement deals with, among other things, the transfer of power to an interim government. The agreement

[16] "The Parties agree that an armed attack against one or more of them in Europe or North America shall be considered an attack against them all; and consequently they agree that, if such an armed attack occurs, each of them in exercise of the right of individual or collective self-defence recognized by Article 51 of the Charter of the United Nations, will assist the Party or Parties so attacked by taking forthwith. Individually and in concert with the other Parties, such action as it deems necessary, the use of armed force, to restore and maintain the security of the North Atlantic area (...)." Article 5 of the The North Atlantic Treaty, 4 April 1949.

[17] See for instance Eric Myjer and Nigel White, 'The Twin Towers Attack: An Unlimited Right to Self-Defence?', (2002) 7 *Journal of Conflict and Security Law*, p. 5–17; Myra Williamson, *Terrorism, War and International Law. The Legality of the Use of Force Against Afghanistan in 2001*, Farnham: Ashgate 2009.

[18] S/RES/1368 (2001).

[19] S/RES/1373 (2001).

[20] Bibi van Ginkel, *The Practice of the United Nations in Combating Terrorism from 1946 to 2008, Questions of Legality and Legitimacy*, Antwerp: Intersentia, p. 245–253, in particular on p. 246: "The Council demanded from all states that they should prevent and suppress the financing of terrorist activities, as well as criminalizing the willful provision or collection of funds for such acts. The latter obligation can be seen as an order to legislate, which was unprecedented in the practice of the Security Council".

[21] S/Res/1386 (2001).

[22] Agreement on Provisional Arrangements in Afghanistan pending the Re-establishment of Permament Government Institutions, <http://unama.unmissions.org/Portals/UNAMA/Documents/Bonn-agreement.pdf>.

makes clear that "the responsibility for providing security and law and order throughout the country resides with the Afghans themselves".[23] However, since it may take some time before the new Afghan 'security and armed forces' will be fully constituted and functioning, the United Nations Security Council was requested to consider authorising the early deployment to Afghanistan of a United Nations mandated force.[24] This came to be ISAF, which is meant to provide security both for the Interim government and different UN (and other) operations.

Up to the present day, the mandate of ISAF has been renewed regularly,[25] and its area of operation has been gradually expanded from the Kabul area to the whole of Afghanistan. The resolutions whereby the mandate was extended show a remarkable development in the relationship between ISAF and the Enduring Freedom self-defence operation. From 2003 onwards, ISAF is called upon to work in close consultation with the OEF Coalition in the implementation of the force mandate.[26] And from the way in which Operation Enduring Freedom is mentioned in all successive resolutions in relation to ISAF, we can note an increasing 'closeness' between both operations, namely from close consultation,[27] closer operational synergy,[28] to increased[29] continued coordination.[30] We find this development confirmed in a Report of the US Department of Defense,[31] from which the conclusion can be drawn that the only substantial difference in activity between both operations is the element of counterterrorism. This close cooperation between Operation Enduring Freedom and ISAF also follows from the fact that since 2010, there even exists a joint (US) command of both NATO-led ISAF forces, and the US-led OEF forces.[32]

With regard to the ISAF operations, it can therefore be concluded that gradually such a far-reaching cooperation has emerged between the ISAF Operations and the OEF self-defence coalition, that the operations can no longer be viewed separately. One might even get the impression that both

---

[23] Ibid., annex 1.

[24] Ibid.

[25] By S/RES/1413 (2002); S/RES/1444 (2002); S/RES/1510)2003); S/RES/1563 (2004); S/RES/1623 (2005); S/RES/1707 (2006); S/RES/1776 (2007); S/RES/1833 (2008); S/RES/1890)2009);S/RES/1943 (2010).

[26] S/Res/1510 (2003)

[27] S/Res/1510 (2003), S/Res/1563 (2004); S/Res/1623 (2005); S/Res/1707 (2006); S/Res/1776 (2007); S/Res)/1833 (2008); S/Res/1890 (2009); S/Res/1943 (2010).

[28] S/Res/1659 (2006) (This is not a resolution whereby the mandate of ISAF is extended but a resolution endorsing the Afghan Compact of 31 January 2006).

[29] S/Res/1707 (2006).

[30] S/Res/1776 (2007); S/Res/1833 (2008); S/Res/1890 (2009); S/Res/1943 (2010);

[31] *Progress toward Security and Stability in Afghanistan*, Department of Defense, January 2009, Report to Congress in accordance with the 2008 National Defense Authorization Act (Section 1230, Public Law 110–181), p. 27.

[32] 'NATO to run U.S. Forces in Afghanistan', CBSNews, March 17, 2010, <http://www.cbsnews.com/stories/2010/03/17/world/main6307408.shtml>.

operations have become part of the same action. This observation concerning the development of the relationship between both operations is important, for it shows that the Security Council measures have taken the upper hand over the Enduring Freedom self-defence operation. We also see this reflected in the present numbers of troops, approximately 130,000 ISAF and 10,000 OEF.[33]

When and how can it be concluded that the Security Council has taken the necessary measures, and that therefore there is no longer a legal basis for the OEF self-defence operation? In the case of Afghanistan this translates into a question of whether the ISAF operations and the other measures taken by the Security Council, such as the United Nations Assistance Mission (UNAMA), or measures to combat terrorism in response to the 9/11 use of force are, at present, almost 10 years later, sufficient to have taken over the Enduring Freedom self-defence operation. Given that the 'necessary measures' criterion is a material one, making such an assessment is not exclusive to the Security Council. A different question, however, pertains to the proper supervisory mechanism within the UN which is applicable to the article 51 rule.

In order to establish whether the measures of the Security Council can be regarded as the necessary measures as meant in article 51, they will have to be tested against what can be regarded as a 'normal' self-defence operation. This means that, as with a self-defence operation, such measures must answer both to the criteria of proportionality, necessity and immediacy, as well as to the legitimate aim of the self-defence operation. To do this, one has to refer to the starting point of Operation Enduring Freedom, namely 9/11, and to the US claim in initiating its self-defence action that Al Qaeda was central in the attack, and that the Taliban regime allowed Al Qaeda to use part of Afghanistan as a base.[34]

To determine whether the necessary measures (material) criterion has been fulfilled, one has to look at the sum of the measures taken by the Security Council over a period of almost 10 years. As our concern here is the use of force element in both operations, this will be the predominant focus. From the long list of resolutions adopted by the Security Council, it is clear that the Security Council has been very active. Furthermore, there have been a number of conferences[35] and two elections in Afghanistan, after which a legitimate

[33] See for instance BBC, Q&A, 18 November 2010, 'Foreign forces in Afghanistan', <http://www.bbc.co.uk/news/mobile/world-south-asia-11371138>.

[34] "The attacks on 11 September 2001 and the ongoing threat to the United States and its nationals posed by the Al-Qaeda organization have been made possible by the decision of the Taliban regime to allow the parts of Afghanistan that it controls to be used by this organization as a base of operation.", Letter from Ambassador John Negroponte, Permanent Representative of the USA to the UN in New York, to the President of the Security Council, S/2001/946, 7 October 2001.

[35] E.g. the Bonn Conference (2001); the London Conference on Afghanistan (31 January – 1 February 2006) leading to the Afghanistan Compact; The The Hague International Conference

government was installed. As has been seen above, ISAF is not the classic peace operation, only using force in self-defence, but is primarily about creating a secure environment in order to allow for a normalisation of the situation in Afghanistan. This object seems to have been realised since Al Quaida no longer enjoys 'hospitality' in Afghanistan, a regime change has been realised and the Taliban government has been expelled. For that reason, it can no longer be held that there is an armed conflict between the US and Afghanistan, and that the US is still defending itself against the latter. Furthermore, on the basis of mutual respect, both under US president George Bush[36] and president Barack Obama, official arrangements have been made, also concerning Operation Enduring Freedom.[37]

The factual situation also points to a Security Council that has taken its task under article 51 of the UN Charter seriously. As we have seen, ISAF is both an extensive and complex operation. In combination with Afghan security forces, ISAF has extended its presence over the whole of Afghanistan.

The sum of the measures taken by the Security Council fulfils the legitimate goal of the self-defence operation, can be regarded as necessary, and is certainly proportional. Furthermore, all these measures have been taken with the active cooperation and full consent of the US. A logical conclusion is therefore that the Security Council has indeed taken the necessary measures, and that therefore self-defence as the legal basis for Operation Enduring Freedom has ended.

Having established that the necessary measures criterion appears to be fulfilled on all accounts, we then face the question of how to ensure that such an assessment is made by the relevant supervisory body of the UN, since no attempt has been made to let the Security Council make such determination.

Given that Operation Enduring Freedom is predominantly an operation of the US, one of the P5 members of the Security Council with a veto-right, it seems unlikely that such determination, in the form of a resolution, would be adopted by the Security Council. In that respect, the Security Council is not fulfilling its role as supervisor of the system of collective security as embodied in the UN Charter. This might lead to an erosion of the Charter rules, both as regards the ban on the use of force in article 2 (4), and the clear strictures of article 51. Since article 51 is quite often used to cloak the use of force for

on Afghanistan (31 March 2009); the London International Conference on Afghanistan (28 January 2010); the Kabul International Conference on Afghanistan (20 July 2010).

[36] Compare the *Joint Declaration of the United Sates – Afghanistan Strategic Partnership* between President George W. Bush and Hamid Karzai, 23 May 2005, The White House, <http://merln.ndu.edu/archivepdf/afghanistan/WH/20050523-2.pdf>.

[37] Compare the Joint Statement by Hamid Karzai, President of Afghanistan, and Barack Obama, President of the United States of America, May 12, 2010, <http://www.whitehouse.gov/the-press-office/joint-statement-president-and-president-karzai-afghanistan>.

offensive purposes, this is especially worrisome. The parallel becomes apparent with the question of the Joint Dutch Advisory Committees of seeking a legal base for humanitarian intervention outside the UN system of collective security in case the Security Council is deadlocked. Only in our case, it is not about providing a mandate to use force, but about establishing that the legal basis for the legitimate use in self-defence has lapsed. Looking for ways to correct a possible supervisory deadlock points us therefore to the principle of approximate treaty application.

4. *Supervision and the Relevance of the Principle of Approximate Treaty Application*

In cases where it is highly likely that that the necessary measures criterion, as a material criterion, has been fulfilled, but where the issue is not expressly addressed within the UN system of collective security, we are faced with a situation where not only effective supervision is lacking, but supervision *per se*. This is a serious matter, for it may concern the continuing use of force by a state or states in (collective) self-defence where, on the basis of a provisional assessment, the legal basis for such an operation appears to be lacking. This may appear paradoxical, since the necessary measures criterion concerns the very measures taken by the Security Council. What is at issue is a situation where the Security Council is unable or unwilling to draw conclusions from its very actions.

Supervision is about ensuring "(...) respect for the law and the realization of rules of law as well as the regular functioning of public service within the limits laid down in these rules of law. Supervision is an organic function which makes it possible for errors (either in the assessment of a situation or in taking action) which might jeopardize the stability and security of social existence to be rectified. It therefore serves to ensure public order".[38]

International supervision can be regarded as having four functions,[39] namely the collection function, the review function, the creative function and the correction function.[40] The collection function refers to the collection of the relevant data. The review function is about judging state behaviour for its conformity with an agreed rule of law. The creative function is about the interpretation or clarification of the rules, and the correction function is about the

[38] M. Kaasik, 'Le contrôle en Droit International' (1933), quoted by G.J.H. van Hoof and K. de Vey Mestdagh, Mechanisms of International Supervision', in: P. van Dijk et al. (eds.), *Supervisory Mechanisms in International Economic Organisations*, The Hague: T.M.C. Assser Instituut, p. 7.

[39] Van Hoof and de Vey Mestdagh distinguish three functions (ibid., p. 11), namely the review function, the creative function and the correction function.

[40] See Eric Myjer (ed.), *Issues of Arms Control Law and the Chemical Weapons Convention*, Leiden-Boston: Martinus Nijhoff Publishers 2001, p. 104 ff.

correction of state behaviour when it is established that it has violated an international obligation.

All these different functions may come into play when looking at the issue under discussion. To start with, the fact that the situation described above may arise is not for lack of a supervisory mechanism in the system of collective security as embodied in the UN Charter. The primary role of the Security Council for the maintenance of international peace and security is clearly described in article 24, and the General Assembly's secondary role follows from article 11 and 12 UN Charter. Furthermore, it is clear that the Security Council is not violating a rule by not deciding that it has taken the necessary measures under article 51. Yet the necessary measures are a material criterion, and if it appears that the Security Council has taken the necessary measures we may rightly assume that if a state is still acting in self-defence this no longer has a legal basis under article 51 UN Charter. Such a state thereby acts in violation of the ban of the use of force under Article 2 (4) UN Charter. This is a clear issue of peace and security, for the maintenance of which the Security Council has the primary responsibility. The primary duty of supervision of a possible breach of these norms therefore lies clearly with the Security Council. It will, however, be clear that a Security Council that is unwilling or unable to take the non-obligatory decision under article 51 that it has taken the necessary measures, will most likely also not do so under its general competence for the maintenance of peace and security. This has all the traits of a vicious circle that needs to be broken.

It is here that the principle of approximate treaty application comes into focus. As for example in the case of granting permission for the application of the use of force under circumstances of urgent need when the Security Council is blocked by a veto, it appears logical to look to the General Assembly as the UN's secondary supervisory body of the system of collective security. It is in establishing this supervisory role of the General Assembly and the ensuing competences that the importance of the principle of approximate treaty application becomes apparent. The need for the application of this principle follows from the special character of public international law.

In advance, it should be noted that the interrelationship between values, rules and principles is a complicated one. Values are of a general character and may lead to principles and rules. Principles may inform rules of law by providing the necessary framework for interpretation of rules of law.[41] There is a close relationship between principles and rules. This does not mean, however, that principles are as easily discernable as rules. One cannot always find the principles in written form. Certain principles may be traced back to a set of

---

[41] Arend Soeteman, 'Hercules aan het werk. Over de rol van rechtsbeginselen in het recht', (1991) 40 *Ars Aequi* (special issue), at p. 35.

rules which they underlie. In that respect within a system of law based on the *trias politica*, i.e. national systems of law like those found in Europe, the said principles of law will mostly be ones established by the judiciary. Since international law is however not based on this *trias politica*, with judicial supervision taking place on a voluntary basis instead, principles are to a lesser extent judge-found principles. This does not, however, mean that within public international law, and for that matter, sub-areas of public international law, principles are of lesser importance.

Lauterpacht described a central principle of public international law, namely that of approximate treaty application. It concerns a crucial principle, for it points at the interpretative character of public international law:

> It is a sound principle of law that whenever a legal instrument of continuing validity cannot be applied literally owing to the conduct of one of the parties, it must, without allowing that party to take advantage of its own conduct, be applied in a way approximating most closely to its primary object. To do that is to interpret and to give effect to the instrument – not to change it.[42]

Although Lauterpacht mentions a situation whereby a legal instrument cannot be applied *literally*, owing to the conduct of one of the parties, he refers to what he calls a sound principle of law, that the legal instrument *be applied in such a way as to approximate most closely its primary objective*. This is done via *interpretation* of that legal instrument. This is what Dworkin would view as an essential function of the judge, namely applying the law by using legal principles that, next to rules of law, form part of the positive law, and therefore have legal authority for the judge.[43]

The application of the principle of approximate treaty application in the case of humanitarian intervention described above[44] concerned the division of responsibilities between the Security Council and the General Assembly, in case the Security Council would be prevented from taking a decision because of one of the P5 casting a veto. Notwithstanding the fact that this very veto-power is an essential element of the system of collective security, and no doubt

---

[42] Separate opinion of Sir Hersch Lauterpacht, in *Admissibility of Hearings of Petitioners by the Committee on South-West Africa*, ICJ Reports 1956, p. 46. Also quoted in the *Gabčíkovo-Nagymaros* case, 25 September 1997, par. 75, where this opinion of Sir Lauterpacht, described as "the principle of approximate application", was invoked by Slovakia, where it claimed that this is a principle of international law and a general principle of law. At par. 76, the Court decided that in this particular case "it is not necessary for the Court to determine whether there is a principle of international law or a general principle of law of 'approximate application' because, even if such a principle existed, it could by definition only be employed within the limits of the treaty in question. In the view of the Court, Variant C does not meet that cardinal condition with regard to the 1977 Treaty".

[43] Arend Soeteman, 'Ronald Dworkin', in: Paul Cliteur and Marc Loth (eds.), *Rechtsfilosofen van de Twintigste Eeuw*, Arnhem: Gouda Quint 1992, p. 168.

[44] In the first section of this contribution.

for the 'super-powers' a precondition to agree on the system of collective security of the United Nations, the very nature of issues related to conflict and security renders the possible application of principles to break a deadlock crucially important. This is what led the Joint Dutch Advisory Committees to apply the principle of approximate treaty application in the instance of a humanitarian disaster necessitating, in the opinion of some states, action involving the use of force, even unilaterally.

The current question is of similar importance, and also concerns the use of military force. At which point can it be assumed that the Security Council has taken the necessary measures in a case where a state has reacted unilaterally in self-defence in response to an armed attack? The consequence of a deadlocked Security Council is likely to be that the defending state takes the position that the Security Council has evidently not taken the necessary measures, and that therefore, under article 51, the state continues to be entitled to use force in self-defence. The likely result is a continuation of unchecked use of force by this state.

Given that the central purpose of the United Nations system of collective security is the control of the use of force, the supervisory organs of the system have a duty to prevent the possibility of uncontrolled use of force. Assuming that the Security Council, as the primary supervisory body of the UN system of collective security, is unable to perform this function, it behoves one to apply the principle of approximate treaty application to the UN Charter.

5. *In Conclusion: Breaking the Deadlock and the Principle of Approximate Treaty Application*

In the particular case of a deadlocked Security Council when trying to establish whether the necessary measures under article 51 UN Charter have been taken, one has to conclude that the Charter of the United Nations cannot be applied fully in giving effect to the core principles of its system of collective security. These principles are the ban of force embodied in article 2 (4) of the UN Charter and its concomitant duty to settle disputes peacefully ex Article 2 (3). In order to realise the effectiveness of the system of collective security we therefore need to apply the United Nations Charter in a way most closely approximating its primary objective. Since the primary object of the system is the control of the use of force, and the Security Council as the primary supervisory organ is failing its duty, the General Assembly as the secondary supervisory organ of the United Nations appears to constitute the logical alternative. Of course, the General Assembly is not supposed ex article 12 to make any recommendations when the Security Council is involved in such a case, but an Emergency Special Session of the UN General Assembly could be foreseen, invoking the *Uniting for Peace* resolution. The criteria are clearly fulfilled, since an uncontrolled use of force has an impact on international peace and security.[45] Such an emergency special session could even be used to request the International Court of Justice to give an advisory opinion on a point of law, as the 10th Special Emergency Session of the General Assembly did with regard to the issue of the wall in the Occupied Palestinian Territory.[46] Such a request might, for instance, concern the issue of the necessary measures criterion, as a material criterion, to put beyond doubt that the General Assembly is also entitled to make such an assessment. Thereby, the International Court of Justice would perform its creative supervisory function.

This procedure might also be relevant in other use of force cases, such as a case in which a revocation of a given mandate by the Security Council under chapter VII to use military force ("all necessary means") seems in order since the continued use of force might lead to a disaster, but where this is not possible due to a deadlocked Security Council.

In order to invoke an emergency special session, the submission of two Security Council resolutions, and if possible a General Assembly resolution pronouncing thereon, would be necessary. In applying the principle of approximate treaty application, one stays within the system of the Charter and complies with the rules of international law, as long as all these steps are capable of being assessed. In parallel with our opinion in the report of the Advisory Committee,[47] the following procedure would appear logical:

1. The Security Council must primarily pronounce on the question of whether it has taken the necessary measures by giving its opinion on a substantive draft resolution;
2. If such a resolution is vetoed, the General Assembly must pronounce on it on the basis of its secondary (shared) responsibility for peace and security;

[45] "Resolves that if the Security Council, because of lack of unanimity of the permanent members, fails to exercise its primary responsibility for the maintenance of international peace and security in any case where there appears to be a threat to the peace, breach of the peace, or act of aggression, the General Assembly shall consider the matter immediately with a view to making appropriate recommendations to Members for collective measures, including in the case of a breach of the peace or act of aggression the use of armed force when necessary, to maintain or restore international peace and security. If not in session at the time, the General Assembly may meet in emergency special session within twenty-four hours of the request therefor. Such emergency special session shall be called if requested by the Security Council on the vote of any seven members, or by a majority of the Members of the United Nations." A/Res 377A(V), ('Uniting for Peace') of 3 November 1950. Under the resolution an 'emergency special session' can be convened within 24 hours. See <http://www.un.org/en/ga/sessions/emergency.shtml>.

[46] A/RES/ES-10–14 of 12 December 2003.

[47] Supra, n. 5.

3. In order to pronounce on the resolution, the General Assembly must be convened in an emergency special session by means of a procedural resolution based on the Uniting for Peace resolution (see General Assembly Resolution 377 A(V) 'Uniting for Peace' (3 November 1950), UN Doc. A/1775), for which a majority of nine members of the Security Council is in practice sufficient.[48]

[48] Cf. Christoph Eick, in: Bruno Simma (ed.), *The Charter of the United Nations, A Commentary*, Oxford: Oxford University Press 2002, p. 384: "Hence, there now appears to exist a rule that the convening of special sessions is a procedural matter not affected by the right of veto."

CHAPTER FIVE

MR KADI AND MRS PROST: IS THE UN OMBUDSPERSON GOING TO FIND HERSELF BETWEEN A ROCK AND A HARD PLACE?

Laurence Boisson de Chazournes and Pieter Jan Kuijper

1. *Introduction*

Karel Wellens has devoted quite an important part of his academic and professional life to working inside the ILA on the vital issue of the accountability and responsibility of international organisations.[1] Some years ago he dedicated a perceptive study to this subject.[2] One of the important themes in this field of study is the question if and how international organisations can be made accountable for their alleged breaches of fundamental rights of individuals. Ironically this question has come to the surface recently *inter alia* as a consequence of the fact that UN economic sanctions which traditionally were directed against states and thus hit the whole population of states, were considered to be of doubtful legality and political legitimacy insofar as they also hurt – and often in disproportionate fashion – vulnerable groups in society, such as children and sick people.[3]

This led to the rise of individualised sanctions or 'smart sanctions', that is to say sanctions that were directed originally against members of the government, or high civilian or military personnel of the government, of the sanctioned country and later, after the rise of Al Qaeda, the Taliban and international terrorist groups, also against individuals without government affiliation, but with a link to such terrorist groups.[4] The sanctions imposed on the persons listed in the annexes to the relevant resolutions were mostly of economic or financial nature, principally so-called asset freezes, which made it

[1] Karel Wellens, 'ILA Committee on Accountability of International Organisations', International Law Forum du droit international, Final Report adopted at the Berlin ILA Conference in August 2004.

[2] Karel Wellens, *Remedies against International Organisations*, Cambridge: Cambridge University Press 2002.

[3] The sanctions imposed on Iraq are an emblematic example. As to the side effects thereof on the Iraqi civil population, see F.G. Gause, 'Getting It Backward on Iraq', *Foreign Affairs*, May/June 1999, p. 54; Center for Economic and Social Rights, *UN Sanctioned Suffering: A Human Rights Assessment of the United Nations Sanctions on Iraq* (1996), p. 42.

[4] See particularly UNSC res. 1267, 15 October 1999 and UNSC res. 1373, 28 September 2001. See also UNSC res. 1390, 28 January 2002; UNSC res. 1526, 30 January 2004; UNSC res. 1617, 29 July 2005; UNSC res. 1735, 22 December 2006; UNSC res. 1822, 30 June 2008.

impossible for them to dispose of their financial resources except insofar as they were necessary for their basic subsistence.[5]

As is well known from the literature,[6] these sanctions were imposed without any warning or hearing on the facts which were supposed to show that the persons targeted belonged to, supported, financed, delivered arms to, or were otherwise affiliated with such terrorist groups. If that was still considered acceptable, given that the money that was going to be blocked could be removed in a second, as soon as the person concerned would have been advised of the reasons for the incipient freezing of his/her assets,[7] it was highly doubtful if, once the measures had been imposed, such persons should also remain bereft of any opportunity to be heard about the reality of such links or even about such a simple issue as a possible confusion of identities. Even if such "hearing" was granted, the information to be had was often minimal, since the various national intelligence agencies that originally pushed for inclusion of these persons on the sanctions list, were very intent on protecting their sources.[8]

It is remarkable that many of the court cases concerning the breach of fundamental rights by international organisations in the course of imposing individual sanctions come from the courts of regional organisations or from courts charged with interpreting a regional international agreement, such as the European Court of Human Rights and the Court of Justice of the European Union. In this way, these cases also raise the issue of the relationship of the jurisdictions of regional organisations to organisations at the world level, in particular the UN and its organ for the maintenance of international peace and security, the Security Council.

---

[5] See, for instance, paragraph 4 (b) of UNSC res. 1267, which reads: "[All states shall] freeze funds and other financial resources, including funds derived or generated from property owned or controlled directly or indirectly by the Taliban, or by any undertaking owned or controlled by the Taliban, as designated by the Committee established by paragraph 6 below, and ensure that neither they nor any other funds or financial resources so designated are made available, by their nationals or by any persons within their territory, to or for the benefit of the Taliban or any undertaking owned or controlled, directly or indirectly, by the Taliban, except as may be authorized by the Committee on a case-by-case basis on the grounds of humanitarian need."

[6] See Christina Eckes, *EU Counter-Terrorist Policies and Fundamental Rights. The Case of Individual Sanctions*, Oxford: Oxford University Press 2010.

[7] This was normally justified by the courts that had to decide such issues on the basis of the provisional or conservatory nature of the asset freezing technique; see Case T-315/01 *Yassin Abdullah Kadi v. Council of the European Union and Commission of the European Communities* [2005] ECR II-3649, par. 248, 274 (hereafter, *Kadi 2005*); see also Joined Cases C-402/05 & C-415/05 P, *Kadi and Al Barakaat International Foundation v. Council and Commission* [2008] ECR I-06351, par. 101, 358 (hereafter, *Kadi 2008*).

[8] The reluctance to disclose the information on the basis of which an individual or an entity was added to the list is confirmed by the arguments raised by the EU institutions and the intervening Member States in the recent *Kadi* judgment of the General Court; see in particular par. 97–111. As to the answer provided by the Court, see particularly par. 132–137, 157–164, Case T-85/09, *Kadi v. Commission* [2010], Judgment of the General Court of 30 September 2010 (hereafter, *Kadi 2010*).

For these reasons, it is fitting to contribute this paper on questions of accountability of international organisations, questions which at the same time raise issues of hierarchy between international organisations, to this volume in honour of Karel Wellens. We hope that it will also shed some light on the direction in which these fundamental questions will evolve.

In the following we will first recall the situation as it evolved through different cases until the end of the summer of 2010. This will be done briefly and cursorily, since we believe that these cases are widely known. This will result in an evocation of the situation as it was in September 2010. Secondly, we will then analyse the further developments during autumn and winter of 2010 with a view to assessing the situation at present and to discussing in which direction it is likely to evolve. This will cause us to review in particular the creation of the office of the UN Ombudsperson and the first steps of Mrs Kimberley Prost who was appointed to this new office, as well as the judgment of the EU General Court in the Kadi 2010 case and what might be the likely consequences of these developments.

2. *The Varying Approaches of the European Court of Human Rights and the European Court of Justice to Sanctions Measures*

Both the European Court of Justice and the European Court of Human Rights have taken positions in respect of sanctions decided by the Security Council, which have varied over time. The European Court of Human Rights (ECtHR) has taken two somewhat different approaches to measures of the Security Council, but both showing degrees of deference varying between moderate and total.

Insofar as it concerned sanctions measures taken by the Security Council and implemented by the European Community – at the time not yet in the nature of individual sanctions - the ECtHR has applied a kind of variant of the so-called "solange" approach practiced by the German Constitutional Court (*Bundesverfassungsgericht*) in respect of European Community measures with human rights dimensions. In the so-called *Bosphorus* case, the ECtHR took the position that, *as long as* (in German "solange")[9] the European Court of Justice broadly afforded a level of judicial protection equivalent to that provided by the ECtHR itself, it would presume such implementing measures to be in conformity with the Convention, unless there was a reason in an

[9] In respect of the *solange* doctrine of the German Constitutional Court, see *Solange I*, 29 May 1974, BVerGe 37, 271 and *Solange II*, 22 October 1986, BVerGe 75, 339. As to an application of this doctrine between European regional courts, see for instance Nikolaos Lavranos, 'The Solange-dialogue between the ECJ and ECrtHR' (2008) 11 *European Law Reporter*, p. 384.

individual case to review the taking of such measures in detail for reasons of human rights.[10]

However, in a later case concerning the responsibility for serious accidents resulting from the omission by UNMIK to clear unexploded anti-personnel weapons and excessively long detention by French and Norwegian troop contingents of KFOR,[11] the ECtHR constructed the line of command between these national troop contingents and the UN so generously that only the UN might ultimately be held responsible for these actions and omissions. Since the ECtHR had no jurisdiction *ratione personae* over the UN, the practical result was total judicial indulgence in respect of the two national troop contingents. All the more so, since the national jurisdictions of the countries involved in the Kosovo operation would in all likelihood follow the example of a Dutch Court which declared an action of the so-called "Mothers of Srebrenica" against the state inadmissible, precisely because the Dutch contingent in Srebrenica during the Bosnian actions was under UN command and the UN enjoyed immunity in the Dutch courts.[12]

It is also important to recall that the ECtHR devoted specific reasoning to its lack of jurisdiction over the UN beyond the simple consideration that the UN as organisation was not a party to the European Convention. The Court advanced the view that actions within the framework of UN authorized operations were vital for the accomplishment by the Security Council of its specific tasks that it was charged with under chapter VII of the Charter. Thus they were vital to the achievement of the fundamental objective of the UN to maintain international peace and security.[13] The Court suggested here that its 'solange test' as applied in the *Bosphorus* case was not applicable in the framework of chapter VII operations. In other words: fundamental rights can be abridged by the UN Security Council in certain situations.[14]

The Court of Justice of the European Union, in its different incarnations as the Court of First Instance and the European Court of Justice as *cour de cassation*, also showed different degrees of deference to the European implementation of "smart sanctions" taken by the Security Council for reasons linked to

---

[10] See *Bosphorus Airways v Ireland* no. 45036/98, para. 155, ECHR 2005-VI.

[11] See *Behrami and Behrami v. France, Saramati v France, Germany and Norway, (dec.)* [GC], Nos. 71412/01 and 78166/01, 2 May 2007 (hereafter, *Behrami*).

[12] See *Mothers of Srebrenica v. Netherlands*, Hague Court of Appeals, 30 March 2010, see www.haguejusticeportal.net/Cache/DEF/7/776.html, last visited 20 February 2011.

[13] See *Behrami* (n.11), par. 149.

[14] See contra, Erika de Wet, 'Human rights Considerations in the Enforcement of Security Council Sanctions in the EU Legal Order' in: Bardo Fassbender (ed.) *The United Nations Security Council and Human Rights*, Oxford: Oxford University Press (forthcoming); 'Holding the United Nations Security Council Accountable for Human Rights Violations through Domestic and Regional Courts: A Case of "Be Careful What you Wish For?", in: Jeremy Farrall and Kim Rubenstein (eds.), *Sanctions, Accountability and Governance in a Globalised World*, Cambridge: Cambridge University Press 2009; see also Antonios Tzanakopoulos, *Disobeying the Security Council: Countermeasures against Wrongful Sanctions*, Oxford: Oxford University Press 2011.

the latter's fundamental responsibility for the maintenance of peace and security in the world.

In the famous *Kadi* case, concerning the implementation of Security Council (UNSC) sanctions that demanded the freezing of Mr Kadi's assets, the Court of First Instance (CFI, now called the General Court since the entry into force of the Lisbon Treaty) went even further than the ECtHR in accepting that measures taken for the implementation of Security Council resolutions under chapter VII of the Charter would be exempt from judicial review in case of alleged breaches of fundamental rights. The CFI struggled mightily with the relationship between the Security Council resolution placing Mr Kadi on the so-called sanctions list and the European Community acts implementing this resolution, because it believed that they were *de facto* indistinguishable and that quashing the EC implementation measure implied that the Security Council resolution was also undermined. The CFI felt that even by implication it should not review a Security Council resolution, except possibly on the basis of *ius cogens* to which in its view the Security Council was bound just as much as any subject of international law.[15] Where the CFI went further than the ECtHR in *Behrami & Saramati* was in giving great weight to articles 25 and 103 of the Charter as creating obligations (even if indirectly through the Member States) for the Community. In this way the binding character of the resolution (article 25) and the supremacy of the resolution of the Security Council over not just other treaties, but also over Community primary law, would weigh just as much on the Community as on UN Member States. This recognizes the Community on the one hand as a separate entity under the UN system[16] but on the other hand makes it entirely subservient to the UN policy on peace and security, even if that policy has been laid down in Security Council resolutions in a manner so as to put in peril the fundamental rights of Community citizens.

It is this conception of the Community as, on the one hand, autonomous to a certain degree, but on the other hand, as subservient to the UN Security Council that became an issue in the appeals procedure before the European Court of Justice launched by Mr Kadi. Stimulated by the radical position of its Advocate-General, Miguel Poiares Maduro, the ECJ took the view that the

---

[15] See *Kadi 2005* (supra n. 7), par. 226. It should be noted in passing that the CFI gave an extra-ordinarily broad interpretation to the notion of *ius cogens*, including in it by implication the right to property and the fundamental rights of procedure of Mr Kadi, only to come to the conclusion that even in this (overly) broad conception of *ius cogens* these rights had not been violated.

[16] This is in contrast to the conception of article 103 of the Charter, which sees this provision essentially as a principle determining the hierarchy of treaties and according to which the obligations under chapter VII fall on the member states. This would have to leave Community law, including its fundamental rules of a primary nature, to one side under the edict of article 103 in favour of the UN Charter and the UNSC resolutions based on it.

relative autonomy of the European Community/Union in respect of the UN ought to have consequences for its acceptance of implementing measures of Security Council resolutions, which breached the fundamental rights of Mr Kadi where it concerned his right to a proper procedure and his right to property.[17] Here the Court relied on the formal distinction that the CFI had so struggled with, namely the distinction between the UNSC resolution and the Community implementation measures. The Court emphasised that it confined its judgment strictly to the legality of the Community implementation measures and that this was no reflection on the Security Council resolution, even if the contents of the latter were in reality largely identical to those of the former. However, as Mr Maduro had already stressed, there was no alternative to taking one's own legal order seriously and, at least within it, protecting the Community citizens against any breach of their fundamental rights. Thus in the end the maintenance of individual rights within a 'regional' organisation[18] should prevail over the claims to the maintenance of world order issuing from the United Nations. There is little doubt that this can create great tensions between the regional and world-wide levels of the international legal order. We will come back to this below.

3. *From 'Avoidance' to 'Engagement': The Political and Judicial Dialogue between the UN and Regional Institutions on the Implementation of Sanctions*

As we have seen, the judicial decisions reviewed so far seem to be premised on different approaches, ranging from subordination to autonomy. Yet, independently of the approach taken, courts have tended to avoid tackling the legal issues raised by the chapter VII resolutions of the Security Council. Indeed, whether we take the ECJ's rhetoric on the autonomy of the EU legal order – inspired by the position of Advocate General Maduro – or we look at the ECtHR's and CFI's attitude of (more or less nuanced) subordination towards the norms or values enshrined in the international legal order, we end up confronted with a number of legal techniques crafted to avoid entering into a dialogue between the regional and the UN legal order.[19] That has entailed a dearth of reflection as to the possible ways to reach systemic coherence and to

[17] See *Kadi 2008* (supra n. 7), par. 334, 361, 368–370.

[18] The authors use the word 'regional' here strictly in a factual sense and express no viewpoint on whether the EC/EU in the past or the EU at present can be regarded as a 'regional organisation' within the meaning of article 53 Charter, which entails a consequential subordination *ab initio* to the Security Council for the organisation in question.

[19] Although certain passages of the ECJ's *Kadi 2008* decision may hint at a sort of dialogue between the regional and the UN legal order; see particularly par. 321 and 374.

preserve a balance among those values fundamental for a smooth functioning of the international legal system.[20]

In the light of the foregoing, a reflection as to the causes of such an attitude of avoidance seems to be warranted. Could this attitude be due to the limited competence of regional courts? The articulation of a framework for judicial review of Security Council action (even if only indirectly by review of regional implementation measures) meets obstacles of a systemic character, having to do with the shaping of the international judicial space. Regional courts by their nature can only act within the confines of their (regional) competence. Therefore, almost by definition they cannot fully apprehend and judge the totality of the measures ordered by the Security Council and their underlying rationale. Thus they retreat behind formal mechanisms of avoidance.

This is, however, not entirely satisfactory as an explanation. It suffices to note that a similar attitude of avoidance surfaces also in the *Sayadi* decision taken by the Human Rights Committee.[21] The review of national measures exercised by the Committee is potentially universal in scope and based on a set of uniform standards. That offers an advantage compared to the circumscribed protection afforded by regional judicial instances. Yet, the Committee seems to have been reluctant to fully grasp this opportunity. The reasoning expounded in *Sayadi* is rather simplistic: the Committee confines itself to analysing the conduct of the defendant state in light of its obligations under the International Covenant on Civil and Political Rights (hereinafter: ICCPR), glossing over the issue of normative conflict between the Covenant and the UN Charter and, even more tellingly, omitting any reference to article 103 of the Charter. In the end, one is left with another missed opportunity to spell out the relationship between the UN legal order and norms for the protection of human rights.[22]

---

[20] In this respect, it has been noticed that principles such as those of subsidiarity and of complementarity may help in addressing the incoherence stemming from the growing complexity of the international legal order. This goal may also be fostered through a number of legal techniques, such as that of the national margin of appreciation or that of formal equivalence. On this point, see for instance Mirelle Delmas-Marty, 'Avant-propos', in: Edouard Dubout and Sébastien Touzé (eds.), *Les droits fondamentaux: charnières entre ordres et systèmes juridiques*, Paris: Pedone 2009, p. 9.

[21] See, *Sayadi v. Belgium*, CCPR/C/94/D/1472/2006 (29 December 2008) (hereafter: *Sayadi*). The applicants had been blacklisted by the 1267 Sanctions Committee on the basis of their alleged ties with Al-Qaida. The request to the Human Rights Committee has come after a series of proceedings intended in Belgian domestic courts.

[22] For a similar view, see Marko Milanovic, 'The Human Rights Committee's Views in *Sayadi v. Belgium*: A Missed Opportunity', (2009) 1 *Goettingen Journal of International Law*, p. 519.

4. *The Strategy of 'Conforming Interpretation'*

In spite of the remarks made above, the *Sayadi* case offers some clues on a more elaborate strategy, aimed at addressing the legal issues posed by the practice of the Security Council's blacklists. We refer in particular to the position on conforming interpretation[23] contained in Sir Nigel Rodley's Individual Opinion attached to the *Sayadi* decision. According to Sir Nigel, the Committee should pronounce itself on the existence of a normative conflict between the obligations under the UN Charter and those under the Covenant. On the basis of this analysis, it shall be decided whether article 103 has to be applied or not. The crucial point here is how to define a normative conflict.

Sir Nigel puts forward four main criteria for such a definition, formulated as interpretative presumptions about the Council's intention of derogating from human rights norms. To start with, he refers to a general presumption of conformity between human rights norms and Security Council resolutions if their wording does not exclude such conformity explicitly. Next, he posits a presumption of conformity between Security Council resolutions and *ius cogens* and with the non-derogable rights contained in the Covenant. Finally, a presumption of strict necessity and proportionality is invoked, when it comes to the restriction of rights from which derogation is not allowed under the Covenant. As it appears, it is particularly through the third and fourth criteria that Sir Nigel attempts to spell out the relationship between the ICCPR and the UN Charter. Indeed, by making reference to the non-derogable character of certain rights and to the standards governing the possibility to derogate from certain other rights, he seems to take into account the situation of emergency arising in connection with international terrorist activities.

---

[23] On conforming interpretation, see Marko Milanovic, 'Norm Conflict in International Law: Whither Human Rights?', (2009) 69 *Duke Journal of Comparative and International Law*, p. 98–102. See also Andrea Bianchi, 'Assessing the Effectiveness of the UN Security Council's Anti-Terrorism Measures: The Quest for Legitimacy and Cohesion', (2006) 17 *European Journal of International Law*, p. 881, p. 912–914, p. 916. The notion of conforming interpretation has also been employed in the *Al-Adsani* case before the ECHR. According to the Court "(...) [t]he Convention should so far as possible be interpreted in harmony with other rules of international law of which it forms part, including those relating to the grant of State immunity', see par. 55, *Al-Adsani v. United Kingdom*, No. 35763/97, par. 24, ECHR 2001-XI. It is important to stress that this interpretative presumption can refer to the conformity of national/regional measures vis-à-vis general international law and UN law or to the conformity of universal measures vis-à-vis regional rules on human rights protection. This type of interpretation may come close an implicit amendment of the measure at stake. On this point, Tzanakopoulos makes reference to the interpretation by the English High Court in *Regina (on the application of Othman) v. Secretary of State for Work and Pensions* [2001] EWHC Admin 1022, par. 57; see Antonios Tzanakopoulos, 'From Interpretation to Defiance: *Abdelrazik v Canada* and United Nations Sanctions in Domestic Courts', (2010) 8 *Journal of International Criminal Justice*, p. 249, p. 253–254, p. 260–261.

In our view, Sir Nigel Rodley's approach goes to the heart of the complex relationship between the Security Council and regional judicial organs engaged in the protection of human rights provoked by the Council's action against international terrorism. Indeed, it demonstrates the importance of respecting the rule of law at the UN level. When applied to the Security Council, this means that, above all, the Council must accept that its action is subject to the legal limits imposed by fundamental rights. Indeed, as recalled by by the ICTY in the *Tadić* case: "In any case, neither the text nor the spirit of the Charter conceives of the Security Council as *legibus solutus* (not bound by law)'.[24] Even more importantly, the 2005 World Summit Outcome envisages that:

> Sanctions should be implemented and monitored effectively with clear benchmarks and should be periodically reviewed, as appropriate, and remain for as limited a period as necessary to achieve their objectives and should be terminated once the objectives have been achieved.[25]

5. *The 'Carrot and Stick' Strategy*

The requirement to guarantee the respect for the rule of law has inspired a further 'positive' strategy, emerging in the pronouncements of a few domestic courts[26] and in a series of diplomatic initiatives taken within the Council of Europe.[27] We could speak of it as a 'carrot and stick' approach.

---

[24] ICTY, Decision on the Defence Motion for Interlocutory Appeal on Jurisdiction, *Prosecutor v. Dusko Tadić 'Dule'*, IT 94-1-AR72 A. Chamber, 2 October 2005, par. 28.

[25] *World Summit Outcome*, GA Doc. A/60/L. 1, 20 September 2005, par. 107 (see also par. 108–109).

[26] See *R. (Al-Jedda) v. Secretary of State for Defence,* [2005] EWHC 1809 (Admin); R. (Al-Jedda) v. Secretary of State for Defence, [2006] EWCA Civ. 327, [2007] UKHL 58; *A, K, M, Q & G v. HM Treasury* [2008] EWHC 869 (Admin); *Hay v. HM Treasury* [2009] EWHC 1677 (Admin); *Abdelrazik v. Canada (Minister of Foreign Affairs)* 2009 CF 580, [2010] 1 R.C.F. 267.

[27] See Iain Cameron, *The European Convention on Human Rights, Due Process and United Nations Security Council Counter-Terrorism Sanctions*, Report prepared for the Council of Europe, 6 February 2006, available at <http://www.coe.int/t/legal_affairs/legal_co>. See also *UN Security Council Black Lists*, Committee on Legal Affairs and Human Rights, Council of Europe Parliamentary Assembly, AS/Jur (2007), 19 March 2007. This work contains a Memorandum introducing the Report by Dick Marty and a Working Document entitled 'Certains comportements récents du Conseil de sécurité des Nations Unies en matière de droits de l'homme', prepared by Symeon Karagiannis concerning the black lists of the Sanctions Committees. See also the Report by Dick Marty, *UN Security Council and EU Blacklists*, doc. 11454, 16 November 2007 and the addendum thereto of 22 January 2008, available online at <http://www.statewatch.org/news/2007/may/coe-marty-un-lists.pdf>. These reports are part of a series of initiatives concerning the impact of UN sanctions on human rights. On this topic, see also Bardo Fassbender, *Targeted Sanctions and Due Process. The Responsibility of the UN Security Council to Ensure that Fair and Clear procedures Are Made Available to Individuals and Entities Targeted with Sanctions under Chapter VII of the UN Charter*, Study commissioned by the United Nations, Office of Legal Affairs, available at <http://www.un.org/law/counsel/Fassbender_study.pdf>.

A number of national tribunals have explored indirect forms of control over Security Council resolutions, by reviewing the measures transposing them into domestic law. A telling example is provided by the *Abdelrazik v. Canada* decision rendered by the Canadian Federal Court.[28] Before dealing with the impugned domestic act, the Court indulged in a harsh critique of the sanctions regime imposed by resolution 1267 and deemed it "a denial of basic legal remedies" and "untenable under the principles of international human rights". As it appears, this reasoning entails a twofold dimension. While criticising the Council, the Court finally opts for a review of the domestic measure of implementation only, omitting to deal with the legality of the resolution at stake. The blending of these two attitudes suggests the endorsement of a 'carrot and stick' approach, though in the concrete case the stick comes first. This approach has found an echo also in other decisions of national courts and has not been overlooked by the Security Council. On the contrary, it is likely that these pronouncements have triggered the improvements to the sanctions regime recently made by the Council.[29]

Leaving aside the judicial context, a 'carrot and stick' approach has surfaced also in the Council of Europe, especially through the expert reports dealing with the Council's practice of blacklisting. The Marty Report, for instance, proposes that the Secretary General of the Council of Europe shall require information from Member States as to the application of the ECHR. Additionally, the report calls upon the Parliamentary Assembly "s'en prendre directement et à loisir aux résolutions du Conseil qu'elle jugerait contraires aux droits de l'homme" and to exercise its influence over the states responsible for the elaboration of resolutions that might have even more direct and immediate effects.[30]

Admittedly, this 'carrot and stick' approach is somewhat heterodox. A more conventional way for regional organisations to communicate their position would have entailed a direct exchange of views between them and the UN during the period of conception of the sanctions regime. That could have happened on numerous occasions, such as the meetings between the Security Council and regional organisations or the high-level meetings among the UN,[31] regional and other intergovernmental organisations organized by the

[28] See *Abdelrazik v. Canada* (supra n. 26), par. 50–52.

[29] The Council has considered the domestic proceedings mentioned above in several occasions; see for instance S/2008/324, 14 May 2008, par. 39–41 and Annex I; S/2009/245, 13 May 2009, par. 19–25 and Annex I; S/2009/502, 2 October 2009, par. 36–38 and Annex I.

[30] See *Marty Report* (supra n. 27), p. 32.

[31] The first meeting gathering the UNSC and representatives of regional organisations took place in 2003, see S/PV.4739, 11 April 2003 (*The Security Council and Regional Organizations: Facing the New Challenges to International Peace and Security*); a second meeting was held in 2010, see S/PV.6257, 13 January 2010 (*Cooperation between the United Nations and Regional and Sub-Regional Organisations in Maintaining International Peace and Security*).

UN Secretary General.[32] However, these opportunities have repeatedly been missed and today the Council is caught into an indirect dialogue, obliging it to react to the allegations of illegality coming from domestic jurisdictions and from regional political fora. A response by the Council, in fact, becomes urgent, since the very respect for the measures adopted by it is put in question and, therefore, potentially hampered.

6. *The Reaction of the Security Council: the Creation of the Office of the Ombudsperson*

In response to the above-mentioned critiques and to a number of other diplomatic initiatives,[33] the Security Council has adopted resolution 1904 (2009),[34] which potentially heralds a new era in the implementation of anti-terror sanctions. The rationale behind this resolution is fairly straightforward: the functioning of the sanctioning regime is seen as depending not only on the effectiveness of the adopted measures, but also on the existence of procedures guaranteeing their pertinence *in casu*. Along these lines, resolution 1904 innovates from previous resolutions by introducing an Ombudsperson,[35] charged with examining the requests for delisting submitted by sanctions-affected individuals and entities. The Ombudsperson, in fact, has more powers than the so-called Focal Points set up by resolution 1730.

As is well known, the Focal Points mainly operate within an interstate framework; which is confirmed by the following elements. First, any request for delisting received by a Focal Point has to be communicated to the government(s) responsible for the complainant's inscription on the list as well as to the State of nationality and of residence of the listed person or entity.[36] Any of these States can recommend the removal of the complainant's name from the list. If, after a certain time, none of these States has taken an initiative in this sense, *any* member of the Sanctions committee can take over and

---

[32] Between 1994 and 2006, the SG has conveyed seven meetings entailing the participation of other international organisations. These meetings have covered a broad range of substantive issues concerning the relations between the UN and regional organisations.

[33] The initiatives taken at UN level have been promoted by Switzerland, Sweden and Germany. See particularly *Supplementary Guidelines for the Review of Sanctions Committees' Listing Decisions*, Discussion Paper available at <http://www.liechtenstein.li/en/pdf-fl-aussenstelle-newyork-discussionpaper-delisting-workshop-2007-11-8.pdf>, Explanatory Memorandum by Michael Bothe, available at <http://www.liechtenstein.li/en/pdf-fl-aussenstelle-newyork-explanatory-memorandum-prof-bothe-delisting-workshop-2007-11-8.pdf>.

[34] UNSC res. 1904, 17 December 2009.

[35] As to previous attempts of amelioration of the sanctioning regime, see Irène Couzigou, 'La lutte du Conseil de sécurité contre le terrorisme international et les droits de l'homme', (2008) 43 *Revue générale de droit international public*, p. 49–84.

[36] UNSC/Res/1730, par. 5 and 6 (a).

recommend the removal of the complainant's name from the list.[37] If, after one month from the receipt of the request, no Committee member recommends such de-listing, it shall be deemed rejected and the Chairman of the Committee shall inform the Focal Point accordingly.[38]

The provisions of resolution 1904 (2009) on the Ombuds-person improve this process in several respects. Overall, the tasks entrusted to the Ombuds-person are designed to foster the efficacy of the information gathering process and to improve the interaction among the actors involved in the phase of decision-making. The work of the Ombudsperson, after receipt of a de-listing request, is divided into three parts of each two months' duration.[39]

First there is a period of information gathering, during which the Ombuds-person does not need to rely exclusively on information given to her by the complainant and the states concerned, but can also herself search for additional information.[40] The second two months' period is devoted to dialogue and engagement. The Ombudsperson will establish a dialogue with the complainant and can also act as go-between between the complainant and the states concerned.[41] At the end of the second period – which may, if necessary, be prolonged with another two months – the Ombudsperson will issue a so-called comprehensive report on the request for delisting.[42] This report will be drawn up with the help of the Monitoring Team, but since it concerns matters that require an independent assessment, is written by and issued under the responsibility of the Ombudsperson alone.[43] Given the way it has been prepared, this report to the Committee gives access to a broader range of information than was hitherto the case, thus allowing a more accurate analysis of each case.

After this second period, a third period follows during which the Sanctions Committee must arrive at a decision on the request for de-listing. This will involve intensive discussions with the Ombudsperson, who will herself present her report to the Sanctions Committee. "After the Committee consideration, the Committee shall decide whether to approve the delisting request through its normal decision-making procedures."[44] In this way, the fate of a request is less dependent on the discretion of the Committee members entitled to take action according to resolution 1730. Indeed, since the Committee

37 UNSC/Res/1730, par. 6 (c).
38 Ibid.
39 For this procedure, see Annex II, UNSC res. 1904.
40 See ibid., Annex II, par. 1–4.
41 See ibid., Annex II, par. 6.
42 See ibid., Annex II, par. 7.
43 On this division of work on the Comprehensive *Report see S/2011/29, Report of the Office of the Ombudsperson pursuant to Security Council Resolution 1904 (2009)*, Appendix, I (hereafter, *Report Ombudsperson*).
44 Annex II, UNSC res. 1904, par. 10.

is bound to take a formal decision, silence in case of inaction by any of the Committee members is no longer enough to quash a request for de-listing. On the whole one can say that the functions vested in the Ombudsperson are conceived so as to create an independent third party, enjoying a certain freedom in the collection of information and thereby giving the impression of acting according to a transparent and fair procedure.

7. *The Reaction of National Courts, the EU General Court and a UN Special Rapporteur to the Creation of the Office of the Ombudsperson*

It is to be noted at the outset of this section that the European national courts and the Court of First Instance (later the General Court) had been much more at ease in judging cases concerning people placed on the lists linked to UNSC resolution 1373. In that system of sanctions resolutions, relating to international terrorism other than Al Qaeda and the Taliban, the UN list was ultimately based on requests from national governments, which had to use official criminal investigations, accusations or convictions (*in absentia*) as the basis for communicating names to the UN. This made it much easier for national courts or quasi-judicial authorities[45] to insist on full review and criticise or even delegitimize the actions of the national authorities. This, in turn, made it much simpler for the CFI and later the General Court, basing themselves on such rulings at the national level, to wipe cases, in which national authorities just went on placing the persons or organisations concerned again on the list, off the table with some gusto. This was the case with Mr Sison in the Netherlands[46] and with the PMOI/OMPI in the UK and France.[47] Such cases also did not carry the same risk of inexorably opposing the EU to the UN Security Council decision to put somebody on the list, as in the Al Qaeda and Taliban sanctions system. In such cases the General Court was at ease using more stick than carrot.[48]

[45] In the UK for example the authority referred to in the PMOI cases, the Proscribed Organisations Appeals Commission (POAC), see *Lord Alton of Liverpool and Others v. Secretary of State for the Home Department* [2008] EWCA Civ 443; [2008] WLR (D) 141.

[46] See Case T-341/07, *Sison v. Council* [2009] ECR II-03625. In this case the CFI could rely on a judgment of the Council of State, which related to Mr Sison's status as a refugee, but was in no way proof of his terrorist links.

[47] See Case T-256/07, PMOI *v. Council*, [2008] ECR II-03019, in which the CFI could rely on the fact that in the UK the POAC (see n. 45 supra) had ruled that the PMOI could no longer be regarded as a terrorist organisation.

[48] It is remarkable to see how this tendency changes if the national authorities, for instance a prosecutor's office, insist on regarding somebody as a suspect in a terrorist case. Deference to that national authority seems to be the reaction prevailing in such cases. This was the case in the case of Sofiane Fahas, against whom a provisional arrest warrant for terrorist activities had been issued by the prosecuting judge (*juge d'instruction*) in Naples; see Case T-49/07 *Sofiane Fahas v. Council*, Judgment of the General Court (Second Chamber) 7 December 2010, n.y.r.

The same lack of patience with the Union's institutions that meekly accepted again and again such flawed proposals for the terrorist list from some Member States, can also be felt in the General Court's reaction when it was called upon to rule again on Mr Kadi's continued placing on the Al Qaeda terrorist list (*Kadi 2010*). This was after the Union's authorities had gone through the motions of following the Court of Justice's negative judgment of 2008 (*Kadi 2008*) by subjecting Mr Kadi to a new procedure in response to his request to be taken off the list, at least in Brussels.

The General Court initially followed the Court of Justice's judgment in *Kadi 2008* only reluctantly and protesting a bit too much,[49] but later in its judgment it saw many parallels between how the Court of Justice dealt with *Kadi 2005* and how it itself threw out the PMOI II case.[50] Thus the General Court did not hesitate to draw the conclusion that Kadi's rights of defence had been infringed once again.[51] This was based on the fact that Mr Kadi was put through a new procedure both at the UN and at the EU level before the Office of the Ombudsperson became operational. Therefore his procedure followed the Focal Points mechanism in the UN, which had already been implicitly rejected by the Court of Justice in Kadi 2008 as inadequate. Moreover, he had only be advised of a summary of the reasons why he was placed on the list. The General Court also pointed to the important difference between the procedures followed in cases based on resolution 1373 (terrorist activities other than Al Qaeda and the Taliban), such as the OMPI and PMOI cases, where at least judicial review at the national level had been possible, and the present case where the procedure at Community level is marked by an absence of effective judicial review that can remedy or sanction the lack of a guarantee of the rights of defence at the level of the administrative procedure.[52]

In the end the General Court thus came easily to the conclusion that Mr Kadi had once more been the victim of a breach of his rights of defence

[49] If one reads par. 112–122 of the General Court's judgment full of implicit and not so implicit barbs at the Court of Justice, one is inevitably reminded of President's Sarkozy's snide remark in another context, "*Elle a raté une occasion de se taire*" ("It lost an opportunity to stay silent"). One may wonder, moreover, by what (mal)chance it fell to the same President of Chamber and *Judge-Rapporteur* to be in charge of this judgment as had been dealing with the same case at the outset in 2005.

[50] *Kadi 2010*, par. 138.

[51] *Kadi 2010*, par. 176–184.

[52] *Kadi 2010*, par. 186–187. This confirms our earlier remark in footnote 46 above to the effect that the General Court felt very reassured by such review at the national level, even if exercised by somewhat unconventional judicial authorities such as POAC in the UK, but essentially showed deference when the competent national authorities, such as a prosecutor or a judge, persisted in their assessment of a person as being linked to terrorism. Only the wish to show deference to the national courts in procedures linked to resolution 1373 can explain the difference in tone and outcome as between the *Fahas* case and the judgments in *PMOI II* and *Kadi 2010*.

and of judicial protection and that also his right to property had been infringed in breach of the principle of proportionality.

The impression that also in *Kadi 2010* the General Court was wielding the stick rather than proffering the carrot to the UN is confirmed by a number of other pronouncements by the Court relating directly or indirectly to the office of the Ombudsperson and its functioning.

First of all, the Court recalled what it said in PMOI II about communication to the Court of elements contained in the national file communicated by a Member State to the Council and/or the Commission.[53] The Court repeated that if the Member State in question is not willing to authorise the communication of such file to the Community judicature whose task it is to review the lawfulness of the Community decision based on that file, and *even rejects communication to the Court alone*,[54] the ineluctable conclusion must be that the Court is unable to review the lawfulness of that decision and thus the right to judicial protection is denied.[55] On the positive (carrot) side, it can be noted that it would seem that the Union's judicial authorities are at least considering the possibility of *ex parte* communication of the national file.

The Court made another interesting remark of principle. It put in doubt whether after the more than 10 years during which Mr Kadi had been subject to an asset freezing decision, it and other courts could still continue to rely on the preventative, provisional and temporary character of such asset freezing.[56]

Finally – and here it is again the stick that dominates the General Court's approach – it thinks fit to give a shot across the bow of the Office of the Ombudsperson at a time when the occupant of that Office, Mrs Kimberley Prost, a former *ad litem* judge in the ICTY, had been in office for barely four months. The Court notes that, in spite of the Ombudsperson's presence, the removal of a person from the list still takes consensus, even if now a positive vote is necessary, as signalled above. The disclosure of the evidence to the person on the list remains a matter entirely in the hands of the Member State who proposed the person for inclusion in the list in the first place. The person in question has no right to even know the name of the proposing State and there is no guarantee that the information, if it is given, is sufficient for the person to mount his defence effectively. "For those reasons", the Court concluded, "the creation of (…) the Office of the Ombudsperson cannot be equated with the provision of an effective judicial procedure for review of the decisions of the Sanctions Committee".[57]

---

[53] *PMOI II*, par. 76–78.

[54] Italics added.

[55] *Kadi 2010*, par. 145.

[56] Ibid., par. 150.

[57] Here the Court relies on the UK Supreme Court's Judgment in the Case of *HM Treasury v. Mohammed Jabar Ahmed et al*, Judgment given on 27 January 2010, that is to say slightly over two months after the adoption of UNSC resolution 1904 (2009). In fact the Supreme Court

Finally, the UN Special Rapporteur on the promotion and protection of human rights while countering terrorism, Martin Scheinin, also expressed doubts about the adequacy of the office of the Ombudsperson from a perspective of fundamental rights. This is linked to the opinion he already expressed in his 2008 report, namely that the listing of a person because of the severity of the sanction (the indefinite freezing of one's assets) amounted to a criminal charge.[58] Even though the Special Rapporteur welcomed the creation of the Office of the Ombudsperson in his 2010 report, given his view of the regime based on SC Res 1267 (1999) he could not possibly be fully satisfied with the powers granted to this Office by SC res. 1904 (2009). In his opinion, it is necessary, as a minimum, to give the Ombudsperson quasi-judicial powers. This would imply that she would have the power to overturn a listing decision by the Committee established pursuant to SC Res 1267 (1999). But that, of course, is not what SC res. 1904 (2009) decided: the Ombudsperson cannot even make formal recommendations to the Committee and in the end it is that Committee, a political organ, that decides on the basis of confidentiality and by consensus and without much transparency vis-à-vis the listed person or the general public whether a person will be delisted. There is no guarantee that the report of the Ombudsperson on a case will be published.[59]

These considerations bring Special Rapporteur Scheinin to the conclusion that the sanctions regime of SC Res 1267 (1999) is based on an *ultra vires* act of the Security Council, exceeding its powers under chapter VII of the Charter. That will remain the case unless and until the Ombudsperson or the Council itself is equipped with quasi-judicial powers. As long as the Ombudsperson is not equipped with decision-making power, she "cannot be regarded as a tribunal within the meaning of article 14 of the International Covenant on Civil and Political Rights". In the meantime, individuals and entities listed have no other remedies than those provided by domestic or regional judicial review of the national or regional implementing measures, such as that provided by the UK courts and by the European Court of Justice.[60]

8. *The First Months of the Office of the Ombudsperson*

On 3 June 2010 Mrs Prost was appointed by the UN Secretary-General to the Office of the Ombudsperson. In late October she unveiled a bit of her approach to her office in a briefing to an informal meeting of the legal advisors of the

judges could not do much more than signal that the Ombudsperson did not guarantee the equivalent of a judicial review procedure at the UN level. For the rest the Supreme Court was largely on the line of the Court of Justice in the *Kadi 2008* judgment.

[58] UN doc. A/63/223, par. 16.

[59] UN doc. A/65/258 par. 55–56

[60] Ibid., par. 57–58

Member States,[61] in late January 2011 she published her first biannual report on her activities to the Security Council[62] and in late February she planned to finalise her first comprehensive report to the Sanctions Committee on the first case of the seven that have been submitted to her so far.[63]

From Mrs Prost's statement to the legal advisors and from her first report to the Security Council it is clear that she has a robust approach to her office. She quite rightly takes the Supreme Court of England and Wales and the EU General Court to task for having declared her office inadequate at a moment that it was not or only barely functioning and without giving her a fair hearing.[64] Thus the dialogue with the national and regional courts seems to begin with an exchange of stick strokes. It is interesting to note, however, that she does not react to the criticism contained in Martin Scheinin's report.

In reality, the dialogue has been well engaged, since Mrs Prost is clearly aware where the difficult points in the Sanctions Committee procedure are located according to the national and regional courts in question. From her briefing and her report to the Security Council one gets the strong impression that she hopes that, perhaps in an unorthodox fashion and with herself as intermediary, she can achieve the equivalent of a fair hearing for people who apply to be de-listed under the regime of Security Council resolution 1267. She fully realizes that if she does not succeed in this, the Security Council regime of 'smart sanctions' may be in peril.[65] Thus, she hopes to extend a carrot to the courts that have rejected her Office seemingly out of hand, which they might find difficult to refuse.

Mrs Prost is trying to get the Member States, particularly those which have regularly proposed persons or entities to be placed on the list, to move on two points that have been important, for instance, to the General Court in *Kadi 2010*. First of all, from her Report it transpires that she is trying to make these states budge on their policy of refusing the disclosure of their identity to the person who seeks to be de-listed. She states that this policy puts the listed person at a disadvantage in answering the case against him and that disclosure may even be useful to other Member States in helping them to obtain more information on the case. If the Ombudsperson is not in a position to reveal the proposing state's identity, "it constitutes a potential impediment to due process" in her view.[66] There can indeed be little doubt about that.

[61] See www.un.org/en/sc/ombudsperson/presentations.shtml, last visited 16 February 2011 (hereinafter, *Briefing*). Note that late October is normally the time that the chief legal advisers from the Foreign Offices of Member States congregate at UN Headquarters in New York for the meetings of the General Assembly's Sixth, legal, Committee.

[62] See *Report Ombudsperson* (supra n. 43).

[63] This report is confidential and will only be published if the Committee established pursuant to SC Res 1267(1999) will so decide.

[64] See *Briefing*, p. 7.

[65] See *Briefing*, p. 5.

[66] See *Report Ombudsperson* (supra n. 43), par. 51–52.

Secondly, Mrs Prost is seeking a way to gain access to classified and confidential information from the proposing states. To this end, she is looking for mechanisms that will give these states assurances that such information will be sufficiently protected by her Office, while enabling her to form the best possible answer to the question: "Is this individual or entity on the list today on a sufficient basis?"[67]

The big question is, of course, whether she will succeed in all of this, and as proof of that success, on the one hand get a certain number of the petitioners delisted, and on the other hand be put in the position by the Committee to publish a convincing report in those cases where persons are not delisted. If the Ombudsperson succeeds in doing all of that, will it all be enough, as she put it in her briefing? She will certainly have provided a number of answers to the qualms of the General Court in *Kadi 2010*. That Court also seemed willing to entertain the idea of contemplating *ex parte* information under protective arrangements. Would it be willing to do so with information received under protective orders by the Ombudsperson, *ex parte* once removed, so to say? That is uncertain, but at least the dialogue seems to be well and truly engaged.

9. *Conclusions*

Thus the dialogue between the regional level and the worldwide level is continuing. It is now the turn of the UN level, through the Ombudsperson, to proffer a carrot to the regional level. Whether she will be able to do so remains uncertain at the time of writing and will only become really clear after she has treated a number of cases. If the proposing states do not give her a chance to succeed (by not collaborating in protective mechanisms under which the Ombudsperson can consult classified information from their files and by not consenting that their identity shall be made known to the petitioner), the conclusion is foregone and the UN sanctions system will be in dire straits, as the national and regional courts will see no reason to show flexibility on their part.

If Mrs Prost succeeds, however, the question is whether the regional and national courts must keep to their strict approach, according to which only full judicial control at Security Council level is enough. If such judicial control were to remain limited to cases where the rights of individuals are at stake, it might not be entirely outside the realm of the possible. The possibility of full

[67] *Briefing*, p. 6. It is interesting to note that in her Report, at par. 25, she states that she is still seeking for a defined standard by which this question can be answered and that "properly reflects the serious nature and particular context of decisions of the Al Qaeda and Taliban Sanctions Committee and at the same time recognizes the significant effect of the sanctions on the listed individuals and entities". This promises to be a difficult balancing test.

judicial control in such cases has been introduced for example in the EU's Common Foreign and Security Policy.[68] Nevertheless, even such a system may be a bridge too far for the Security Council. Would the regional courts then take the risk of blowing up *de facto* the Security Council system of sanctions against individuals, which has been set up for reasons related to modern day terrorism on an international scale? If the UN system of sanctions is indeed, as Mrs Prost has put it, unique and therefore deserves to be treated as such, also by the judicial powers of Member States and regional organisations, why should these Courts not look for a system providing an "adequate level of protection",[69] if this can be guaranteed in practice by the Office of the Ombudsperson and possibly a further exchange of information between the Ombudsperson and the national and regional courts?

The crucial point in all of this is that the dialogue between the regional level and the universal level should contribute to establishing a working system that demonstrates that the accountability of the international organisations and the courts involved in the system at both levels is seriously improved. This includes the necessary minimum transparency. It is submitted that even a less than perfect system that does not deliver full judicial review of sanctions imposed on individuals under full transparency, may still contribute to a degree of accountability that would meet the requirement of an 'adequate level of protection'.

On the other hand, a cleaner solution may well be the one suggested, though as yet a bit *sotto voce*, by Special Rapporteur Martin Scheinin.[70] Is it worth it to continue to tinker with the 'unique' Security Council system of freezing of assets, whilst the International Convention for the Suppression of the Financing of Terrorism of 1999 has now been ratified by 173 States[71] and provides for a normal criminal law approach to this phenomenon? Perhaps the time is there to drop the Security Council approach to the financing of terrorism and revert to the Convention that was created at about the same time as SC res. 1267 was adopted.[72]

As stated above, the dialogue between the regional and universal level on the protection of the fundamental rights of individuals in the process of the fight against the kind of terrorism that constitutes a threat to international

---

[68] See Art. 24 (1) of the Treaty on European Union and Art. 275 of the Treaty on the Functioning of the European Union.

[69] The term 'adequate level of protection' comes from EU data protection law and indicates that the EU will only be able to exchange electronic data with third States that have an 'adequate level', but not an 'identical' level of data protection laws on the books. See Directive of the Council and Parliament No. 95/46/EC, Art. 25(1). It is obvious that this would be an approach that is again close to the 'solange' test.

[70] UN doc. A/65/258, par. 52

[71] See <http://treaties.un.org>.

[72] This requires a careful further study of the Convention in relation to the SC sanctions regime, which might well benefit from Karel Wellens' expertise.

peace and security is well and truly engaged. It is difficult to predict the outcome. Above we have referred to a number of elements that could play a role in the solution. However, there can be little doubt that, whatever happens, the Ombudsperson will be for some time between a rock and a hard place and that it will require all Mrs Prost's skill to extricate herself from there and bring us closer to a satisfactory solution.

CHAPTER SIX

CERTAIN OTHER PERSPECTIVES FOR A REFORM OF THE UNITED NATIONS SECURITY COUNCIL

Eric Suy

1. *Introduction*

On Monday, 8 November 2010, President Barack Obama, speaking before the Indian Parliament in New Delhi, announced that the United States would back India's campaign for a permanent seat on an expanded United Nations Security Council. The President said: "The just and sustainable international order that America seeks includes a United Nations that is efficient, effective, credible and legitimate (…) That is why I can say today, in the years ahead, I look forward to a reformed U.N. Security Council that includes India as a permanent member". One can imagine that, if the President had been on an official visit to Brazil, Japan, South Africa or Germany, he could have used exactly same words thus creating expectations for those countries.

During the last four decades, the reform of the United Nations Security Council has been the subject of numerous debates and proposals, both in official bodies of the United Nations and in non-governmental and academic circles. Discussion papers and multiple proposals on this issue have been published worldwide. Perhaps the most surprising thing to emerge from analysis of those debates and the conclusions and proposals for a reform is that nearly all aspects of the Council's reform seem to be confined to the question of the Council's composition. This major issue may be a simple one: is there a need to increase the membership of the Security Council? The difficulty, however, lies in giving this aspiration concrete form.

Membership of the Security Council though is only one, and to some perhaps the most important aspect of a possible reform. The *de facto* review and the constant improvement of the working methods of the Council, and its relationship with the General Assembly, are some of the other aspects of the reform that are less in the limelight in the usual debates. Most of these 'lesser' reforms proceed from the insight gained by the direct actors – i.e. the members, both permanent and non-permanent of the Council – based on their daily experience of the working of this principal organ entrusted with the maintenance of international peace and security. It is sometimes surprising that reforms are accepted without major challenges as regards their conformity with the United Nations Charter. The same goes for conformity of the *de facto* reforms with the Rules of Procedure of the Security Council. These Rules have in any event continued to be 'provisional' for the last sixty-six years. They can, therefore, be changed and adapted at random by the members of the Council, although I know of no particular case when a formal change to these Rules has taken place. In a first section I will therefore discuss certain aspects of the changing of the working methods of the Council. The question of membership of the Council will be dealt with in the second section.

2. *Changing the Working Methods of the Security Council*

This section will briefly address certain aspects of the Council's working methods that have largely contributed to making the Council either more efficient or more transparent, i.e. the prior consultations leading to decision-making, the practice of the presidential statements, and the relationships between the Security Council and the General Assembly.

2.1. *The Prior Consultations*

It is obvious that the decision making process in all institutions, organisations or other bodies with multiple membership should be preceded by genuine and intensive consultations among their members or participants. This is a prerequisite for an enduring and successful outcome of any decision or action. This is also applicable to the Security Council whose members cannot but work in team in the search for viable solutions to issues and disputes through resolutions. Ideally, the consultations will start between the permanent members in order to ensure their support for any draft text of a future resolution. A consensus among the permanent members is a strong incentive for non permanent members to go along with a draft in the knowledge that it will not be vetoed, thereby leading to either a unanimous vote, a consensus or, at the very least, the requisite nine votes for the valid adoption of a resolution. Alternatively, a recalcitrant or hesitant permanent member may be induced to go along with a draft or at least abstain if consultations seem to indicate that the position adopted by this member means that it is isolated. By and large, the pattern of prior consultations will vary depending on the change in data and situations specific to any issue before the Council.

In the early years of the United Nations it was normal practice for the Security Council to hold a public debate in the Council's chamber around the so called 'horse shoe table'. This debate is not necessarily restricted to Members of the Security Council. Article 31 of the Charter of the United Nations states that "[a]ny Member of the United Nations which is not a member of the Security Council may participate, without a vote, in the discussion of any question brought before the Security Council whenever the latter considers that the interests of that Member are specially affected". It is interesting to note that rule 37 of the still Provisional Rules of Procedure of the Security Council repeats article 31 of the Charter, but adds the words "or when a Member brings a matter to the attention of the Security Council in accordance with article 35 (1) of the Charter". This is a rare example of amendment to the Charter (article 31) through an addition to the Rules of Procedure (rule 37).

Following the numerical expansion of membership in the Organization, the requests by non-members to participate in the discussions in the Security Council grew accordingly. Consequently, the consideration of any issue by the Security Council sometimes led to lengthy debates spreading over several sessions and meeting days. This was felt by the fifteen Members of the Council to impose a serious burden on their "primary responsibility for the maintenance of international peace and security". Permanent and non-permanent Members alike gradually saw the opening of the discussions in the Security Council to non-members as seriously impeding "prompt and effective action by the United Nations" (article 24 of the Charter). From the middle of the 1970s onwards, the decision-making therefore moved from the limelight in the Council's room to a new venue, i.e. a new caucus room for the fifteen Members of the Council. This room was built next to the Council's meeting room and is still the place where the 'brewing' takes place, although this procedure has been criticised as being undemocratic and contrary to the requirement of transparency. After 1994, a number of adjustments took place when the Members of the Council agreed to open the forum of the private consultations to Member States directly affected by the issue under discussion. This is *inter alia* the case with the troop contributing countries when the renewal of a Peacekeeping Operation is due.

If the outcome of the private consultations is a draft resolution acceptable to all, or to a majority of at least nine Members including the Permanent Members, the further procedure will then shift to a formal meeting of the Security Council where the President of the Council will announce that an agreement has been reached on a draft resolution which will be put to the vote. The President will then call on the Members for any explanations of vote. Those formal meetings of the Security Council are usually relatively brief. However, if the informal meetings do not lead to an acceptable result, the President of the Council may issue a statement reflecting the general feeling of the Council provided there have not been any objections. I will now briefly turn to certain aspects of these Presidential Statements.

2.2. *The Presidential Statements*

Professor Karel Wellens was the first author who collected and systematically edited the Statements of the Security Council in his indispensable *Resolutions and Statements of the Security Council (1946–1992)*.[1] In his view "[t]he role

[1] Karel Wellens, *Resolutions and Statements of the Security Council (1946–1992)*, The Hague: Martinus Nijhoff Publishers 1993.

played by these 'Presidential statements' in the Council's handling of a particular problem cannot be under-estimated and certainly should never be overlooked".[2]

The Provisional Rules of Procedure of the Security Council contain several rules referring to the functions of the President of the Council. There is even a special chapter IV dealing with the Presidency (rules 18–20). None of these texts, however, confer upon the President the powers or the authority to make substantive statements on behalf of the Council. And yet, in the course of the last four decades coinciding with the practice of the prior consultations, Presidents of the Council have issued numerous statements reflecting the discussions on items in the Council which did not come to fruition in the form of a resolution. Two questions arise in this respect: 1) what is the legal significance of those Presidential Statements? 2) under what authority does a President act when making a Statement?

The legal value of these Statements is somewhat uncertain. If the discussions during the private consultations do not lead to a resolution, this is most likely because no consensus exists and one or more Permanent Members have fundamental objections, or support by the requisite nine Members is absent. Where this is the case, the role of the President is somewhat delicate since it will be intended as a makeshift, reflecting a failure by the Security Council to act. It is, however, always possible for an issue to be brought before the Security Council without a draft resolution having been tabled. This situation could arise when a Member State that is not a member of the Council brings a matter to the attention of the Security Council under article 35 (1) of the Charter. Where this is the case, the President is in a more comfortable position when he summarises the debates and indicates the general tenure and consensus, including decisions by the Council. His Statement, while indicating the general feeling and concern of the Council's members, will primarily have moral and political weight, and this may be precisely what the initiators expected. He will anyhow, as in the previous case, seek the agreement of the Council or of its Members to proceed with a Statement and will have to consult the Members on the substance of any such Statement.

The position of the President of the Security Council is different from that of the President of the General Assembly. The latter has a role of arbiter and exercises his function in a neutral manner. The President of the Security Council, on the other hand, still acts in the capacity of a representative of his country while, at the same time, he is supposed to conduct the business of the Council in an impartial way. This role of the President is a typical case of *dédoublement fonctionnel* (role-splitting): the President wears two hats. In making a Statement, the President definitely does not act as a representative of

---

[2] Idem, at p. x.

his country. But does he really act on behalf of the Council? This may perhaps be the case when the Council holds a debate that does not imply a discussion of a draft resolution. But if the Security Council is unable to reach an acceptable outcome, the President is not entitled to make a Statement on behalf of the Council. This would amount to an abuse of authority. In practice, the formula used in the Presidential Statements is variable. Usually, the official document starts with a sentence clearly indicating that the following Statement is made "on behalf of the Security Council". Sometimes, however, the President announces that his Statement is made "on behalf of the Members of the Security Council". There are also cases when certain Statements are referring to "Members of the Council" or to "a majority of the Members". I even came across one Statement made "as President of the Council", without any further reference. One may therefore conclude that, as a rule, most Statements are made on behalf of the Security Council, but that the practice reveals certain exceptions the meaning of which must be analyzed in the light of the outcome of the discussions in the Council.

2.3. *The Relationships between the Security Council and the General Assembly*

To a certain extent, the reform of the working methods of the Security Council also touches on the relations with the General Assembly. It is well known that the relationship between these two principal organs of the United Nations mainly affects the cooperation in elections in the broadest sense. Thus, the General Assembly elects the non-permanent members of the Security Council (Charter, article 23). The members of the International Court of Justice are elected by the Security Council and by the General Assembly in a simultaneous procedure (Statute of the ICJ, article 4). The Secretary-General of the Organization is appointed by the General Assembly on the recommendation of the Security Council (Charter, article 97). The admission of new members of the Organization is effected by a decision of the General Assembly on the recommendation of the Security Council (Charter, article 4). Both bodies also cooperate in the field of the maintenance of international peace and security (Charter, articles 10, 11 and 12) although primary responsibility in this respect rests with the Security Council (Charter, article 24). In its most recent Advisory Opinion of 22 July 2010 (the so-called *Kosovo Opinion*), the International Court of Justice, while discussing its jurisdiction and the discretion to accede to the request by the General Assembly to give an Opinion, extensively dealt with the interpretation of the articles mentioned above.[3]

While the foregoing areas of interaction between the two bodies do not affect the working methods of the Security Council, this does not seem to be the case when it comes to the more controversial issue of accountability.

[3] ICJ Kosovo Opinion, 22 July 2010, in particular paragraphs 29 to 48.

It is somewhat reluctantly that I use the word 'accountability'. In 2002, Karel Wellens published a remarkable book on *Remedies against International Organisations* dealing with the accountability of international organisations for infringements of the mainly legal norms governing their activities.[4] What are the possibilities and venues for individuals, staff members, national and foreign companies and even States for obtaining, mostly judicial, redress against an international organisation? In the following discussion, I will use 'accountability' to refer to 'parliamentary' control of the executive branch by the assembly of member states. Basically, the structure of an international organisation is similar to that of a democratic state in a parliamentary system. This structure may even be compared to that of a company in private law with its Board of Directors (or Executive Board) and the General Meetings of shareholders. Similarly, in the constitutions of democratic States, the executive branch (the Government) is subject to control by a Parliament or the Assembly of elected representatives. In the United Nations Organization, the Security Council is the executive branch, whereas the General Assembly is the Parliament of the member states. In all these cases, the executive powers or authorities are accountable to a controlling authority represented by the general assembly. One may, therefore, conclude that there is a general principle of law – and hence, also of international law – under which the executive branch is accountable to the 'controlling' entity. The power of the controlling entity, though, may differ depending on the constitution applicable.

The Charter of the United Nations deals with the accountability of the Security Council to the General Assembly in two brief articles, without further details in the Provisional Rules of Procedure of the Council and in the Rules of Procedure of the General Assembly. Article 15 of the Charter states that the General Assembly shall receive and consider annual and special reports from the Security Council; these reports shall include an account of the measures that the Security Council has decided upon or taken to maintain international peace and security. Article 24 of the Charter, dealing with the Functions and Powers of the Council, states in its paragraph 3: "The Security Council shall submit annual and, when necessary, special reports to the General Assembly for its consideration". These two articles deal with exactly the same situation, i.e. the report by the Security Council, but seen from the different perspective of both the Council (in article 24) and the Assembly (article 15). It should perhaps be noted that the qualitative requirement of the reports as formulated in article 15 should logically have been included in article 24. The substance of any report is an issue for the reporting authority, whereas the controlling authority, while considering the report, will look at

[4] Karel Wellens, *Remedies against International Organisations*, Cambridge: Cambridge University Press 2002.

the completeness and correctness of the information while leaving open the possibility for substantive remarks or suggestions to be made.

The most important words in these two articles are "consider" and "for its consideration". What is the meaning of these words, and what is their purpose? The French text of article 15 uses the expression "étudie", whereas "consideration" in article 24, paragraph 3, becomes "pour examen". It appears, however from the preliminary works that all these expressions are to be deemed synonymous. Moreover, the practice of the General Assembly indicates that its controlling function – if it ever existed – is mitigated and practically reduced to taking note of the Security Council's Report. At one point, though, both principal organs seemed to be on a collision course over the substance of the Report. The Annual Report of the Security Council, covering the highly important period between 16 June 1991 and 15 June 1992 following the Gulf War, was submitted to the General Assembly with considerable delay in 1993. During discussion of the Report on 22 June 1993, Members of the Assembly took offence at the late submission of the Report. Furthermore, they criticised its content as being a bare enumeration of the items dealt with by the Council, of the number of meetings held and of the adopted Resolutions. In other words, the Report was a mere documentary compendium already available in previously published official documents of the Council. The harshest criticism came from the Representative of Egypt, Dr Nabil ElAraby, who referred to the articles of the Charter indicating that, in his view, the Assembly had supremacy and that the Security Council was bound by accountability. He concluded: "The Council is not above the law and should keep that in mind".[5] The Representatives of Indonesia and Brazil made similar critical remarks during consideration of the Council's Report at the next session of the General Assembly in 1994.[6] Summarising the general feeling of most of the Member States participating, it is of benefit to quote the remarks of the Representative of Tanzania in a similar debate in 1993 on the equitable representation and increase in the membership in the Council: "Most of the Council's work is, increasingly, being conducted in informal sessions, with formal meetings becoming correspondingly fewer and little more than occasions to rubber-stamp decisions reached at informal meetings".[7]

Meanwhile and fortunately, the Security Council adopted various practical improvements to its working methods, thus rendering the functioning of the Council more transparent. In June 1993, the Council had already established an Informal Working Group on Documentation and other Procedural Questions. In August 2008, and for the first time in fifteen years, the Council organised a thematic debate on its working methods during the

[5] The verbatim text of the full debate can be found in Doc. A/47/PV.106, p. 17–75.
[6] A/49/PV.48, 31 October 1994, p. 1 *et seq.*
[7] A/48/PV.64, 24 November 1993, p. 21.

Belgian presidency. Regular consultations with non-members of the Council, such as troop contributing countries and countries directly affected by a particular agenda item, briefings by the President on issues before the Council, and briefings of the Member States of the Council by members of the Secretariat, were some of the salient improvements albeit that they mainly concern the private consultations.

Also in 1993, the United Nations General Assembly decided to establish a 'Open-ended Working Group on the question of Equitable Representation on and Increase in Membership of the Security Council and Other Matters Related to the Security Council'. Actually, this body only dealt with the question of an expanded Membership in the Council. Yet this issue cannot be seen as a precondition for improving the working methods.

3. *Membership of the Security Council: A Never-Ending Fairytale*

The purpose of this brief section is not to repeat what has been said and written during the last three decades on the subject of increasing the membership of the Security Council. The discussions are based on a few considerations relating to the changing overall picture of the world at the dawn of the twenty-first century. This world does no longer reflect the situations that existed at the end of World War II when the victorious five major Allied Powers carved out for themselves a dominant and privileged position as Permanent Members of the Security Council of the then newly created United Nations Organization. These '5Ps', as they came to be known, not only permanently occupy a seat in the Council, but also granted to themselves the right to veto all actions of the Council that might adversely affect their direct interests or those of their allies and friends. Furthermore, under article 108 of the Charter, the 5Ps have the power to prevent the entry into force of any amendment to the Charter.

After the major decolonisation period in the late 1950s and the early 1960s and the ensuing increase in membership of the Organization from 51 in 1945 to close to 100 in 1963, an amendment to the Charter was adopted enlarging membership of the Security Council from eleven to fifteen. This amendment came into force on 31 August 1965. The 5Ps could easily go along with this amendment since it did not affect their privileged position as "*primi inter pares*". After nearly fifty years, membership of the Organisation stands at 193, and the Security Council, still with fifteen members, seems to be working more or less according to the book and, therefore, is more efficient than in the past. A mere glance at the number of resolutions and the few trifling vetoes adopted during the last two decades confirms this finding. The picture of international relations also underwent significant changes. Regional organisations in Europe, Africa, Asia and Latin America have become more influential as economic and trade partners. Some have even ventured into common foreign and security policies that may impact on the position of some of their members in the Security Council. Furthermore, the implosion of the Soviet Empire, and the ensuing cooperation between the former opposing Cold War members, has contributed to a total change in the East-West relations. But the 5Ps saw no reason to give up or share their privileged position with others. On the contrary, the end of the Cold War was seen precisely as a unique opportunity to improve the cooperation within the Security Council which was, ultimately, successful.

The louder the calls for a reform of the Security Council, the more flexible the reaction of the 5Ps became. At one point they even seemed to admit that increasing the number of permanent members could be envisaged on the basis of a consensus package among the various regional groups, thus putting the ball back in the latter's court. The 5Ps were highly confident that this consensus would not materialise. This deadlock continues to exist even in 2011; in Africa, Nigeria, Egypt and South Africa still are the contenders for a permanent seat at the Council's table. The situation is no different for Latin America where Argentina, Brazil and Mexico are still in the running for a regional seat. India, Pakistan, Indonesia and Japan claim to be the ideal candidates for an Asian seat. Finally, and although Germany seems to be the most important candidate in Western Europe, Italy and Spain have not yet abandoned their ambitions. Under these circumstances, the 5Ps have no need to worry about their privileged positions. They can continue making promising statements without committing themselves, thus keeping the fairy tale going for all contenders. The following observations and queries on certain of the legal and practical aspects of an expanded membership of the Security Council seem to be in order. They deal with the requirement for an effective Security Council and with a largely overlooked aspect of 'equitable representation' in the Council.

Under article 24, paragraph 1, the Members of the United Nations expect the Security Council to take "prompt and effective" action. They, therefore, confer on the Council primary responsibility for the maintenance of international peace and security. Would it be too far-fetched to interpret this provision as implying that the composition of the Council could also affect prompt and effective action? This action was clearly frustrated during the Cold War period. At present, however, and for the last two decades, the Council has acted promptly and effectively. The many Resolutions adopted by the Security Council since 1990 under chapter VII of the Charter, and the very few instances when a Permanent Member has used its right to veto, are clear indications that a new era in the life of the United Nations has been reached. No wonder, therefore, that more Member States want to become part of this success story. But is an enlargement of the Membership of the Council the appropriate response to a question that does not call for a solution, except in the mind of the eager contenders? Why change a team that has proved that it is able to act promptly, effectively and, it should be added, more or less successfully, for the last two decades? A proverb in American slang is even more blunt: "if it ain't broke, don't fix it". It is very doubtful whether the decision-making process in the Security Council with, say twenty-five members, ten of which are permanent members, will be any smoother than the process is today. Negotiations and consultations to reach a workable outcome will definitively become more lengthy and difficult than they are today. Would this fit the requirement for 'prompt and effective action'?

It is both interesting and encouraging to observe an emerging tendency by the member states to elect non-permanent members of the Security Council on the basis of – generally but not universally – unanimous proposals by the regional groups. These groups may, indeed, have an interest in being represented at regular intervals by some of their most prominent, important or 'great' members rather than being represented forever by one of them as a permanent member. If it were followed systematically and faithfully, this practice could have the advantage of forestalling a Charter amendment which might have unpredictable consequences for the 'prompt and effective action' by the Security Council. The Council might even be paralysed if new permanent members should benefit from the provision of article 27, paragraph 3, of the Charter.

If the present status quo in the membership of the Council is maintained, with or without the improvements to the practice suggested above of always nominating and electing 'major' non-permanent members, it is tempting to point to another paradox. A glance at the composition of the Security Council over the past two decades reveals that four and sometimes five of its members – non-permanent and permanent members alike – are also members of the European Union, and that five and possibly six are members of the North Atlantic Treaty Organization. In order to achieve an equitable distribution of seats in the Security Council, there may perhaps be scope for reviewing the present criteria based on geographical regions that, nowadays, sometimes overlap with more powerful regional organisations. In this connection, a final and perhaps disquieting observation may be made. The European Union has now established a common diplomatic service under its Commissioner for Foreign Affairs, Lady Ashton. This is the ultimate implementation of the common foreign and security policy already agreed upon in principle by the Union and its members more than twenty years ago. The European permanent members of the Security Council felt that, for them, this common policy stopped at the doorstep of the Security Council. The United Kingdom and France argued – and they still do – that, as Permanent Members, their responsibilities are universal and go beyond the European dimension. If this position were to be followed in the Security Council also by the non-permanent members of the EU, a most delicate and difficult situation will arise in implementing the common foreign and security policy at a worldwide level. All EU members in the Council should, therefore, agree to adopt and abide by a common position lest the ideal of a common EU policy becomes a mere chimera with a negative effect on the EU members' position in the negotiations and consultations with the other members of the Security Council.

4. *Conclusion*

This chapter started with a reference to President Obama's statement supporting India's application to become a Permanent Member of the Security Council. Since then, India has been elected by the General Assembly for a two-year term as a non-permanent member (2011–2012). It is expected that, during this tenure, India will prove to be a worthy applicant for permanent membership. The policy of Germany, also elected as a non-permanent member for the same two-year term, will equally be inspired by the same endeavour. As observed earlier, the regular election of 'major' or 'important' members of the various regional groups as non-permanent members could be a solution for breaking the existing and continuing deadlock. This deadlock is based on the premise that an increase in the number of Permanent Members in the Council must be based on a consensus package covering all new applicants from the regional groups. This package is supported by both the potential candidates and by their respective regional groups because it prevents an imbalance favouring one applicant or one region as compared with another. But this package also suits, and is supported by, the existing 5Ps who feel that a consensus in the regional groups on five applicants for permanent membership is not feasible. Meanwhile, the 5Ps continue to enjoy their privileged and comfortable position within the United Nations.

However, the package deal is not a hard and fast rule. Assuming that both India and Germany succeed in obtaining the agreement of the existing 5Ps in favour of their permanent membership of the Security Council, it is to be expected that other regional groups will likewise put their act together and agree on a single applicant. As indicated above, it is doubtful that a Security Council with ten Permanent Members is an ideal solution because regional groups may not agree to be represented forever by the same member. Furthermore, the obsession with an increase in Permanent Members does not solve the question of filling the gap of five more new non-permanent members. Why therefore drag on a never ending and frustrating exercise that has almost reached the stage of surrealism?

PART II

CONVERGING AND DIVERGING NORMATIVE TRENDS IN THE INTERNATIONAL COMMUNITY

CHAPTER SEVEN

INTEGRATING THE FRAGMENTED INTERNATIONAL PUBLIC ORDER: A THEORETICAL PERSPECTIVE

Teruo Komori

1. *Introduction*

Set off against the rules of traditional international law, conventions governing global environmental protection, international protection of human rights and the institutionalisation of international crimes (e.g. the International Criminal Court) have complicated and diversified not only the interests protected by the rules and the addressees of those rules, but also the procedures for dispute settlement and implementation thereof. This diversification in the making and the implementation of international rules has resulted in the so-called 'fragmentation' of the international legal order. At present, a significant problem facing international lawyers, both at a theoretical and a practical level, is how to characterise this phenomenon, and how to resolve the problem this fragmentation seems to represent. This chapter both deals with this characterisation and with the question how to integrate the fragmented international order.

2. *Characterising the Fragmentation of Public International Law*

2.1. *Aspects of Fragmentation*

So far, two aspects of the phenomenon of the fragmentation of public international law have taken centre stage: conflicting norms and conflicting authorities. The first of these concerns the problem of when norms of different legal regimes are in conflict. The application of one norm may constitute a violation of another conflicting norm, thus making it difficult to apply these conflicting norms consistently in the international community as a whole. The other aspect of fragmentation is concerned with the situation in which inconsistencies arise in the application and interpretation of a rule, or in the characterisation of conflicting rules, between the dispute settlement mechanisms of different legal regimes that are not hierarchically organised. Here, the problem arises from the conflict of competing authorities that purport to prioritise their own legal regimes.

As regards the first aspect of fragmentation (hereafter referred to as 'norm fragmentation'), there are two situations that have produced this phenomenon. One is that norms of legal regimes lack consistency among themselves. Multilateral environmental agreements serve as an example. Each legal regime of global environmental protection was adopted separately with its own purpose and without the harmonisation of rules. The other situation resulted from conflicts of norms between e.g. a human rights protection regime, or a trade regime and between an environmental protection regime and a trade regime – that is to say, instances where each organ of a treaty regime is likely to give priority to its own regime or to consider its interpretation of rules more legitimate than that of another regime. However, when seeking a solution to the conflict of norms in this second situation (hereafter referred to as 'norm integration'), it is necessary to take into account the nature of the conflict of norms, whether the norms themselves are conflicting in principle, or whether or not the conflict relates to a technical issue in the process of application of rules of differing regimes. For example, while in the case of projects against HIV/AIDS in developing countries, the protection of patent rights by TRIPs and the right of access to those medicines protected by patent rights as a human right are in conflict, those two rights are not in conflict in countries having a more advanced social welfare system. When assessing how to integrate the conflicting treaty regimes, such consideration of the nature of the conflict of norms seems very important.

Next, with regard to the second aspect of fragmentation (hereafter referred to as 'authority fragmentation'), there are several cases that illustrate the relevant problems. For example, in the *MOX Plant* case, the same case was dealt with in four different forums (arbitral and judicial tribunals).[1] In the *Tadic* case, the ICTY expressed a view that was rather different view from that of the ICJ in the interpretation of state responsibility.[2]

While the problem of fragmentation has as such been recognised by academic lawyers,[3] it is largely due to authority fragmentation that it has become

[1] ITLOS *MOX Plant* case (*Ireland, v. UK*), Order regarding request for provisional measures of 3 December 2001; UNCLOS arbitral tribunal (Arbitral Tribunal constituted pursuant to Article 287, and Article 1 of Annex VII, of the United Nations Convention on the Law of the Sea for the dispute concerning the MOX Plant, international movement of radioactive materials, and the protection of the marine environment of the Irish Sea), *MOX Plant* case (*Ireland* v. *UK*), Order No. 3, suspension of proceedings on jurisdiction and merits and request for further provisional measures, 24 June 2003; OSPAR arbitral tribunal, Dispute concerning Access to Information under Article 9 of the OSPAR Convention (*MOX Plant* case *(Ireland* v. *UK)*), Final award of 2 July 2003; ECJ Case C-459/03, *Commission v. Ireland* [2006] ECR I-4635.

[2] ICTY, Appeals Chamber, *Tadić*, 15 July 1999 (Case no. IT-94-1-A)

[3] Ian Brownlie, 'The Rights of Peoples in Modern International Law in Modern International Law', in: James Crawford, *The Rights of Peoples*, Oxford: Clarendon Press 1988, p. 15.

a great concern.[4] Because each treaty regime has adopted its own dispute settlement mechanism, such problems as, for example, which jurisdiction should be given priority between the ITLOS and the European Court of Justice, which of the competing interpretations of a rule between the ICJ and the ICTY should take precedence, have turned into real issues to be solved in practice. The problems here emerged mainly because each treaty regime aimed at securing the effectiveness of its own regime, without considering the integration or coordination of conflicting norms between the various different systems.

The situation in which competing jurisdictions give rise to fragmentation of the international legal order, due to the fact that each treaty regime gives priority to the effectiveness of its own system, highlights the need for an overarching theoretical perspective to deal with the phenomenon. As will be explained below, the idea of integrating or coordinating substantive norms of treaty regimes, in terms of clarifying which rules or interests should precede from the perspective of the international community as a whole, seems to play a more important role than the idea of reorganising competing jurisdictions and establishing a hierarchical order. Whereas the former idea mainly pertains to a matter of interpretation regarding the status of treaty regimes in general international law, the second idea is closely related to the political preferences of states with regard to the establishment of international organisations.

2.2. *Approaches to the Problem of Fragmentation of the International Public Order*

2.2.1. *Introduction*

Next to clarifying the relevance of 'norm fragmentation' and 'authority fragmentation', two approaches have been taken to deal with the question of how to characterise the phenomenon of fragmentation of the public international order. One approach, discussed further in paragraph 2.2.2 below, puts emphasis on the analysis of why it came into being. The other, discussed further in paragraph 2.2.3, focuses on the changing character of the international legal order itself. The difference between these two approaches is largely a matter of perspective, in the sense that most analyses refer to both features, and are not mutually exclusive in their understanding of the phenomenon. But, even if the difference between the two approaches is a matter of perspective, the choice of

[4] Gerhard Hafner, 'Risks Ensuing From Fragmentation Of International Law', in: United Nations General Assembly Official Records, 55th Session, Supplement No. 10 (A/55/10), p. 321–325.

the aspect to emphasise is closely related to the choice of method for integrating or coordinating the fragmented international order.

2.2.2. *Focusing on the Factual Aspect of the Phenomenon*

The first approach addresses the phenomenon by focusing mainly on the reasons why fragmentation has occurred in practice. The Report on Fragmentation prepared by the International Law Commission (ILC) states that the rationale for its discussion of fragmentation is that the emergence of new and special types of law, self-contained regimes and geographically or functionally limited treaty-systems creates problems of coherence in international law.[5] It describes the situation in more detail as follows:

> Each rule-complex or "regime" comes with its own principles, its own form of expertise and its own "ethos", not necessarily identical to the ethos of neighbouring specialization. "Trade law" and "environmental law", for example, have highly specific objectives and rely on principles that may often point in different directions. In order for the new law to be efficient, it often includes new types of treaty clauses or practices that may not be compatible with old general law or the law of some other specialized branch. Very often new rules or regimes develop precisely in order to deviate from what was earlier provided by the general law. When such deviations become general and frequent, the unity of the law suffers.[6]
>
> Much of the concern over the fragmentation of international law emerges from the awareness of the "horizontal" nature of the international legal system. The rules and principles of international law are not in a hierarchical relationship to each other. Nor are the different sources (treaty, custom, general principles of law) ranked in any general order of priority. This is a key difference between international and domestic legal systems. Whereas domestic law is organized in a strictly hierarchical way, with the constitution regulating the operation of the system at the highest level, there is no such formal constitution in international law and, consequently, no *general* order of precedence between international legal rules.[7]

Furthermore, in its general conclusion, as background to the concerns with regard to the fragmentation of international law, the Report describes the rise of specialised rules and rule-systems that have no clear relationship to each other.[8] After formulating the issues to be tackled in order to solve the problem of fragmentation, the Report states the aim of the study conducted by the ILC as follows:

> This study has not aimed to set up definite relationships of priority between international law's different rules or rule-systems. To that extent, its results may

---

[5] *Report of the Study Group on the Fragmentation of International Law, finalized by Martti Koskenniemi* (hereinafter: ILC Report 2006), UN Doc. A/CN.4/L.682, par. 15.
[6] Ibid., par. 15.
[7] Ibid., par. 324.
[8] Ibid., par. 481–482.

> seem unsatisfactory or at least inconclusive. However, such priorities cannot be justifiably attained by what is merely an elucidation of the process of legal reasoning. They should reflect the (political) preferences of international actors, above all States. Normative conflicts do not arise as technical "mistakes" that could be "avoided" by a more sophisticated way of legal reasoning. New rules and legal regimes emerge as responses to new preferences, and sometimes out of conscious effort to deviate from preferences as they existed under old regimes. They require a legislative, not a legal-technical response.[9]

Thus, even in seeking answers to the problem, the study focuses mainly on the factual aspect of how international actors, particularly states, respond to the problem, not on elucidating the legal reasoning behind it, although it does indicate that fragmentation causes problems for the coherence and unity of international law.

This approach to the phenomenon of fragmentation, focusing mainly on factual and structural factors in international law-making and its implementation, is also taken by Wolfrum and Matz in their study of conflicts in international environmental law. They point out that conflicts of norms in international environmental law have arisen from the fact that international law on the protection of the environment developed in a sectoral manner, and in different stages. Moreover, the difference between the respective sectors and stages resulted in a substantive overlap of the various international agreements, and in differences between the approaches pursued.[10]

However, this approach that sees the phenomenon as a result of the horizontal nature of the international legal system is not a sufficient reason for taking fragmentation seriously, as a new problem that needs to be resolved. If fragmentation were mainly a result of the horizontal structure of the international legal system, the problem might have to be addressed within the scope of traditional international law. Moreover, the phenomenon is not problematic from the perspective of those assessing the situation of proliferating tribunals and overlapping jurisdictions in positive terms, as it is likely to provide more opportunities for the peaceful settlement of international disputes.

2.2.3. *Focusing on the Changing Character of International Law*

In the second approach, the problematic character of fragmentation is grounded in the perception that the character of the international legal order has been changing. In this approach the question is asked why in the current international order fragmentation of international norms and dispute settlement mechanisms is considered a problem that needs to be solved. The origin of this approach lies in the observation of Koskenniemi and Leino that the

---

[9] Ibid., par. 484.

[10] Rüdiger Wolfrum and Nele Matz, *Conflicts in International Environmental Law*, Heidelberg-Berlin: Springer 2003, p. 209.

core of the problem resides not so much in the emergence of new sub-systems, but in the use of general law by new bodies, representing interests or views that are not identical with those represented in old ones;[11] the general law used by new bodies may be concerned with the protection of common or public interests in the international community as a whole.

Therefore, in this approach, an important cause of the problem of fragmentation is that many international treaties that aim at protecting the common interests of the international community, or global interests, are created under the umbrella of the UN, but implemented by each treaty organ without coordinating regime conflicts. Thus, the approach takes into account that, while international law aims at the formation of public order in the international community, fragmentation of international law, to the contrary, may prejudice its integrity. It considers fragmentation as a problem to be solved, in order to secure the integrity of the public order.

3. *Views on How to Integrate the Fragmented International Order*

3.1. *Introduction*

Various different views exist on how to solve the problem of fragmentation, but not all of them necessarily consider the answer to lie in the integration of the international legal order. As stated above, some scholars see the proliferation of tribunals in a positive light, as increasing the opportunities for peaceful settlement of disputes. Koskenniemi himself, who was in charge of the study group of this problem in the ILC, states that fragmentation is to be characterised rather as an effect of politics, and advocates that it should be resolved in the light of tolerance and pluralism, predicated on the understanding that the universalist voices of humanitarianism, human rights, trade or the environment may echo imperialist concerns.[12]

However, most of the views examining the fragmentation phenomenon in theory and practice seem to resolve it by integrating the legal order in some way or the other. As indicated in the ILC Report, the key issue is to establish how conflicting norms and overlapping jurisdictions should relate to each

[11] Martti Koskenniemi and Paivi Leino, 'Fragmentation of International Law? Postmodern Anxieties', (2002) 15 *Leiden Journal of International Law*, p. 561. This being their recognition of the problem of fragmentation, they are rather passive with regard to the integration of the fragmented order, considering (as pluralists tend to do) that special regimes and new organs are parts of an attempt to advance beyond the political present (which in one way or another has been revealed as unsatisfactory) and that no overall solution (i.e. a single hierarchy) is available. Ibid., p. 578.

[12] Ibid., p. 578–579.

other in specific situations or with regard to the international community as a whole.[13] Solutions have been advanced that rely on concepts such as 'unity', 'hierarchy', 'priority', 'invalidity', 'illegality', 'coherence', and 'coordination'. These may, however, address only parts of the problem, as the issues they deal with are often limited by the tasks they set, or by the types of conflict among treaty regimes.

This section examines the drawbacks of the different views on resolving the problem of fragmentation. It will indicate their weakness in the light of what is necessary for the integration of norms and the international order as such. Hereby, the views will be distinguished in two groups, depending on what they regard as the key aspect of the problem. One group focuses on the integrity of norms, the other pertains to the (level of) respect for the coordination of jurisdictions and processes.

3.2. *Views Respecting the Integrity of Norms*

3.2.1. *Introduction*

The views that respect the integrity of norms can be further divided into two types, depending on the differences in the method they adopt so as to achieve integration. On the one hand there are those views that rely on the method of applying rules in the law of treaties (as e.g. outlined in the ILC Report). On the other hand there is the view that has recourse to the concept of constitutionalism in international law. In the paragraphs below, both are discussed in subsequent order.

3.2.2. *Integration Relying on the Rules of the Law of Treaties*

The views that try to solve the conflict of norms by applying rules from the law of treaties proceed from the idea that most of the rules and institutions of international law are adopted in the form of treaties and conventions. For two reasons the ILC Report restricted its response to the problem of fragmentation to solving the conflict of substantive norms. First, it considered that the issue of institutional competencies was best dealt with by the institutions themselves.[14] Secondly, it considered that most of the new regimes claim binding force from, and are understood by practitioners to be covered by, the law of treaties.[15] Thus, in the Report, the issue of how rules and institutions relate to each other, in terms of the order of priority that exists among them, is addressed by looking at their status within the framework of the law of treaties.

[13] See ILC Report 2006, par. 22–28.
[14] Ibid., par. 13.
[15] Ibid., par. 17.

Underlying this idea is the understanding that the fragmentation of the international legal system into technical regimes, when examined from the point of view of the law of treaties, is not too different from its traditional fragmentation into more or less autonomous territorial regimes called 'national legal systems'. As a result, the Report discusses the problems under the four types of relationships that lawyers have traditionally understood to be involved in normative conflicts: (a) relations between special and general law; (b) relations between prior and subsequent law; (c) relations between laws at different hierarchical levels; and (d) relations of law to its 'normative environment' more generally.[16]

This discussion on the problem in the four types of relationship mentioned above is further endorsed as follows:

> (…) International law's traditional 'fragmentation' has already equipped practitioners with techniques to deal with rules and rule-systems that point in different directions. This does not mean to cancel out the importance of the recent push towards functional specialization of regulatory regimes. But it does suggest that these factual developments are of relatively minor significance to the operation of legal reasoning. In an important sense, 'fragmentation' and 'coherence' are not aspects of the world but lie in the eye of the beholder. What is new and unfamiliar, will (by definition) challenge accustomed ways of thinking and organizing the world. Novelty presents itself as 'fragmentation' of the old world. In such case, it is the task of reasoning to make the unfamiliar familiar by integrating it into received patterns of thought or by amending those patterns so that the new phenomenon can be accommodated. Of course, there will always remain some 'cognitive dissonance' between the familiar conceptual system and the new information we receive from the world.[17]

On this assumption, the ILC Report discusses the integration of fragmented international rules and institutions in terms of, first, the concept of priority, secondly, the concept of invalidity, and thirdly, the concept of coordination and systemic integration.

It would appear, however, that the points made in the assumptions above are not automatically to be taken for granted. They do not, for instance, take into consideration whether newly developed international rules and institutions have changed the character of traditional international law, because the assumption is that the novelty presents itself as fragmentation of the old world. Consequently, there is no consideration of the perspective that should be adopted in examining the problem. It therefore appears that, as a result of that assumption, the Report advances arguments and explanations that are problematic even within the traditional framework. While this is problematic for various reasons, this contribution will just discuss one, which pertains to the relationship between special law and general law.

---

[16] Ibid., par. 17–18.
[17] Ibid., par. 20.

First, with regard to this relationship the Report states that the idea that special enjoys priority over general has a long pedigree in international jurisprudence. It explains why the *lex specialis* rule is a valid maxim of interpretation or conflict-solution technique in public international law by referring to international law scholarship since Grotius. That is, a special rule is more to the point than a general one; it regulates the matter more effectively than general rules or special rules are better able to take account of particular circumstances; they have greater clarity and definiteness and are thus often felt to be "harder" or more binding than general rules which may remain in the background and will be applied only rarely; and, *lex specialis* may also seem useful as it may provide better access to what the parties may have willed.[18] On this basis, the Report examines types of specific/general relationships between international rules and regimes, and shows that the specific has functions as an application of the general, as a modification of the general, and as an exception to the general. The relation between international humanitarian law and international human rights law is also dealt with in this specific/general relationship. Considering, however, that both international humanitarian law and international human rights law are regarded as general international law, their relationship is not a matter to be decided according to the *lex specialis* rule within the framework of the law of treaties. Rather, one needs to address the matter within a different framework, by asking which of two general regimes should be given priority when they are in conflict.

In this regard, the relationship between the specific and the general discussed in the Report is completely different from the relationship between treaty and general rules within the framework of the law of treaties to which the traditional *lex specialis* rule is applied. Therefore, the Report recognises that the character of the specific/general distinction discussed in such a wider scope of international rules must be relational.[19] In a hard case of deciding the priority between rules, in order to be justified, a decision would need to take all of these rules into account by articulating some systemic relationship between them.[20] Instead however, this highlights the difficulty of extending the application of the specific/general relationship to the problem of deciding the priority between conflicting rules of general international law. Moreover, it would seem that the systemic relationship is rather different in character from the specific/general relationship.

The ILC further examines the cases between general law and self-contained regimes, which it insists should be called specific regimes, in a section separate from the *lex generalis* rule. A well-known example concerning the relationship between a specific regime and a general law is the Law on Diplomatic

[18] Ibid., par. 59–60.
[19] Ibid., par. 111–112.
[20] Ibid., par. 118.

Relations. This general law adheres to some unique rules of dispute settlement, without applying the general rules of state responsibility to it. While the specific regimes of that sort are adopted on the basis of the secondary rules concerning law-making and dispute settlement, they are not limited to secondary rules. Specific regimes having priority over general international law may consist of substantive rules.

The reasons why specific regimes have priority over general law are the same as those behind the *lex specialis* rule in general.[21] But, contrary to the case of a *lex specialis* rule, in the examination of specific regimes, the ILC places emphasis on the coordinative relation between specific regimes and general law. It argues not only that most international rules are dispositive, and that 'contracting out' by establishing a regime is possible, limited only by rules of *ius cogens*; it also argues that no legal regime is isolated from general international law, and that a regime can receive legally binding force ('validity') only by referring to rules or principles *outside it*.[22] This is because it substitutes a 'specific regime' for a 'self-contained regime', which stresses the exclusion of general law.

However, it seems doubtful whether these arguments concerning the relationship between specific regimes and general law are useful for the resolution of the problem of fragmentation, since the concepts of specific regime and general law are themselves equivocal. For example, with regard to the relation between specific regimes and the law of state responsibility, alleged to be general law in the Report, there are two possible meanings to that concept of general law. One is that general law is the general principle of the Law of State Responsibility; the other is that the Law of State Responsibility is applied to the international community as a whole. The understanding that the Law on Diplomatic Relations is a specific regime to the Law of State Responsibility is made on the basis of the former meaning, and not the latter meaning of general law. The specific regime is irrelevant to the latter. In contrast, if the general principles of the Law of State Responsibility do not form part of general international law in the latter sense, no problem of priority of specific regimes over general law arises between the Law on Diplomatic Relations and the Law of State Responsibility.

The same is true for the concept of a specific regime. International human rights law and international humanitarian law are specific regimes in the sense that they constitute special branches of international law. Yet, specific regimes in that sense are also part of general international law if they are considered to apply in the international community as a whole. Some regard international human rights as forming a part of the international constitution. Therefore,

[21] Ibid., par. 191.
[22] Ibid., par. 193.

international human rights law and international humanitarian law are specific to the general theory and principles of international law, but can be included in the latter sense of a general international law regime. In this respect, the conflict of norms associated with the problem of fragmentation is not identical to the conflict the ILC identifies within the scope of the relationship between specific regime and general law. The main issue pertains to the priority among rules that have a public law character, not the priority between general and specific regimes. The ILC Report only indicates that a general law having a public law character limits specific regimes, but it does not examine why it does so, and what the laws of public law character actually are.

The ILC also discusses the cases in which a conflict of norms is integrated, in the form that rules conflicting with rules of general international law are invalidated, or in the form that rules of general international law have priority over other conflicting rules by relying on article 103 of the UN Charter, on the concept of *ius cogens* or on obligations *erga omnes*, stating that "the practice of international law has always recognised the presence of some norms that are superior to other norms and must therefore be given effect".[23] Additionally, with regard to the relationship between priority and invalidity, the Report states, taking the relation between measures determined by the Security Council and rules of *ius cogens* as an example, that article 103 of the UN Charter certainly suggests the hierarchically higher status of that document over other parts of international law, while the very idea of *ius cogens* suggests that even UN politics may run against a 'constitutional' limit.[24] On the basis of this argument, it concludes that debates on superior and inferior norms remain a fertile ground for deliberating constitutionalisation and fragmentation, and also, that the importance of the notion of *ius cogens* may lie less in the way the concepts are actually 'applied'; rather *ius cogens* rules can function as signals of argumentative possibilities and boundaries for institutional decision-making, notwithstanding the ongoing disputes on the determination of their exact content.[25]

For the following reasons however, it is necessary to examine carefully the possibility of combining international constitutional law with the notion of *ius cogens*. First, whereas there is no doubt that even UN politics may run against a constitutional limit, the rules and measures adopted within that framework cannot always be invalidated, even when they conflict with principles of international law that are regarded as having a peremptory character. For example, even the principle of sovereign equality of states, which is considered to have a peremptory character as a constitutional principle of international law, cannot

---

23 Ibid., par. 326.
24 Ibid., par. 409.
25 Ibid., par. 409.

invalidate the voting system of the Security Council that deviates from it, because the system is considered to be necessary for the maintenance of international peace and security.[26] Another thing one should keep in mind is that rules of international law having a peremptory character do not necessarily have the status of constitutional law. For example, rules of international criminal law that are valid as general international law have a peremptory character as international *ordre public* rules, but they do not function as constitutional principles of international law. Therefore, when arguing about the effect of the rules having peremptory character, it seems necessary to distinguish between the effect of rules constituting constitutional principles, and of rules constituting public order in the international community. This distinction will be helpful for the resolution of the problem of fragmentation.

Thirdly, with regard to cases where a conflict of norms cannot be dealt with in terms of the application of the *lex specialis* rule or of the doctrine of *ius cogens*, the ILC discusses the issues in the light of coordination or systemic interpretation of conflicting rules. For that purpose, the ILC argues that the integration of conflicting rules can rely on the application of article 31 (3) (c) of the Vienna Convention on the Law of Treaties, on the understanding that the integration of the conflict between treaties cannot be distinguished from the interpretation of treaties. It also argues that article 31 (3) (c) can be taken to express what may be called the principle of 'systemic integration'.[27] This entails that, in the area of framework treaties and implementation treaties, the doctrine of 'treaty parallelism' can be applied, which addresses precisely the need to coordinate the reading of particular instruments or to see them in a mutually supportive light.[28] Moreover, according to the ILC,

> the normative environment cannot be ignored' and 'when interpreting the treaties, the principle of integration should be borne in mind. This points to the need to carry out the interpretation so as to see the rules in view of some

[26] In par. 349 of the ILC Report 2006, two early judgments of the Court of First Instance are mentioned: Case T-306/01, *Ahmed Ali Yusuf and Al Barakaat International Foundation v. Council and Commission*, and Case T-315/01, *Yassin Abdullah Kadi v. Council and Commission*. In *Yusuf*, the Court of First Instance noted that "there exists one limit to the principle that resolutions of the Security Council have binding effect: namely, that they must observe the fundamental peremptory provisions of jus cogens. If they fail to do so, however improbable that may be, they would bind neither the Member States of the United Nations nor, in consequence, the Community" (Case T-306/01, par. 281). The ILC Report also notes that "[i]n its subsequent analysis over the question whether the freezing of applicants' rights constituted a breach of jus cogens, the Court found in the negative" (see par. 350 of the ILC Report 2006). On appeal, the European Court of Justice took a markedly different approach, shirking away from scrutinising the contested measures within the light of *ius cogens*: see Joined Cases C-402/05 P & C-415/05 P, *Yassin Abdullah Kadi and Al Barakaat International Foundation v. Council and Commission*, [2008] ECR I-6351. For further reflections of these cases, see also the contribution of Boisson de Chazournes and Kuijper to this volume.

[27] Ibid., par. 413.

[28] Ibid., par. 417.

> comprehensible and coherent objective, to prioritise concerns that are more important at the cost of less important objectives. This is all that article 31 (3) (c) requires; the integration into the process of legal reasoning – including reasoning by courts and tribunals – of a sense of coherence and meaningfulness.[29]

Further, according to the ILC,

> if [article 31 (3) (c)] is merely the expression of a larger principle – that of the 'systemic integration' – and if that principle, again, expresses a reasonable or even necessary aspect of legal reasoning, then a discussion of its actual and potential uses would constitute a useful contribution to the study of the alleged fragmentation (or diversification) of international law.[30]

The ILC's understanding of the role of article 31 (3) (c) is based on the idea that general international law is concerned with the problem of fragmentation not so much in terms of substantive rules and principles, but as a formal argumentative technique. Importantly, it is this technique that represents what is 'general' in a world of proliferating technical particularities.[31]

There is little doubt that the resolution of conflicts between treaties is hard to distinguish from the interpretation of treaties. Nevertheless, there seem to be various problems with the reading of the ILC. Firstly, is it possible to give article 31 (3) (c) such a significant role, as a technique to systemically integrate conflicting regimes or conflicting rules of general international law? Whereas the interpretation provided in the article concerns establishing the meaning of treaty provisions in the light of other, related treaty rules, systemic interpretation as understood by ILC concerns the systemic application among conflicting regimes and conflicting rules. Secondly, the ILC does not clarify what rules in the international community have an *ordre public* character. If the 'systemic interpretation' taking account of the normative environment comes down to interpretations of applicability among conflicting regimes or rules, this interpretation concerns the determination of the status of each regime or rule in general international law or in the international public order. It will then be necessary to examine the issue concerning the construction of public order in the international community, in addition to that of constitutional principles that may make the application of article 31 (3) (c) relevant from that perspective.

In the foregoing, the method was examined of relying on the rules of the law of treaties, which the ILC used in order to cope with the problem of fragmentation of international regimes. Yet, as the integration of the fragmented international order concerns the integration of international public order as a whole, it seem difficult to resolve the problem by relying on the framework of

[29] Ibid., par. 419.
[30] Ibid., par. 423.
[31] Ibid., par. 455.

the law of treaties, which is mainly concerned with the formation and effect of treaties.[32] Whereas the ILC, in the construction of its argument, refers to the constitutional and public law character of general international law, it equates the issue of resolving norm conflicts to a problem in the phase of dispute settlement, stating that it is not in a position to discuss this problem *in abstracto*. It would not appear logical, however, to conclude that if one refrains from discussing the problem *in abstracto*, the whole analysis remains limited to the framework of the law of treaties.

3.2.3. *Constitutional Approach*

Recently, constitutionalism has become a pressing issue in the study of international law. Most of the studies deal with the issue in the light of the characterisation of the Charter of the United Nations[33] and the rule of law in the international community.[34] There are two different views on the role of constitutionalism as a response to the fragmentation of the international legal order.

Firstly, there is the view put forward by Christian Walter, relying on the conception of a disaggregated constitution, which focuses on the constitutional function of rules in various regimes but requires an abandonment of the idea of a constitution.[35] He argues that unlike a national constitution, in the current decentralised international legal order that corresponds to the disaggregation of public authority, it is not possible to develop a constitution that bundles various constitutional functions into one regime. However, he understands that within sectoral regimes such as international human rights law and international environmental law, each regime has separately developed norms that have constitutional functions. Therefore, he argues, it is necessary to disaggregate the various constitutions in the international legal order.[36] On the basis of this understanding, he explains that, in case international human rights law conflicts with international environmental law or with world trade law, the ECHR has responded by exporting the standards set by the ECHR to the other regimes. More technically, it does so by extending the obligations of the member states from their own legal orders to other regimes they set up in pursuit of their regulatory objectives.[37]

---

[32] Wolfrum and Matz, supra n. 10, p. 129.

[33] James Crawford, 'The Charter of the United Nations as a Constitution', in: James Crawford, *International Law as an Open System*, London: Cameron May 2002, p. 123–136; Bardo Fassbender, 'The United Nations Charter as Constitution of the International Community', (1997) 36 *Columbia Journal of Transnational Law*, p. 529–619.

[34] Ronald St.J. MacDonald and Douglas M. Johnston (eds.), *Towards World Constitutionalism*, The Hague: Martinus Nijhoff Publishers 2005.

[35] Christian Walter, 'Constitutionalizing (Inter)national Governance – Possibilities for and Limits to the Development of an International Constitutional Law', (2001) 44 *German Yearbook of International Law*, p. 170–201.

[36] Ibid., p. 174.

[37] Ibid., p. 199.

This conception of a constitution is a practical construction, which helps to deal with the development of constitutional norms in international law and their role in the resolution of problems caused by conflicting norms. However, this approach is not without its problems. First, it is not clear what should be considered as 'the constitutional function' in international law. The approach illustrates the constitutional function by identifying the fundamental principles of individual regimes. Therefore, the function itself is not determinate, because it depends on the function of fundamental principles in each regime. It may not be the same in international human rights law and environmental law, nor may the role of fundamental principles of each regime be equal for the maintenance of public order in the international community. Secondly, when states decide on the fundamental principles of a regime they establish, the approach disregards whether states are restricted in their decision, whether they are constrained by principles that constitute the fundamental framework of international law.

A different view that adopts the constitutional approach to fragmentation is the one taken by Dunoff and Trachtman, who regard the phenomenon of globalisation and fragmentation as the basis of constitutionalisation in international law. In order to explain the complex phenomenon of international constitutionalisation, they use a functional approach, which directs attention to the purposes that international constitutional norms are intended to serve, thus avoiding definitional problems.[38] In order to describe the three key purposes international constitutional norms serve, they highlight the three functions of those norms: (1) enabling the formation of international law (i.e. enabling constitutionalisation), (2) constraining the formation of international law (i.e. constraining constitutionalisation), (3) filling gaps in domestic constitutional law which arise as a result of globalisation (i.e. supplemental constitutionalisation).[39]

Of these functions, they argue, it is the first and the second one that have a greater role for the integration of fragmented international rules. This is because they think that the first one, by providing the allocation of procedural authorities, can resolve the conflict of norms and the conflict of authorities among international organisations, and because the second can constrain the formation and effect of international rules inconsistent with substantive constitutional norms by giving precedence to the latter.[40]

In order to integrate a fragmented international order, it is no doubt important, as they argue, to place the function of international constitutional law in

[38] Jeffrey L. Dunoff and Joël P. Trachtman, 'A Functional Approach to International Constitutionalization', in: Jeffrey L. Dunoff and Joël P. Trachtman (eds.), *Ruling the World? Constitutionalism, International Law and Global Governmance*, Cambridge: Cambridge University Press 2009, p. 9–10.

[39] Ibid., p. 10.

[40] Ibid., p. 11.

the centre of attention in the integration of norms, and pinpoint the rules that have that function. If we are able to specify the functions of international constitutional law, it will be much easier to advocate the integration of rules that are unequivocally inconsistent with international constitutional law. But, in the present circumstances, in which the number of principles that are considered as international constitutional law is limited and indeterminate, it is difficult to rely on constitutional principles in order to resolve the various kinds of conflict between rules and regimes. For that purpose, it will be necessary not only to focus on international constitutional law, but elucidate the structure of the international public order constructed by general international law in order to protect the common interests of the international community, and the constitutional structure that lies behind that international public order.

3.3. *Views Respecting the Coordination of Conflicting Authorities*

3.3.1. *Introduction*

Next to the approach of systemic integration relying on the law of treaties, and the constitutional approach, there is an approach that does not focus on normative integration, but instead concentrates on the issue of how international organisations and treaty organs respond to the problem of fragmentation and the key issues in that process (hereafter as 'authority integration'). Again two approaches can be distinguished for this 'authority integration'. First, there is the approach that mainly deals with the resolution of authority conflicts between treaty organs; secondly, there is the approach that focuses on the coordination of implementation processes of treaties in terms of the effectiveness of the institutions. Both are discussed in the paragraphs below.

3.3.2. *The Response Focusing on the Allocation of Authority*

In his analysis of the fragmentation problems, Tomer Broude draws attention to the aspect of how the authority of the dispute settlement mechanism of each treaty regime is organised, and how the fragmentation of authorities influences the response to the conflict of substantive norms. Broude indicates that the problems of fragmentation fall into a category dealing with the fragmentation of substantive norms (i.e. the complex interactions caused by the existence of a staggering variety of substantive sources of international law), and into a category dealing with the fragmentation of international authority as regards the distribution of power among the plethora of international and national institutions who produce, interpret, and apply international law. According to him, both categories are the warp and weft of fragmented international law and cannot be separated. The integration of norms and that of authorities are therefore interlocked.[41]

On this understanding, he describes the interaction between the two categories of fragmentation, in the light of their basic correlation, first analysed descriptively, and subsequently in the light of an international decision-maker faced with fragmentation and integration problems of both categories. He considers this second aspect the more important.

With regard to the basic correlation, Broude argues that the significance of authority fragmentation and the seriousness of the problem it presents largely depend on the degree of norm fragmentation, and vice versa.

> Where substantive norms are integrated or harmonized rather than fragmented, identifying the proper forum for producing them or for making determination based upon them is of less importance, the room available to the different for a for manoeuvring between different and potentially conflicting decision is reduced. The normative commonality overcomes institutional difference. (…) Similarly, if decision-making authority were formally more integrated, the fragmentation of norms would be naturally mitigated and, in any case, would not be as problematic.[42]

However, instead of applying that basic correlation in a merely technical manner for the resolution of norm fragmentation, he suggests that, for such a purpose, it is necessary to take account of the political meaning the quest for norm integration has for the structure of the entire system of authority and governance. This is because international decision-makers are sensitive to norm integration, considering that it will lead to authority integration for the following four reasons: 1) to integrate the norms of another system is to acknowledge the authority of that system to produce pertinent norms; 2) to integrate the norms of another system is to assert authority over them; 3) to integrate the norms of another system is to introduce the overlapping authority; 4) problems of overlapping authority agitate towards authority-integrating solutions.[43]

Against this background, Broude argues that normative integration should in practice be dealt with in a manner not to be combined with authority integration. Therefore, he recommends the methods of integration that will be least intrusive and least threatening to authority, for instance the principle of integration in paragraph 4 of the Rio Declaration.[44]

---

[41] Tomer Broude, 'Fragmentation(s) of International Law: On Normative Integration as Authority Allocation', in: Tomer Broude and Yuval Shany (eds.), *The Shifting Allocation of Authority in International Law*, Oxford: Hart Publishing 2008, p. 101–103.

[42] Ibid., p. 105.

[43] Ibid., p. 110–113.

[44] Ibid., p. 120.

This view, which argues for normative integration in terms of the extent to which it can be achieved, may be a very practical response to the fragmentation problem, especially considering that there is no possibility of institutionalising the hierarchical order of sources of law and authority in the present international community. It also provides suggestions for new law-making. But the problem with Broude's view is that normative integration is strongly influenced by a sensitivity to the authority of decision-makers and the method of resolution they use. Thus, if norms of another regime are integrated within the framework of one regime only as an exception, and if one regime is not allowed to integrate norms by balancing the interests of each regime, (as seen in the case of GATT and WTO taking account of environmental rules), integration is likely to occur differently per regime. In that case, the fragmentation problem still remains to be resolved. Thus, to ensure that normative integration by each regime leads to a wholesale integration in the international community, it is essential for decision-makers to share a notion of international public order.

3.3.3. *Integration Relying on Governance Theory*

Yet another different approach relies on methods developed in governance theory. There may be conflicts between treaty organs with regard to the measures taken in the implementation process, due to the fact that agreements have different objects, and conflicts may arise because of overlapping authority. In both these cases, methods of coordination are often used so as to ensure good governance.

Methods of coordination resolve conflicts between treaty regimes involving norms and authorities, e.g. the Convention on Biodiversity and CITES, without giving priority to either of them. The methods of coordination used vary considerably. Examples are the establishment of a joint organ or the set-up of networks, exchanges of memoranda of understanding and cooperation, or the use of constructing partnerships and joint actions. These methods facilitate the exchange of information and experience between treaty organs and secure the efficiency of administrative resources, for instance the Global Environmental Facility that is concerned with the allocation of funds.

In their examination of conflicts in international environmental law, Wolfrum and Matz assert that the different types of coordination in the implementation process have developed not only due to the fact that environmental agreements formulate obligations in a vague manner (so that conflicting obligations can be identified and side-stepped during the negotiation phase), but also because conflicts between multilateral environmental agreements manifest themselves only in the implementation phase, due to the vagueness of the formulations employed. This constitutes a continuing process and not a single event.[45]

As examined by Wolfrum and Matz, there is no doubt that, with regard to the integration of conflicting rules among international environmental agreements, coordination plays an important role. But, in conflicts between international environmental law and other areas of law (e.g. conflicts between human right law and environmental law, or between WTO and environmental law), cases are often brought that need to be settled by interpreting the applicable rules. This goes to show that methods of coordination do not resolve all fragmentation problems, and do not exclude other approaches.

4. *Normative Integration and the Structure of International Public Order*

4.1. *Introduction*

Above, several different views were outlined on the issue of how to integrate the fragmented international order. In the eyes of the present author, the problem common to all of them is that they do not fully recognise that the international legal regime developed to protect the general interests of the international community as a whole has evolved, and so has the character of public order in the international community. In consequence, it is necessary to discuss normative integration and authority integration as means of constituting public order in the international community.

This section will examine theoretical issues on integrating the fragmented international order by way of interpretation, in order to constitute, on the basis of existing international law, the international public order. In advance, two points need to be stressed concerning the structure of the discussion.

The first preliminary point is concerned with how to consider the relationship between normative integration and authority integration in the process of integrating the international public order. What is important in this respect is that normative integration through interpretation will be possible if the theoretical structure of public order is clear. Authority integration, on the other hand, will require changes to the present structure of dispute settlement mechanism, unless one resorts to coordination. Thus, considering that it is cumbersome to (attempt to) amend existing dispute settlement mechanisms, it becomes of greater practical importance to realise a clear theoretical construction of international public order through normative integration. This may also provide us with a framework for evaluating the reasonableness of an interpretation, even when treaty organs deal with normative integration by

45 Wolfrum and Matz, supra n. 10, p. 11–12.

applying article 31 (3) (c) of the Convention on the Law of the Treaties. Thus, I will mainly focus on normative integration here.

The second preliminary point concerns the appropriate theoretical method to construct the international public order through interpretation. The main problem that we are faced with when we discuss normative integration is, to the mind of the author, that general international law is characterised, in principle, as *ius dispositivum*. Moreover, as the legal status of general international law of peremptory character was provided within the framework of the law of treaties, it was characterised as a set of norms that invalidate rules which conflict with it. Consequently, whereas in domestic legal systems, the effects of rules having a peremptory character are distinguished between a private and a public law sphere, in international law, no distinction of effects has been made among international rules of peremptory character. As a result, general rules prohibiting genocide or slave trade have been discussed as examples of *ius cogens* which invalidate any rules that deviate from them.

This notion of general international law would appear to be based on the understanding that the foundation of international law is the consent of states, and that rules of general international law have been developed as customary international law. Having discussed this notion's problematic aspects in detail elsewhere, this section only stresses two essential points. First, the formation of customary law as rules of general international law is not based on the consent of all the states bound by them, and general rules prohibiting genocide or slave trade aim at prohibiting the conduct violating them, not invalidating the treaties that deviate from them.[46] In this respect, it would seem necessary to draw attention to the peremptory character of the rules in a public law sphere in international law as well.

Furthermore, in theory, what is essential for the argument concerning the existence of customary international law as general international law is not to confirm the evidence of the formation of customary rules on the basis of the requirements of customary law. Rather, it would need to be examined on what normative and practical factors the justification of generalisation of rules is based, and how they are authorised.[47] In other words, it is important for the argument concerning the existence of general international law to look at the reasons to legitimise the normative generalisation of rules, and also at the

[46] Teruo Komori, 'A Study on the Nature and Concept of General International Law', (1998) 13 *Chiba Journal of Law and Politics*, p. 8–53 (originally in Japanese). See also Alexander Orakhelashvili, *Peremptory International Norms in International Law*, Oxford: Oxford University Press 2006.

[47] Teruo Komori, 'Reconstructing the Theory of Customary International Law', (2005) 56 *The Hokkaido Law Review*, p. 3 (originally in Japanese). See also Amanda Perreau-Saussine and James B. Murphy (eds.), *The Nature of Customary Law*, Cambridge: Cambridge University Press 2007; Brian Lepard, *Customary International Law. A New Theory with Practical Applications*, Cambridge: Cambridge University Press 2010.

basis to authorise rules. On the basis of this understanding, normative integration is now discussed by way of constituting international public order.

4.2. *Legitimisation of the Generalisation of International Rules*

4.2.1. *Introduction*

Rules of general international law are often recognised as existing even when there is a conflict with regard to the question which rule can be considered generally applicable. Therefore, the judgment on whether a rule qualifies as a rule of general international law is not confined to those cases where all the states consent to it. From the perspective of legitimacy, however, it is necessary to justify why it can be identified as a general rule, despite the disagreement among states with regard to its validity as such.

This justification of the legitimacy or necessity of considering a rule as a general rule can be divided into two phases, corresponding with the different reasons that need to be given for that justification. The first phase concerns the premise or philosophical foundation of why a general rule or a general order is necessary on a specific issue. The second phase is concerned with how rules are formulated in legal regimes that are considered as legitimate or necessary.

4.2.2. *Justification concerning the Necessity of a General International Order*

In turn, justifying the premise or philosophical foundation of the necessity of a general order requires two things. One is intrinsic justification, on the basis of a reason intrinsic to a claim; the other is extrinsic justification, made on the basis of reasons extrinsic to a claim.[48]

Intrinsic justification is required when we insist on the necessity of generalisation of a rule on the basis of universality of its object (as with the universality of human rights), or when we insist that a rule should comply with the idea of justice (for example the principle of common but differentiated responsibility). In other words, when we claim that a rule itself has universality, we have to justify the universality of the rule on the basis of reasons intrinsic to it. Intrinsic justification is substantive and essential for the demonstration of the necessity of a general regime or a general rule that claims universality by itself, because it relates to the philosophical foundation of its object. Thus, the claim demanding that the philosophical foundation of a regime is capable of being generalised is required to provide intrinsic reasons, which in turn may counter claims that try to negate the generalisation of a regime on the ground of

---

[48] Robert Alexy used the conception of internal justification and external justification as a means of legal argumentation, but the role of intrinsic and extrinsic justification relates to the concept of internal justification that is concerned with the justification of law but not with the justification according to law. See Robert Alexy, *A Theory of Legal Argumentation*, Oxford: Clarendon Press 1989.

relativism, individualism, pluralism, etcetera. The claim demanding that the philosophical foundation of a regime is capable of being generalised is also required for answering the question of how it can justify a new regime that tries to reconstruct an established concept of international law such as sovereignty.

Extrinsic justification, on the other hand, is necessary when a rule itself has no intrinsic reason to justify its universality, but when it should be applicable in the community as a whole for reasons extrinsic to it (e.g. driving on a certain side of the road, applied for reasons of traffic safety or stemming from particular historical circumstances). Extrinsic justification is also required when, although there is conflict of views among states concerning which rule should be applied, we insist that it is necessary to have one general rule nevertheless. This extrinsic justification can play a significant role for normative integration in case there is a conflict of views concerning which principle should be adopted as a principle of a regime. Stability of law and order, the requirement of predictability, fair procedure of decision-making, and burden of proof are examples of such extrinsic reasons.[49]

As indicated, in theory, the justification of the validity of a regime, or of a rule as being a rule of general international law, has an intrinsic and an extrinsic component. In the justification of a rule as a rule of general international law, the question which component is more important depends on the character of the rule and the circumstance in which a law is made. In practice, in the law-making process of a regime, it is often the case that, since various factors are concerned with decision-making, both justifications intersect. For the normative integration of conflicting rules of general international law, it is therefore important to examine the justificatory reasons on which conflicting general rules are based.

4.2.3. *Justification concerning the Formulation of a General Rule*

If the premise for the existence of a regime of general international law is justified and general international order is considered necessary for a certain field, then as a matter of institution-building, one needs to discuss the formulation of concrete rules. In this stage of formulation of a regime, justification problems exist with regard to the question of which formulation of a rule is more legitimate as a general rule of international law, how definite it should be, etcetera.

In this second phase of justification, the factors concerned with the justification of a rule as a general rule are *inter alia* consistency with the object of a

---

[49] Tatsuo Inoue addresses this extrinsic reason as second order justification ground. See Tatsuo Inoue, 'What is Publicness?', in: Tatsuo Inoue (ed.), *Legal Philosophy of Publicness*, Tokyo: Nakanishi Publishing 2006, p. 3–27 (originally in Japanese).

regime, the available resources and knowledge for its implementation, its capacity for solving problems, and the fairness of distribution.[50] Furthermore, since the reasons necessary for the justification in this phase are related to practical issues, it depends on the situation which reason has importance in the process, for example, whether among parties there is a common understanding on the idea and object of the regime. For the integration of conflicting rules at this stage, it will therefore be important to consider factors that relate to the justification of rules, and to consider which factor is more important in the particular situation.

4.3. *Normative Integration and the Structure of International Public Law*

4.3.1. *Introduction: Conception of International Public Law*

It was stated above that normative integration should be discussed as a matter of constructing an international public order that consists of international constitutional law and international public law in a narrow sense, which means public law other than constitutional law (hereafter referred to as international public law, to be distinguished from international constitutional law). Moreover, a theory of international public law must be construed under the condition that, unlike a domestic legal system, there is no hierarchical order of public authorities in the international community.

This paragraph will discuss the conception of international public law, the types of reasons that might justify characterising rules and regimes of general international law as international public law, and the reasons that underlie (attempts at) normative integration.

4.3.2. *The Character of International Public Law*

In the legal systems of continental Europe, public law was characterised as law with which a government was able to provide authority to regulate private spheres of nationals for public purposes. But in the international community, there is no central government, and no hierarchical order of public authorities. Therefore, we first need to identify and discuss the key factors for a successful construction of a theory of international public law.

In international law, the necessity of a legal regime protecting the interests of the international community has been argued with reliance on the concept of the common interest or the general interest of the international community. As indicated by Furuya, it is undeniable that those concepts have been misused as a ground to intervene into national legal systems of some states, or to

---

[50] Hermut Breitmeier, *The Legitimacy of International Regimes*, Farnham: Ashgate 2008, p. 19–38.

generalise interests of a group of states.[51] However, it is also undeniable that there are interests like the protection of the environment that are indeed of concern to the international community as a whole. It is therefore necessary to clarify what common interests of the international community are based on legitimate grounds. Here, the common or general interest as the public interest in the international community comes into play: for international public law can be conceptualised as a legal regime protecting the public interest of the international community. This conceptualisation is possible by linking it, on the one hand, to the peremptory character of rules of general international law and, on the other hand, by underlining the object and purpose of a regime as a global issue.

As stated above, the peremptory character of certain law is divided into the public and the private law sphere. In the public sphere, the function of peremptory norms is to invalidate rules conflicting with them, or to make illegal conduct violating them.[52] In this respect, discussing whether a legal regime is a public law regime is made possible by discussing the reasons underpinning the function of general international law: to make rules conflicting with it null and void, or to characterise activities conflicting with it as illegal.

4.3.3. *Reasons Grounding General International Law as Public Law*

In national legal systems, the rules that constitute a system of public law have different functions. Similarly in international law the different regimes have various functions as well. Fundamental principles such as that of sovereign equality of states constitute the framework of the entire international legal system. On the other hand, there are principles that only constitute fundamentals of a specific regime, e.g. the precautionary principle in environmental agreements.[53]

The different function performed by general international law as public law is closely related to the rationale of a specific regime under public international law. We may identify the following five types of reasoning that are used for justifying the validity of regimes as international public law.

The first is when the reasoning is used in order to underpin the constitutional construction of an entire legal system. Any legal system must determine the subject of the system as its main addressee, and the fundamental status of the subject that constitutes its basis, in order for it to function as a system.

---

[51] Shuichi Furuya, 'The International Community as Ideology', in: Onuma Yasuaki (ed.), *Law and Power in International Society*, Tokyo: Nihon Hyoronsha 2009, p. 155–190 (originally in Japanese).

[52] See Shotaro Hamamoto, 'Nullity and its Relation to Responsibility in International Law', (2004) 104 *The Journal of International Law and Diplomacy*, p. 73–102 (originally in Japanese).

[53] Breitmeier, supra n. 50, p. 161–163.

Therefore, it must be argued on an intrinsic basis who is the subject of a legal system and what is the fundamental status of this subject.

The second scenario concerns the case when, as with the protection of the global environment, states intend to create a regime to realise the interests of the international community as a whole, and to regulate activities that might otherwise prevent their realisation. In this case, it is necessary to argue on an intrinsic basis whether the interests that the regime protects are really common interests to the international community, and to argue whether the activities that deviate from the regime's rules disturb the realisation of its objects, or whether double standards are applicable on an extrinsic basis.

The third type can be found when a public order is established to regulate the free use of resources that have the character of public goods, such as the high seas and outer space, in order to secure their free use for all. According to the descriptive definition used in economics, public goods are goods that are non-rivalrous and non-excludable in consumption. If those resources are inexhaustible, there is no need to regulate the utilisation of them publicly, since their use is *de facto* secured to all. But if instead, the available resources are exhaustible, in one way or the other, the non-rivalrous and non-excludable use of them must be secured for everyone. In this respect, the two facets of non-rivalrousness and non-excludability turn into normative grounds for establishing a public regulation. Therefore, in order to regulate the public utilisation of resources and spaces, it is necessary to provide solid reasons, on both intrinsic and extrinsic basis, for why their utilisation must be non-rivalrous and non-excludable.

The fourth type comes up when activities need to be regulated as a matter of public concern in the international community, in cases where those activities damage the rights and status of others without their consent. This is so, for example, when states take unilateral measures to extend an area of regulation, in order to protect resources along their coast, when they pass a law to facilitate free trade, or when states enforce their own regulation of environmental protection against others. In these cases, it is necessary to argue intrinsically whether there exists a legitimate reason for a uniform application of rules.

Finally, the fifth situation is concerned with the determination of the 'public order entity'. On the basis of the fact that current international regulations are applied to the activities of entities other than states, Kingsbury argues that public order in international law should be constructed as inter-public law, law among public entities other than states, instead of as inter-state law, where the only relevant entities are states.[54] He contends that the components

[54] Benedict Kingsbury, 'International Law as Inter-Public Law', in: Henry Richardson and Melissa Williams (eds.), *Moral Universalism and Pluralism*, New York: New York University Press 2009, p. 188.

of publicness are the principles of legality, rationality, the rule of law, and human rights.[55] He advances this idea because he considers that entities such as NGOs possessing specific scientific knowledge have an ever-increasing role in the making and implementation of international administrative law. But, to aid in the construction of a rule of general international law, which is in fact still concerned with the legal status of states in the international community, the relation between inter-public law and inter-state law would need to be developed further.

These different types of reasoning illustrate that the justification of general international law as public law depends on various factors and contexts. To the mind of the present author, when discussing the normative integration of the international public order, it is of great significance to distinguish between these five types of reasoning when justifying the use of international public law.

4.3.4. *Normative Integration and Types of Conflict of Norms*

The fact that it is formally impossible to decide on a hierarchy of sources of international law, due to the lack of a centralised legislative organ and judicial system, is the main cause of the fragmentation of the general international order. Therefore, one attempt to solve the problem is made by relying on the categorical distinction of the characters of international law, i.e. differentiating between the effects of rules belonging to separate categories. Galicki illustrates the hierarchy of rules by referring to norms of *ius cogens*, obligations *erga omnes* and obligations under article 103 of the UN Charter.[56]

This idea is useful as long as the relation between conflicting rules is simple. Yet, overall, its usefulness seems limited, considering that the justificatory reasons for the peremptory norms are not constructed in a consistent manner throughout the entire international legal system. Moreover, norms that have a peremptory character in the broad sense conflict in a rather complicated way in their implementation. Also, the most difficult issue associated with the fragmentation phenomenon is the conflict between two rules that are both enjoying a peremptory character. For resolving such cases, the suggestion of Pauwelyn may be helpful that the solution should correspond with the type of conflict.

Pauwelyn rejects the narrow definition that limits the situation of conflict to conflict of obligation. He takes an open approach, defining the notion of conflict as a case in which one norm constitutes a breach of other norms not

[55] Ibid., p. 178–179.

[56] Zdzislaw Galicki, 'Hierarchy in International Law within the Context of Its Fragmentation', in: *International Law between Universalism and Fragmentation. Festschrift in Honour of Gerhard Hafner*, The Hague: Martinus Nijhoff Publishers 2008, p. 41–59.

consisting of obligations. On the basis of this broader definition of conflict, he describes the multi-layered structure of conflict situations. First, he divides conflicts of norms into inherent normative conflicts, where one norm categorically breaches the other norm at the times of their adoption, and conflicts in the applicable law, where one norm breaches the other norm in the process of allocation, although both norms are continuously valid. He then identifies conflict situations that belong to each group. In the first group, the key issue is whether one norm can exclude the other, rendering it null and void or illegal. In the second group, everything depends on whether one norm is given priority over the other, or whether a state can claim state responsibility of the other if one norm is breached by the other norm, depending on their formulation as either command, prohibition, exemption or permission.[57] Furthermore, after examining multiple WTO cases, he concludes that conflicts of norms in international law are essentially governed by priority rules and state responsibility, not by rules invalidating either of the two conflicting norms.[58]

Irrespective of whether or not WTO law constitutes international public law, the method that differentiates situations of norm conflicts and argues for resolving the problems in accordance with the specific situation is more generally useful, as it addresses the problems that are relevant to norm integration.

4.3.5. *Types of Normative Integration and the Structure of Reasoning*

In order to argue for the normative integration of international public law in its entirety, the relation between specific conflict situations and the relevant reasoning in each situation needs to be examined comprehensively. As will become clear from the following examples, the types of normative integration vary, depending on what one considers to be the key issue in conflict situations.

The first example pertains to the case in which there is a difference of understanding regarding the objects and purposes of conflicting regimes, as is with the conflict between international human rights law and international humanitarian law. International human rights law institutionalises the protection of human rights mainly, but not exclusively, in peacetime, and international humanitarian law institutionalises the protection of individuals to secure basic elements of humanity during armed conflict. Both laws conflict, because activities prohibited in human rights law are permitted in humanitarian law. In this conflict, the view identifying the protection of life on the basis of humanity with the protection of human rights insists on integration, in the

[57] Joost Pauwelyn, *Conflict of Norms in Public International Law*, Cambridge: Cambridge University Press 2003, p. 165–188.
[58] Ibid., p. 436.

form of characterising humanitarian law as a subordinate of human rights law.[59] Other views, however, insist on integration in the form of characterising humanitarian law as the specific law of human rights law, or in the form of implanting human rights into the application of humanitarian law, on the ground that both laws have their own purposes for various reasons; while human rights law is (also) applied in times of peace, humanitarian law is only applied in armed conflict; while human rights law stipulates the relationship between individuals and the state under which jurisdiction they are, humanitarian law stipulates the relationship between individuals and the other belligerent state (in an international armed conflict) and with their own state (in the context of an internal armed conflict) in the form of an obligation.[60] Therefore, in the integration of conflicts of this type, reasons intrinsic to the object of a regime play an important role.

The second example concerns the case in which (as with the conflict between the application of humanitarian law and law on crimes against terrorism at a stage where the terrorist act has triggered an armed conflict), the difference of interpretation with regard to the applicability of a regime pertains to the issue of whether or not there is conflict between the different sets of rules. In a view that takes humanitarian law very strictly as the law to protect the humanitarian order in situations of armed conflict, one interprets the regime as not being applicable to military actions by the terrorist groups, since they do not meet some essential requirements; instead, their actions are characterised as criminal acts to which rules on terrorism apply. Consequently, in this interpretation, there is no conflict between the two regimes.[61] On the other hand, when humanitarian law is applied to terrorist groups, even when consistent with the purpose of those rules, a conflict is bound to arise in the process of their application.[62] Yet, in this conflict, the one regime cannot invalidate nor render the other illegal, since the validity of both sets of rules is generally recognised. Therefore, normative integration follows from giving priority to the one over the other, here for instance in the form of the

---

[59] Koji Teraya, 'Structural Transformation of the Idea of Humanity and Human Rights', in: Shinya Murase et al. (eds.) *International Law of Armed Conflict*, Tokyo: Toshindo Publishing 2004, p. 213–233 (originally in Japanese).

[60] See Rene Provost, *International Human Rights and Humanitarian Law*, Cambridge: Cambridge University Press 2002, p. 3–9, p. 17–41, p. 58–101; James Ross, 'Jurisdictional Aspects of International Human Rights and Humanitarian Law in the War on Terror', in: Fons Coomans and Menno Kamminga (eds.), *Extraterritorial Application of Human Rights Treaties*, Antwerp: Intersentia 2004, p. 9–24. Peter Rowe, *The Impact of Human Rights Law on Armed Forces*, Cambridge: Cambridge University Press 2006, p. 114–162.

[61] Christopher Greenwood, *Essays on War in International Law*, London: Cameron May 2006, p. 428–432.

[62] Shuichi Furuya, 'International Terrorism and the Scope of the Law of Armed Conflicts', in: Shinya Murase et al. (eds.), *Law and Power in International Society*, Tokyo: Nihon Hyoronsha 2009, p. 178–181 (originally in Japanese).

application of criminal law *after* the application of humanitarian law during an armed conflict. Furuya argues that applying humanitarian law to terrorist groups does not exempt them from criminal responsibility against the acts of terrorism, since humanitarian law is applicable to them as a consequence of a limitation in its process of application.[63] In the integration of the conflict of this type, it is therefore important to examine the intrinsic reasons of each regime, in order to justify that each regime is applicable as general international law. At the same time one also needs to consider the extrinsic reasons regarding the choice of the most desirable regime for the maintenance of international security.

The third situation arises in cases where measures taken by one legal regime conflict with the rights provided by another regime. Taking the activities of the United Nations, as an example, there are many cases in which the measures taken by the UN conflict with the protection of human rights. In the aforementioned *Yusuf* and *Kadi* litigation,[64] an enforcement measure by the Security Council freezing the assets of a person who was suspected of links with the Taliban and Al Qaeda network was contested, as it violated the fundamental right to property. One example of UN peacekeeping forces violating human rights is UNISOM II in Somalia and in the Afghan aid programme, the humanitarian aid measures to the government denying their application to women conflicted with rules for the elimination of discrimination against women.[65]

In the *Yusuf* case, in which the plaintiff contended that the EU Regulation implementing a UN Security Council resolution violated the right to property, the Court of First Instance refused to review the Regulation, finding that all the Member States of the EU and the EU itself were bound by chapter VII resolutions, in accordance with article of 103 of the Charter.[66] With regard to the issue of whether the Security Council measures constituted a violation of human rights, the Court found that, while the fundamental peremptory provisions of *ius cogens* needed to be observed,[67] the asset-freezing-measures did not violate *ius cogens*, since they pursued an objective of fundamental public interest for the international community.[68] Moreover, the freezing of funds qualified as a precautionary measure which, unlike confiscation, does not affect the very substance of the right of the persons concerned to property in

---

[63] Ibid., p. 180.

[64] See supra, n. 26.

[65] See in greater detail Guglielmo Verdirame, 'Compliance with Human Rights in UN Operations', (2002) 2 *Human Rights Law Review*, p. 269–275.

[66] Case T-306/01, *Ahmed Ali Yusuf and Al Barakaat International Foundation v. Council and Commission*, par. 239–243.

[67] Ibid., par. 281.

[68] Ibid., par. 298.

their financial assets, but only the use thereof.[69] In the other two cases, in the implementation of measures, attention was drawn to the protection of human rights in some way or the other. After the failed humanitarian operation in Somalia, the Report of the Secretary-General on the implementation of the report of the panel on UN peacekeeping operations proposed producing materials and conducting more training, *inter alia* on international humanitarian and human rights law and on gender issues.[70] In the Afghan aid situation, though unsuccessful, negotiations took place to make the implementation of the aid programs conditional on the elimination of discrimination against women, by characterizing the pertinent rules as non-derogable.[71] Here though, it is difficult to indicate the specific type of conflict between the protection of fundamental rights and the measures of UN organs, since the dependent variables are the human rights provisions relied on in particular disputes, the seriousness of the conflict, and the situation in which the conflict emerged. To arrive at normative integration, it is therefore crucial to take these duly into account. Nevertheless, in these cases, it is generally desirable to make similar solutions when there is a similar type of conflict. Thus, in these cases, normative integration depends on the weight that intrinsic and extrinsic reasons have in each regime in each situation.

In contrast to the other three examples, the fourth and last example requires careful case by case balancing between conflicting obligations from two regimes. In the case of a conflict between the Washington Convention[72] and the Convention on Biodiversity, measures taken in the same area in order to comply with the purpose of one treaty, may be contrary to the purpose of the other treaty. A measure to increase the number of endangered animals, e.g. elephants, in one area may destroy the biodiversity there; vice versa, to preserve biodiversity in one are area may require reducing the number of endangered animals. In such conflicts, what is key for the implementation of measures is not to give priority to one regime over the other, but to ensure that measures are balanced between the two regimes. In this regard, intrinsic reasons and extrinsic reasons of both regimes intersect, depending on the conflicting situations.

5. *Concluding Remarks*

In this contribution, the topic of fragmentation of international law and the normative integration of the international public order has been examined in

[69] Ibid., par. 299.
[70] *Report of the Secretary-General on the implementation of the report of the Panel on United Nations peace operations*, A/55/502, 20 October 2000, responding to Panel on United Nations Peace Operations (Brahimi Report), A/55/305, 21 August 2000.
[71] Verdirame, supra n. 65, p. 269–275.
[72] Convention on International Trade in Endangered Species of Wild Fauna and Flora (CITES).

the light of different justificatory strategies. On the basis of the examination, to conclude and by way of summary, some theoretical observations are made.

First, for the integration of a fragmented international legal order, as a matter of practice, normative integration plays a more important role than authority integration. This is due to the fact that, whereas authority integration has only a limited scope involving coordination in the implementation process of rules, normative integration may be achieved on the basis of the interpretation of legal regimes and rules.

Second, integration of conflicting norms and authorities on the basis of procedures provided in the Convention on the Law of Treaties are rarely made in practice, except for those cases where priority is given to the resolutions of the UN Security Council by relying on the article 103 of the Charter. And even when those resolutions are given priority, the question of what are the legitimate measures and to what extent can they exclude the application of human rights law, must be argued in terms of substantive reasons to justify such exclusion (as illustrated by the *Yusuf/Kadi* litigation and the Afghan aid programme).

Third, since normative fragmentation is often concerned with conflicts between legal regimes that are characterised as the law of the international public order (such as a conflict involving international human rights law and international humanitarian law), in order to realise normative integration, it is necessary to discuss the relationship between legal regimes in terms of priority and coordination. This means that for achieving normative integration – which relates to the priority between regimes in the international public order – a method that simply relies on article 31 (3) (c) of the Vienna Convention on the Law of Treaties is not useful. After all, that article mainly relates to clarifying the meaning of a treaty provision by relying on other relevant rules applicable in the relations between the parties, but it does not indicate which rules should have priority.

Fourth, how norms are integrated varies according to the different types of conflict. Integration may take various forms, such as giving priority to one regime over the other, or coordinating measures taken in the implementation process of both regimes.

Finally, for the normative integration of legal regimes and rules, it is essential to focus on the justificatory reasons that underpin the public character of those regimes. That is to say, it not only needs to be demonstrated that legal regimes and rules have intrinsic reasons that justify their generalisation, but also that the public character of such norms is grounded on extrinsic reasons. Moreover, in the face of conflicting rules or legal regimes it is important to determine what justificatory reasons underpinning the public character of those regimes must be recognised as having greater priority within the international community as a whole.

CHAPTER EIGHT

THE RIGHT TO PEACE AS AN EMERGING SOLIDARITY RIGHT

Theo van Boven

1. *Components of Solidarity*

1.1. *Towards the Law of All Humankind*

In his learned writings Karel Wellens has given prominent attention to the principle of solidarity in international law.[1] He thoroughly analysed the principle of solidarity in the light of common responsibilities of states, international organisations, peoples and nations, and civil society. He outlined these common responsibilities as a basic premise in general international law, but also as an expression of firm commitment anchored in special branches of international law, notably international human rights law, international humanitarian law, refugee law, the law of development and the law on the maintenance of international peace and security. In the concluding words of one of his articles, Karel Wellens brought it all together under the vision of Otto Kimmenich who, referring to global solidarity in refugee protection, expressed some fifty years ago the hope that international law as a result of current insights and endeavours would be transformed from a law of sovereign states into the law of all humankind.[2]

The principle of solidarity may be difficult to define in legal terms as entailing rights and duties, but it is a concept that progressively moves forward in asserting common rights and responsibilities and in the shaping of an international community. Legal and moral notions with strong solidarity contents are, among others, common heritage of mankind, *ius cogens* and obligations *erga omnes*, and the recognition of the universality and the inclusiveness of all human rights. They have in common that they represent values to be attached

---

[1] See e.g. Karel Wellens, 'Solidarity as a Constitutional Principle: Its Expanding Role and Inherent Limitations', in: Ronald St.J. MacDonald and Douglas M. Johnston (eds.), *Towards World Constitutionalism: Issues in the Legal Ordering of The World Community*, Leiden: Martinus Nijhoff Publishers 2005, p. 775 ff.; Karel Wellens, 'Solidarity as a (Re-)Emerging Constitutional Principle: Some Further Reflections', in: Rüdiger Wolfrum and Chie Kojima (eds.), *Solidarity: A Structural Principle of International Law*, Berlin-Heidelberg: Springer 2010, p. 3 ff.

[2] Wellens (2010), supra n. 1, p. 38, quoting Kimmenich: "Es besteht daher die Hoffnung, dass das Völkerrecht durch die Bestrebungen unserer Zeit aus einem Recht der souveränen Staaten zu einem Recht der gesamten Menschheit verwandelt wird."

to the international community as a whole, to the life and basic means of subsistence of present and future generations, and to the development of a democratic and equitable international order.

1.2. *A Democratic and Equitable International Order*

It should be noted that the United Nations Millennium Declaration of 8 September 2000 included as fundamental values essential to international relations in the twenty-first century – among freedom, equality, tolerance, respect for nature –, the principle of solidarity. The General Assembly referred to solidarity in the following terms:

> Global challenges must be managed in a way that distributes costs and burdens fairly, in accordance with basic principles of equity and social justice, that those who suffer or benefit the least deserve help from those who benefit the most.[3]

In the same terms, the UN General Assembly listed in another significant resolution the principle of solidarity as a fundamental value among the constituent elements of a democratic and equitable international order.[4] The General Assembly mentioned, in addition to solidarity, a series of other requirements as constituent elements for the realisation of a democratic and equitable international order, among them the right of all peoples to self-determination; the right of peoples and nations to permanent sovereignty over their natural resources; the right of every human person and all peoples to development; the right of all peoples to peace; the right to equitable participation of all, without any discrimination, in domestic and global decision making; the right of every person and all peoples to a healthy environment; the enjoyment by everyone of ownership of the common heritage of mankind.[5] Further, the resolution stressed, in the same words as the Vienna Declaration adopted by the World Conference on Human Rights in 1993, that all human rights are universal, indivisible and interdependent and interrelated.[6]

As is evident from the wording of the General Assembly, basic principles of equity and social justice are core values of national and international solidarity. They are intrinsic components of composite rights combining individual and collective aspects. Among these rights are the right to self-determination, the right to development, the right to peace and the right to a healthy environment. These composite rights are by their nature linked with the principle of solidarity as a fundamental value, and may well be qualified as solidarity rights.

---

[3] United Nations Millennium Declaration, General Assembly resolution 55/2, par. 6 (8 September 2000).

[4] UN General Assembly resolution 59/193, par. 4 under (f) (20 December 2004).

[5] UN General Assembly resolution 59/193, par. 4 (20 December 2004).

[6] UN General Assembly resolution 59/193, par. 6 (20 December 2004).

1.3. *Human Rights and International Solidarity*

A growing attachment to the principle of international solidarity may also be inferred from the appointment in 2005 by the UN Commission on Human Rights of an independent expert on human rights and international solidarity. The work of the independent expert, whose mandate was renewed by the UN Human Rights Council, is aimed at the preparation of a draft declaration on the right of peoples and individuals to international solidarity. As the independent expert argued, obligations based on international solidarity, where they concern the most fundamental human rights, go beyond the limits of state borders "as they are owed erga omnes rather than inter partes."[7] In a series of resolutions relating to the work of the independent expert on human rights and international solidarity, the UN Human Rights Council reaffirmed the recognition, set forth in the Millennium Declaration,[8] of the fundamental value of solidarity essential to international relations in the twenty-first century.[9] As will be indicated further below, a clear relationship may be construed between the right to peace and the principle of solidarity – or, to put it in a broader perspective, a case is to be made in favour of the right to peace as an emerging solidarity right.

2. *Development, Peace and Security, Human Rights*

2.1. *The Three Pillars of the UN System*

The right to peace is a recurring notion and theme in resolutions of United Nations bodies, notably the General Assembly as the largest representative organ of the World Organisation. Most notable is the Declaration on the Right of Peoples to Peace which "solemnly proclaimed that the peoples of our planet have a sacred right to peace".[10] The Charter of the United Nations prominently lists the maintenance of international peace and security among the purposes of the Organization. While the United Nations Charter, according to the opening words of its preamble, was proclaimed in the name of "We the Peoples of the United Nations", this constitutional document is largely state-oriented, and presupposes and prescribes inter-state cooperation. Against this background, it is noteworthy that where UN statements make reference to the right to peace, this right is attributed to peoples as the beneficiaries. But, pursuant

[7] *Human Rights and International Solidarity*, Report of the Independent Expert to the Twelfth Session of the UN Human Rights Council, UN doc. A/HRC/12/27, par. 42 (22 July 2009).

[8] See n. 3 supra.

[9] UN Human Rights Council resolutions 6/3 (27 September 2007), 9/2 (24 September 2008), 12/9 (1 October 2009).

[10] UN General Assembly resolution 39/11 (12 November 1984).

to the Declaration on the Right of Peoples to Peace, the preservation of this right and the promotion of its implementation constitute a fundamental obligation of each state.[11]

In order to explore the contextual framework of the right to peace as an emerging solidarity right, the concepts of development, peace and security and human rights command themselves. In this regard, the visionary report of former UN Secretary-General Kofi Annan entitled *In Larger Freedom: Towards Development and Human Rights for All* offers pertinent insights.[12] It builds on the principal notions of freedom from want and freedom from fear which, as part of F.D. Roosevelt's heritage, are intrinsically interrelated, and found their normative and ethical expression in the Universal Declaration of Human Rights. The report stresses the inextricable link between development, security and human rights as basic preconditions for peoples, nations and individuals to conduct life in larger freedom. A fundamental assumption reads: "Larger freedom implies that men and women everywhere have the right to be governed by their own consent, under law, in a society where all individuals can, without discrimination or retribution, speak, worship and associate freely. They must also be free from want – so that the death sentences of extreme poverty and infectious disease are lifted from their lives – and free from fear – so that their lives and livelihood are not ripped by violence and war. Indeed, all people have the right to security and to development".[13] The document then continues and heralds:

> We will not enjoy development without security, we will not enjoy security without development, and we will not enjoy either without respect for human rights.[14]

The same words were thereupon echoed in the Outcome Document of the 2005 World Summit which stated:

> We acknowledge that peace and security, development and human rights are the pillars of the United Nations system and the foundations for collective security and well-being. We recognize that development, peace and security and human rights are interlinked and mutually reinforcing.[15]

2.2. *Human Security*

A striking element that figures prominently in these quotations is the notion of 'security', or more precisely 'the right to security'. It is obvious that the right to security and the right to peace, though not identical, are closely connected,

---

[11] Ibid., par. 2.
[12] UN doc. A/59/2005.
[13] Ibid., par. 15.
[14] Ibid., par. 17.
[15] UN General Assembly resolution 60/1, par. 9 (16 September 2005).

and in many ways overlapping. Nevertheless, the concept of security carries also adverse connotations. It must be recalled that authoritarian regimes massacred, tortured and deported people in the name of national security. Even democratic regimes disregarded non-derogable human rights in the name of national security. However, this is not the type of security that is to be associated with the right to peace. In fact, a secure state is necessary to protect all its inhabitants, but any argument which may actually imply that human rights must necessarily be subordinated to the security of the state must be met with the greatest circumspection. The security to be closely linked to the right to peace is human security. While security in this sense is to be considered an essential underlying component of the right to peace, it forms part of a wider spectrum that also comprises development and human rights. These three pillars mutually reinforce one another, and their further implementation is a common responsibility to be carried by states, civil society and the international community.[16]

2.3. *Responsibility to Protect*

A very special responsibility with direct implications for the right to peace is the protection of populations from the most conscience-shocking atrocity crimes: genocide, war crimes, ethnic cleansing and other crimes against humanity. Building on a recommendation in a report of the High-Level Panel on Threats, Challenges and Change,[17] the Secretary-General emphasised in his own *In Larger Freedom* report the need to take action against actual or imminent large-scale human rights violations under the name of Responsibility to Protect (RtoP). In the process leading to the 2005 UN World Summit, he urged the Heads of State and Government to embrace RtoP and stated that it is first and foremost the responsibility of individual States to protect persons within their jurisdictions, but that this responsibility shifts to the international community if a State is unwilling or unable to provide such protection.[18] The UN World Summit did thereupon reach agreement on a text outlining and conditioning RtoP. It followed in essence the recommendation of the Secretary-General, and RtoP was thus included in the Summit Outcome Document.[19] RtoP as a newly emerging principle of international law can be considered – to quote a report of the Netherlands Advisory Council on International Affairs – as

[16] See also Wellens (2010), supra n. 1, p. 27.

[17] *UN High-Level Panel on Threats, Challenges and Change, A More Secure World: Our Shared Responsibility*, United Nations, New York, 2004.

[18] UN doc. A/59/2005, Annex, For decision by Heads of State and Government, par. 7 (b).

[19] UN General Assembly resolution 60/1, par. 138–139.

> an overarching principle that defines the entire fabric of legal, moral and political obligations and responsibilities of States and the international community in the case of specific, actual or imminent, large-scale human rights violations.[20]

The RtoP principle is based on a progressive, people-oriented interpretation of the UN Charter principle of national sovereignty that not only implies the notion of non-intervention, but also, and above all, the responsibility to protect the lives and the security of people. Such protection is the primary duty of states, separately and jointly, but in situations where national authorities are manifestly failing to protect populations from genocide, war crimes, ethnic cleansing and other crimes against humanity, the international community should step in to take collective action, in a timely and decisive manner, through the Security Council, in accordance with the UN Charter. RtoP puts great emphasis on preventive measures as a means to forestall mass atrocity crimes, and attributes preventive and protective responsibilities to regional and international capacities as constituent parts and partners of the international community.

The responsibilities of states to ensure respect for human rights of all persons under their jurisdiction are fairly well anchored in international law, although as Karel Wellens quite rightly observed: "(…) the general State responsibility regime is not very satisfactory from a solidarity point of view".[21] In fact, the law on the responsibility to protect persons living under the jurisdiction of other states is still in a stage of evolution. Here the responsibility of the international community, as embodied in the membership of the United Nations as a whole, comes into play. The responsibility to defend and protect community interests has strong roots in the principle of solidarity which, as it now stands, combines profound ethical values with growing legal implications. This combination of ethical and legal aspects is inherent in the notion of 'international community' which, as Karel Wellens asserted, is to be distinguished from 'international society'.[22]

3. *The Human Right to Peace*

3.1. *The Role of Civil Society*

Many human rights instruments were conceived in the minds, and in pursuit of the aspirations, of interested and committed sectors of civil society.

[20] Advisory Council of International Affairs, *The Netherlands and the Responsibility to Protect: The Reponsibility to Protect People from Gross Atrocities*, Report No. 70, June 2010, p. 17.

[21] Wellens (2010), supra n. 1, p. 27.

[22] Ibid., p. 7–9. In fact, this distinction between international community and international society is most clearly expressed in the German vocabulary: 'Internationale Gemeinschaft' and 'Internationale Gesellschaft'.

They brought their concerns to the United Nations and other international fora. Thus, the origins of standards to enhance the rights of women, children, migrants, disabled persons, indigenous peoples can be traced back to initiatives of civil society actors, who succeeded in seeing their concerns and aspirations translated into international normative pronouncements. The outcome of such processes involving civil society attained broad legitimacy. Similarly, important sectors of the human rights movement worked closely together with the peace movement in campaigns against weapons of mass destruction and other cruel and inhuman devices having indiscriminate and fatal effects on innocent human beings. This led to treaties outlawing land mines and cluster bombs.[23] A process of the same kind is underway with a view to clarify and codify the right to peace and to give substance to its scope and its implementation as a common endeavour. This process is taking shape through interactions between a coalition of engaged sectors of civil society, with the Spanish Society of International Human Rights Law as the principal initiator and actor, and the UN Human Rights Council together with its Advisory Committee.

In a series of resolutions the UN Human Rights Council underscored the promotion of the right of peoples to peace.[24] The Council repeatedly reaffirmed the solemn proclamation of the 1984 Declaration of the Right of Peoples to Peace to the effect that "the peoples of our planet have a sacred right to peace". The Council also continued to emphasise the well-known pronouncement of the 2005 World Summit Outcome Document that "peace and security, development and human rights are the pillars of the UN system and the foundation for collective security and well-being". The Council further repeated, in a resolution on the promotion of a democratic and equitable international order, much of the content of a General Assembly resolution[25] on the same subject matter, which enumerated a series of constituent requirements of a democratic and equitable international order, among them the 'right of all peoples to peace' and 'international solidarity, as a right of peoples and individuals'.[26] As one commentator aptly observed, the Council approached the development of the right to peace as an emerging right from a perspective of international collective and individual solidarity.[27]

---

[23] See e.g. 1997 Convention on the Prohibition of the Use, Stockpiling, Production and Transfer of Anti-Personnel Mines and on their Destruction, concluded in Oslo, opened for signature in Ottawa, entered into force 1 March 1999 (156 state parties as of April 2011); 2008 Convention against Cluster Munitions, entered into force 1 August 2010, 55 ratifications and 53 additional signatories (as of April 2011).

[24] UN Human Rights Council resolutions 8/9 (18 June 2008), 11/4 (12 June 2009), 14/3 (17 June 2010), 17/16 (15 July 2011).

[25] See n. 4 supra.

[26] UN Human Rights Council resolution 8/5, para. 3 (d) en 3 (f) (18 June 2008).

[27] Carlos Villán Durán, 'The Human Right to Peace in the Work of the Human Rights Council', in: Carlos Villán Durán and Carmelo Faleh Pérez (eds.), *Contribuciones Regionales para una Declaración Universal del Derecho Humano a la Paz*, Luarca: Asociación Española para el Derecho Internacional de los Derechos Humanos 2010, p. 275.

It is one way to carry on a process relating to the right to peace in general and contextual terms, as is apparent in declarations and statements of the UN General Assembly and the Human Rights Council, but it is another more constructive way to give concrete content to the right to peace in terms of rights and responsibilities. It is the latter approach that committed sectors of civil society are pursuing with the cooperation and input of independent experts from a variety of legal, educational and cultural backgrounds. This is a process aimed at unfolding the normative content in a legal instrument on the human right to peace. Such focus on the human right to peace, as distinct from the right of peoples to peace, reveals different orientations and approaches which, as is argued further below, are not mutually incompatible. Successive stages of civil society standard-setting efforts relating to the human right to peace led to the Luarca Declaration (October 2006), the Bilbao Declaration (February 2010), the Barcelona Declaration (June 2010) and, ultimately, the Santiago Declaration adopted by an international congress held in Santiago de Compostela in December 2010.[28]

3.2. *Towards Codification of the Right to Peace*

It is noteworthy that the activities of civil society organisations for the promotion of the right to peace and towards the codification of this right found recognition by the Human Rights Council.[29] Thus, the Council requested the Office of the UN High Commissioner for Human Rights to convene a workshop on the right of peoples to peace that had as one of its tasks the further clarification of the content and scope of this right.[30] Further, the Council requested its Advisory Committee, in consultation with Member States, civil society, academia and relevant stakeholders, to prepare a draft declaration on the right of peoples to peace, and to report on the progress thereon to the Council at its June session of 2011.[31] For that purpose the Advisory Committee established a drafting group of four of its members. The progress report submitted by the Advisory Committee to the June 2011 session of the Human Rights Council is significant for various reasons.[32]

---

[28] For extensive background information, see Carlos Villán Durán and Carmelo Faleh Pérez (eds.), *Contribuciones Regionales para una Declaración Universal del Derecho Humano a la Paz*, Luarca: Asociación Española para el Derecho Internacional de los Derechos Humanos 2010; for the text of the Santiago Declaration, see <www.aedidh.org>.

[29] See Villán Durán, supra n. 27.

[30] UN Human Rights Council resolution 11/4 (17 June 2009). For the report of the workshop, held in December 2009, see UN doc. A/HRC/14/18.

[31] UN Human Rights Council resolution 14/3 (17 June 2010).

[32] *Progress Report on the Right of Peoples to Peace*, UN doc. A/HRC/17/39 (28 March 2011).

First, the progress report suggests to conceive peace as both the absence of organised violence within a country or between countries, as well as the comprehensive and effective protection of human rights, gender equality and social justice, economic well-being and free and widespread expression of different cultural values, without discrimination and restraints.[33]

Second, eleven guiding dimensions of the draft declaration are proposed, namely international peace and security; disarmament; human security; resistance to oppression; peacekeeping; conscientious objection and freedom of religion and belief; private military and security companies; peace education; development; the environment, in particular climate change; the rights of victims and vulnerable groups.[34]

Third, the progress report does not content itself by enumerating guiding dimensions, but makes great efforts to translate them into an elaborate series of proposed standards, thus providing a normative framework for the right to peace and setting out a number of options for monitoring and implementation.[35] A review of the guiding dimensions together with the proposed standards reveals that the authors of the progress report relied in many ways on standard-setting work already performed by civil society organisations and experts, which culminated, as mentioned above, in the Santiago Declaration on the Human Right to Peace.[36] The progress report provides ample proof of interaction between civil society and the UN Human Rights Council and its Advisory Committee. In fact, the report acknowledges the important contribution of civil society to the international codification of the right to peace within the United Nations, and pays particular tribute to the world campaign on the human right to peace carried out by the Spanish Society for International Human Rights Law with the support of a large number of non-governmental organisations.[37]

A fourth significant aspect of the progress report is its reaffirmation that the right to peace has its legal basis in the Charter of the United Nations, in international human rights law and numerous resolutions approved by the General Assembly, the Commission on Human Rights and the Human Rights Council.[38]

3.3. *Peoples and Individuals as Rights Holders*

The progress report recognises that the right to peace has a double dimension – collective and individual –, and that the rights holders should be

[33] Ibid., par. 17.
[34] Ibid., par. 18–64.
[35] Ibid., par. 65–71.
[36] See n. 28 supra.
[37] Advisory Committee, Progress Report, par. 12.
[38] Ibid., par. 3–4 and par. 18–23.

both peoples and individuals.[39] As mentioned earlier in this chapter, this double dimension of the right to peace raises questions as to the legal nature of this right. Is it a human right or a right of peoples? The latter is standard UN terminology, while the former is propounded in codification work of civil society. Or does the right to peace have a double dimension as a collective and individual right? This appears to be the assumption of the Human Rights Council's Advisory Committee.

There are indeed good arguments to attach to the right to peace both a collective dimension in the sense of a right of peoples and an individual dimension as a human right. This dual ownership of a right is also inherent in the right to development, as is clearly expressed in the UN Declaration on the Right to Development.[40] Article 1 (1) of this Declaration states:

> The right to development is an inalienable right by virtue of which every human person and all peoples are entitled to participate in, contribute to, and enjoy economic, social, cultural and political development, in which all human rights and fundamental freedoms can be fully realized.

Article 2 (1) of the same Declaration reads: "The human person is the central subject of development and should be the active participant and beneficiary of the right to development". In the more recent UN Declaration on the Rights of Indigenous Peoples[41] numerous articles refer to indigenous peoples and to indigenous individuals as rights holders, separately or in conjunction. It may well be argued that composite rights (or 'third generation rights'), such as the right to self-determination, the right to development, the right to an healthy environment and the right to peace, imply by their nature collective and individual dimensions. Recognition of the dual nature of the right to peace as a human right and a peoples' right could be an important step so as to reach wider political acceptance of the right to peace as an emerging solidarity right.

4. *Concluding Remarks*

It is submitted in this contribution that the right to peace falls in the category of emerging solidarity rights, under the umbrella of the international community as the overarching fabric of all humankind. Human security is an essential component of the right to peace. It is also understood that the right to peace has strong underlying moral and ethical values, but that such right would create ephemeral illusions if not anchored in international and domestic law. Therefore, the steps now undertaken to shape and define the contents

[39] Ibid., Annex II B.
[40] UN General Assembly resolution 41/128 (4 December 1986).
[41] UN General Assembly resolution 61/295 (13 December 2007).

and the implications of the human and peoples' right to peace, in terms of rights and obligations and of right holders and duty-holders, together with concrete measures of implementation, merit constructive support. However, the process now underway is still facing reservations along the lines of traditional North-South divide. It follows a pattern of the past when other composite (or 'third generation') rights were brought into the realm of human rights, notably the right to self-determination and the right to development. Now that the right to peace is brought to the fore, previous counter-arguments are repeated, such as the impropriety of human rights forums to deal with the matter and the mixing up of individual and collective rights. It would seem, however, that these differences are not insurmountable. If further codification of the right to peace goes in the direction – as the Santiago Declaration and the Human Rights Council's Advisory Committee are indicating – of recognising the dual nature of the right to peace as a human right and a peoples' right, such development may well bring about a broader consensus.[42] In final analysis, the right to peace not only symbolises but also strengthens solidarity among nations, peoples and human beings. It is universalist and inclusive; it is based on the premise that human rights, security and development must go hand in hand.

[42] See in more detail Carlos Villás Durán, supra n. 27, p. 287–291.

CHAPTER NINE

THE EVOLUTION OF *LIBERTÉ, ÉGALITÉ* AND *FRATERNITÉ* IN THE INTERNATIONAL COMMUNITY

Rein Müllerson

1. *Introduction*

An ideal society, like an ideal world, is an impossibility not only in practice but also in theory, as an ideal, since there are as many ideals as there are philosophers, politicians or lawyers, not to mention different religions, cultures and civilisations. Then, the schemes of ideal societies like John Rawls' 'justice as fairness' society drawn up by people acting under 'the veil of ignorance' (where the participants do not know whether they are men or women, black or white, Christians, Jews, Muslims or atheists) or other contract theories of society are at best suitable for a particular type of society on which the analysis is based, i.e. a Western society. Moreover, as Amartya Sen has convincingly shown,[1] only by comparing concrete societies and not by building abstract models can we come to tentative conclusions about which society is more just, better responding to various needs and interests of their members.[2] John Rawls's 'transcendental institutionalism', looking for a perfect society using abstract theorising, is not only theoretically weak; its application in practice concentrates attention on building perfect institutions without analysing what is feasible and whether these institutions work in varying contexts.[3] There are

[1] Amartya Sen, *The Idea of Justice*, London: Allen Lane 2009.

[2] Shortly before his death in 2007, Richard Rorty wrote: "Followers of Dewey like myself would like to praise parliamentary democracy and the welfare state as very good things, but only on the basis of invidious comparison with suggested concrete alternatives, not on the basis of claims that these institutions are truer to human nature, or more rational, or in better accord with the universal moral law, than feudalism or totalitarianism" (Richard Rorty, *Philosophical Papers* (Volume 1), Cambridge: Cambridge University Press 2007, p. 211). One of his arguments used to be: it is theocracies that lose refugees to us, and not vice versa.

[3] One has to consider the situation in Sudan, Afghanistan, Somalia etc. to see the weaknesses of Rawls' theories. Even if we take 'easier' cases such as Kyrgyzstan, Tajikistan or Uzbekistan, we clearly see the limits of the application of Rawls' criteria or other liberal-democratic concepts. It is true that in one of his last works, *The Law of Peoples*, Cambridge (Mass.): Harvard University Press 1999, Rawls distinguished between liberal-democratic societies, decent hierarchical societies, outlaw states, burdened societies and benevolent absolutisms and did not extend his liberal concepts to all these societies. My rejection of some basic premises of Rawls' theory of justice (here I find myself in the good company of Amartya Sen, John Gray and others) does not mean that I do not appreciate Rawls' contribution to moral and political philosophy as well as law and enjoy the depth of his insights. Such an attitude can be explained by the fact that the

no axioms or laws of nature waiting to be discovered from which to start measuring different societies. All the yardsticks human beings use to evaluate dissimilar societies are historical and comparative, even if we consider them theoretical. All the attempts of creating abstract axioms, universal in time and space, only reflect particular preferences of their authors.[4] In practice, all the attempts to build an ideal society have led to tyranny. As practice is at the end of the day the only source from which we can draw theoretical conclusions, this is an additional argument in favour of our point that an ideal society is not only practical but also a theoretical impossibility.

However, this does not mean that there cannot be any blueprints of fairer and better societies that may serve as guidelines to be adapted, mutatis mutandis, to particularities of various societies. Using such historical and comparative approach it seems to be intuitively correct (and every intuition has its roots in one's own or humankind's practice) that the holy trinity of the French Revolution: *liberté, égalité and fraternité* are all necessary qualities or characteristics of any modern society. Although in human history there have been societies where none of these qualities have flourished, today a society that completely or substantially lacks any of these characteristics is not a comfortable place to live in and in extreme cases it may even forfeit its right to be called society. Of course, these characteristics come in different proportions and combinations; moreover they often clash and sometimes even try to cancel each other out; however, in today's world no society worthy of its name can completely sacrifice them.

2. *The End of the Cold War and the Triumph of* Liberté *over* Égalité

The collapse of the Soviet Union and the communist ideology occurred at the time when Thatcherism and Reaganomics, i.e. free market ideologies and practices, were prevalent in the Western world. This had not always been the case. The post-WWII Europe had for long periods and to a great extent been social-democratic (and flourishing as such) and even in the much more

legacy of talented and honest thinkers is often of lasting import even if some of their premises may be rejected.

[4] All values, morals, ethical norms as well as social theories are historical phenomena and social constructs; even if today we consider some of them axiomatic and natural, take them for granted, do not question their validity and are unable to discover their origins at the dawn of human evolution. They all have emerged because they have served, were deemed to serve or continue to serve some instrumental purposes. The American philosopher Daniel Dennett insightfully observes that "[b]iology insists on delving beneath the surface of 'intrinsic' values and asking why they exist, and any answer that is supported by the facts has the effect of showing that the value in question is – or once was – really instrumental, not intrinsic, even if we do not see it that way" (Daniel Dennett, *Breaking the Spell: Religion as a Natural Phenomenon*, London: Penguin 2007, p. 69).

individualistic United States the Rooseveltian New Deal, John Kennedy's "Ask not what your country can do for you – ask what you can do for your country", and Lyndon Johnson's Great Society, on the one hand, and Reaganomics continued by Presidents Clinton and especially George W. Bush, on the other, seemed to belong not only to different eras but also to different continents. It has to be emphasised that both the American programmes to eliminate poverty and racial injustice or those addressing medical and educational problems and policies of European social-democratic governments were not in any way steps towards communism, as their opponents claimed; on the contrary, they were, *inter alia*, pre-emptive anti-communist (anti-totalitarian) measures. The unfettered market's opposite has been state socialism and communism. The welfare state and development of economic and social rights was a response of Western European capitalism to the spectre of communism haunting Europe[5] at the time when Russia's fate was sealed by the communist response.

However, as the collapse of communism happened when the West was in one of its libertarian[6] phases, most post-communist countries also embarked on this road, seeing in it not only the most promising but as their only possible way of development. Moreover, when one extreme (in this case the state-dominated planned economy) fails it is quite natural for many to seek refuge in another extreme that seems to be as far away from the previous extreme as possible. Not paying enough attention to the fact the world is not flat, that even in an allegorical sense it is round and curvy (where opposite extremes may be closer to each other than some mid-way stations), many post-communist societies chose Thatcherism or Reaganomics as their lodestars. To an extent it may have been even necessary; if one wants to straighten something up it is often necessary to bend it in the opposite direction far over the median line. What is wrong is the belief that this new situation is normal or the only correct one. Unfortunately, this is what many politicians and social

---

[5] One of John Maynard Keynes' biographers, Peter Clark writes that Keynes, who "saw antiquated anti-capitalist dogmas as no better than the dogma of *laissez-faire*" wanted "to save capitalism from itself" (P. Clark, *Keynes: The Twentieth Century's Most Influential Economist*, London: Bloomsbury 2009, p. 68). The British welfare state, writes Anthony Giddens, "[was] created partly to dispel the socialist menace" (Anthony Giddens, *The Third Way*, Cambridge: Polity Press 1998, p. 111). This does not mean, however, that the traditional welfare state as it was known in Europe is necessarily a proper answer to today's challenges. In many cases, the welfare state has turned into what is sometimes called a 'nanny state' in need of substantial reforms.

[6] In this chapter, I use closely related terms such as liberalism, libertarianism and neo-liberalism, not always strictly distinguishing between them. To put it in a general and simplified way, which hopefully suffices for the purposes of this contribution, it may be said that neo-liberalism is a political, legal, and economic doctrine premised upon a rethinking and reassertion of classical liberalism as defined in writings of John Locke, John Stewart Mill and others, which became influential in the 1980s. Libertarians are the most prominent neo-liberals and enthusiastic advocates of the rights the individual against those of the 'coercive state'.

theorists believe.[7] For them, ideology replaces pragmatic approaches based on the study of facts. What will happen in such a case warned *The Economist*. A year ago it wrote of Margaret Thatcher: "She was much more of a pragmatist than is often credited; it was when she ditched that approach to pursue the Platonic ideal of Thatcherism that she was undone."[8] Thatcherism failed when the British Prime Minister became a convinced Thatcherite and started to believe that Hayek's theories (or her interpretation of Hayek) and Keith Joseph's policies were if not universally true then at least what Britain needed now and forever.

Moreover, social recipes that are based on the analysis of some societies are not necessarily transferable to other societies. Speaking of the widening stratification of the Estonian society, Märt Väljataga for example, writes that what makes the increasing inequality especially saddening is the fact that the principle of equality seems to have been historically programmed in our national idea.[9] In my opinion, this comments rings true also for many other societies, which have borrowed recipes that had worked in different contexts. It is important to note that most libertarian theories have their origins in the Anglo-Saxon philosophical, political and legal thought. Lord Raymond Plant has argued that neo-liberal theories and practices are "closely related to ideas about the spontaneous order, the private law, the common law, the negative liberty, the market order, the fragmented and dispersed nature of knowledge, etc. together with the claim that both common law and legislation should be guided more in the direction of the rule of law than has been the case under socialist and social democratic regimes".[10] The context of elaboration of such theories means that they are not necessarily universal or even universalisable, i.e. fit to be applied in all societies irrespective of their history, religion and political, ethical or aesthetic background. Another British philosopher, Michael Oakeshott, has shown that ideas of liberty and individualism are not metaphysically grounded, are not universal like laws of nature, but are based on historical peculiarities of European development.[11]

---

[7] The current financial and economic crisis has renewed interest in intellectual giants of the past. Left leaning liberals have found inspiration in the works of John Maynard Keynes and Karl Marx while those on the right have rediscovered Friedrich von Hayek, Joseph Schumpeter or even Ayn Rand. Reprints of their works abound and new biographies are regularly published. The first are used to show the dangers inherent in 'free market' while the latter warn against what will happen if the market is distorted by state's interference. Such widespread use of dead philosophers and economists means that often ideology is replacing independent analysis and research. We can find a great deal of that also in Estonia where many, having rejected Soviet style collectivism and internationalism that were not only imposed but also distorted, today find solace in right-wing and nationalistic ideologies.

[8] 'The Tories' Futile Quest to Find an Ideology', *The Economist*, 20 August 2009.

[9] Märt Väljataga, 'In Three Years from Idyll to Crisis', *Sirp*, 1 April 2010, p. 3.

[10] Raymond Plant, 'The Neoliberal State', Oxford: Oxford University Press 2009, p. 24.

[11] Michael Oakeshott, 'On Human Conduct', Oxford: Clarendon Press 1975.

In this context and because of the influence of neo-liberal ideas in many Eastern and Central European countries, including Estonia, it is of interest to note that grand-fathers of the neo-liberal thought such as Ludwig von Mises, Friedrich Hayek, Joseph Schumpeter, Karl Popper and Peter Drucker were all of Central European origin (three of them came from Vienna) who found political refuge from totalitarianism in the Anglo-Saxon world. There they found their intellectual refuge in the generalisation and universalisation of the Anglo-Saxon libertarian ideas, often making them more extreme, straightforward, less nuanced and balanced than originals elaborated by, say, Adam Smith or John Stewart Mill. And those Central Europeans were intellectual giants who sought a remedy from the totalitarian serfdom in another extreme – libertarianism without properly analysing whether these ideas could take root in societies with different histories, traditions, religions etc. The reaction of today's Eastern and Central European Thatcherites and Reaganites to the totalitarian past of their countries has been much more reflexive and much less learned.

This may be, at least in the case of Estonia, partly explained, by the incompetence (or the lack of intellectual capacity) of market liberals. In such a case libertarian economic policies may have some justification; sometimes it may be better not to govern at all than to govern incompetently. In the foreign policy of our country such incompetence or the lack of capacity can be seen in having two quite distinctive strands. In our relations with the West we often follow what the most hawkish (in politics) and libertarian (in economics) forces prescribe (sometimes, though not always, we simply lack the freedom of manoeuvre); in our dealings with our former boss – Russia – we are invariably negative, if not hostile. It is not only our admiration for all things Western and rejection of what comes from the East what explains such attitude. Partly it can be also explained by the easiness and simplicity of such knee-jerk policies. It is quite obvious that Russia is not an easy partner, especially for her much smaller neighbours whom she still regards as ungrateful relatives. The lack of independent foreign policy capacity and incompetence, combined with negative historical memories, causes some of those Russia's neighbours that were recently under her sway to have reflexively negative attitude towards whatever Russia says or does. In that respect the recent warming of the relations between Poland and Russia may be a sign of Poland (and to an extent Russia probably too) becoming more mature and self-confident, since often it is the lack of self-confidence that makes one prickly.

James Dale Davidson and Lord William Rees-Mogg (the former editor-in-chief of *The Times*) at the end of the 1990s, when the prevailing ideology was 'the freer the market, the merrier', published a book 'The Sovereign Individual', a kind of neo-liberal Manifesto, where they advocated unfettered markets.[12] They saw it as inevitable, as a universal blessing. In the world the authors saw emerging, they welcomed the fact that there would be no citizens, only customers. Among those customers there was to be a small minority of 'sovereign individuals' and other 'rational individuals' who would flee jurisdictions that tax them. The nation-state – "the main parasite and predator upon the individual at the end of the twentieth century"– they predicted, "will become feeble". The United Nations would be liquidated soon after the turn of the millennium, and it would be a 'winners take all world' where most people are losers and only 'sovereign individuals' will be winners. "[D]emocracy as it has been known in the nineteenth and twentieth centuries is destined to disappear," they prophesied.[13] True, much of this reads like social science fiction. Albeit that, as in many a 'sci-fi' novel, Davidson and Rees-Mogg, though quite grotesquely, did grasp some of the world's potentially dangerous tendencies. One thing they did not mention, or did not want to notice, was that such 'paradise' was at that time being realized in Yeltsin's Russia where emerging 'sovereign' individuals (most sovereign amongst them became called 'oligarchs') transferred their billions of dollars to off-shore bank accounts and built for themselves enclosures beyond the perimeters of which they were often gunned down; there was a small group of winners (quite within the percentages described by the authors) who took it all, while the majority of the population were losers many of whom lost everything. Most former KGB agents worked not for the Government but for 'sovereign' individuals (maybe it is not even ironic that it took also a former KGB officer to start straightening up the anarchy Russia was descending into and in the process quite predictably bent it to the opposite direction). But the point is that these authors not only did not see any ethical or moral problems in welcoming their predicted paradise for 'sovereign individuals' (obviously hell for the rest), they did not even think of possible responses of those who would not be lucky (clever, talented, ruthless, unscrupulous) enough to belong to the chosen. This is what happens when liberté, especially if understood as economic liberties, prevails over other components of the trinity.

Moreover, libertarians and neo-liberals understand liberty in its negative sense only as 'freedom from', freedom from outside interference, be it by the state or somebody else. This is also a typically Anglo-Saxon approach, though also mostly advanced by those for whom the Anglo-Saxon world gave political refuge (e.g. Isaiah Berlin[14]). However, so-called 'positive freedom' or 'freedom to', i.e. freedom to do whatever individuals chose to do with their lives is not

---

[12] James Dale Davidson, William Rees-Mogg, *The Sovereign Individual*, London: Macmillan 1997.

[13] Ibid., p. 331.

[14] See his 'Two Concepts of Liberty', in: Isaiah Berlin, *Four Essays on Liberty*, Oxford: Oxford University Press 1969.

less important for individual autonomy. People are unfree not only when the state interferes with their choices, their life-styles. They are unfree also when they are uneducated, unemployed or otherwise disenfranchised or incapacitated. Therefore a society that cares only about 'freedom from' is not only unequal; for the majority of the people it is also unfree.[15]

3. Égalité *as a* Conditio Sine Qua Non *of Democracy*

The opposite of the totalitarian state that controls and attempts to regulate everything is not the liberal-democratic state but the situation where the life of men, according to Thomas Hobbes, was solitary, poor, nasty, brutish, and short. There was no contract between those nasty and brutish men to establish a commonwealth, as Hobbes called it; general interests of survival of all and particular interests of those who were nastier and more brutish forced the latter to develop more and more sophisticated institutions. In today's world most societies have institutions that on this spectrum are somewhere between the totalitarian state and the Hobbesian anarchical *bellum omnium contra omnes*. From time to time some societies descend into the pre-state anarchy while a few are still totalitarian. Many states are today liberal democracies while some may be called illiberal democracies or semi-democracies (semi-autocracies). An important point is that without the state there will be the Hobbesian original state of affairs. When the role and the power of the state decline below a certain level, the society may find itself in a free-fall. If the functions of the state is curbed beyond a certain point those who are cleverer, luckier, stronger, nastier, more ruthless will gain the upper hand. We saw it in Yeltsin's Russia where the oligarchs, organised crime groups and privatised KGB men ruled the country; we have seen it recently in Kyrgyzstan that recently had been the Western darling in the Central Asia;[16] we saw it also, of course in a different

[15] Libertarians strictly separate rights and liberties from capabilities. However, authors such as Amartya Sen, Martha Nussbaum, Raymond Plant and others have shown that such a separation is not even theoretically possible, to say nothing about the fact that in practice rights and liberties without the ability (capacity) to enjoy them are meaningless for those who lack such ability. Capabilities, Amartya Sen affirms, are "notions of freedom in the positive sense: what real opportunities you have regarding the life you may lead" ('The Standard of Living: Lecture I, Concepts and Critiques', 'The Standard of Living: Lecture II, Lives and Capabilities', in: Geoffrey Hawthorn (ed.), *The Standard of Living*, Cambridge: Cambridge University Press 1987, p. 36. Raymond Plant writes that "if the value of freedom is explained in terms of what I am able to do with it, then it becomes quite difficult to maintain that freedom and ability are totally separable" (Plant, supra n. 10, p. 232), while John Gray believes that "without the 'positive' freedoms conferred by enabling welfare institutions, the 'negative' liberties of the market are of limited value" (John Gray, *Gray's Anatomy*, London: Allen Lane 2009, p. 37).

[16] In its 2007 world freedoms' map, the world's main democracy watchdog had coloured the whole of Central Asia, with the exception of Kyrgyzstan, as not free (see the *Map of Freedom 2007*, available at <http://www.freedomhouse.org>).

way, in George W. Bush's de-regulated and privatised America where investment bankers, hedge-fund managers, private military contractors and many others benefited from financial deregulation, from wars in Iraq and Afghanistan while the majority of Americans bore the brunt of the economic crisis as well as the human and financial costs of wars in far-away places.

The concepts, as well as practice, of democracy are closely, I would say, inherently linked with the state. There is no democracy in international, especially in inter-state, relations and I am quite sceptical about this concept's applicability in that domain (is it a one-man-one-vote, one-state-one-vote or one-democracy-two-votes-one-dictatorship-zero-votes system?). Therefore, weakening the state, undermining its ability to respond to different challenges will also be the end of democracy. Davidson and Rees-Mogg are not wrong when they speak of the disappearance of democracy, as we know it, in the case of the triumph of their vision of the evolution of the world.

If *liberté* is the essence of liberalism, *égalité* is the essence of democracy. Emmanuel Wallerstein writes "that liberals give priority to liberty, meaning individual liberty, and that democrats (or socialists) give priority to equality. (...) Liberals do not merely give priority to liberty; they are opposed to equality, because they are strongly opposed to any concept measured by outcome, which is the only way the concept of equality is meaningful".[17] Does this mean that the more there is democracy, the less there are liberties? Not necessarily, of course. Only by absolutising the importance of equality[18] or vice versa liberty can one come to the conclusion that one necessarily negates the other. Since *égalité* is a necessary component of democracy, a society that becomes too unequal endangers its democratic achievements. In a liberal-democratic state, liberty and equality have to be balanced.

The spread of market economy and democracy – the concepts that are considered by many as obvious as God, motherhood and apple-pie – in practice often turns out to be a mixed blessing. If the planned economy of the Soviet type left everybody and society as a whole poor and market freedoms may indeed be one of the preconditions for political freedoms and personal liberties[19] – the shock introduction of markets, especially unfettered markets,

---

[17] Immanuel Wallerstein, 'Liberalism and Democracy: *Frères Ennemis?*', available at <http://fbc.binghamton.edu/iwfrenn.htm>.

[18] As with liberty or freedom, there are many definitions and approaches to equality as well. Today very few would advocate equality of outcome that would call if not for grand utopian projects like communism then at least for something quite marginal like the kibbutz style combination of Zionism and socialism in the early years of Israel. Now most champions of equality advocate equality of opportunity. Such understanding of equality is close to liberty understood not only as negative freedom (freedom from) but also as positive freedom (freedom to). Means called to guarantee equal opportunities for all also help all be freer and more autonomous in their life-choices.

[19] However, lest it lead to absurd conclusions, one should not absolutise or accept this assertion without qualifications. This is what was done, for example, in a recent collection of

makes a few extremely rich while many become even poorer than they were under the previous system. As one of the central tenets of democracy (with some important qualifications of course) is that the voices of the many count more than those of the few, it should be clear that economic 'shock therapy' and political democracy are incompatible and one either has a shock or one has democracy; they do not come together. Cambridge economist Ha-Joon Chang goes even further writing that 'free market and democracy are not natural partners'.[20] One of the most persistent market-friendly advocates of political freedoms, Karl Popper, already half a century ago incisively wrote: "Even if the state protects its citizens from being bullied by physical violence (as it does in principle, under the system of unrestrained capitalism), it may defeat our ends by its failure to protect them from the misuse of economic power. In such a state, the economically strong is still free to bully one who is economically weak, and to rob him of his freedom. Under these circumstances, unlimited economic freedom can be just as self-defeating as unlimited physical freedom, and economic power may be nearly as dangerous as physical violence."[21] Indeed, unfettered economic freedoms are as damaging for individual liberties as their absence in totalitarian states. Tony Judt's remark that "the market, over time, is its own worst enemy"[22] contains an important truth, though, as colourful remarks often do, it also simplifies the matter. The truth is that the market, like many other institutions, may, under certain circumstances, indeed become its worst enemy, its opposite.

It seems that free market (capitalism) and liberal democracy, phenomena that on the one hand presume each other, are at the same time also in constant rivalry or competition. The freer is a market, the greater is the economic

---

libertarian essays published in the UK. One of the authors claims that "private property is vital to individuals' abilities to defend themselves and their liberties" (Elaine Sternberg, 'Ethical Capitalism and Classical Liberalism', Michael James (ed.), *Classical Liberalism in the 21st Century. Essays in Honour of Norman P. Barry*, London: The University of Buckingham Press 2010, p. 50). From this claim logically follow some conclusions that are hardly acceptable even (or especially) for proponents of liberalism. First, this assertion is, to a great extent true: the more money one has, the more liberties one enjoys. Rich former football star and actor O.J. Simpson, who was accused of having killed his former wife and her lover, was acquitted in the criminal case in 1995 because he could afford to have the best defence team money could buy (in 1997, the civil court found him liable for the wrongful death of the same persons and O.J. was ordered to pay $ 33 million in damages). Thousands other African-Americans are sentenced every year and at least some of them only because they do not have enough private property to hire best defence lawyers. Secondly, this assertion seems to call for a radical redistribution of property since only in such a case would it be possible to guarantee equal protection of rights and liberties for all. This, of course, is not a conclusion libertarians would like to draw.

[20] Ha-Joon Chang, *Bad Samaritans. Rich Nations, Poor Policies & the Threat to the Developing World*, London: Random House 2007, p. 18.

[21] Karl Popper, *The Open Society and Its Enemies* (Volume 2), London: Routledge 1996, p. 124.

[22] Tony Judt, *Ill Fares the Land*, London: Allen Lane, 2010, p. 204.

inequality; the greater inequality, the less would there be democracy, and vice versa. Strong democracy attained by curbing inequality almost inevitably also bridles market freedoms. Economic inequality *de facto* and inevitably also increases political inequality, while political equality puts breaks on the widening economic inequality. Democracy tries to make a society more equal, while unbridled market increases inequality. The result of such constant balancing is that in Western European liberal democracies these two spheres (political and economic), while supporting each other, also constantly temper each other and soften each other's impacts. The United States, in that respect too, differs considerably from Europe. Cambridge Professor John Dunn writes that "America today remains a society uncomfortable with every surviving vestige of explicit privilege, but remarkably blithe in face of the most vertiginous of economic gulfs, and comprehensively reconciled to the most obtrusive privileges of wealth as such. Behind this outcome lies the continuing vitality of its economy, the real source of the victory of the partisans of distinction, or the English school of economists".[23] There the market has prevailed over democracy while, say, in Sweden, ruled for long periods by social democrats, there has been less room, as Dunn puts it, for "distinctions and opulence",[24] i.e. democracy has exercised greater constraints on the market.

John Dunn also observes that within the liberal democratic movement 'the partisans of the order of egoism', i.e. capitalists, have defeated 'the partisans of equality'[25], i.e. democrats. One of the important causes of equality's defeat in the hands of economic egoism has been that in the long run the uncompromising instruments for attempting to realize equality and the rigidities inherent in its pursuit have blunted equality's appeal as a goal.[26] Both the French and especially the Russian revolutions, where contrary to the American revolution, the aim was not, as Hannah Arendt put it, the 'freedom from oppression' but 'freedom from want', and one of the main requirements therefore was *égalité* (equality), have contributed to such a balance (or imbalance) within today's understanding of the balance between democracy and liberty. Arendt wrote that 'the inescapable fact was that liberation from tyranny spelled freedom only for the few and was hardly felt by the many who remained loaded down by their misery. These had to be liberated once more, and compared to this liberation from the yoke of necessity, the original liberation from tyranny must have looked like child's play'.[27] The fact that radical attempts of liberation from 'the yoke of necessity' and creation of more equal societies have led to tyranny should in no way compromise these values in the eyes of

---

[23] John Dunn, *Setting the People Free. The Story of Democracy*, London: Atlantic Books 2005, p. 127.
[24] Ibid., p. 130.
[25] Ibid., p. 134.
[26] Ibid., p. 129
[27] Hannah Arendt, *On Revolution*, London: Penguin 1965, p. 74.

thoughtful individuals.[28] It is possible to abuse all values and norms but this does not mean that we should therefore reject them. What is needed is a critical mind able to distinguish between a value and its abuse. Today, advanced liberal democracies have in principle got rid of the 'yoke of tyranny' and have alleviated the 'yoke of necessity' for most of their people, though one cannot be complacent since not only there are too many poor people in rich societies but the 'war on terror' is attempting to bring back also the 'yoke of tyranny'. However, for many other societies both tasks still constitute formidable challenges and even mature democracies constantly have to find new balances between freedom and equality.

4. Fraternité *and* Égalité *Supporting Each Other*

It is politically correct and fashionable to refer to the classics, though too often we use intellectual giants of the past selectively. In a way, this is understandable, since even the most consistent thinkers have not always been at their best and not all of their ideas have withstood the test of time. However, our selectivity has to be principled and not opportunistic. Libertarians who often refer to John Stewart Mill[29] to prove their points forget that this great liberal thinker

[28] It has become popular in Estonia to draw parallels between the crimes of communist and fascist regimes. It is true that communist regimes, especially the USSR under Stalin, Cambodia under Pol Pot and others have exterminated more of their own people than fascist regimes that were in power for far shorter periods. In practice, both totalitarianisms – fascism and communism – were indeed in many respects quite similar. However, their ideologies were rather different. If fascism represented moral nihilism and ideas of supremacy of a race and nation, communism was a morally utopian creed, which due to its humane ideas had wide attraction. In a way, communist ideology, due to its benevolent and compassionate nature and universal appeal, has been more infectious than fascist ideology (the road to hell paved with good intentions). Reinhold Niebuhr concluded that communism as "the corruption of the good" can be in human history even more dangerous than "explicit evil" in the form of fascism (Reinhold Niebuhr, *The Irony of American History (with a new introduction by Andrew Bacevich)*, Chicago: University of Chicago Press 2008, p. 128). However, this also means that we should not throw away ideas and ideals only because of their association with or exploitation by a totalitarian system. For example, the first draft of the new Russian Constitution under President Yeltsin, which had a chapter dedicated to human rights, did not contain any economic or social rights. Only later, after domestic criticism and comments from abroad, did the authors include economic and social rights as rights protected under the Constitution. One of the authors of the text of the Constitution, Professor Sergei Alekseyev, who in the 1970s had written a lot on the primacy of economic and social rights over civil and political rights, in the 1990s denied that the former even existed. When Estonia, after the restoration of its independence in 1991, adhered to the International Covenant on Economic, Social and Cultural Rights, some Estonian commentators, referring *inter alia* to the fact that Washington had not ratified the Covenant, accused the author of this article, who at that time worked as Deputy Foreign Minister of the country, of dragging our society back to communism. Such simplistic interpretations of history are hardly helpful; they certainly can be used as brakes on social progress and well-being of people.

[29] It is also necessary to keep in mind that Adam Smith, before he published one of the most famous and quoted books 'The Wealth of Nations' (1776), where he spoke of the 'invisible hand'

also wrote: "(…) the idea is especially repulsive of a society held together only by the relations and feelings arising out of pecuniary interest".[30] Not only is such an idea repulsive for many; if market relations were the only ones that connect people, Margaret Thatcher would be right that there is no such thing as society, only individual men and women and their families.[31] However, it is not accidental that practically all governments, political elites and opinion leaders of all countries are in the search of a national idea that would consolidate society, strengthen or restore societal bonds damaged by individualistic practices. Without some feeling of fraternity there can be neither Britain nor Estonia. Tony Judt is right that "if we remain grotesquely unequal, we shall lose all sense of fraternity; and fraternity, for all its fatuity as a political objective, turns out to be the necessary condition of politics itself".[32]

If the contradictions and the need of constant balancing between liberty and equality have received significant attention, the third component of the trinity – *fraternité* – has received much less consideration. However, in today's societies this neglected characteristic plays more important role than in yesterday's world that may have been more heterogeneous externally, i.e. as to the characteristics of individual countries (in today's globalising world countries actively borrow from each other whatever works better and therefore in some important respects the world is becoming more homogeneous) but internally those countries were usually more homogenous than today (that is why they became called nation-states – the term that nowadays is becoming increasingly oxymoronic) and they were also much more bonded.[33] Is not this neglect

of the market that made individuals and also nations rich, wrote 'The Theory of Moral Sentiments' (1759) where the great thinker, using the term 'invisible hand' for the first time, concentrated his study on matters such as fellow-feeling, compassion, pity and sympathy for others. There he expressed contempt for wealth 'abstracted from merit and virtue'.

[30] John Stuart Mill, *Principles of Political Economy with Some of Their Application to Social Philosophy (Edited and with an Introduction by Stephen Nathanson)*, Indianapolis: Hackett Publishing, 2004, p. 193.

[31] Margaret Thatcher, Interview to Women's Own Magazine, 31 October 1987 (available at <http://www.margaretthatcher.org/speeches/default.asp>).

[32] Judt, supra n. 22, p. 185.

[33] One of the increasingly acute problems in many liberal democracies is the question of how liberals will deal with increasing ethnic, racial and religious diversity. Traditionally liberal thought has been divided into 'universalists' (Locke, Kant, Rawls) and advocates of 'peaceful coexistence' (Hobbes, Hume, Berlin). The first see their society and potentially all societies becoming more liberal (as people start behaving more rationally they inevitably choose the best social arrangement, i.e. liberal democracy). The second, the proponents of peaceful coexistence do not believe in the possibility of such a rational consensus and therefore the best what can be achieved is peaceful coexistence between people and groups that have differing interests and hold dear different, often conflicting, values. John Gray has persuasively exposed the limits of universal liberalism. He writes that "it is a mark of an illiberal regime that conflicts of value are viewed as signs of error. Yet liberal regimes which claim that one set of liberties – their own – is universally legitimate adopt precisely that view" (supra n. 15, p. 39). Gray advocates a *modus vivendi* project, which would allow to exist side by side, and not only in the world as a whole but within a single 'nation-state', various communities, some of whom may even embrace illiberal

of the role of fraternity in our individualistic age partly due to the fact that it rather supports equality and somewhat counterbalances liberty? Be as it may, but the loosening of social bonds today concerns many societies, especially in the West.

However, political and intellectual leaders often look for the national idea not in the brotherhood of their people, not in efforts to overcome divisions between the affluent and poor, city and country dwellers, black and white, heterosexuals and homosexuals but in the opposition to external and internal Others (immigrants, people of different religion, race or sexual orientation, neighbouring nations). Nationalism, xenophobia, religious extremism, homophobia and other such ideas and ideologies are used to bring people together. This is a brotherhood or friendship against somebody else. Hatred and fear of the external or internal Other has deep historical and psychological roots. That is why, it is easy to exploit these characteristics (as recently done in Southern Kyrgyzstan, where the Kyrgyz and Uzbeks violently clashed) and very difficult to overcome them. Today, when all societies are increasingly becoming heterogeneous, the Other is more and more often not somebody in another country but in one's own neighbourhood. Therefore demonisation and stereotyping people of different religion or ethnic origin raises us not only against other countries but also against our immediate neighbours. Especially explosive are situations where ethnic or racial divides overlap with divisions between more prosperous and less affluent people or regions within the same country.

This brings us to the issue of the union between economic (market) liberalism and social conservatism.[34] Within the British Conservative Party

---

values. Such social arrangements have to accommodate almost incompatible values, like the need to tolerate intolerance. If some Western European societies, like the United Kingdom, which have for some time enjoyed (or have not much enjoyed) cultural diversity, are through processes of trial and error finding various *modi vivendi*, in the Eastern part of Europe, for example, in Estonia, all this seems to be too exotic to be thought about seriously. In our country differences in life styles and perceptions between the native Estonians and the Russian speaking minority are indeed very small. Exaggerated and exploited by Estonian and Russian nationalists such Freudian 'narcissism of small differences' has created a society that is rather intolerant towards social diversity, to say nothing about seeing in the rich tapestry of cultures the splendour of humankind. When our politicians often and enthusiastically speak of 'European values' they have in mind something quite narrow and characteristic of yesterday's Europe that excludes tolerance towards and enjoyment of social diversity in its manifold manifestations. When the Estonian Human Development Report of 2009 finds that "the decrease of social mobility in Estonia indicates that in parallel with liberal welfare state Estonia is acquiring characteristics of the corporate state and moving towards a closed society" (Eesti Inimarengu Aruanne 2009, Eesti Koostöö Kogu, 2010, p. 105) the authors of the report based such a conclusion on the increasing social and economic stratification only. Importantly, Estonia is remaining a relatively closed society also in terms of the attitude towards racial, ethnic and religious diversity.

[34] As a European, it is quite natural that I use the term 'liberalism' not in a pejorative sense, as often done in the US. The American Professor John Kekes in his book *Against Liberalism* (Ithaca (N.Y.), Cornell University Press 1997) well expresses the view on liberalism prevalent in

(the Tories) this combination of market liberalism and social conservatism has been quite distinctive. So-called 'One Nation Conservatives' (led, for example, by Prime Ministers Harold Macmillan and Edward Heath), who tried to combine liberal economy with social programmes aimed at the eradication of poverty, unity of citizenry and harmony between social classes, were quite different from the Thatcherite conservatives. The emergence of the term and doctrines of 'compassionate conservatism', which was meant to overcome one-sidedness of Thatcherite and Reaganite market liberalism and social conservatism, also indicates that traditional conservatism is not attractive enough and leads to social divisions that damage bonds holding societies together.

In Estonia today we have a coalition government of the Reform Party liberals and IRL (Fatherland-Republican Union) conservatives. The latter claim that they differ from their coalition partners because for the liberals 'the money is the only value'[35] and differently from those on the left of the political spectrum, they value liberty over equality. They emphasise the role of national culture, history and traditions in today's politics. It is not accidental that among IRL politicians many are historians, and quite a few politicians have taken up writing on historical issues. For them history is a servant that has to govern today's affairs.[36] Politically they are market liberals and social

his country. This is an attack of a social conservative and market liberal on those who value "autonomy, freedom pluralism, rights, equality, and distributive justice" higher than "order, civility, peace, a healthy environment, security, happiness, and law-abidingness" (p. 43). For him there is no difference (or big difference) between social liberalism and social democracy. From Kekes' point of view, liberals blindly believe that human nature is basically good and evil stems from extraneous sources (e.g., poverty, oppression) while "the facts are that evil is prevalent in all human societies: the vices of selfishness, greed, malevolence, envy, aggression, prejudice, cruelty, and suspicion motivate people just as the contrary virtues do" (p. 39). Therefore, the more autonomy and freedom there are in society, the more easily can vices prevail. Kekes asks: "Why could a considerable increase in law-abidingness not justify some reduction in pluralism?" (p. 43). He believes that "if a liberal society wishes to curtail the prevalence of evil that exists in it, then it must be committed to decreasing, rather than increasing, the autonomy of many people living in it" (p. 32). It is of import to note that Kekes not at all criticises market liberalism. It would be wrong to outrightly reject all Kekes' points. He certainly makes some valid observations. What is wrong is that he does not subject his own views to the same critical scrutiny to which he subjects the views of his opponents. In today's developed world societies have to balance different values and interests. Notonly are there many people who hold dear liberal, social democratic or conservative values; as these values, in different proportions and combinations are genuinely needed, no society can completely neglect them. Their proportions depend on time and space. It would be too good to be true if all good things would harmoniously coexist and all the people regard the same things as good or evil.

35 The dismantling of the Soviet-era monument in Tallinn in the spring of 2007 indicates that the liberal Reform Party does not lack nationalistic instincts, though this and other similar policies may be due more to political opportunism (forthcoming elections) than strong ideological preferences. Ideas often and ideology almost always are used as a cover for certain interests and this is not even necessarily always done cynically or hypocritically. Politicians very often deceive not only others but become involved in self-deception when they start to believe what they say.

36 Recently reading Philip Pullman's novel *The Good Man Jesus and The Scoundrel Christ*, I saw more clearly than ever that time and again history plays the role either of a servant or a

conservatives for whom in social life traditions and nation reign supreme while in economic affairs money is what matters.

Such a combination of economic liberalism and social conservatism, whether it exists within one political party (the Tories in the UK) or in a governing coalition (the current Estonian Government) has its strains and limits. Policies of those for whom 'only the money matters' make society less coherent and more divided while of those for whom the nation and historical traditions reign supreme put breaks on money-making ability through restrictions on migration, restrictive citizenship and language legislation or sacrificing beneficial economic cooperation for politically motivated hostility towards foreign countries against whom they have historical grievances or whose regimes they do not like. If for liberals the state has to be a 'nomocracy' (a rule-governed order that is not devoted to the attainment of any particular social goals), social conservatives, who may be market liberals, support certain social goals, purposes or ends in their policies, i.e. they are proponents of a 'telocratic order'.[37] Here, we see, conservatives have something in common with social democrats though their goals are usually rather different.

Recently there has been much debate about 'the third way' between unfettered capitalism and state interventionism. Actually, over the years most liberal democracies already have developed a kind of third way as a result of a

---

governor and not often enough of that of a teacher. Too frequently authorities try to interpret or reinterpret history to further their political agenda, i.e. they use history as their servant. In such a case, for people history becomes, due to their historic grievances and memories that often contain negative stereotypes of other nations as well as fears exploited by the political elites, a governor. We see this happening in many parts of the world and this tendency is quite noticeable in countries that belonged to the former Soviet bloc whether it is the creation of the Presidential Commission to Counter Attempts to falsify History to the Detriment of Russia in Moscow or the attempts of Estonian, Georgian or Ukrainian officials to give their only true interpretation of historical events. Neither side sees any irony in the fact that they are doing the same thing: using history for political purposes. In Estonia it finds its expression in the misreading of Russia's assertiveness, exaggerating its aggressiveness, uncritically accepting whatever Washington (especially during the last Bush Administration) says or does. In Russia it perpetuates the denial of crimes committed by the communist regime and distorts understanding of historical perspectives held by Russia's neighbours. Teaching legal and political issues of terrorism for years at London University for students from various countries for many years it became clearer and clearer for me that the famous (or infamous) saying "one man's terrorist is another man's freedom fighter" has a limited explanatory value in more than one sense. A terrorist indeed can be a freedom fighter (or independence fighter, which is not the same thing) if she uses terror tactics. Similarly, when the advancing Soviet troops in 1944 pushed the Germans out of the Baltics they liberated them and the world from fascism, but at the same time they also reoccupied them, deprived them of their independence. The problem is that too many people see only one aspect of this event. It would be wrong to call to leave history for historians only but it would be appropriate to invite politicians to stay away from politicising history.

[37] See e.g. Plant, supra n. 10, p. 6. If nomocratic order (nomocracy) emphasises the role of institutions that facilitate the pursuit of different private ends without attempting to have any common goals or generally agreed concepts of the good, telocratic policies (telocracy) imply that there are some important overriding goals for the society to achieve and there is an agreement on the common good.

pendulum style vacillation between the Scylla of unbridled markets and deregulation and the Charybdis of state interference and nationalisation. Whether it will be possible to steer a more sensible course instead of having things result principally from left-to-right and right-to-left vacillations is not clear. The nature of politics in liberal democracies, or the nature of politics in general, makes the implementation of any of such a third way problematic.[38] At best, developed countries have moved so far like a sail boat tacking against the wind – navigating to the left from the direct line towards the point of destination and then as a counterbalance turning to the equal degree to the right in order to straighten the course.

5. *On the Possibility of Progressive Liberalism*

In the post-World War II Europe, with the exception of strong communist parties in France and Italy, social democrats were the main advocates of equality. Being democrats, they did not deny the role of social, political and economic freedoms though they were ready to restrict economic liberties through the redistribution of wealth for the sake of various social goals and programmes. Social democratic policies have always faced two serious problems or accusations from the part of both liberals and conservatives: (1) redistribution increases state bureaucracy and the state itself becomes paternalistic, more and more interfering in everyday life of the people (the emergence of so-called 'nanny state'); (2) redistribution of wealth from the more affluent to the more needy means that there are fewer resources for investment which is a brake on economic growth.

These traditional criticisms of social democracy, though having grains of truth, are not completely sincere. First, the state's role and interference in the life of the individual grew also on the watch of free-marketeers such as Margaret Thatcher, George W. Bush and Tony Blair, though in the case of the last two leaders this may have been partly due to the specific circumstances of the 'war on terror', which however do not justify excesses such as 'extraordinary rendition', torture through 'waterboarding' and other violations of human rights and unnecessary interference with liberties. Secondly, social-democratic Sweden or Germany had at times economic growth higher than

[38] Richard Bronk, *Progress and the Invisible Hand. The Philosophy and Economy of Human Advance*, London: Little, Brown and Company, 1997, p. 238, writes that since the eighteenth-century Enlightenment, there has been in Europe "a fertile mix of conflicting ideas", and that none of them prevailed for long. There has been a constantly shifting balance between the belief in collective action, faith in individual liberty, competition between ideas of rational planning and *laissez-faire* policies, respect for civic duty and individual self-interest. Believing that this has made this period so successful, Bronk doubts whether at the age of globalisation this balance between the collectivist and individualistic traditions will be sustainable.

those democracies that were governed by conservatives or market liberals. Moreover, as the experience of Hong Kong, Singapore, Malaysia, South Korea and now China testifies, democracy is not needed at all for economic growth. Martha Nussbaum, referring to concrete statistical studies, concludes: "Political liberty, health and education are all poorly correlated with growth".[39] However, there is a new and more serious problem for social democracy – globalisation.

The nation-state and national market economy – these cradles of human rights and democracy – are both in the process of radical change. The world market is no longer a sum-total of national markets; it is becoming more and more a real common market. The state has lost not only its ability to control world financial markets but also its ability to protect its own population from negative effects of fluctuations in the world market. The unfettered global market tends to drag down the protection of economic and social rights to the level of the lowest common denominator (e.g. cheap labour and longer working hours in many Asian societies are certainly affecting employment and social protection in the OECD countries). Jack Donnelly writes: "The globalisation of production is weakening state-centric schemes for implementing economic, social and cultural rights, most dramatically in the wealthier countries of the Northern Hemisphere. It does not, however, seem to be creating viable alternative mechanisms".[40] Donnelly correctly also emphasises that economic growth due to globalisation and the new division of labour should not be confused with the growth of economic and social rights since "human rights are about assuring minimum distributions of goods, services and opportunities to all, something that is by no means assured by economic growth".[41] Civil and especially political rights are not unaffected either by the process of globalisation. The inability of democratically elected governments to protect their constituencies from negative global effects (e.g. from the crash of financial markets or from the effect of cheap child labour in some Asian countries) means that democracy has become less effective and political rights less important. The dilemma which globalisation has caused for social democrats has been well summarised by Dominique Strauss-Kahn, a leading French socialist and former minister in the Mitterrand and Jospin governments: "The success of post-war democracy rests on the equilibrium between production and redistribution, regulated by the state. With globalization, this equilibrium is broken. Capital has become mobile: production has moved

[39] Martha Nussbaum, *Not for Profit: Why Democracy Needs the Humanities*, Princeton: Princeton University Press 2010, p. 14.

[40] Jack Donnelly, 'Social Construction of International Human Rights', in: Tim Dunne and Nicholas J. Wheeler (eds.), *Human Rights in Global Politics*, Cambridge: Cambridge University Press 1999, p. 94.

[41] Ibid., p. 95.

beyond national borders, and thus outside the remit of state redistribution. (…) Growth would oppose redistribution; the virtuous circle would become the vicious circle."[42]

The creation after WWI of the International Labour Organization (ILO) was the world's (at the time the Western world was the only one that mattered) response to two problems: the workers movements for their rights, in which many saw 'the spectre of communism' haunting the Western world, and to the need to level the playing field for competing national capitals. The establishment of the ILO – the only specialised agency of the UN that was created before WWII, whose mandate has been the promotion of social and economic rights, which are considered to be the second generation rights (if human rights at all) vis-à-vis the first generation (civil and political) rights, before human rights became an international issue (this happened together with the creation of the UN in 1945) is a significant fact indicating that these were not so much human rights but other interests that guided the founders of the ILO. International concern for workers' rights was not so much due to the unease about the welfare of the workers, though they naturally benefited from it. It was for the sake of the survival of capitalism and to mitigate rivalry between employers from different Western countries by creating for them more equal costs of labour (approximately the same working hours and conditions, paid holidays, etc). Such an arrangement was possible between the countries that were approximately at the same level of economic and social development. Can it be repeated today on a world scale? Of course, the ILO is an organisation with universal membership but it is not a big secret that working conditions, worker's pay and other labour factors hugely differ between countries and regions.

These negative effects of globalisation can be mitigated only through purposeful international efforts on the part of governments. Today it is not Orwell's 1984 that, at least for the Western world, is the most realistic and immediate danger; in many parts of the world, as we are seeing today, the failure or total collapse of states, not their strength and stability, has been the main cause of massive human suffering. The clear and present danger is, rather, that the unfettered global market, without any democratic control, may become a 'big brother' whose interference with individual liberties, though more anonymous and less direct than that of the state, may prove equally or even more nefarious. One of the most important tasks of the state is now the management of global issues such as the globalised economy, the prevention of environmental degradation, the maintenance of national and international security, and qualified, contingent and contextual promotion of democracy

[42] Dominique Strauss-Kahn, 'What is a Just Society?', in: *Where now for European Social Democracy?*, London: Policy Network 2004, p. 14.

and human rights.[43] It is sometimes said that states are too big for small things and too small for big things. However, if there are entities ready to take over some of the smaller things, there is nothing yet available to resolve big things. The rise of China and other Asian countries, where the role of the state has been instrumental in guaranteeing this rise, is a further evidence that it is too early to resign the state to the dustbin of history, as Marxists dreamed, or cut it down to the size of a mere night watchman, as libertarians or neo-liberals would like.

6. *Instead of Conclusions*

John Ruggie, one of the most prominent political scientists and a former UN Assistant Secretary-General, has written that "the strength of each approach is also the source of its major weakness".[44] The opposite may also be true; there may be a strength in the weakness. Without some one-sidedness a study may lack passion and depth. Andrei Makin, contemporary French writer of Russian origin, wrote about Freud, Marx and Lacan, that "they have very limited vision, which they develop to excess".[45] I do not want to judge the fairness of this comment concerning these very different individuals, but the point made can be appreciated: limited vision that is developed to excess has both positive and negative aspects. In a pianist it may cause the whole world to applaud, while in a politician it may lead to expensive mistakes or terrible tragedies. The study of social phenomena needs various theories and there can hardly be a single grand theory attempting to explain equally well all the aspects of the complicated reality. Rather, like a world-class tennis player who combines a strong serve with excellent returns and uses, depending on circumstances, with equal skill both backhand and forehand, a social scientist (both as a practitioner and academic) has to be ready to use, depending on the subject-matter and concrete tasks, different intellectual tools, that is to say, different theories and theoretical approaches. The latter are like the petals of a flower that all explain some aspects of the reality, while in the centre of the flower there is not a grand 'theory of everything', but there is the capitulum on which most theories or theoretical approaches can agree upon. Bertrand Russell once observed: "No one has yet succeeded in inventing a philosophy at once credible and self-consistent. Locke aimed at credibility, and achieved it at the expense of consistency. Most of the great philosophers have done the opposite. A philosophy that is not self-consistent cannot be wholly true, but a

[43] See Rein Müllerson, *Democracy – A Destiny of Humankind? A Qualified, Contingent and Contextual Case for Democracy Promotion*, New York: NovaSciencePublishers 2009.
[44] John Ruggie, *Constructing the World Polity. Essays on International Institutionalism*, London: Routledge 1999, p. 36.
[45] *The Independent*, 24 July 1999, The Week-End Review, p. 9.

philosophy which is self-consistent can very well be wholly false. The most fruitful philosophies have contained glaring inconsistencies, but for that very reason have been partially true."[46]

There may be, of course, objections to selective use of different theories. One may be accused of being eclectic. However, is eclecticism necessarily such a bad thing? If a choice of strong points from different theories is open, conscious and can theoretically be justified (e.g. if it can be shown that a phenomenon under study, or an aspect of it, can be better explained not by a single theory but by the use of various theories) eclecticism may become a principled approach to research. There is, however, a more serious problem with using eclectical approaches: not everybody is open-minded and flexible enough (though some may call it unprincipled enough) to use them. James Rosenau and Mary Durfee question: "[A]re we not so locked into our preferred theory that it is virtually impossible to shift back and forth between models as circumstances warrant and our interests change?"[47] And they believe that "usually we are locked into the theory with which we are most comfortable. It gives meaning to any and all discrepancies. It infuses order into seemingly disparate developments, highlights the central actors, clarifies their motives, and explains their successes and failures".[48]

There is a good deal of truth in this comment. However, social theories are not philosophical or religious world-views that help the individual to distinguish between the good and evil, moral and immoral, and that, in general terms, explain the world and our place in it. Our personal philosophies (be they subconscious or well articulated) are, indeed, rarely perceptible to sudden change (though this cannot be completely excluded either). Although social theories are dependent on our wider world-views, this dependency is not absolute and rigid. Therefore, it is not impossible that a person can use different approaches for the explanation of social phenomena. What is important is that politicians avoid being locked into theoretical and ideological constructs, which they, ignoring reality, mindlessly use. Various liberal theories of society, like social-democratic and conservative concepts have all their strengths and weaknesses and none of them is able to encapsulate the 'eternal truths'. All of them have their strenghts and weaknesses, their limits in time and space. Not only would it be wrong to judge Plato's or Aristotle's views with the yardstick of today's morality and law; I would also not advise to discuss liberal theories of society seriously when trying to find solutions for situations in, say, Darfur, or the Helmand province in Afghanistan.

---

[46] Bertrand Russell, *History of Western Philosophy and its Connection with Political and Social Circumstances from the Earliest Times to the Present Day*, London: Allen & Unwin 1946, p. 637.

[47] James Rosenau and Mary Durfee, *Thinking Theory Thoroughly. Coherent Approaches to an Incoherent World*, Oxford: Westview Press, 1995, p. 140.

[48] Ibid.

CHAPTER TEN

THE SOVEREIGNS ARE DEAD, LONG LIVE THE SOVEREIGNS – REFLECTIONS ON STATE SOVEREIGNTY AND INTERNATIONAL LAW

*André de Hoogh**

1. *Introduction*

At an early stage on my path towards academics, during my PhD research in Nijmegen, I remember having a conversation with Karel Wellens discussing approaches to international law. He suggested that I was more of a positivist, whereas he considered himself more of a realist. Though the memory plays tricks on us, and possibly I do not remember the words accurately, I would certainly say that his characterisation of my attitude towards international law is correct. And possibly this explains why claims of the decline of sovereignty as the fundamental tenet explaining the workings and content of international law have seemed premature to me.

Reflecting for instance on human rights law, it has been argued that the sovereignty of states is no longer sufficient to explain the reality of international law.[1] New actors, new threats, new rules, new principles, all chip away at the autonomy of states and highlight the erosion of their independence. All in all, the increases of obligations of states, in particular those affecting the exercise of their authority in the internal legal order, whether through participation in treaties or binding decisions of international organisations, is followed by an assessment that the times of sovereignty have passed.

And yet there is something unsatisfying to those claims, if only because a proper understanding of the concept of sovereignty will require a detailed assessment as to the extent to which sovereignty, as *the* foundation of international law, must be considered *passé*. This contribution intends, in a rather limited fashion, to make good on this, and will consider both the traditional conceptualisation of sovereignty as well as such developments as may be said to erode the authority of states. Those developments will be viewed 'looking up', i.e. by assessing to which extent states are bound to decision-making at a

---

* This contribution is based in part on a presentation given to the International Workshop on Kelsen, Schmitt and Arendt and the possibilities of (international) law, 11 September 2009, Vienna. Many thanks to Marcel Brus, Michiel Duchateau, Antenor Hallo de Wolf, Gerhard Hoogers and Jörg Kammerhofer for their critical reading and helpful comments.

[1] Cf. Javaid Rehman, *International Human Rights Law*, Harlow: Pearson 2010, p. 3–4.

higher level, and looking down, i.e. by assessing to which extent states may no longer control events within their territory and could be considered displaced in their exercise of authority over territory and population.

For this purpose, the second section of this contribution reflects on the traditional understanding of the sovereignty of states as signifying the existence and exercise of the highest authority over territory and population. The third section will consider longstanding rules that protect the authority of states, especially regarding and within their own territory. In the fourth section the focus will be on the position of individuals in relation to the authority of the state, whereas the fifth section will address some aspects of decision-making by the Security Council of the United Nations.

2. *The Concept of Sovereignty*

The advent of sovereignty as a concept is widely credited to Jean Bodin, who in the first book of his *Les six livres de la république* stated: "La souveraineté est la puissance absolue et perpétuelle d'une République (…)."[2] Bodin begins his argument by identifying the quality of a republic in terms of sovereignty, which he identifies as the absolute and perpetual power. In discussing the perpetual nature of such power, he moves from the republic to sovereign Princes in order to explain that those who possess only temporally limited power cannot be considered sovereign.[3]

With respect to the matter of absolute power, Bodin claims that a Prince who is granted sovereignty under charge, and subject to conditions, is not truly sovereign and has not received absolute power.[4] Furthermore, those who are sovereign must not be subject to command by another, and they may give laws to their subjects and may cancel or change pointless laws in order to

[2] Jean Bodin, *Les six livres de la république*, Livre Premier, Paris: Fayard 1986, p. 179 (first published in 1577).

[3] Ibid., p. 179–187. Bodin's qualification of sovereignty implying the existence of perpetual power is somewhat vexing, in that placing the *locus* in a natural person will of necessity entail the nullification of his or her power with the passing away of that person (which of course Bodin realises, ibid 191). Only the attachment of sovereignty to a natural person in a combination with hereditary succession (cf. ibid. p. 225–226) or to a body could avoid this consequence. In international law, by contrast, sovereignty may be wholly or partially alienated. Cf. *Customs Régime between Germany and Austria* (Advisory Opinion), PCIJ Reports 1931, Series A/B, No. 41, p. 44–52 (hereinafter: *Customs Régime* opinion); James Crawford, *The Creation of States in International Law*, Oxford: Oxford University Press 2006, p. 45.

[4] Bodin, supra n. 2, p. 187. He adds that a certain power is absolute, and sovereign, because it is subject to no other condition than God's law and the law of nature. Ibid., p. 188. Moreover, if one were to say that only he possesses absolute power who is subject to no laws, this would imply that none of the Princes in the world would be sovereign, considering that all are subject to God's law, and to nature, and to various human laws common to all peoples. Ibid., p. 190; see also p. 192–193.

provide others.[5] Moreover, as the Prince is exempted from the laws of his predecessors, *a fortiori* he is also not held to the laws and orders of his own making. Though one may receive law from another, it is impossible to give law or command to oneself on a matter that is dependent on one's own free will.[6]

In chapter X, Bodin continues to discuss the true marks of sovereignty that allow one to identify a sovereign Prince. He posits that these marks are not held by the Prince in common with other subjects and cannot be alienated.[7] Bodin identifies five in total: 1. to give law to all in general, and each in particular, without the consent of those more great, similar or equal, or less;[8] 2. to commence a war or to make peace;[9] 3. to appoint the principal officers and magistrates;[10] 4. to act as a final instance of appeal in respect of judgments;[11] 5. to pardon those subject to sentence.[12]

This very brief introduction to Bodin's thoughts serves to direct attention to the situation in international law, which has discarded any intention to identify any specific person, institution, body or group within a state as sovereign.[13] Indeed, any attempt to identify the locus of sovereignty in another state is bound to be controversial, the more so when precisely that question would be a matter of conflict within that state.[14] Instead, international law has strongly affirmed the sovereignty of the state, as a legal person,[15] and developed rules to ensure that a state does not meddle in the internal affairs of another state.

---

[5] Ibid., p. 191, where he adds that this cannot be a person who is subject to laws, nor any who may be commanded by him. He specifies further that the law stipulates that the Prince is absolved from the power of the laws. Later on, he specifies that the Prince is not subject to his laws, but that he is subject to just and reasonable conventions in whose observance his subjects in general or particular have an interest. Ibid., p. 194, and further on p. 217–219.

[6] Ibid., p. 192.

[7] Ibid., p. 295 and p. 298–299.

[8] Ibid., p. 306–309. Bodin notes that all other marks of sovereignty are comprised within this first one (ibid., p. 309). With respect to the imposition of extraordinary charges, discussing the situation in England, Bodin notes that the estates do not accept those without the consent of Parliament. However, generalizing the matter, he then claims that in any case "si la nécessité est urgente, en ce cas le Prince ne doit pas attendre l'assemblée des états, ni le consentement du peuple, duquel le salut dépend de la prévoyance, et diligence d'un sage Prince (…)." Ibid., p. 201.

[9] Ibid., p. 310–315.

[10] Ibid., p. 315–318.

[11] Ibid., P. 319–325.

[12] Ibid., p. 325–327.

[13] Though at times phrases reminiscent of earlier times may be noted, such as in the reference to *sovereign* immunity. Cf. Malcolm Shaw, *International Law*, Cambridge: Cambridge University Press 2008, p. 697–701.

[14] For a study retracing the development of the theory on sovereignty, see Charles Merriam, *History of the Theory of Sovereignty Since Rousseau*, New York: Columbia University Press 1900.

[15] Following similar movements as in domestic constitutional theory. Ibid., p. 85–129. See also Wouter Werner, 'State Sovereignty and International Legal Discourse', in: Ige F. Dekker and Wouter G. Werner (eds.), *Governance and International Legal Theory*, Leiden-Boston: Martinus Nijhoff Publishers 2004, p. 137–138.

For the purposes of this contribution it is important to clarify the essential characteristics of the concept of sovereignty, as it pertains to states as legal persons. Where Bodin speaks of power (*puissance*; which could also be translated as 'might'), authors in the field of international law are wont to use the word 'authority'. This change in language is important in that it favours the normative or legal component over factual control or power.[16] Authority in this respect is intended to reflect that there is a relationship of command and obedience between an entity considered sovereign and its subjects, the one entitled to command and the others bound to obey.

Furthermore, Bodin qualifies such power by the adjectives 'absolute' and 'perpetual', where later authors are inclined to use qualifications for authority such as 'ultimate' or 'highest'. Overall therefore authors consider states to be sovereign, signalling that the state, as a legal person, constitutes the highest authority.[17]

To an extent, however, this begs the question, because to be able to assess whether an entity is 'sovereign' will require an assessment whether it is a state.[18] For that purpose authors most commonly consider four elements to be relevant, namely that the entity possesses: 1. a more or less defined territory; 2. a certain population (more or less permanent) living on that territory; 3. a government that exercises stable and effective control over that territory and population; and 4. the capacity to enter into international relations.[19] In essence then an entity may be considered a state when that entity is politically organised through a government, that government controls a territory and its population, and holds the capacity to enter into international relations.

The capacity to enter into international relations may be approached from both an internal perspective and external perspective. From the internal perspective, such capacity signifies that an entity is not part of a bigger one from which the source of its own authority is derived. Thus the phrase 'capacity to enter into international relations' may be argued to convey the notion that an entity is self-sufficient in the sense that such capacity originates from its own constitution rather than the constitution of a larger entity. By way of example, this in effect distinguishes federal states as constituent parts from the federation as the legal person of which they form part.[20] This phrase may, at the same

---

[16] Cf. Werner, supra n. 15, p. 132–133.

[17] Cf. the orthodox view referred to, but not necessarily endorsed by, Hans Kelsen, *Principles of International Law*, New York: Rinehart & Company 1952, p. 108.

[18] Cf. Crawford, supra n. 3, p. 37–40, who notes that the terms 'state' and 'statehood' have gone without satisfactory definition for a long time.

[19] In this respect reference is made, usually, to article 1 of the Convention on the Rights and Duties of States, (1934) 28 *American Journal of International Law* (Supplement), p. 75. For a discussion of these criteria, see Crawford, supra n. 3, p. 45–62, who continues by discussing the additional criteria of sovereignty and independence and other factors (ibid., p. 62–95).

[20] In other words, the capacity to enter into international relations derives from a legal document that is self-contained, i.e. not dependent for its validity on another legal document.

time, serve to stress the element of independence that must apply, though this is more commonly linked to the external perspective.

From the external perspective, the entity concerned must be independent, meaning that it is not subject to some other authority, whether to other states or, rather more uncommon, to an international organisation.[21] Certain classical cases have confirmed this view, primary among them Huber's statement in the *Palmas* case that:

> Sovereignty in the relations between States signifies independence. Independence in regard to a portion of the globe is the right to exercise therein, to the exclusion of any other State, the functions of a State. The development of the national organisation of States during the last few centuries and, as a corollary, the development of international law, have established this principle of the exclusive competence of the State in regard to its own territory in such a way as to make it the point of departure for settling most questions that concern international relations.[22]

The crucial factor therefore is that of a government exercising the highest authority over territory and populationand hence the entity concerned is not subjected to the authority of any other state(s) or entity. Though the elements or criteria to determine the existence of a state refer to stable and effective *control* over territory and population, it is to be noted that such control must be the result of an exercise of *authority*, as may be seen from this statement by Kelsen:

> 'Authority' is usually defined as the right or power to issue obligating commands. The actual power of forcing others to a certain behavior does not suffice to constitute an authority. The individual who is or has the authority must have received the right or power to issue obligating commands, so that other individuals are obliged to obey. Such a right or power can be conferred on an individual only by a normative order.[23]

Hence, when sovereignty is used as shorthand for 'highest authority' this denotes the competence and legal power to issue commands or norms.

Cf. Vaughan Lowe, *International Law*, Oxford: Oxford University Press 2007, p. 157–158, though he does not specifically make this point.

[21] Consider especially the administration of the territories of Kosovo and East Timor by respectively the United Nations Mission in Kosovo (UNMIK) and the United Nations Transitional Administration of East Timor. Cf. UNSC resolution 1244 (10 June 1999) UN doc. S/RES/1244; UNSC resolution 1272 (25 October 1999) UN Doc S/RES/1272. The ICJ in its advice on Kosovo did not address the question whether Kosovo had become a state. *Accordance with international law of the unilateral declaration of independence in respect of Kosovo* (Advisory Opinion) (22 July 2010) 19–20, par. 51, available on <http://www.icj-cij.org/docket/files/141/15987.pdf>.

[22] *Island of Palmas case (Netherlands v. USA)*, (1928) 2 *Reports of International Arbitral Awards*, p. 838.

[23] Cf. Kelsen, supra n. 17, p. 440.

Factual control or power does not equal authority but rather order absent law; though of course the one may, and some would say must, coincide with the other.

Here it may be noted that this contribution uses the word 'authority' in connection to a body or person, whether natural or legal, and not with respect to (international) law. If sovereignty involves a relationship of command and obedience, one might be inclined to see the law as command and for that reason international law as an authority above states.[24] Such a position could perhaps be read into the observations of judge Anzilotti regarding the *Customs Régime between Germany and Austria* opinion:

> Independence as thus understood is really no more than the normal condition of States according to international law; it may also be described as *sovereignty* (*suprema potestas*), or *external sovereignty*, by which is meant that the State has over it no other authority than that of international law.[25]

However, (international) law itself is made by (or through) authority, and though authority can only be assigned by law to begin with,[26] this contribution takes as a starting-point that such authority must be 'personified' in the sense that a certain body or natural or legal person must be able to exercise such authority by virtue of attributed competences and (legal) powers.

This leads to a critical examination of the question to what extent sovereignty, as a legal concept, is undermined by previous or current developments in international law. It is this question that is examined in the remainder of this contribution. It may be noted that this question excludes from the examination the extent to which sovereignty might be undermined by internal, that is national, constitutional developments, nor does the question concern the extent to which sovereignty is undermined by factual or social developments that weaken the control of governments over their territory and population or diminish their freedom of action. The analysis will instead focus on developments in international law which undermine the 'highest authority' embodied in states. Before initiating that investigation, the next section will reflect upon the protection provided by international law to sovereign states.

3. *The Protection of Sovereignty in International Law*

Although sovereignty became a popular theory rapidly after its conceptualisation by Bodin, entailing both the denial of higher authority on the part of the

---

[24] Cf. Kelsen, supra n. 17, p. 438–444, who argues that states cannot be sovereign, since they are subject to the supreme legal authority of international law, though he admits of the logical possibility that one national legal order, i.e. one state, could be considered sovereign to the exclusion of all others.

[25] *Customs Régime* opinion, Individual Opinion of Judge Anzilotti, p. 57.

[26] Kelsen, supra n. 17, p. 439–440. The authority assigned by law, mentioned in the main text, relates to the concept of constituted powers, as distinct from the concept of constituent power,

Pope and the Holy Roman Emperor,[27] as well as the mutual recognition of many different authorities as sovereigns, legal protection under international law lagged behind. Starting from the premise of all sovereigns possessing absolute power, international law became dominated by a positivist and consensualist attitude best expressed in the oft quoted, and criticised, statement of the Permanent Court in the *Lotus* case:

> International law governs relations between independent States. The rules of law binding upon States therefore emanate from their own free will as expressed in conventions or by usages generally accepted as expressing principles of law and established in order to regulate the relations between these co-existing independent communities or with a view to the achievement of common aims. Restrictions upon the independence of States cannot therefore be presumed.[28]

In the 18th and 19th century, states generally accepted the absence of rules of international law outlawing the use of armed force by one against the other, and instead considered the 'right' to wage war an attribute of a sovereign state.[29] This development was neither predestined by the theory of sovereignty, nor inevitable as a matter of law. Bodin had already stipulated that a sovereign was bound by Divine and natural law and various human laws common to all peoples,[30] whereas the Treaty of Münster, part of the Peace of Westphalia, stipulated that those breaking the treaty or the public peace would be considered infringers and subject to punishment and restitution and reparation. Moreover, everyone was enjoined to have recourse to means of ordinary justice, and to pursue one's right by force and arms was prohibited to any state (of the empire).[31]

The attitude towards the use of armed force between states shaped in the 18th and 19th century only changed direction at the beginning of the 20th century. With the adoption of the 1907 Porter-Drago Convention,[32] the 1919

which essentially concerns who or which body or bodies may create or modify a legal order acting outside the bounds of the law of that order.

[27] Cf. Bruno de Witte, 'Sovereignty and European Integration: The Weight of Legal Tradition', in: Anne-Marie Slaughter, Alec Stone Sweet, J.H.H. Weiler (eds.), *The European Court and National Courts – Doctrine and Jurisprudence. Legal Change in its Social Context*, Oxford: Hart Publishing 1998, p. 279.

[28] *The Case of the S.S. "Lotus"* (Judgment), PCIJ Reports 1927, Series A, No. 10, p. 18 (hereinafter: *Lotus* case).

[29] Cf. Albrecht Randelzhofer, 'Article 2 (4)', in: Bruno Simma (ed.), *Charter of the United Nations: A Commentary* (Volume I), Oxford: Oxford University Press 2002, p. 114–115. Note that measures short of war, i.e. armed reprisals, were subject to legal regulation. Cf. *Arbitrage entre le Portugal et l'Allemagne, Affaire Naulilaa*, (1928) 2 *Reports of International Arbitral Awards*, p. 1011; *Arbitrage entre le Portugal et l'Allemagne, Affaire Cysne*, (1930) 2 *Reports of International Arbitral Awards*, p. 1035.

[30] Bodin, supra n. 2, p. 190.

[31] Cf. article CXXIV and more broadly articles CXXI to CXXV of the Treaty of Münster, 24 October 1648, available at <http://avalon.law.yale.edu/17th_century/westphal.asp>.

[32] The 1907 (Hague) Convention (II) Respecting the Limitation of the Employment of Force for the Recovery of Contract Debts, (1908) 2 *American Journal of International Law* (Supplement), p. 81.

Covenant on the League of Nations,[33] the 1928 Kellogg-Briand Pact,[34] and finally the 1945 Charter of the United Nations,[35] international law prohibited recourse to war and armed force by one state against another. The significance of this development does not lie only with the restriction of the freedom of action of states as such, that is states no longer being able to 'lawfully' use armed force, but rather with the protection this entailed for the *sovereignty* of states, that is the authority states possess over their territory and population.

Where in the preceding centuries states could suffer from complete or partial loss of title to territory through conquest, that is through use of brute force, this is no longer legally allowed due to the prohibition of the use of armed force between states. Significantly, article 2 (4) of the Charter prescribes, among others, abstention of use of force against the *territorial integrity or political independence of any state*.[36] The precursor of this provision, article 10 of the Covenant of the League of Nations, brought out more strongly that the object was to protect states and their sovereignty, since the members undertook *to respect* and *preserve as against external aggression* the territorial integrity and political independence of all members. Furthermore, the prohibition of article 2 (4) of the Charter has been strengthened by a complementary norm denying the possibility of acquiring territory through aggression or the use of armed force.[37] That norm, moreover, does not apply only to the acquisition of territory by *unlawful* armed force, but also applies where the territory concerned would (purportedly) be acquired by a *lawful* use of armed force, for instance in self-defence.[38]

The particular protection provided by the prohibition of the use of armed force has been complemented by the prohibition of intervention in the

[33] The 1919 Covenant of the League of Nations, (1919) 13 *American Journal of International Law* (Supplement), p. 128.

[34] The 1928 General Pact for the Renunciation of War, (1928) 22 *American Journal of International Law* (Supplement), p. 171.

[35] The 1945 Charter of the United Nations, (1945) 39 *American Journal of International Law* (Supplement), p. 190.

[36] This specification was inserted at the behest of smaller states, which demanded protection precisely against the power politics of bigger states in disposing of the rights of other states. Cf. Randelzhofer, supra n. n. 29, p. 123–124. Recently the International Court of Justice opined that "(…) the scope of the principle of territorial integrity is confined to the sphere of relations between States": see the *Kosovo* opinion, par. 80.

[37] Principles that States shall refrain in their international relations from threat or use of force, paragraph 10, Declaration on Principles of International Law concerning Friendly Relations and Co-operation among States in accordance with the Charter of the United Nations, UNGA res. 2625 (XXV) (24 October 1970) (hereinafter: Declaration on Principles); article 5 (3) Definition of Aggression, UNGA res. 3314 (XXIX) (14 December 1974) (hereinafter: Definition of Aggression).

[38] Cf. Principles that States shall refrain in their international relations from threat or use of force, paragraph 10; Declaration on Principles; article 5 (3) Definition of Aggression. Note that this norm is further strengthened by requiring states not to recognise as legal any territorial acquisition resulting from the threat or use of force or from aggression.

internal or external affairs of states, which may be said to protect a state's freedom with respect to its actions and the policies it pursues regarding its own population and other states. The extent to which the internal or external affairs of a state are protected through the prohibition of intervention, depends on whether a certain matter remains within the domestic jurisdiction of a state or instead is regulated by international law.[39] Furthermore, not all interference is prohibited under international law, but only such as is coercive in character, as was made clear by the International Court of Justice in the *Nicaragua case*:

> A prohibited intervention must accordingly be one bearing on matters in which each State is permitted, by the principle of State sovereignty, to decide freely. One of these is the choice of a political, economic, social and cultural system, and the formulation of foreign policy. Intervention is wrongful when it uses methods of coercion in regard to such choices, which must remain free ones. The element of coercion, which defines, and indeed forms the very essence of, prohibited intervention, is particularly obvious in the case of an intervention that uses force, either in the direct form of military action, or in the indirect form of support for subversive or terrorist armed activities within another State.[40]

In respect of the question of coercion, the Court was mostly concerned with acts of (indirect) armed force (financing, training, arming of, providing intelligence and logistics to, the *contras*), but it also discussed the claim of Nicaragua that certain economic measures of the United States constituted a breach of the prohibition of intervention. The Court, with a noticeable lack of supporting argument, did not see such action as a breach of the prohibition.[41] Regarding the US claim of violation of human rights, the Court first suggested that such claims could be assessed at the regional level and could have led to decisions of competent OAS organs, and then noted:

> (…) while the United States might form its own appraisal of the situation as to respect for human rights in Nicaragua, the use of force could not be the appropriate method to monitor or ensure such respect.[42]

Though this claim has at times been interpreted as a rejection of humanitarian intervention,[43] the specific examples of use of force then mentioned by the Court "mining of ports, destruction of oil installations, and the training, arming and equipping of the *contras*" (the latter were themselves accused of violating human rights and international humanitarian law),[44] which it considered

[39] Cf. *Nationality Decrees Issued in Tunis and Morocco* (Advisory Opinion), PCIJ Reports 1923, Series B, No. 4, p. 24 (more broadly p. 21–26).
[40] *Military and Paramilitary Activities in and against Nicaragua (Nicaragua v. United States of America)* (Merits), ICJ Reports 1986, p. 108, par. 205 (hereinafter: *Nicaragua* case).
[41] Ibid., p. 125–126, par. 244–245 (see also p. 69–70, par. 123–125).
[42] Ibid., p. 134, par. 268.
[43] E.g. Randelzhofer, supra n. 29, p. 131, footnote 156.
[44] Cf. *Nicaragua* case, p. 134, par. 268, and p. 63–69, par. 113–122.

incompatible with the humanitarian objective of protection of human rights, militate against a generalisation of this kind.[45]

As to matters regarding which choices must remain free ones, the Court considered US support for the *contras*, which were intent upon overthrowing the Nicaraguan government, a breach of the prohibition.[46] Moreover, the Court considered pledges of the Nicaraguan government to organise free elections, and concluded that it could not find an instrument with legal force whereby Nicaragua had committed itself in respect of the principle or methods of holding elections.[47] In a related matter, with respect to the claim of the US Congress that the Nicaraguan government had moved into the direction of becoming a "totalitarian Communist dictatorship",[48] the Court found that, however one were to characterise Nicaragua's policies, it could not contemplate a new rule allowing intervention on the grounds of choice for certain ideologies or political system.[49] In this connection the Court also noted that foreign policy was protected and that international law did not prevent a state from conducting it in cooperation with another state.[50] Finally, the Court noted that, absent rules accepted by states under treaties or otherwise, international law knows no rules by which the weaponry of a state can be limited.[51]

However, the prohibitions of use (and threat) of armed force and intervention do not exhaust the protection that international law provides to states. The sovereignty of a state over its territory also entails the attribute of territorial jurisdiction, which is in principle unlimited (barring limitations under international law) and plenary in character. Though it is possible for another state to adopt legislation applying to persons, property or events abroad,[52] and of course in that sense a state's territorial jurisdiction is not exclusive, this also constitutes the outer limit of jurisdiction as the Permanent Court made clear in the *Lotus* case:

> Now the first and foremost restriction imposed by international law upon a State is that – failing the existence of a permissive rule to the contrary – it may not exercise its power in any form in the territory of another State. In this sense jurisdiction is certainly territorial; it cannot be exercised by a State outside its

[45] Ibid., p. 134–135, par. 268.
[46] Ibid., p. 123–124, par. 240–242.
[47] Ibid., p. 132, par. 261. The Court's finding is odd, because in 1980 Nicaragua had acceded to the International Covenant on Civil and Political Rights, which in article 25 stipulates that all citizens shall have the right to vote and be elected in genuine periodic elections. The 1966 International Covenant on Civil and Political Rights, 999 *UN Treaty Series*, p. 171; for ratification status, see <http://treaties.un.org/Pages/Treaties.aspx?id=4&subid=A&lang=en>.
[48] *Nicaragua* case, p. 133, par. 263.
[49] Ibid., and p. 134, par. 266.
[50] Ibid., p. 133, par. 264.
[51] Ibid., p. 135, par. 269.
[52] Cf. Shaw, supra n. 13, p. 659–686.

> territory except by virtue of a permissive rule of international law derived from international custom or from a convention.[53]

Overall therefore states are not merely protected against factual, physical conduct or coercive action,[54] but international law requires a state not to display any authority in the territory of another state without the proper consent of the competent organs of that state.

Finally, as all states deny the existence of any higher authority and mutually recognize each other as sovereign, this implies the equality of all states to each other. In view of such equality, affirmed for instance in article 2 (1) of the Charter, one state cannot exercise authority over another (captured by the Latin maxim *par in parem non habet imperium*). Consequently any decisions taken by (the authorities of) a state do not bind another state (except by consent). It is this feature that explains the existence of long-standing norms of state immunity that inhibit the exercise of jurisdiction by courts of a state over the (official) acts of other states. Though the norms on state immunity have suffered from erosion, immunity being denied for acts that have commercial or private law character (*acta iure gestionis*), immunity for acts that typify the sovereignty of the state (*acta iure imperii*) persists. Matters that concern derived state immunity, that is those that concern the immunities of persons representing the state, will be considered in the next section.

4. *Authority over Individuals*

One development in international law commonly invoked to support the thesis that state sovereignty is no longer sacrosanct is the protection of the human rights of individuals.[55] A second development, less frequently raised and possibly the more invasive, lies with the imposition of responsibility on individuals for violations of international law.

With respect to the first development, it is pertinent to mention, first of all, that there is nothing inherently contradictory between the sovereignty of a state and the assumption of obligations under international law that bind it to exercise its authority in a certain manner. As much was already affirmed by the Permanent Court in its first judgment ever, the *Wimbledon case*,[56] and this

---

[53] *Lotus* case, p. 18–19. Note that the ICJ in the *Nicaragua* case (p. 111, par. 212), considered respect for territorial sovereignty to be linked to the principles of non-use of force and non-intervention. Cf. also *Corfu Channel* (*United Kingdom v. Albania*) (Judgment), ICJ Reports 1949, p. 32–35 (hereinafter: *Corfu Channel* case).

[54] Cf. *Nicaragua* case, p. 111, par. 212–213, concerning sovereignty and placement of mines in the internal and territorial waters of a state.

[55] Cf. Jarat Chopra and Thomas G. Weiss, 'Sovereignty Is No Longer Sacrosanct: Codifying Humanitarian Intervention', (1992) 6 *Ethics and International Affairs*, p. 95.

[56] *Case of the S.S. "Wimbledon"* (Judgment), PCIJ Reports 1923, Series A, No. 1, p. 25.

was echoed by the ICJ in the *Nicaragua* case.[57] What this implies is that the number of matters falling within, or exclusively within, the internal or external affairs of any particular state, varies according to the presence or absence of rules of customary international law, the treaties to which a state may be a party and the decisions of international organisations to which it may be bound as a member (or any other international obligation).

This implication may lead to the further observation that since 1945 the number of matters falling within the domestic jurisdiction of states has, overall, decreased dramatically. And this is nowhere as apparent as regarding the acceptance by states of obligations for the protection of human rights. Such obligations are concerned not with the protection of the rights of foreign nationals within a state but with the rights of all individuals within a state, and in particular with the goal of protecting nationals of a state against the actions of their own government.[58] Consequently, many issues previously within the internal affairs of states are now subject to international obligations and hence to international scrutiny. If therefore states have lost a considerable quantum of freedom in their treatment of nationals and foreigners within their territories, does this conversely entail that they can no longer be considered to constitute the highest authority with respect to such individuals present within their territory? The answer must, on the whole, be negative.[59]

From the development of human rights standards and supervision some have argued that the sovereignty of states has been compromised through the existence of universal human rights standards,[60] or that sovereignty is now shared between states and various international institutions due to international supervision of the observance of human rights, the recognition of the individual as a subject of international law independent of state consent and

[57] *Nicaragua* case, p. 131, par. 259: "A State, which is free to decide upon the principle and methods of popular consultation within its domestic order, is sovereign for the purpose of accepting a limitation of its sovereignty in this field."

[58] It may be noted that the obligations in the general human rights conventions were intended to apply, first and foremost, to individuals within the territory or (territorial) jurisdiction of a state. Cf article 1 of the European Convention for the Protection of Human Rights and Fundamental Freedoms, 213 *UN Treaty Series*, p. 221; article 2 (1) of the ICCPR. Controversies over the scope of application of these treaties, however, abound. See e.g. the contributions in F. Coomans and M.T. Kamminga (eds), *Extraterritorial Application of Human Rights Treaties*, Antwerp: Intersentia 2004; M.J. Dennis, 'Application of Human Rights Treaties Extraterritorially in Times of Armed Conflict and Military Occupation', (2005) 99 *American Journal of International Law*, p. 119.

[59] It is not possible to say that the increase of obligations assumed by the state equals an inverse decrease in sovereignty. See Werner, supra n. 15, p. 133–134.

[60] Rod Jensen, 'Globalization and the International Criminal Court: Accountability and a New Conception of the State', in: Ige F. Dekker and Wouter G. Werner (eds.), *Governance and International Legal Theory*, Leiden: Martinus Nijhoff Publishers 2004, p. 170, p. 173–174, but he also notes that such standards do not necessarily impact upon the autonomy of the state to set its own policies.

the participation of NGOs in the treaty-making process.[61] However, some of the conclusions drawn appear to be overstated.

A preliminary observation is that it is primarily for states to live up to, perform and implement obligations to respect human rights. This follows already from article 2 (1) ICCPR which stipulates that states parties shall ensure and respect the human rights of individuals within their territory and subject to their jurisdiction. Furthermore, it is for states to adopt measures, whether legislative or otherwise (for instance judicial or administrative) for the actual implementation of the obligations of the Covenant (article 2 (2), including the provision of effective remedies for human rights violations (article 2 (3–4)). Such provisions provide the basis for requiring individuals to exhaust all available domestic remedies (article 2 Optional Protocol to the Covenant).[62]

Moreover, international institutions by and large do not determine the content of the internal law of a state. International courts and tribunals, whether in the field of human rights or otherwise, do not displace national courts in decisions of a civil, administrative or criminal character and, most importantly, do not act as courts of appeal with respect to such decisions.[63] And quite obviously the authorities of a state are in place to enforce law and order, for which there is no substitute at the international or regional level (barring UN administration of territories, such as occurred in Kosovo and East Timor). Thus, there is no actual displacement of authority when it comes to the concrete exercise of powers by states.

The argument has been made that states are increasingly subject to international supervision, both at a political level and through judicial intervention. Within the United Nations a member state's performance in the field of human rights may be subject to consideration by the Human Rights Council and more generally ECOSOC and the General Assembly. However, such supervision does not lead to binding decisions, nor to the (mandatory) imposition of sanctions against states violating human rights (unless the Security Council gets involved and exercises its powers under chapter VII of the Charter). Moreover, judicial intervention plays out foremost at the regional level, in Europe, the Americas and Africa, and not quite at the international level, since the (quasi-judicial) treaty bodies established under universal human rights conventions do not possess the power to adopt binding decisions.[64] It is

[61] Israel de Jesús Butler, *Unravelling Sovereignty: Human Rights Actors and the Structure of International Law*, Antwerp: Intersentia 2007.

[62] The 1966 Optional Protocol to the International Covenant on Civil and Political Rights, 999 *UN Treaty Series*, p. 171.

[63] See Sarah Joseph, Jenny Schultz and Melissa Castan, *The International Covenant on Civil and Political Rights: Cases, Materials, and Commentary*, Oxford: Oxford University Press 2004, p. 22–23, par. 1.47-1.48; *LaGrand (Germany v. United States of America)* (Judgment), ICJ Reports 2001, p. 485–486, par. 50–52.

[64] Contrary De Jesús Butler, supra n. 62, who at p. 85–88 and p. 135–140 comes to the conclusion that it is for the UN and supervisory bodies to determine the scope, content and

precisely for this reason, the lack of authority, more precisely the lack of a relationship of command and obedience, that one cannot see the competences and activities of universal human rights bodies as legally encroaching on the sovereignty of states.

Finally, it should be noted that although human rights may be invoked by a person at the national level, this does not provide individuals with justification to violate their own national law. In essence, a state's recognition of human rights obligations at the international level does not affect its internal regulation of the relationship between international law and national law. For this reason, the extent to which an individual may invoke his or her human rights at the national level may vary from state to state.

In a particular sense, one may see human rights law also as an attempt to bind the state, the highest authority, to the collectivity of individuals (or citizens) of a state through the lens of political representation. For that purpose article 25 of the International Covenant on Civil and Political Rights stipulates that all citizens of a particular state have the right:

> [t]o vote and be elected at genuine periodic elections which shall be by universal and equal suffrage and shall be held by secret ballot, guaranteeing the free expression of the will of the electors.

It seems plausible to regard the reference to the will of the electors as an endorsement of the theory of popular sovereignty. Although no reference is made to the idea that government ought to be based on the outcome of such elections, this would seem to underlie the various conditions formulated – genuine periodic, universal and equal suffrage, secret ballot, free expression of the will of the electors – with respect to such elections.

From the will of the electors it is but a small step to the right of self-determination of peoples, embodied in article 1 of the Covenant, which allows a people to freely determine its political status. Precisely the internal dimension of that right has been said to lie with the right of the people of any given state to freely determine its political status and to freely pursue its economic, social and cultural development. Thus *free* determination and *free* pursuit are the crux here, and the right to self-determination needs to be read in conjunction with article 25 ICCPR (and together with other freedoms, such as that of article 19 ICCPR).[65]

Taken together these developments have been at the heart of another one, which is intent upon denying the legitimacy, and legality, of the violent

---

interpretation of human rights obligations. From this flows, in conjunction with the obligation of states to perform their obligations in good faith and to cooperate with supervisory bodies in good faith, that a state would not be entitled to impose its own understanding of its human rights obligations on an individual (ibid., p. 135).

[65] Antonio Cassese, *Self-determination of Peoples: A Legal Reappraisal*, Cambridge: Cambridge University Press 1995, p. 52–55.

overthrow of governments, and more broadly speaking of government denial of the outcome of elections and consequent refusal to relinquish power.[66]

As to the second development, the imposition of criminal responsibility on individuals for violating international law, this may be said to have started with the Nuremberg Charter and the trials held pursuant thereto.[67] Prior to this war crimes had been prosecuted by such belligerent parties that could get hold of suspected individuals,[68] and the Allies after World War I had wanted to prosecute the German Emperor for committing "a supreme offence against international morality and the sanctity of treaties".[69] The trials at Nuremberg were different in that for the first time an international (military) tribunal had been established, with its jurisdiction extended from war crimes to crimes against the peace and crimes against humanity. Moreover, the Charter specifically denied the possibility for a defendant of invoking his or her official position, even as head of state, or the fact that the act concerned had been ordered by the government or a superior.[70] In its judgment, the Tribunal observed, by reference to article 7 of the Charter which denied the possibility of defence based on official position, that:

> (…) the very essence of the Charter is that individuals have international duties which transcend the national obligations of obedience imposed by the individual state. He who violates the laws of war cannot obtain immunity while acting in pursuance of the authority of the state if the state in authorising action moves outside its competence under international law.[71]

The significance of the Nuremberg Charter and the Nuremberg Judgment does not lie with the trial of individuals before an international tribunal as such. This may be done by states acting collectively, provided that such states would be entitled under international law to establish jurisdiction. Nor does it

---

66 Cf. Brad R. Roth, *Governmental Illegitimacy in International Law*, Oxford: Oxford University Press 1999; Karel Wellens, 'The UN Security Council and New Threats to the Peace: Back to the Future', (2003) 8 *Journal of Conflict and Security Law*, p. 46–47, p. 66. For two recent examples, see par. 1 and par. 8 of UNSC res. 1962 (20 December 2010), UN doc. S/RES/1962 (Ivory Coast), urging respect for "the will of the people and the outcome of the election"; par. 1 of UNSC res. 1970 (26 February 2011), UN doc. S/RES/1970 (Libya), referring to the "legitimate demands of the population".

67 Charter of the International Military Tribunal to be found in the 1945 Agreement for the prosecution and punishment of the major war criminals of the European Axis, 251 *UN Treaty Series*, p. 284 (Nuremberg Charter); *Judgment of the Nuremberg International Military Tribunal 1946* (1947) 41 *American Journal of International Law*, p. 172 (hereinafter: *Nuremberg* judgment).

68 Cf. article 228 of the 1919 Treaty of Peace with Germany, (1919) 13 *American Journal of International Law* (Supplement), p. 151 (Treaty of Peace with Germany), in which Germany recognised the right of the Allies to bring persons to military trial for having committed violations of the laws and customs of war.

69 Cf. article 227 of the Treaty of Peace with Germany.

70 Articles 7 and 8 of the Nuremberg Charter.

71 *Nuremberg* judgment, p. 221, more broadly p. 216–221.

lie with the trial of individuals in a general sense, since the rules of international law concerning the establishment of jurisdiction provide ample opportunities to proceed with such trials.[72] No, the significance lies with the fact that the acts and omissions concerned were committed by individuals that represented the state and that they constituted an exercise of the state's authority, that such acts and omissions were considered criminal and were qualified as crimes under international law – that is, crimes against the peace, war crimes, and crimes against humanity – and that on trial the individuals in question were denied the immunities due to representatives of states under international law.

And all of this, seen from the perspective of sovereignty, leads to that one sentence in the *Nuremberg* judgment which had such far-reaching effects, that individuals have duties under international law that transcend obligations of obedience to the state. That states are required to perform their obligations under international law has long been uncontroversial.[73] However, aside from the originally rather limited possibility of prosecuting soldiers for war crimes by a belligerent party to a war, international law had not known of the responsibility of an individual for committing a violation of international law, and hence the authority of the state and the duties of individuals under its law were unchallenged.

This was the case for various reasons. First of all, individuals were not considered subjects of international law and did not have obligations under international law, but at most under domestic law. Secondly, to the extent that certain individuals could be considered to have committed crimes under domestic law, states argued that these individuals could not be prosecuted if they had been acting as the agents of the states. This was the case, notoriously, with the prosecution of McLeod, who had boasted to have been involved in the capture of *The Caroline* in 1837, in setting it on fire and in sending it off over the Niagara Falls.[74] And as much was true as late as the mid-1980s when France argued, equally notoriously, that its (external security) agents Mafart

[72] Shaw, supra n. 13, p. 659–686.

[73] Cf. article 27 of the 1969 Vienna Convention on the Law of Treaties, 1155 *UN Treaty Series*, p. 331; and articles 3 and 32 of the 2001 Draft on the Responsibility of States for Internationally Wrongful Acts, (2001) *Yearbook of the International Law Commission*, Volume II, Part Two, p. 26 (for commentaries, see p. 36–38 and p. 94).

[74] See Kenneth Shewmaker (ed.), *The Papers of Daniel Webster: Diplomatic Papers, Volume 1, 1841–1843*, Hanover: University Press of New England 1983, p. 651, p. 656, letter of Lord Ashburton, and also ibid., p. 669, p. 670, letter of Secretary of State Webster of the United States, where McLeod was being prosecuted, in which he observed: "This Government has admitted, that for an act committed by the command of his sovereign, *jure belli*, an individual cannot be responsible, in the ordinary courts of another State. It would regard it as a high indignity if a citizen of its own, acting under its authority, and by its special command, in such cases, were held to answer in a municipal tribunal, and to undergo punishment, as if the behest of his Government were no defence or protection to him."

and Prieur could not be prosecuted by the New Zealand authorities for having placed a bomb on board *The Rainbow Warrior* in the harbour of Auckland.[75]

However, the Nuremberg Charter and Judgment initiated a development by which certain crimes came to be recognized as crimes under international law, and which on that basis disallowed any plea of justification under internal law (including the defence of superior orders). The principles involved were early on affirmed by the General Assembly,[76] and later the International Law Commission gave legal form to the Nuremberg Principles.[77] Moreover, one of the more important principles formulated related to the official position of individuals, whether as heads of state or government officials, which would not absolve such persons from responsibility nor mitigate punishment. Seen from this perspective, it stood to reason that immunities that might apply – a matter not as such addressed in the Principles – would also have to give way, since to affirm responsibility on the one hand but then to respect immunities on the other hand would render the principle of personal responsibility nugatory.

The developments set out above remained inconsequential, as no international tribunal was established for over 45 years. Although the end of the Cold War already sparked renewed interest, the creation of the Yugoslavia and Rwanda Tribunals by the Security Council in 1993 and 1994 moved everything into hyperspeed.[78] The International Law Commission prepared a draft statute for an international criminal court and the Draft Code of Crimes against the Peace and Security of Mankind,[79] the General Assembly established a Preparatory Committee to draft a convention for an international criminal court,[80] after which the Rome Conference adopted the Statute of the International Criminal Court.[81] The principles underlying the responsibility of the individual under international law were therefore extended from its application to defeated states and specific circumstances, to cover all states that are parties to the ICC Statute, and this has generalised the rules concerned and evidences their general acceptance.

---

[75] See *Case concerning the differences between New Zealand and France arising from the Rainbow Warrior affair*, (1986) 19 *Reports of International Arbitral Awards*, p. 208, par. 4, p. 210–211, par. 9 (for decision, see p. 213–214, par. 3).

[76] UNGA res. 95 (I) (11 December 1946).

[77] See Principles VI, and I, II, and IV of the 1950 Principles of International Law Recognized in the Charter of the Nürnberg Tribunal and the Judgment of the Tribunal, (1950) *Yearbook of the International Law Commission*, Volume II, p. 374.

[78] UNSC res. 827 (25 May 1993), UN doc. S/RES/827; UNSC res. 955 (8 November 1994), UN doc. S/RES/955.

[79] Draft statute for an international criminal court, (1994) *Yearbook of the International Law Commission*, Volume II, Part Two, p. 26; Draft Code of Crimes against the Peace and Security of Mankind, (1996) *Yearbook of the International Law Commission*, Volume II, Part Two, p. 17.

[80] UNGA res. 50/46 (18 December 1995), UN doc. A/RES/50/46.

[81] The 1998 Rome Statute of the International Criminal Court, 2187 *UN Treaty Series*, p. 90 (hereinafter: ICC Statute).

Articles 12 and 13 of the Statute do not as such allow for the exercise of jurisdiction based on universality, aside from the case where the Security Council refers a situation to the ICC,[82] but rather on the basis of nationality and territoriality. Objections have nevertheless been raised with respect to the application of the Statute to nationals of non-states parties that committed crimes in the territory of a state party.[83] However, the primary reason for arguing encroachment of sovereignty on this score lies in the perceived lack of consent of non-party states to the ICC Statute.[84] This particular objection misses the mark since the rules of international law on establishing and exercising jurisdiction have never required consent by the states of nationals subjected to such jurisdiction.

Another objection raised is that in judging individuals for committing war crimes, crimes against humanity and genocide, one would in reality be judging state behaviour since the individuals concerned will have acted on behalf of the state.[85] This objection is similar to those recounted above regarding the prosecutions of McLeod and of Mafart and Prieur, and amounts to saying that the conduct of the state should not be held against an individual. That objection seems no longer accepted with full force,[86] though it does raise questions regarding the scope of derived immunities under international law.

The ICC Statute has adopted, in articles 25, 27 and 33, the same principles of individual responsibility as were applied in the past. However, when looking at the question of immunities a slightly different picture emerges. Article 27 (2) of the Statute does specify that immunities under international law will not bar the Court from exercising its jurisdiction. However, when an exercise of jurisdiction would concern a national of a non-state party to the Statute, article 98 (1) of the Statute stipulates that the Court shall not issue a request for surrender or assistance if this would require the requested state to disregard the diplomatic or state immunity of a person of a third state, unless it could obtain a waiver of that third state.

No doubt this rather more conservative provision has been motivated by the perceived differences between earlier international criminal tribunals and the ICC. The Nuremberg and Tokyo Military Tribunals tried nationals of

---

[82] Two referrals have been made, first in relation to the situation of Darfur in Sudan and this year in relation to the violence in Libya. See § 1 UNSC res. 1593 (31 March 2005), UN doc. S/RES/1593; § 4 UNSC res. 1970 (26 February 2011), UN doc. S/RES/1970.

[83] E.g. Diane Marie Amann, 'The International Criminal Court and the Sovereign State', in: Ige F. Dekker and Wouter G. Werner (eds.), *Governance and International Legal Theory*, Leiden: Martinus Nijhoff Publishers 2004, p. 185.

[84] Ibid., p. 190–194, p. 208–211.

[85] Ibid., p. 198.

[86] Cf. Francisco Messineo, 'The untidy dystopias of anti-terrorism: Italian State Secrets, CIA Covert Operations, and the Criminal Law in the Abu Omar Judgment', available at <http://www.ejiltalk.org/the-untidy-dystopias-of-anti-terrorism-italian-state-secrets-cia-covert-operations-and-the-criminal-law-in-the-abu-omar-judgment/#more-2532>.

states that had unconditionally surrendered at the end of World War II. The ICTY and ICTR have been created by binding decisions of the Security Council, and UN members have agreed to accept and carry out decisions of the Council (article 25 Charter). The ICC Statute, however, is a treaty and due to its conventional character binds only the parties.[87] Hence, though the ICC exercises jurisdiction over natural persons only (article 25 (1) ICC Statute), its decisions will not bind third states and, crucially, to ignore the immunity benefiting a national of a third state is to ignore the immunity of that third state.[88]

If a rule of customary international law were to exist that would allow states to ignore the immunity of nationals of a state committing international crimes, this could justify a rule different from the one put down in article 98 (1) ICC Statute. However, in the *Arrest Warrant* case the International Court of Justice held that, as diplomatic and consular agents, certain persons holding high-ranking office, such as heads of state and government and ministers of foreign affairs, benefit from immunities.[89] The immunities benefiting current ministers of foreign affairs before national courts, the Court concluded, do not suffer any form of exception in case of war crimes or crimes against humanity.[90] However, it held that immunity does not imply impunity and observed, among others and referring to article 27 (2) ICC Statute, that such persons could be prosecuted before international criminal tribunals such as the ICC.[91]

At the same time the usefulness of the Court's judgment is limited by the fact that it only considered the immunities of current, that is incumbent, high-ranking officials, who it held enjoy full immunity with no distinction to be made according to the official or private character of his or her acts or presence in another state.[92] With respect to the possibility of prosecution after leaving office the Court mentioned that such officials could be prosecuted for acts before and after that period of office and for private acts committed during office.[93] For that reason, *a contrario*, official acts of high-ranking state authorities could not lead to prosecution before national courts. Yet this

---

[87] Article 34 VCLT.

[88] Hence the debate that has followed the decision of the Pre-Trial Chamber of the ICC to issue an arrest warrant for incumbent president Al Bashir of Sudan, a debate especially intense in view of the rather inadequate argument why president Al Bashir would not benefit from immunity under article 98 ICC Statute. *Prosecutor v. Omar Hassan Ahmad Al Bashir* ICC-02/05-01/09 (application for arrest warrant) (4 March 2009), par. 40–45. See Paola Gaeta, 'Does President Al Bashir Enjoy Immunity from Arrest?', (2009) 7 *Journal of International Criminal Justice*, p. 315; Dapo Akande, 'The Legal Nature of Security Council Referrals to the ICC and its Impact on Al Bashir's Immunities', (2009) 7 *Journal of International Criminal Justice*, p. 333.

[89] *Arrest Warrant of 11 April 2000 (Democratic Republic of the Congo v. Belgium)* (Judgment), ICJ Reports 2002, p. 20–21, par. 51.

[90] Ibid., p. 24, par. 58.

[91] Ibid., p. 26–27, par. 61, without, however, mentioning the limitation(s) provided under article 98 ICC Statute.

[92] Ibid., p. 22, par. 54–55.

[93] Ibid., p. 26, par. 61.

suggests, as the Court denied the existence of a rule of customary international law allowing the setting aside of immunities in case of international crimes by incumbent high-ranking authorities,[94] that the immunity for official acts of other representatives of a state of lower rank might perhaps persist also.[95]

The jurisdiction of the International Criminal Court is limited to crimes of most serious concern to the international community as a whole, which tend to implicate state authorities at the highest level. Important in this respect is the principle of complementarity, as stated in the preamble of the ICC Statute, which enjoins states to exercise their primary responsibility to deal with situations in which individuals are suspected of having committed crimes within the jurisdiction of the Court.[96] However, considering the likely suspects of such crimes it cannot be excluded that a state, barring a change of government, will be unable or unwilling to deal *genuinely* with persons committing such crimes. This has provided the motivation to include in article 20 (3) of the Statute, an exception to the prohibition of double jeopardy (*ne bis in idem*), which may allow the Court to proceed with a trial of a person already tried or acquitted by another (national) court. Unlike other rules intended to allow the Court to investigate or try persons when a state is unwilling or unable to deal with such persons at the national level, the exception of article 20 (3) permits one to view the ICC not as a kind of appellate jurisdiction, but as a body that is enabled to overrule a specific exercise of authority by the state.[97] Otherwise, the Court does possess wide-ranging powers to solicit the cooperation of the parties for the investigation and prosecution of persons suspected of having committed crimes within its jurisdiction.[98]

There are nevertheless various reasons why the ICC should not be viewed as a higher authority either. First, its competence is limited in that the crimes subject to its jurisdiction are the most serious ones of concern to the international community and relate to situations in which a breakdown in (international) law and order is current. Consequently, the Court will exercise its powers in crisis situations rather than with respect to the ordinary, normal state of affairs. Moreover, even then the Court's jurisdiction is complementary to that of the state(s) directly concerned.

In the second place, the Court may exercise its jurisdiction only, aside from a Security Council referral, when such exercise is triggered by a person

[94] Ibid., p. 24, par. 58.

[95] The Court at some point referred to obligations under treaties to establish and exercise criminal jurisdiction to prevent and punish, and to prosecute or extradite, certain serious crimes, adding in the same breath that such treaties do not affect immunities under customary international law. Ibid., p. 24–25, par. 59.

[96] Jensen, supra n. 60, p. 180–181.

[97] Ibid., p. 179–180

[98] Articles 86–102 ICC Statute.

committing a crime within the territory of a state party or by one of its nationals (article 12 ICC Statute). As a result, the powers of the Court to request cooperation by the parties are incidental to its exercise of jurisdiction over natural persons. As such the Court does not possess the competence to address any matter pertaining to the responsibility of a state (cf. also article 25 (4) ICC Statute), including the attribution of conduct to that state, and in particular cannot claim cessation, reparation (restitution, compensation or satisfaction) or guarantees against repetition of such a state.

Finally, the Statute recognises the possibility of a party to withdraw, with effect after a year (article 127 ICC Statute), thus allowing a state to escape the Court's authority unless the Security Council were to refer a situation. Strikingly Members of Parliament in Kenya have voted to withdraw from the ICC Statute in response to the ICC Prosecutor's request to a Pre-Trial Chamber to issue summonses to appear for six Kenyan citizens in relation to the post-election violence in 2007–2008.[99]

5. *The Security Council as a Modern-Day Sovereign?*

Moving from the sphere of criminal jurisdiction to the maintenance of international peace and security, it has not gone unnoticed that the end of the Cold War enabled the Security Council to exercise its chapter VII powers. What made many raise an eyebrow was the novel way in which the Security Council used its powers. Among the developments provoking fierce debate have been the creation of the two ad hoc international criminal tribunals,[100] and its resolutions on the financing of terrorism and the proliferation of weapons of mass destruction which may deemed to amount to acts of international legislation.[101] Before going into the Council's legislative exercise, it is opportune to mention just a few examples of its practise with respect to the more typical enforcement measures, since these have ventured into targeting specific individuals.

It is generally accepted that demands made of targeted states or entities by the Council are binding upon those states or entities, as may be illustrated by reference to the ICJ's observation in the *Certain Expenses* opinion:

> To this end, it is the Security Council which is given a power to impose an explicit obligation of compliance if for example it issues an order or command to an

[99] BBC, 'Kenya MPs vote to leave ICC over poll violence claims' (23 December 2010), <http://www.bbc.co.uk/news/world-africa-12066667>; ICC Press Release, 'Kenya's post election violence: ICC Prosecutor presents cases against six individuals for crimes against humanity' (15 December 2010), <http://www.icc-cpi.int/NR/exeres/BA2041D8-3F30-4531-8850-431B5B2F4416.htm>.

[100] See supra, n. 79.

[101] UNSC res. 1373 (28 September 2001), UN doc. S/RES/1373; UNSC res. 1540 (28 April 2004), UN doc. S/RES/1540.

> aggressor under Chapter VII. It is only the Security Council which can require enforcement by coercive action against an aggressor.[102]

Where the Security Council first invoked its powers to adopt coercive measures against member states (South Africa) or state-like entities (Southern Rhodesia),[103] it later extended the circle of targets to encompass measures against governments (the Taliban regime in Afghanistan) and armed opposition groups (UNITA in Angola).[104] From this it went on to target terrorists groups (Al-Qaida) and persons associated with such groups, but most importantly it decided to request the relevant Sanctions Committee to compile a list of names of such persons, whose funds would be frozen by any member in a position to do so upon inclusion on that list.[105] Similar measures targeted at individuals have been adopted, for instance, in relation to the nuclear programme of Iran.[106]

Resolutions 1373 and 1540 of the Security Council have a few features that appear to give them the appearance of acts of international legislation. First, contrary to its earlier and later practise of tying its determination to a concrete situation, the resolutions affirm that acts of international terrorism and proliferation of weapons of mass destruction constitute threats to international peace and security. Consequently abstract phenomena are held to constitute threats, rather than any concrete event or situation. Furthermore, in the past the Council has asserted that the "non-military sources of instability in the economic, social, humanitarian and ecological fields have become threats to peace and security".[107] If the Council were to determine actual threats to the peace on this basis, the scope of its competence would be significantly expanded.[108] Secondly, the measures specified are decisions that apply generally and place obligations on all members rather than target any particular (member) state or entity or individual. Thirdly, the Council decided that the financing of terrorism, when engaged in wilfully by individuals, must be criminalised, whereas in the case of the proliferation of weapons of mass destruction it placed an obligation on (member) states to enforce various measures by appropriate criminal or civil penalties. All these

---

102 *Certain expenses of the United Nations (Article 17, paragraph 2, of the Charter)* (Advisory Opinion), ICJ Reports 1962, p. 163; cf. also *Questions of Interpretation and Application of the 1971 Montreal Convention arising from the Aerial Incident at Lockerbie (Libyan Arab Jamahiriya v. United Kingdom)* (Provisional Measures), ICJ Reports 1992, p. 15, par. 39.

103 E.g. UNSC res. 232 (16 December 1966, Southern Rhodesia), UN doc. S/RES/232; UNSC res. 418 (4 November 1977, South Africa), UN doc. S/RES/232.

104 UNSC res. 864 (15 September 1993, Angola), UN doc. S/RES/864; UNSC res 1268 (15 October 1999, Afghanistan), UN doc. S/RES/1268.

105 See par. 8 (c) of UNSC res. 1333 (19 December 2000), UN doc. S/RES/1333.

106 See par. 12 and Annex of UNSC res. 1737 (27 December 2006), UN doc. S/RES/1737.

107 UNSC (31 January 1992), UN doc. S/23500, p. 3.

108 Cf. Wellens, supra n. 66, p. 28–29.

features have led quite a few authors to argue the Council legislated for the members.[109]

The issue under consideration here is not whether the Security Council is bound to conform to human rights obligations and whether it violates such obligations,[110] but whether in exercising its powers it acts as an authority over and above UN member states. When it comes to the maintenance of international peace and security the Security Council possesses a primary responsibility (article 24 Charter), and under chapter VII of the Charter it may decide on measures under articles 41 and 42 subject to a determination of the existence of a threat to the peace, breach of the peace or act of aggression. Furthermore, it is generally recognised that the measures adopted may be binding and will have to be implemented by the members, as they have agreed to accept and carry out decisions of the Council (article 25 Charter).

Clearly then, by virtue of the Council's functions and powers, it could be considered an authority higher than that of the UN members, since the relationship between the Council and UN members may be characterised as one of command and obedience. Moreover, in view of the Security Council's legislative activity, its establishment of international criminal tribunals,[111] and its enforcement powers, the Council's broad competence seems to comprise all such powers as might typify a 'sovereign' (though not evidencing all the marks

---

[109] Cf. André J.J. de Hoogh, 'Attribution or Delegation of (Legislative) Power by the Security Council? The Case of the United Nations Transitional Administration in East Timor (UNTAET)', (2001) 7 *International Peacekeeping. The Yearbook of International Peace Operations*, p. 1; Jurij Daniel Aston, 'Die Bekämpfung abstrakter Gefahren für den Weltfrieden durch legislative Maßnahmen des Sicherheitsrat – Resolution 1373 (2001) im Kontext', (2002) 62 *Zeitschrift für Ausländisches Öffentliches Recht und Rechtsvergleichung*, p. 257; Roberto Lavalle, 'A Novel, if Awkward, Exercise in International Law-Making: Security Council Resolution 1540 (2004)', (2004) 51 *Netherlands International Law Review*, p. 411; Stefan Talmon, 'The Security Council as World Legislature', (2005) 99 *American Journal of International Law*, p. 175; Michael Fremuth and Jörn Griebel, 'On the Security Council as a Legislator: A Blessing or a Curse for the International Community,' (2007), 76 *Nordic Journal of International Law, p.* 339.

[110] See on this topic e.g. the chapter by Boisson de Chazournes and Kuijper in this book; Iain Cameron, 'UN Targeted Sanctions, Legal Safeguards and the European Convention on Human Rights', (2003) 72 *Nordic Journal of International Law*, p. 159; Clémentine Olivier, 'Human Rights Law and the International Fight against Terrorism: How do Security Council Resolutions Impact on States' Obligations Under International Human Rights Law? (Revisiting Security Council Resolution 1373)', (2004) 73 *Nordic Journal of International Law*, p. 399.

[111] The suggestion has even been made that the Security Council could, in the exercise of its chapter VII powers, enjoin states to submit their dispute to the International Court of Justice, which would on this basis have jurisdiction under article 36(1) of its Statute as a matter "specially provided for in the Charter of the United Nations". Christian Tomuschat, 'Article 36', in: Andreas Zimmermann, Christian Tomuschat and Karin Oellers-Frahm (eds.), *The Statute of the International Court of Justice: A Commentary*, Oxford: Oxford University Press 2006, p. 617–618. For the contrary view, Jörg Kammerhofer and André de Hoogh, 'All Things to All People? The International Court of Justice and its Commentators', (2007) 18 *European Journal of International Law*, p. 974–975. The 1945 Statute of the International Court of Justice, (1945) 39 *American Journal of International Law* (Supplement), p. 215.

of sovereignty put forward by Bodin). However, there are different reasons why such a conclusion would be inappropriate.

First, the implementation of decisions of the Security Council is the responsibility of the members and the effects of its decisions in their legal systems is not predetermined by the Council. As much can be gleaned from, for instance, the judgment of the General Court of the European Union in the *Kadi* case quashing once more the regulation implementing the decisions of the Council targeting individuals on the Resolution 1267 Committee's list.[112]

Secondly, to the extent that sovereignty would equate either absolute or ultimate power, the Security Council's powers are generally considered limited both by specific provision (for instance article 24 (3) of the Charter stipulating that the Council's exercise of powers must remain faithful to the purposes and principles of the United Nations),[113] as well as by the principle of speciality which limits an international organisation to the (express or implied) powers that the states which created them intended them to possess, and excess of which might lead one to the conclusion that an act was adopted *ultra vires*.[114]

Thirdly, states as founding fathers may grant powers to an international organisation, but they may also take them away. In other words, the member states of the United Nations possess power over the Charter. The amendment procedure of the Charter testifies to this, though amendment is a tall order requiring ratifications by two thirds of all the UN members including those of the permanent members of the Security Council (articles 108–109 Charter). More generally all the parties to a treaty acting together are entitled, after proper consultation, to suspend or terminate it,[115] but this requires unanimous approval and thus this will constitute an even taller order.

Finally, as a collective will to limit the Council's competence or powers, or to escape from its authority, may be inadequately formed or lacking altogether, a right to withdraw unilaterally from the United Nations could perhaps provide redress to a state fearing for its sovereignty. Article 56 of the Vienna Convention on the Law of Treaties disallows this, unless it can be established that the parties intended to allow for withdrawal or when this may be implied by the nature of the treaty.

The *travaux préparatoires* of the Charter evidence that withdrawal would be possible in exceptional circumstances, for instance if the UN would fail its responsibility to maintain international peace and security or could do so only by sacrificing law and justice.[116] Whether other circumstances could warrant

---

[112] Case T-85/09, *Yassin Abdullah Kadi v European Commission*, [2010] ECR II-1998.

[113] Cf. ICTY, *Prosecutor v. Tadić* (Jurisdiction) (2 October 1995), (1996) 35 *International Legal Materials*, p. 42–43, par. 28–29.

[114] *Legality of the Use by a State of Nuclear Weapons in Armed Conflict* (Advisory Opinion), ICJ Reports 1996, p. 78–79, par. 25, and p. 82–83, par. 29.

[115] Articles 54 (b) and 57 (b) VCLT.

[116] UNCIO doc. 1210, 27 June 1945, volume I, p. 612, p. 616.

withdrawal,[117] and whether a right of withdrawal exists under customary international law,[118] is controversial. Yet certainly when the matter at issue concerns the withdrawal from a treaty establishing an international organisation, in particular when that organisation possesses the power to adopt decisions binding upon its members, a right of unilateral withdrawal could turn out to be a final guarantee and the ultimate backbone of the sovereignty of its member states.

6. *Conclusions*

This contribution has started out by discussing the traditional notion of sovereignty, as conceptualized by Bodin, though with certain adaptations drawn from the theory and body of international law. Under international law, sovereignty is inherent in states and signifies that they possess authority over their territory and population and that they do not recognise any other entity as a higher authority. Authority is taken to imply a relationship by which an entity possesses the power to issue commands to its subjects which are bound to obey. Furthermore, the mere existence of law that binds a certain entity is not sufficient to assume the existence of a higher authority; an authority must be 'personified' in that powers are exercised by a certain body or natural or legal person.

After the conceptualisation of sovereignty and its acceptance by and application to the European entities in the 17th century, international law lagged behind in protecting the new authorities. Recourse to war became accepted as an attribute of sovereignty and no (small) State was safe from being conquered by its peers. In the 20th century all of this changed with the prohibitions of war, of the use of force, and of forceful intervention. Otherwise international law also stipulated the exclusivity of territorial jurisdiction (at least insofar as the actual display of authority is concerned), and protected the sovereign equality of states by barring the exercise of jurisdiction over acts of states (*par in parem non habet imperium*) under rules of state immunity.

After World War II, a major transformation took place through two developments related to the position of the individual under international law.

[117] Consider the purported withdrawal of Indonesia from the United Nations in February 1965, in protest of the election of Malaysia as a non-permanent member of the Security Council, only to be followed by a resumption of full cooperation in September 1966. Cf. Yehuda Z. Blum, 'Indonesia's return to the United Nation', (1967) 16 *The International and Comparative Law Quarterly*, p. 522.

[118] Cf. Herbert W. Briggs, 'Unilateral Denunciation of Treaties: The Vienna Convention and the International Court of Justice', (1974) 68 *American Journal of International Law*, p. 51; Kelvin Widdows, 'The Unilateral Denunciation of Treaties Containing No Denunciation Clause', (1982) 53 *British Yearbook of International Law*, p. 83; Yogesh Tyagi, 'The Denunciation of Human Rights Treaties', (2008) 79 *British Yearbook of International Law*, p. 86.

First, states started to accept that individuals within their territory and/or subject to their jurisdiction possess human rights, assumed obligations concerning the treatment of their own population, and also agreed to international supervision of the performance of such obligations. However, the assumption of obligations by states in the field of human rights does not undermine their sovereignty, since it remains their primary responsibility to perform such obligations and their authority over territory and population is not actually substituted at the international level. Moreover, the supervision exercised at the universal level by the UN or treaty bodies, in view of the lack of binding force, cannot be considered an exercise of authority.

Secondly, the Nuremberg Tribunal following its Charter posited that international law imposes duties upon individuals, which when violated lead to criminal responsibility. Since such duties are owed under international law, certain defences recognised under national law, such as superior orders, would not be available. As the sovereign state is the highest authority, entailing a relationship of command and obedience between that authority and its subjects, the claim of international criminal law – that individuals must either disregard their duty of obedience or risk being held responsible for committing crimes under international law – is an assault on sovereignty if ever there was one. Moreover, as such crimes are most likely to be committed by persons acting on behalf of the state, disregard of the official status and elimination of immunities of such persons before international tribunals may prove the most revolutionary of all advances.

Of more recent origin is the unprecedented expansion of activities by the Security Council of the United Nations. Armed with broad powers under chapter VII of the Charter, it has progressed from the adoption of coercive and enforcement measures, to the creation of international criminal tribunals, and to legislating for the members. Gathering all unseparated but separable powers into its own hands, the Security Council might well be considered a new modern-day sovereign. However, such a conclusion would be inappropriate, if only because the power to change the Charter lies with the members of the United Nations rather than with the organization itself. Yet the requirements for amending, suspending or terminating the Charter are so demanding that the preservation of the sovereignty of its member states may, ultimately, necessitate recognition of a unilateral right of withdrawal from the United Nations.

All this is not to say that the freedom of states is unfettered, unopposed and subject to no outside influence or interference. Quite the contrary. Norms are set increasingly at the international level, states appear more willing, at least in the last twenty years, to subject themselves to binding dispute settlement in special contexts,[119] though the enforcement of law and order in the international community remains problematic. This contribution has considered various developments that could be seen to undermine the sovereignty of states, but in the end the conclusion reached should be that it is premature to conduct a post-mortem on the concept of sovereignty.

[119] Though, historically, the number of states parties accepting the compulsory jurisdiction of the International Court of Justice (presently sixty-six) has remained stable at about one third of all parties to the Statute. Cf. <http://www.icj-cij.org/jurisdiction/index.php?p1=5&p2=1&p3=3>.

PART III

SHIFTING PATTERNS IN INTERNATIONAL DISPUTE SETTLEMENT

CHAPTER ELEVEN

ISSUES OF SHARED RESPONSIBILITY BEFORE THE INTERNATIONAL COURT OF JUSTICE

*André Nollkaemper**

1. *Introduction*

While most instances in which the international responsibility of states is engaged, involve wrongful acts committed by individual states, international responsibility also may arise out of the acts of two or more states. Examples can be found in the context of multinational military operations,[1] extra-territorial migration policies,[2] or acts that contribute to climate change or other transboundary environmental problems.[3] In these cases, responsibility may be shared between two of more states.[4]

The principles applicable to cases of shared responsibility are not well developed. The International Law Commission (ILC), both in its work on responsibility of states and the responsibility of international organisations, recognised that attribution of acts to one state or organisation does not exclude the possible attribution of the same act to another state or organisation.[5] But it has

---

* This contribution is written as part of the SHARES project, a research project on Shared Responsibility in International Law funded by the European Research Council and carried out at the Amsterdam Center for International Law (ACIL) at the University of Amsterdam. I thank Christiane Ahlborn, Jean d'Aspremont, Nienke van der Have, Dov Jacobs, Erik Kok, and Isabelle Swerissen for assistance in preparing this chapter and for useful comments on earlier drafts. The topic is chosen in recognition of the important contribution that Karel Wellens has made to the law of international responsibility, and the essay is written in his honour.

[1] See generally Tom Dannenbaum, 'Translating the Standard of Effective Control into a System of Effective Accountability: How Liability Should be Apportioned for Violations of Human Rights by Member State Troop Contingents Serving as United Nations Peacekeepers', (2010) 51 *Harvard International Law Journal*, p. 113.

[2] Bernard Ryan and Valsamis Mitsilegas (eds.), *Extraterritorial Immigration Control: Legal Challenges*, Leiden-Boston: Martinus Nijhoff Publishers 2010.

[3] See e.g. Phoebe N. Okowa, *State Responsibility for Transboundary Air Pollution in International Law*, Oxford: Oxford University Press 2000, p. 195, discussing "Responsibility and Multiple State Actors".

[4] For further clarification of the term 'shared responsibility', see section 2 infra.

[5] International Law Commission (hereinafter: ILC), *Draft Articles on Responsibility of States for Internationally Wrongful Acts* (2001) UN GAOR Supplement No. 10 (A/56/10) ch. IV.E.1 (hereinafter: Articles on State Responsibility), article 19: "This chapter is without prejudice to the international responsibility, under other provisions of these articles, of the State which commits the act in question, or of any other State", and ILC, *Draft Articles on the Responsibility of International Organizations*, Report of the Sixty-First Session (2009) UN GAOR (A/64/10)

provided limited guidance to the allocation of responsibility or reparation in such cases. Article 47 of the Articles on State Responsibility stipulates that where several states are responsible for the same internationally wrongful act, the responsibility of each state may be invoked in relation to that act. However, the article raises several questions, and the ILC left aside many aspects of the problem of shared responsibility.[6] The principles of international law on the basis of which such allocation should proceed are, in the words of Brownlie, 'indistinct',[7] and may not provide clear answers for the intricate questions that arise in practice.

A lack of clarity in the law pertaining to shared responsibility is a matter of practical significance. It can hamper redress for injured parties, who may not be able to determine to whom a claim should be addressed, and may find that actors who are responsible for part but not all of the injury pass the buck. It also may undermine the preventative effects of responsibility when the law of responsibility cannot be implemented towards all states that participate in wrong and injury.[8] Finally, it may endanger legal certainty, as states can be held responsible on the basis of a remote connection to a wrongful act committed by another state, where responsibility could not be foreseen.[9]

Against this background, it is useful to examine the few principles of responsibility that have been formulated by the International Court of Justice (ICJ) in relation to shared responsibility. Judgments of the ICJ and its predecessor the Permanent Court of International Justice (PCIJ) on questions of international responsibility almost invariably have been attributed much authoritative weight, and large parts of the law of international responsibility,

---

chapter IV–C (hereinafter: Articles on the Responsibility of International Organizations), article 62: "This Part is without prejudice to international responsibility, under other provisions of these draft articles, of the international organization which commits the act in question, or of any other international organization."

[6] See e.g. ILC, Report on the Work of its Fifty-Second Session, (2000) UN GAOR Supplement No. 10 '(A/55/10), p. 46, par. 252: "[T]he draft articles could not deal with all of the procedural ramifications of situations of multiple responsibility." and ILC, Summary Records of the 2662nd Meeting, 52nd session, (2000) *Yearbook of the ILC*, Vol. I (A/CN.4/SER.A/20000), p. 396 par. 59: "[T]he articles did not address the question of how responsibility was shared when several States were responsible for the same wrongful act."

[7] Ian Brownlie, *Principles of Public International Law*, Oxford: Oxford University Press 2008, p. 457. See also Okowa (supra n. 3), p. 200, noting that: "[N]o definitive principles can be delineated from this limited international practice. Indeed, there is little evidence to suggest that international law already recognizes that in appropriate circumstances responsibility may be joint and several. Such evidence as exists is far from conclusive. It is therefore suggested that the principles which ought to determine the apportionment of responsibility can only be suggested as part of the progressive development of the law." See also Alexander Orakhelashvili, 'Division of Reparation Between Responsible Entities', in: James Crawford, Alain Pellet, Simon Olleson, (eds.), *The Law of International Responsibility*, Oxford: Oxford University Press 2010, p. 664, noting that the law is currently "uncertain, unsatisfactory and even chaotic".

[8] See Orakhelashvili (supra n. 7).

[9] Ibid., p. 649.

including the principle of responsibility itself,[10] attribution of conduct to states of *de facto* organs[11] and attribution of conduct based on acknowledgement[12] are largely based on this case law.[13]

In quite a few cases, the Court has been confronted with situations where two or more states, and sometimes also other subjects of international law, were involved in internationally wrongful acts. Notable examples are the *Corfu Channel* case,[14] *Certain Phosphate Lands in Nauru*,[15] the *East Timor* case[16] and the *Legality of the Use of Force* cases.[17] While these cases do not provide comprehensive discussion of the problems raised by shared responsibility, they do contain pronouncements on a few particular aspects, and as such provide some useful building blocks for a comprehensive theory of shared responsibility.[18]

The aim of this chapter is to systematise the case law of the ICJ and to assess how the ICJ has treated certain core aspects pertaining to shared responsibility. After a brief explanation of the main terms and concepts (section 2), it will discuss some hurdles of a procedural nature, faced by the Court in dealing with problems of shared responsibility (section 3). It will then discuss the case law on shared responsibility involving two or more states (section 4) and the implications of shared responsibility for reparation (section 5). Section 6 discusses questions of shared responsibility involving states and non-state actors. Section 7 contains brief conclusions.

---

[10] *Case Concerning the Factory at Chorzów* (*Germany v. Poland*) (Jurisdiction), PCIJ Reports 1927, Series A, No. 9, p. 21 and (Merits), PCIJ Reports 1928, Series A, No. 17, p. 47; Article 1 of the Articles on State Responsibility.

[11] *Military and Paramilitary Activities in and against Nicaragua (Nicaragua v. United States of America)* (Merits) ICJ Reports 1986, p. 14 (hereinafter: *Nicaragua* case); Article 8 of the Articles on State Responsibility.

[12] *Case Concerning United States Diplomatic and Consular Staff in Tehran (United States v. Iran)* (Merits), ICJ Reports 1980, p. 3 (hereinafter: *Consular Staff in Tehran* case); Article 11 of the Articles on State Responsibility.

[13] See generally on issues of responsibility before the ICJ: Rosalyn Higgins, 'Issues of State Responsibility before the International Court of Justice', in: Malgosia Fitzmaurice and Danesh Sarooshi (eds.), *Issues of State Responsibility Before International Judicial Institutions*, Oxford: Hart Publishing 2004, p. 1; Rosalyn Higgins, 'The International Court of Justice: Selected Issues of State Responsibility', Maurizio Ragazzi (ed.), *International Responsibility Today: Essays in Memory of Oscar Schachter* Leiden-Boston: Martinus Nijhoff Publishers 2005, p. 271.

[14] *Corfu Channel (United Kingdom of Great Britain and Norther Ireland (hereinafter UK) v Albania)* (Merits) [1949] ICJ Rep 4; ICGJ 199 (ICJ 1949) (hereinafter: *Corfu Channel* case).

[15] *Certain Phosphate Lands in Nauru (Nauru v. Australia)* (Preliminary Objections), ICJ Reports 1992, p. 240 (hereinafter: *Nauru* case).

[16] *East Timor (Portugal v. Australia)* (Merits), ICJ Reports 1995, p. 90 (hereinafter: *East Timor* case).

[17] *Legality of the Use of Force (Yugoslavia v. USA)* (Provisional Measures), ICJ Reports 1999, p. 916 *(Legality of the Use of Force* cases).

[18] Karel Wellens discussed these cases, involving a plurality of responsible states and cases of joint state action, as well as distinct wrongful acts, from the perspective of the principle of solidarity. See Karel Wellens, 'Revisiting Solidarity as a (Re-)Emerging Constitutional Principle: Some Further Reflections', in: Rüdiger Wolfrum and Chie Kojima (eds.), *Solidarity: A Structural Principle of International Law*, Berlin-Heidelberg-New York: Springer 2010, p. 22–28.

2. *Conceptual Issues*

2.1. *Forms of Shared Responsibility*

It is the premise of this contribution that shared responsibility causes certain complex questions of determination and allocation of responsibility and reparation that are different from situations where only one state is responsible. As such, shared responsibility represents a useful analytical category for examining questions of international responsibility.

In this article I use the term shared responsibility to refer to situations where two or more states have committed an internationally wrongful act and these two wrongs result in, or contribute to, a single injury. As both states are then responsible in respect of the same injury, the responsibility, and thus also the obligation to provide reparation to an injured party, is shared. Contrary to what perhaps may be suggested by the term, such responsibility does not fall on these states as a collectivity, but falls on each of them as individual states.[19]

We can distinguish three situations in which such shared responsibility can exist.[20] First, the term covers two independent wrongs, arising out of separate acts that are attributable to two states, that result in a single injury. An example from the case law of the ICJ are the facts leading to the *Corfu Channel* case, where it appeared that Yugoslavia and Albania committed separate wrongful acts, resulting in damage to a British ship.[21] Another example, based at least on one reading of the facts of the *Oil Platforms* case, are the independent wrongful acts of Iran and Iraq consisting of placing mines in the Persian Gulf, leading to injury for the United States in that its ability to engage in free navigation through the Gulf was impaired.[22] In such cases, it can be said that each state is individually responsible for its own wrongdoing, and that they are concurrently responsible.[23] Yet, it is not improper to say, certainly from the perspective of the injured state, that the responsibility for the injury is shared between the two wrongdoing states.[24]

---

[19] See Larry May, *Sharing Responsibility*, Chicago: University of Chicago Press 1992, p. 38, noting that it is precisely the fact that responsibility distributes to individual states rather than to them collectively, that is the defining feature of shared responsibility.

[20] One possible form of shared responsibility that I leave out of consideration concerns the sharing of responsibility between the responsible state and the injured state, raising issues of contributory fault. This relationship has been considered in terms of shared responsibility. See in particular the statement made by Mr Mahiou in the discussions at the 2171st meeting of the proposals of Special Rapporteur Arangio-Ruiz on reparation, in: *Yearbook of the ILC 1990*, Vol. I (A/CN.4/SER.A/1990), p.166, par. 68.

[21] See section 4.1.

[22] See section 4.3.

[23] Stefan Talmon, 'A Plurality of Responsible Actors: International Responsibility for Acts of the Coalition Provisional Authority in Iraq', in: Paul Shiner and Andrew Williams (eds.), *The Iraq War and International Law*, Oxford: Hart Publishing 2008, p. 212.

[24] Christian Dominicé, 'Attribution of Conduct to Multiple States and the Implication of a State in the Act of Another State in The Law of International Responsibility', in: James Crawford,

The examples of the *Corfu Channel* Case and the *Oil Platforms* case make clear that there is no absolute opposition between shared responsibility and what the ILC named 'independent responsibility'. The latter term refers to the principle under which each state is responsible for its own internationally wrongful conduct, that is: for conduct attributable to it under the principles of attribution set forth in chapter II of the Articles on State Responsibility, and which is in breach of an international obligation of that state in accordance with chapter III of those articles.[25] Two cases of independent responsibility can combine to result in a single injury, and thus can be treated as a case of shared responsibility.

The second situation covered by the term shared responsibility is the situation where one act is attributed to two or more states. An example is the situation where the organ of one state acts on the joint instructions of its own and another state, or where two or more states may have committed a single wrongful act by acting through a joint or common organ that functions as an organ of both states.[26] An act of that organ is then attributable to each of the states in question.[27] This was the situation in the *Nauru* case, where Australia, New Zealand and the United Kingdom were designated as the joint Authority which was to exercise the administration of Nauru. The acts of the Authority could be attributed to each of these three states.[28] We then can say that the act is shared, as is the resulting responsibility. It is this multiple attribution of a single act that is the essential distinction with the first category. In the arguments of Serbia and Montenegro in the *Legality on the Use of Force* cases, this also was the situation for the bombing of Belgrade carried out by NATO member states.[29]

Third, there is a category that consists of situations in which one state commits a wrongful act in conjunction with another state. This category contains such a wide variety of situations that each may present a separate subcategory. Yet for present analytical purposes these can be grouped together on the basis of the relationship between two wrongful acts. The category includes the situations where a state aids or assists in the wrongful act of another state or another entity, as was considered by the Court in the *Bosnian Genocide* case;[30]

Alain Pellet and Simon Olleson (eds.), *The Law of International Responsibility*, Oxford: Oxford University Press 2010, p. 284.

[25] ILC, 'Draft Articles on Responsibility of States for Internationally Wrongful Acts, with commentaries', in: *Yearbook of the ILC 2001*, Vol. II (A/CN.4/SER.A/2001/Add.1) (Part 2) (hereinafter: Commentaries to the Articles on State Responsibility), p. 64, par. 1.

[26] Commentaries to the Articles on State Responsibility, Commentary to article 6, p. 44, par. 3.

[27] Ibid.; see also Ian Brownlie, *State Responsibility*, Oxford: Clarendon Press 1983, p. 191–92.

[28] See section 4.4.

[29] See section 4.3.

[30] See section 6.

directs or controls the wrongful act by another state;[31] or coerces another state in committing a wrongful act.[32] It is to be added that is rather unclear whether or not in case of direction and control and coercion we speak of two separate wrongs or of one wrongful act that is attributed to both states. This in itself requires further analysis. This category also includes the situations where one state places an organ at the disposal of another state without that organ falling under the exclusive control of the receiving state.[33] Whereas in the cases of aid and assistance two wrongful acts are committed, in this situation, there would be only one.

An additional scenario falling in this category involves cases where a state commits a wrongful act in conjunction with an international organisation, for instance by 'using' an international organisation to commit a wrongful act, that then may lead to responsibility of both the state and the organisation,[34] or by acting wrongfully by implementing a decision of an international organisation, thereby contravening an international obligation.[35]

2.2. *Shared and Joint (and Several) Responsibility*

Sometimes some, or even all, of these situations of 'shared responsibility' are referred to by the term 'joint responsibility' or 'joint and several responsibility'. For instance, Orakhelashvili refers to the concept of joint and several responsibility as the principle under which the responsibility of a state is not reduced, even if another state is involved in the perpetration of that wrongful act.[36] Brownlie uses the term to refer to particular situations where one state aids or assists another state in the commission of a wrongful act.[37]

If the term joint, or joint and several, responsibility is to be used in international law, it is to be used as a formal category recognised by existing secondary rules and to which specific legal effects are attached. Whereas shared responsibility is used here as an analytical category to bring together cases that have certain common features, to say that states are jointly, or jointly and severally, responsible, is to imply certain consequences.[38] If the term joint responsibility as a legal category is to be useful, such legal consequences have to differ from the legal consequences of independent responsibility. Whether and to

[31] Article 17 of the Articles on State Responsibility.
[32] Article 18 of the Articles on State Responsibility.
[33] ILC Special Rapporteur James Crawford, *Third Report on State Responsibility*, 52nd session (2000) UN GAOR A/CN.4/507/Add.2), par. 267.
[34] Article 60 of the Articles on the Responsibility of International Organizations.
[35] Article 16 of the Articles on the Responsibility of International Organizations.
[36] Orakhelashvili, supra n. 7, p. 657.
[37] Brownlie, supra n. 27, p. 191.
[38] It is to be noted that *Black's Law Dictionary* (8th edition, 2004) defines 'joint liability' in very general terms as "liability shared by two or more parties".

what extent in international law a distinct category of joint responsibility indeed exists and what its features are, is a matter of some uncertainty.

It has been said that, as far as joint responsibility is concerned, this consequence would be that the responsibility of each of the states is not reduced by the involvement of another state.[39] However, that is simply another way of phrasing the principle of independent responsibility: each state is responsible for its own wrongs, and for the damage caused thereby. The qualification of an action or responsibility as 'joint' then does not carry any additional legal consequences. It also has been suggested that when two (or more states) were engaged in a single wrongful act, these states can only be held responsible as a collectivity. This was the argument of Australia in the *Nauru* case, which however was rejected by the Court.[40] Perhaps the most relevant (potential) legal consequence of the qualification of a situation as joint responsibility arises if it would not just be joint, but joint and several responsibility. The consequence would then be that injured parties could bring a claim against each of the states that are part of the joint action, irrespective of whether the other party would also be sued: possibly (though that is a matter of some uncertainty) it could also mean that the injured state then could obtain full compensation from each of the co-responsible parties. Particular treaty regimes do provide for such joint responsibility,[41] but the question whether it exists as a matter of international law is uncertain.[42]

The term joint responsibility has been applied to each of the three situations discussed above. First, it has been applied to refer to two independent wrongs resulting in a single injury.[43] Second, it has been used to refer to a situation where a wrong by one state necessarily also is the wrong of another state, because the act is doubly attributed to both states. And third, it has been used to refer to cases where two wrongful acts are related to each other, as in the

---

[39] Orakhelashvili, supra n. 7, p. 657–58.

[40] See section 4.3.

[41] See e.g. Agreement on the Promotion, Provision and Use of GALILEO and GPS Satellite-Based Systems and Related Applications (European Community - USA) (28 June 2004), <http://ec.europa.eu/enterprise/policies/satnav/galileo/files/2004_06_21_eu_us_agreement_en.pdf>. Article 19 par. 2 states: "If it is unclear whether an obligation under this Agreement is within the competence of either the European Community or its Member States, at the request of the United States, the European Community and its Member States shall provide the necessary information. Failure to provide this information with all due expediency or the provision of contradictory information shall result in joint and several liability."

[42] See e.g. *Eurotunnel Arbitration* (*Channel Tunnel Group Ltd and France-Manche SA v. France and UK*) (Partial Award) (Permanent Court of Arbitration, 30 January 2007), par. 165–69.

[43] All examples from national law discussed in the separate opinion by Judge Simma in the *Oil Platforms* case (see section 4.3) relate to liability arising out of acts of independent wrongdoers, and this was indeed the focus of his analysis of the independent wrongs of Iran and Iraq.

case of aid or assistance.[44] However, joint responsibility is not a term of art in international law. The ILC did not use it in its Commentary to the Articles on State Responsibility, and warned against assuming that

> internal law concepts and rules in this field can be applied directly to international law. Terms such as "joint", "joint and several" and "solidary" responsibility derive from different legal traditions and analogies must be applied with care. In international law, the general principle in the case of a plurality of responsible States is that each State is separately responsible for conduct attributable to it in the sense of article 2. The principle of independent responsibility reflects the position under general international law, in the absence of agreement to the contrary between the States concerned.[45]

The ILC did include article 47, providing that where two or more states are responsible for the same internationally wrongful act, the responsibility of each state may be invoked in relation to that act. However, it stated in its Commentary that paragraph 1 of article 47 "neither recognizes a general rule of joint and several responsibility, nor does it exclude the possibility that two or more States will be responsible for the same internationally wrongful act".[46]

In contrast, the commentary of the first draft of the Articles on the Responsibility of International Organizations expressly uses the term 'joint responsibility'. It states that "[t]he joint responsibility of an international organization with one or more States is envisaged in articles 13 to 17, which concern the responsibility of an international organization in connection with the act of a State, and in articles 57 to 61, which deal with the responsibility of a State in connection with the act of an international organization".[47] These are cases that would fall in the third category identified above. However, the Commentary does not provide a concise definition, and it is unclear whether it meant to say that two independent wrongs that result in a single injury cannot be qualified as joint responsibility.

Whether or not the use of the phrase joint responsibility has an added conceptual value, and whether it is actually related to a particular legal category, requires further analysis.[48] In part it is answered by the conclusions of

[44] Brownlie, supra n. 27, p. 191; Christine Chinkin, 'The Continuing Occupation? Issues of Joint and Several Liability and Effective Control', in: Paul Shiner and Andrew Williams (eds.), *The Iraq War and International Law*, Oxford: Hart Publishing 2008, p. 164.

[45] Commentaries to the Articles on State Responsibility, Commentary to article 47, par. 3.

[46] Ibid., par. 6.

[47] ILC, *Text of the Draft Articles on the Responsibility of International Organizations with Commentaries Thereto*, Report of the sixty-first session (2009) UN GAOR Supplement No.10 (A/64/10), chapter IV-C.2, Commentary to article 47, par. 1. See also Caitlin A. Bell, 'Reassessing Multiple Attribution: The International Law Commission and the Behrami and Saramati Decision', (2010) 42 *New York University Journal of International Law and Policy*, p. 517–518.

[48] A more comprehensive analysis will be provided by separate publications of the SHARES project.

the substantive analysis of this body of international law, and it is suggested that in the present unclear state of the law, the issue is best approached inductively. Also for that reason, we now will examine the use of terms and concepts by the ICJ.

3. *Procedural Hurdles in the ICJ*

The possibility that the ICJ considers questions of shared responsibility and contributes to the development of the relevant principles is somewhat limited by the Court's dependency on sovereign states' readiness to submit their behaviour to the scrutiny of the Court, states being able to decide for themselves whether or not they consent to its jurisdiction. As a result, the Court lacks the power to direct that a third state, that does not consent to it, be made a party to the proceedings.[49]

One consequence of this dependency is that the Court's jurisdiction is in the hands of the parties. A state (allegedly) injured by acts of multiple states that may share the responsibility for such acts, may choose whether or not to bring a case against all states (assuming that they all have accepted the jurisdiction of the Court), or may proceed separately. This raises the question of the possible impact of the absence of (one of the) responsible parties for the ability of the Court to rule on the conformity with international law of their behaviour.

This point was raised in connection to the various proceedings relating to the conflict in Nicaragua in the 1980s, when Nicaragua brought separate proceedings against the United States, Costa Rica and Honduras. The latter state objected to this process of 'serial application', and said that this created an "artificial and arbitrary dividing up of the general conflict existing in Central America" that moreover would have "negative consequences for Honduras as a Defendant State before the Court, since it affects the guarantee of a sound administration of justice and undermines the principle laid down in Article 59 of the Statute of the Court".[50] The Court rejected this argument, stating that "it is for the parties to establish the facts in the present case taking account of the usual rules of evidence, without it being possible to rely on considerations of *res judicata* in another case not involving the same parties".[51]

---

[49] In *Military and Paramilitary Activities in and Against Nicaragua (Nicaragua v. USA)* (Jurisdiction and Admissibility), ICJ Reports 1984, p. 392, par. 86, the Court observed that it did not possess the power to direct that a third state be made a party to the proceedings. See also Okowa, supra n. 3, p. 200.

[50] *Border and Transborder Armed Actions (Nicaragua v Honduras)*, Memorial of Honduras, par. 2.05, 35; see also (Jurisdiction and Admissibility), ICJ Reports 1988, p. 69; ICGJ 102 (ICJ 1988) (*Border and Transborder Armed Actions* case), par. 53.

[51] Ibid., par. 54.

The Court referred to article 59,[52] and it indeed would seem that only a strict application of article 59, including to findings of fact, would protect the interests of a state that, while allegedly being one of multiple responsible states, is brought to the Court individually rather than jointly.[53]

The more general point is that article 59 in principle allows the Court to exercise jurisdiction, and that the possible effects of a judgment on a third state do not affect its exercise of jurisdiction. A state which is not a party to a case is free to apply for permission to intervene in accordance with article 62 of the Statute.[54] But, in principle, the absence of such a request does not preclude the Court from adjudicating upon the claims submitted to it. Where it does act, the interests of the third state which is not a party to the case are protected by article 59 of the Statute of the Court. However, there is one major exception to this starting point. This is the indispensable parties principle.

3.1. *The Indispensable Parties Principle*

In the *Monetary Gold* case, the Court formulated an exception to the principle that the absence of a state that is concurrently or jointly responsible for a wrongful act does not preclude its exercise of jurisdiction.[55] The case is of fundamental importance for the role of the Court in cases of shared responsibility, and needs to be considered at some length. The Court was requested to decide that the three respondent states (France, United Kingdom, United States) "should deliver to Italy any share of the monetary gold that might be due to Albania under the Paris Act of January 14th, 1946",[56] in partial satisfaction for the damage caused to Italy by an Albanian law that expropriated Italian property. The Washington Agreement[57] by which the parties had agreed to submit the case to the ICJ, specified in advance one of the purposes of Italy's Application, namely, the "determination of the question whether, by reason of any right which she claims to possess as a result of the Albanian law of 13th January, 1945, or under the provisions of the Italian Peace Treaty,[58] the gold

[52] Statute of the International Court of Justice (adopted 26 June 1945, entered into force 24 October 1945) (hereinafter: ICJ Statute), article 59: "The decision of the Court has no binding force except between the parties and in respect of that particular case."

[53] See on this point also: Separate Opinion of Judge Schwebel in the *Border and Transborder Armed Actions* (supra n. 50), ICJ Reports 1988, p. 126–32.

[54] ICJ Statute, article 62 (1) providing that: "Should a State consider that it has an interest of a legal nature which may be affected by the decision in the case, it may submit a request to the Court to be permitted to intervene."

[55] *Monetary Gold Removed from Rome in 1943 (Italy v. France, UK and USA)* (Preliminary Question), ICJ Reports 1954, p. 19 (ICJ 1954) (hereinafter: *Monetary Gold* case).

[56] Agreement on Reparation from Germany, on the Establishment of an Inter-Allied Reparation Agency and on the Restitution of Monetary Gold (adopted 14 January 1946, entered into force 24 January 1946), 555 *United Nations Treaty Series*, p. 69.

[57] Agreement for the Submission to an Arbitrator of Certain Claims with Respect to Gold Looted by the Germans from Rome in 1943 (France-UK-USA) (signed 25 April 1951), 100 *United Nations Treaty Series*, p. 21.

[58] Treaty of Peace with Italy (signed 10 February 1947), 49 *United Nations Treaty Series*, p. 3.

should be delivered to Italy rather than to Albania". As Italy believed that she possessed a right against Albania for the redress of an international wrong which, according to Italy, Albania has committed against her, the Court found that in order to determine whether Italy is entitled to receive the gold, "it is necessary to determine whether Albania has committed any international wrong against Italy, and whether she is under an obligation to pay compensation to her; and, if so, to determine also the amount of compensation."[59] The Court then held that since Albania had not consented to the jurisdiction of the Court, it could not exercise jurisdiction; doing so would run counter to the principle that the Court can only exercise jurisdiction over a state with its consent.[60] Crucially, it found that "Albania's legal interests would not only be affected by a decision, but would form the very subject-matter of the decision. In such a case, the Statute cannot be regarded, by implication, as authorising proceedings to be continued in the absence of Albania".[61]

The Court thus said that it could not exercise jurisdiction when the principal issue requires a determination of the legal position of a third state that is not a party to the proceedings.[62] Only when such a prior determination of a legal position of a third state is at issue, the legal interest of that state forms the subject-matter of a decision, and only when the legal interest of a third state forms the subject matter of a dispute, exercising jurisdiction would run counter to the principle that the Court can only exercise jurisdiction over a state with its consent. In such a case, the third state is an indispensible party, and we can therefore refer to the principle expressed by the Court as the indispensible parties principle.

Although this aspect of the *Monetary Gold* case did not concern a question of shared responsibility, the principle of indispensable parties that the Court formulated in this case may have implications for particular scenarios of shared responsibility. Indeed, in almost all cases before the Court which raised questions of shared responsibility, the indispensable parties principle was at one stage of the procedure invoked. Only in one of these cases, the *East Timor* case, the Court found that the indispensible parties principle precluded it from exercising jurisdiction.

The *East Timor* case presented issues of shared responsibility, since Portugal had brought a claim in respect to a wrongful act allegedly committed by Australia that consisted in the conclusion of a treaty with Indonesia in respect

[59] *Monetary Gold* case, par. 42.
[60] Ibid., par. 43.
[61] Ibid., par. 45. Albania
[62] Shabtai Rosenne, 'International Courts and Tribunals, Jurisdiction and Admissibility of Inter-State Applications', in: Rüdiger Wolfrum (ed.), *The Max Planck Encyclopedia of Public International Law*, available at <www.mpepil.com> (article was last updated March 2006), par. 7.

to exploration of oil and gas off the coast of East Timor. The right breached (the right of self-determination) was accepted by the Court to be a right *erga omnes*, thus imposing obligations on both Australia and Indonesia.[63] The implication was that both Australia and Indonesia were obliged to refrain from interfering with this right – *erga omnes* rights are by definition the corollary of multilateral obligations.[64] From that perspective, the case involved the possible shared responsibility of Australia and Indonesia. Since Indonesia was not a party to the proceedings, the question was whether the Court could individualise the wrong committed by Australia (which was said to consist of the conclusion of a bilateral treaty with Indonesia) and exercise jurisdiction. Portugal said on this point that its Application was concerned exclusively with the objective conduct of Australia, which consists in having negotiated, concluded and initiated performance of the 1989 Treaty with Indonesia, and that this question was perfectly separable from any question relating to the lawfulness of the conduct of Indonesia. While the Court did not as such reject this latter proposition, it did find that before being able to adjudicate this particular claim, it should first determine the rights of Indonesia over the disputed territory. In view of the absence of Indonesia from the proceedings, it then found that the *Monetary Gold* rule barred the exercise of jurisdiction. It noted that

> the effect of the judgment requested by Portugal would amount to a determination that Indonesia's entry into and continued presence in East Timor are unlawful and that, as a consequence, it does not have treaty making power in matters relating to the continental shelf resources of East Timor. Indonesia's rights and obligations would thus constitute the very subject-matter of such a judgment made in the absence of that State's consent.[65]

The Court added that the *erga omnes* character of a norm and the rule of consent to jurisdiction are two different things: "Whatever the nature of the obligations invoked, the Court could not rule on the lawfulness of the conduct of a State when its judgment would imply an evaluation of the lawfulness of the conduct of another State which is not a party to the case. Where this is so, the Court cannot act, even if the right in question is a right *erga omnes*."[66]

---

[63] East *Timor* case, par. 29.

[64] Dissenting Opinion of Judge Weeramantry in the *East Timor* case, ICJ Reports 1995, p. 172, par. (iii), emphasising the individual nature of obligations flowing from *erga omnes* rights. He noted that "an *erga omnes* right is a series of separate rights *erga singulum*, including inter alia, a separate right *erga singulum* against Australia, and a separate right *erga singulum* against Indonesia. These rights are in no way dependent one upon the other. With the violation by any State of the obligation so lying upon it, the rights enjoyed *erga omnes* become opposable *erga singulum* to the State so acting".

[65] *East Timor* case, par. 34.

[66] Christine M. Chinkin, 'The East Timor Case (Portugal v. Australia)', (1996) 45 *The International and Comparative Law Quarterly*, p. 712–713 and p. 716–722; René Lefeber and

This decision has been subjected to considerable critique.[67] Application of the indispensible parties principle may seem logical if the fundamental question of the case is construed, as presented by Australia, as the question whether "in 1989, the power to conclude a treaty on behalf of East Timor in relation to its continental shelf lay with Portugal or with Indonesia".[68] But it is questionable whether that indeed was the fundamental question of the case. Surely an answer to Portugal's submission that Australia by concluding the treaty has infringed the right to self-determination of the people of East Timor would not seem to depend on the treaty-making power of Indonesia.[69]

The application of the indispensible parties principle by the Court in the *East Timor* case casts considerable doubt on the Court's ability to adjudicate certain questions of shared responsibility, notably in cases involving aid and assistance and direction and control.[70] This also might apply in respect to the responsibility of an act of a state that is coerced in the commission of a wrongful act and would, in view of such coercion, plead for mitigation of reparation. The Court then would have to determine that there indeed was an act of coercion, implicating the responsibility of the coercing state.[71] In such cases, the application of substantive principles pertaining to shared responsibility may be hampered by the procedural principles governing the functioning of the Court. On the other hand, the apparent increase in the number of cases involving shared responsibility,[72] and the development of substantive principles of responsibility in respect to such cases, may lead to an undesirable conflict between the substantive and the procedural law of the ICJ, seriously limiting the degree in which the ICJ could give effect to the policy rationale underlying the system of responsibility. Perhaps induced by this consideration, in quite a few other cases, the Court has narrowly construed the indispensible parties principle in other situations of shared responsibility. These may be grouped in two categories: situations of concurrent independent

---

David Raič, 'Frontiers of International Law Part One: The Chechen People', (1996) 9 *Leiden Journal of International Law*, p. 6–7.

[67] Dissenting Opinion of Judge Weeramantry in the *East Timor* case, ICJ Reports 1995, p. 139–223, p. 172 par. (iii). See also Orakhelashvili, supra n. 7, p. 664.

[68] *East Timor* case, par. 27.

[69] A more relevant question on this point, as noted by Judge Oda in his Separate Opinion, is how exactly, if at all, Australia by doing so would breach an international obligation, but that is a different matter.

[70] Commentaries to the Articles on State Responsibility, Commentary to article 16, par. 11. On the former, the ILC recognised that the *Monetary Gold* rule may well apply to cases involving aid and assistance.

[71] Compare Crawford, *Third Report on State Responsibility* (supra n. 33), par. 267, recognising the possibility that the coerced state invokes a circumstance precluding wrongfulness.

[72] See Separate Opinion of Judge Shahabuddeen in the *East Timor* case, ICJ Reports 1995, p. 119–128, par. 3 noting that "[p]roblems of this kind are apt to arise from the fact that, in the increasingly complex character of international relations, legal disputes between States are rarely purely bilateral".

wrongdoing, on the one hand, and situations of double attribution, on the other.

3.2. *The Indispensable Parties Principle in Cases of Concurrent Independent Wrongful Acts*

The indispensable parties principle does not prevent the Court from exercising jurisdiction in case of two concurrent independent wrongful acts. This can be inferred from the Court's exercise of jurisdiction in the *Corfu Channel* case. The fact that Yugoslavia was not a party to the dispute did not preclude the Court from exercising its jurisdiction under the indispensable parties principle. While the Court had to make some determinations that would at least have indirect legal relevance in hypothetical legal proceedings against Yugoslavia (such as its pronouncements on the legality of the navigation of the British warships), the possible wrongfulness of the acts of Yugoslavia did not constitute the very subject matter of the dispute between Albania and the United Kingdom. For the Court to pronounce on the responsibility of Albania in the *Corfu Channel* case it was not necessary to make a determination on the responsibility of Yugoslavia, and as such the responsibility of Yugoslavia was not the subject matter of the dispute.[73] From this case one can infer that in a situation of two concurrent independent wrongful acts, the Court can independently determine responsibility of each of the wrongdoing states without them being simultaneously party to the proceedings.[74]

The Court's discussion of the indispensable parties principle in the *Nicaragua* case points in the same direction. It had been alleged that Honduras also had acted wrongfully against it by allowing their territory to be used as a staging ground for unlawful uses of force against Nicaragua.[75] It could be inferred that responsibility for the attacks against Nicaragua was shared between the United States and Honduras. The United States used this shared responsibility aspect to argue for application of the *Monetary Gold* rule, on the ground that adjudication of Nicaragua's claim would necessarily involve the adjudication of the rights of third states with respect to their rights under article 51 of the UN Charter.[76] The Court rejected that claim, noting that where claims of a legal nature are made by an applicant against a respondent in proceedings before the Court, the Court has in principle merely to decide upon those submissions, with binding force for the parties only, and no other state, in accordance with article 59 of the Statute. Other states that consider that

---

[73] Ibid., par. 7.

[74] Of course the *Corfu Channel* case preceded the *Monetary Gold* case, but in view of the later *Nicaragua* and *Nauru* cases, discussed in section 3.3, it can safely be concluded that the Court would not decide this aspect of the *Corfu Channel* case differently today than it did at the time.

[75] *Nicaragua* case (Jurisdiction and Admissibility), supra n. 49, par. 86.

[76] Ibid., par. 86.

they may be affected are free to institute separate proceedings, or to employ the procedure of intervention, but "[t]here is no trace, either in the Statute or in the practice of international tribunals, of an 'indispensable parties' rule of the kind argued for by the United States, which would only be conceivable in parallel to a power, which the Court does not possess, to direct that a third State be made a party to proceedings". The Court added that the "circumstances of the *Monetary Gold* case probably represent the limit of the power of the Court to refuse to exercise its jurisdiction; and none of the States referred to can be regarded as in the same position as Albania in that case, so as to be truly indispensable to the pursuance of the proceedings".[77] This part of the judgment confirms a narrow construction of the *Monetary Gold* rule, which essentially does not preclude the Court from exercising jurisdiction in cases of shared responsibility, where a judgment against one state may have implications for other states whose responsibility is not decisive for the outcome of the proceedings concerned. In other words, the outcome does not depend on a prior determination of their legal position.

Judge Simma drew the same conclusion in his Separate Opinion in the *Oil Platforms* case. He noted that it would be possible to hold Iran responsible for the undivided wrongful act that it committed together with Iraq, and on that basis to pronounce on the generic counterclaim against Iran. For doing so it would not have been necessary to make a determination on the legality of acts of Iraq.[78] A contrary argument was made by Italy in the *Legality of Use of Force* cases. It noted that the implication of holding all NATO Member States, without distinction, responsible for the 'Allied Force' action, was that it requested the Court to deliver a judgment on the merits, which would inevitably prejudge the legality of the conduct of states not parties to these proceedings. On this basis, Italy requested the Court to find that the application of Serbia and Montenegro is inadmissible.[79] The Court did not pronounce itself on this argument, but there is little doubt that, on the basis of the interpretations in *Nicaragua* and *Nauru*, it would fail to satisfy the *Monetary Gold* standard.

3.3. *The Indispensable Parties Principle in Cases of Multiple Attribution*

The Court also has excluded from the scope of the *Monetary Gold* rule cases of double attribution, that is: responsibility arising out of an act of a joint organ that can be attributed to two or more states.

[77] Ibid., par. 88.

[78] Separate Opinion of Judge Simma in *Oil Platforms (Islamic Republic of Iran v. USA)* (Merits), ICJ Reports 2003, p. 324–61 (Separate Opinion of Judge Simma in the *Oil Platforms* case); see further section 4.

[79] *Legality of Use of Force (Serbia and Montenegro v Italy)* (Oral Proceedings) [Public Sitting 22 April 2004] *Compte Rendu* 2004/22, par. 34–35.

If an act of a common organ is attributable to each state involved, a pronouncement on the responsibility of that common organ, or of a state acting on behalf of that common organ, necessarily is a determination of the responsibility of all states involved. Yet, in *Certain Phosphate Lands in Nauru (Nauru v. Australia)*, the Court concluded that in such cases the Court can exercise jurisdiction against a single responsible state. Nauru alleged a breach of the Trusteeship Agreement by Australia. The Trusteeship Agreement for Nauru, which was concluded pursuant to article 77 of the UN Charter, provided for an Administering Authority. Article 2 of the Trusteeship Agreement stated that:

> The Governments of Australia, New Zealand and the United Kingdom (hereinafter called 'the Administering Authority') are hereby designated as the joint authority which will exercise the administration of the territory.[80]

The acts performed by Australia involved both 'joint' conduct of several states, and day-to-day administration of a territory by one state acting on behalf of other states as well as on its own behalf.[81] Australia relied on article 2 to support the argument that it was under no separate obligation:

> the trusteeship obligations rest on the Administering Authority. The three Governments together constituted that 'Administering Authority', as a form of 'Partnership' (…) Accordingly, any breach of the obligations of the Administering Authority would be, *prima facie*, the joint responsibility of the Governments of Australia, New Zealand and the United Kingdom.[82]

It then argued that a finding of responsibility against one state would be a simultaneous determination of the responsibility of all three states and that such a determination would be precluded by the fundamental reasons underlying the *Monetary Gold* decision. The Court concluded, however, that the *Monetary Gold* rule did not act as a bar to its jurisdiction over Australia. It said that "the interests of New Zealand and the United Kingdom do not constitute the very subject-matter of the judgment to be rendered on the merits of Nauru's Application". It recognised that a finding by the Court regarding the existence or the content of the responsibility attributed to Australia by Nauru "might well have implications for the legal situation of the two other States concerned, but no finding in respect of that legal situation will be needed as a

[80] Trusteeship Agreement for the Territory of Nauru (Australia - UK - New Zealand) (approved by the General Assembly on 1 November 1947) 10 *United Nations Treaty Series*, p. 3 (Trusteeship Agreement), article 4: The three governments had arranged that Australia would, unless otherwise agreed, "continue to exercise full powers of legislation, administration and jurisdiction in and over the Territory".

[81] Commentaries to the Articles on State Responsibility, chapter IV, p. 64, par. 3.

[82] *Certain Phosphate Lands in Nauru (Nauru v. Australia)* (Preliminary Objections of the Government of Australia), (December 1990) Written Proceedings, Vol. I, par. 321.

basis for the Court's decision on Nauru's claims against Australia. Accordingly, the Court cannot decline to exercise its jurisdiction".[83]

This judgment has been subject of substantial criticism that illustrates the difficult relationship between procedural issues of jurisdiction and substantive issues of (shared) responsibility. President Jennings maintained that, inasmuch as the three states formed the joint authority which exercised the administration of Nauru, the legal interest of New Zealand and the United Kingdom were so inextricably bound up with those of Australia in this matter that they would form the very subject-matter of the decision.[84] Judge Schwebel considered that a judgment by the ICJ on the responsibility of Australia would appear to be tantamount to a judgment on the responsibility of New Zealand and the United Kingdom, which were not before the court.[85]

In particular, it seems difficult for the Court to determine the share of the liability falling upon a state that was involved through a common organ if the other states involved would not be present before the court.[86] It appears that it was in this respect that Judge Ago stated that "it is precisely by ruling on these claims against Australia alone that the Court will, inevitably, affect the legal situation of the two other States, namely, their rights and their obligations. If, when dealing with the merits of the case, the Court were to recognize that responsibility and accordingly seek to determine the share of the responsibility falling upon Australia, it would thereby indirectly establish that the remainder of the responsibility would fall upon the two other States. Even if the Court were to decide – on what would, incidentally, be an extremely questionable basis – that Australia was to shoulder in full the responsibility in question, that decision would, equally inevitably and just as unacceptably, affect not only the 'interests' but also the legal situation of two States that are not parties to the proceedings. In either case, the exercise by the Court of its jurisdiction would be deprived of its indispensable consensual basis".[87]

The Court noted on this point that its ruling on the *Monetary Gold* objection did not prejudge the merits.[88] It thus left open the possibility that even though its jurisdiction may not be limited by the shared nature of responsibility, its possibility to award full reparation would in fact be restricted by such shared responsibility. The question remains, whether any determination on that point would not in fact involve a determination implicating the legal interests of the other states to such an extent that this would be the very subject

[83] *Nauru* case, par. 55.

[84] Dissenting Opinion of President Sir Robert Jennings in the *Nauru* case, ICJ Reports 1992, p. 301–2.

[85] Dissenting Opinion of Judge Schwebel in the *Nauru* case, ICJ Reports 1992, p. 329–43.

[86] Talmon, supra n. 23, p. 209–11.

[87] Dissenting Opinion of Judge Ago in the *Nauru* case, ICJ Reports 1992, p. 326–28.

[88] *Nauru* case, par. 56.

matter of the dispute.[89] Perhaps the Court's practice of reserving such questions to the merits is induced by the general expectation that the Court will not reach a liability phase at all. But that approach would be more of a pragmatic than of a principled nature.

3.4. *The Indispensable Parties Principle in Cases of Responsibility of International Organisations*

The *Legality of Use of Force* cases raised the question whether the *Monetary Gold* rule should be applied in cases of a responsibility that is shared between states and international organisations. Serbia and Montenegro argued that if two or more states together take joint action to the detriment of a third state, they are co-authors of any internationally wrongful act derived from their joint action, and that each of the states would be responsible for that action.[90] In this respect, the claim was not dissimilar from the basis of the claim of Nauru against Australia. The main difference was that in this case, as also agreed by the applicant, the joint action took place in the framework of an international organisation with legal personality (NATO). The applicant argued on this point that the respondent states were jointly and severally responsible for the actions of the NATO military command structure, which constitutes an instrumentality of the respondent states.[91] Several states, including Portugal, noted that responsibility of Member States would presuppose NATO's conduct being regarded as unlawful. It considered that this would be a matter of the responsibility of the Member States by virtue of the acts of an international organization and that the Court could never rule on Portugal's responsibility without first having ruled on the legality of NATO's conduct.[92]

The argument raises the question whether the *Monetary Gold* standard applies at all to cases of indirect responsibility of member states for acts of international organisations, for instance in case of the principle proposed by the ILC that a state member of an international organisation "incurs international responsibility if it seeks to avoid complying with one of its own

[89] Dissenting Opinion of President Sir Robert Jennings in the *Nauru* case, ICJ Reports 1992, p. 301–2. This was in fact suggested by Ago and also by Jennings, who noted: "Moreover, one must contemplate the situation that must arise if, on the merits, there should be any question of assessing the reparation that might be due from Australia (see para. 48 of the Judgment). If the obligations from which the liability arises are held to be solidary (joint and several) so that Australia is liable for the whole, or whether, alternatively, Australia is held liable only for some proportion of the whole sum, it is clear in either case that the Court will unavoidably and simultaneously be making a decision in respect of the legal interests of those two other States."

[90] Dominicé, supra n. 24, p. 282.

[91] *Legality of Use of Force (Serbia and Montenegro v. UK)* (Oral Proceedings) (Public Sitting 10 May 1999), *Compte Rendu* 1999/14, par. VII.

[92] *Legality of Use of Force (Serbia and Montenegro v. Portugal)* (Preliminary Objections of the Portuguese Republic) (July 2000), par. 145; *Legality of Use of Force (Serbia and Montenegro v. Portugal)* (Preliminary Objections), ICJ Reports 2004, p. 1160, par. 22.

international obligations by taking advantage of the fact that the organization has competence in relation to the subject matter of that obligation, thereby prompting the organization to commit an act that, if committed by the State, would have constituted a breach of the obligation so-called abuse of the legal personality of the organization".[93] According to the logic of the ILC Articles on the Responsibility of International Organizations, which should not be considered the final word on this, in such cases there could be shared (or what the ILC calls joint) responsibility between the member states and the organisation.[94] The question then is whether the Court can adjudicate a claim against the state in the absence of an organisation.

The Court has not decided on this issue, but a few points can be noted. The question pertains to the proper foundation of the indispensable parties principle: is it to be recognised in the sovereign equality of states (in which case it would not be applicable to international organisations), or is it a procedural mechanism that safeguards the quality of the decision-making of the Court? The Court has not been in a position to address the question, but it has been suggested that the principle should equally be applicable to (in any case non-UN) organisations.[95] It can be recalled that in the *Monetary Gold* case itself, the Court ultimately based the indispensible parties principle on the principle that the Court can only exercise jurisdiction over a state with its consent.[96] That argument is grounded in the consensual character of the Court's jurisdiction.[97] While the Court has always formulated this principle with respect to its (lack of) jurisdiction over particular states, in principle it would also seem applicable to international organisations, which (as evidenced in the practice of the European Union) can also only be submitted to the jurisdiction of an international court if they consent to such jurisdiction.

It seems doubtful however whether the *Monetary Gold* rule is applicable to international organisations. The Statute does not give contentious jurisdiction to the Court for adjudicating disputes involving international organisations.[98] It follows that acts of international organisations are, as a matter of principle,

---

[93] ILC, Text of draft articles 3, 3bis, 28, paragraph 1, 61, 62, 63 and 64, adopted by the Drafting Committee on 2 June 2009, article 28, A/CN.4/L.743/Add.1, p. 2

[94] Article 60 and 62 of the Articles on the Responsibility of International Organizations.

[95] See Jean d'Aspremont, 'Abuse of the Legal Personality of International Organizations and the Responsibility of Member States', (2007) 4 *International Organizations Law Review*, p. 117, noting that in such a case, the responsibility of the organisation will be part of the "very subject matter" brought before the tribunal concerned, thus requiring the appearance of the international organisation. The absence of jurisdiction *ratione personae* of the ICJ over international organisations should lead the Court to dismiss claims based on the responsibility of states for abuse of the legal personality of the organisation at the decision-making level.

[96] *Monetary Gold* case, par. 43.

[97] See also Andreas Zimmermann, Christian Tomuschat and Karin Oellers-Frahm (eds.), *The Statute of the International Court of Justice: A Commentary*, Oxford: Oxford University Press 2006, p. 604.

[98] Article 34 of the Statute.

not justiciable before the Court, as the Statute does not give contentious jurisdiction to the Court for adjudicating disputes involving them. Hence, the Court by definition cannot determine the legal position of such organisations, and on that basis the *Monetary Gold* rule does not seem to apply. In that sense, the ICJ Statute excludes the application of *Monetary Gold* to international organisations.

The *Monetary Gold* rule in any case would not apply to instances where an incidental assessment of the conduct or responsibility of UN institutions may have to be made: "The United Nations is not a sovereign entity. Institutionally, since the Court is one of its own organs, it must be deemed to be debarred from arguing that no judicial determination on its rights and obligations may be carried out in its absence."[99]

3.5. *Other Procedural Hurdles*

Apart from the *Monetary Gold* rule, questions of shared responsibility may encounter other procedural hurdles in the ICJ. The *Nicaragua case* is a prominent example. The United States had argued that it was primarily for the benefit of El Salvador, so as to help it in its defence against an armed attack, that the US claimed to exercise its right of collective self-defence. To the extent that several states were involved in a collective act of self-defence, the possible wrongfulness of such self-defence would in fact be a collective wrongdoing, and raise an issue of shared responsibility. In contrast to the earlier rejection of the argument based on *Monetary Gold*, this intertwining of collective self defence by El Salvador and the United States, in fact limited the exercise of the Court's jurisdiction. The United States' (then) acceptance of jurisdiction under article 36(2) of the Statute included the so-called multilateral treaty reservation, that excluded from its application "disputes arising under a multilateral treaty, unless (1) all parties to the treaty affected by the decision are also parties to the case before the Court, or (2) the United States of America specially agrees to jurisdiction". The Court distinguished this procedural aspect from that of the operation of the *Monetary Gold* rule,[100] found that any decision on the US claims would affect El Salvador, and on that basis found itself without jurisdiction in regard to the claims based on the multilateral treaties in question (notably the UN Charter).[101] This part of the judgment is not without problems.[102] In any case, it is so tied to the rather unique US reservation that

---

[99] Zimmermann, Tomuschat and Oellers-Frahm, supra n. 97, p. 604.
[100] *Nicaragua* case, par. 54.
[101] Ibid., par. 56.
[102] See James Crawford, 'Military and Paramilitary Activities in and against Nicaragua Case (Nicaragua v United States of America)', in: Rüdiger Wolfrum, *The Max Planck Encyclopedia of Public International Law*, Oxford: Oxford University Press 2011, available at <www.mpepil.com> (article was last updated August 2006), par. 13–17.

it is unlikely to have broader implications for the power of the Court to adjudicate questions of shared responsibility.

Finally, it is to be observed that the procedural hurdles caused by the bilateral nature of dispute settlement before the Court obviously do not apply in Advisory Opinions. If the question put to the Court in *Accordance with International Law of the Unilateral Declaration of Independence in Respect of Kosovo (Request for Advisory Opinion)* had been formulated differently, the Court may well have had to consider the consequences of possibly wrongful (collective) recognition by states.[103] The *Monetary Gold* rule would not be relevant in such a case – indeed, it seems inherent to the procedure that, for instance, the General Assembly can ask questions that require the Court to express itself on rights and obligations of states. Legal consequences of any statement on such rights and obligations for states would already be precluded by the advisory nature of the opinion.

4. *Principles of Shared Responsibility in the Case Law of the Court*

Against the background of the procedural limitations of the Court, we can now examine what principles the Court has been able to develop in its case law on questions of shared responsibility.

4.1. *Concurrent Responsibility between independent wrongdoers*

In the *Corfu Channel* case, the Court had occasion to pronounce on what at first sight is the least controversial scenario of shared responsibility: that of an injury resulting out of two independent wrongful acts by two states. The Court determined that Albania had acted wrongfully for its failure to comply with the obligation to warn the United Kingdom of the presence of the mines, thus allowing the mines to damage the British warships.[104] The failure to warn led to the sinking of two warships and loss of lives, for which Albania had to pay compensation. Albania had, however, not itself laid those mines. The United Kingdom suggested that in fact Yugoslavia had laid those mines.[105] The Court

---

[103] *Accordance with International Law of the Unilateral Declaration of Independence in Respect of Kosovo* (Advisory Opinion) 22 July 2010, available at <http://www.icj-cij.org/docket/files/141/15987.pdf>. The possibility to consider questions of joint responsibility in advisory proceedings is also illustrated by: *Responsibilities and Obligations of States Sponsoring Persons and Entities with Respect to Activities in the Area* (Advisory Opinion) (Seabed Disputes Chamber of the International Tribunal for the Law of the Sea), Case No. 17, 1 February 2011 <http://www.itlos.org/start2_en.html>, par. 190–192.

[104] *Corfu Channel* case, par. 43 and par. 49–56.

[105] Ibid., par. 36–37, par. 78, and Annex 1, par. 84, par. 110; the UK's contention that the mines were laid by two Yugoslav war vessels was never proven since it was based only on circumstantial evidence. See for suggestion that the mines were laid by Yugoslavia also Andrea

did not find sufficient proof of this, but in any case did not suggest that the alleged role of Yugoslavia would diminish the responsibility of Albania. The *Corfu Channel* case thus stands for the principle that in a situation where two states act independently from each other in contravention of an international obligation, the responsibility of each participating state is determined individually, on the basis of its own conduct and by reference to its own international obligations. The ILC indeed primarily relied on the *Corfu Channel* case in support of this principle. Such responsibility would be neither precluded nor diminished by the possible responsibility of the other state.[106]

The *Corfu Channel* case sometimes is attributed more relevance for the topic under consideration than it can bear. It has been suggested that the judgment is an application of the principle of joint and several liability.[107] However, the Court only found Albania responsible for its own wrongdoing, and it is not clear that classifying this finding as a case of joint and several liability adds anything to the legal situation. The situation may have been different if there would have been a case of collusion, or concerted action between Albania and Yugoslavia, as suggested by the United Kingdom.[108] Perhaps this scenario underlies statements to the effect that the *Corfu Channel* case would be an example of a situation where 'one course' of wrongful conduct is attributable to multiple states and each of these states is responsible for it.[109] It then may have been argued that Albania should not only have been responsible for its failure to warn but also for the laying of the mines itself. The existence of some form of collusion was not, however, proven before the Court,[110] and in this respect the *Corfu Channel* case is not a case of joint responsibility for a single course of conduct.

In contrast, the question of joint (or joint and several) responsibility – in the sense of a legal principle with distinct consequences –, was relevant to the facts of the *Oil Platforms* case. The Separate Opinion of Judge Simma in this case is one of the texts of the ICJ jurisprudence that contains the most lengthy analysis of the problem of shared responsibility. Simma's Opinion takes the holding of *Corfu Channel* one step further, in that it argues that a state can be

---

Gattini, 'Breach of the Obligation to Prevent and Reparation Thereof in the ICJ's Genocide Judgment', (2007) 18 *European Journal of International Law*, p. 710–11.

[106] Commentaries to the Articles on State Responsibility, Commentary to article 47, par. 8.

[107] Okowa, supra n. 3, p. 200; Philip Wendel, *State Responsibility for Interferences with the Freedom of Navigation in Public International Law*, Berlin-Heidelberg-New York: Springer 2007, p. 137.

[108] *Corfu Channel* case, par. 33; the UK had argued that: "[T]he minelaying operation was carried out by two Yugoslav warships at a date prior to October 22nd, but very near that date. This would imply collusion between the Albanian and the Yugoslav Governments, consisting either of a request by the Albanian Government to the Yugoslav Government for assistance, or of acquiescence by the Albanian authorities in the laying of the mine."

[109] Bell, supra n. 47, p. 526.

[110] *Corfu Channel*, par. 37.

held responsible, if it has committed an independent wrong that together with an independent wrong of another state has caused injury, even if it is not proved what the causal connection of either state to the injury was. The issue arose as a result of the United States' counterclaim, to the effect that because of the accumulation of attacks on US and other vessels, laying mines and otherwise engaging in military actions in the Persian Gulf, Iran made the Gulf unsafe, and thus breached its obligation with respect to freedom of commerce and freedom of navigation which the United States should have enjoyed under Article X, paragraph 1, of the 1955 Treaty. The problem was that acts that made the Gulf unsafe had also been undertaken by Iraq, and it proved difficult (indeed too difficult for the Court) to determine what acts were attributable to Iran. The somewhat unsatisfactory outcome is then that, because it was impossible to determine precisely who did what, neither of the two states could be held responsible.[111] Judge Simma argued that even though responsibility for the impediment caused to United States commerce with Iran could not be apportioned between Iran and Iraq, Iran should nevertheless have been held in breach of its treaty obligation to protect the freedom of commerce under the 1955 treaty.[112] To arrive at this conclusion, he invoked the principle of the joint and several liability, according to which multiple tortfeasors can be held responsible individually even when the damage cannot be apportioned among them, which he found to be a 'general principle of law' within the meaning of Article 38, paragraph 1 (c), of the Statute of the ICJ.[113]

Joint and several responsibility in national legal systems commonly sees to two or more acts that result in the same wrongful act or the same injury. Judge Simma observed that this condition was satisfied, since in the context of the generic counter-claim, "the 'internationally wrongful act' is constituted by the creation of negative economic, political and safety conditions in the Gulf rather than by a specific incident. The bringing about of this environment, taken as a whole, is attributable to both States, as it is common knowledge that they both participated in the worsening of the conditions prevailing in the Gulf at the time".[114] It then would follow that the two states were both responsible for the same act: the creation of dangerous conditions for shipping and doing commerce in the Gulf. As a result, the United States could invoke the responsibility of either state, that is, also of Iran, individually.

The main difference with *Corfu Channel* was that in that case the wrongful acts, and the damage, were divisible, and that it therefore could be adjudicated on the basis of the principle of independent responsibility. The qualification of joint and several responsibility in that case has no additional value. Yet in *Oil*

[111] Separate Opinion of Judge Simma in the *Oil Platforms* case, par. 65.
[112] Ibid., par. 74.
[113] Ibid.
[114] Ibid., par. 77.

Platforms the situation was different, as the injury was caused by a combination of acts that could not be divided – indeed, it might not be possible to find that either of the states individually had committed a wrongful act. To hold either state responsible, as Judge Simma argued, it then was necessary not just to look at individual causation, but to take resort to the general principle that in cases of indivisible damage, all states can be held responsible individually even when the damage could not be apportioned among them. The question may be raised, though, whether this was indeed the 'same wrongful act' (the treaty was only binding on Iran, and at best there could be a case of parallel, identical wrongful acts). In any case, the Court did not follow the line of argument suggested by Simma. It rejected the claim of the United States, as it found that "the United States has not demonstrated that the alleged acts of Iran actually infringed the freedom of commerce or of navigation between the territories of the United States and Iran".[115] It thus appeared to base itself on the principle of independent responsibility – the burden imposed on the United States was to demonstrate that Iran individually infringed the obligation under the 1955 Convention.

4.2. *Responsibility of States Acting in Concert*

Both the *Corfu Channel* case, on the facts as found by the Court, and the *Oil Platforms* case presented cases of injury arising out of concurrent independent action. A different scenario is presented by situations where two states act in collusion. This was what, according to the United Kingdom, in fact happened in the *Corfu Channel* case.[116] Several other cases have been brought to the Court where the applicant argued that two or more other states, acting in concert, had committed an internationally wrongful act. In *Treatment in Hungary of Aircraft and Crew of United States of America (United States of America v. Hungarian People's Republic and Union of Soviet Socialist Republics)*, the United States of America instituted separate proceedings against Hungary and the Soviet Union. It submitted that the Soviet Union "in concert with and aided and abetted by" Hungary caused the seizure of a United States Air force C-47 type aircraft, together with its crew of four American nationals and its contents, after which both governments engaged in unlawful actions against the crew and the United States, constituting both serious violations of existing treaties as well as manifest denials of justice and other international wrongs. The United States asked the Court to decide that the governments are "jointly and severally liable" to the United States for the damage caused.[117]

[115] *Oil Platforms* case, par. 123.
[116] *Corfu Channel* case, par. 33–40.
[117] *Treatment in Hungary of Aircraft and Crew of United States of America (USA v. Hungarian People's Republic and Union of Soviet Socialist Republics)*, Written Application of 16 February 1956, p. 42–43, par. 3.

However, the Court removed the cases from its list, since neither Hungary nor the Soviet Union had accepted the jurisdiction of the Court in the matter.[118]

An – in some respects – similar claim was made by Serbia and Montenegro in the *Legality of the Use of Force cases*. It argued that if two or more states together take joint action to the detriment of a third state, they are co-authors of any internationally wrongful act derived from their joint action, and that each of the states would be responsible for that action.[119] The respondent states would be jointly and severally responsible for the actions of the NATO military command structure, which constitutes an instrumentality of the respondent states.[120] Brownlie argued for the applicant that the North Atlantic Council directed the war against Yugoslavia as a joint enterprise and that "[i]t would be a legal and political anomaly of the first order if the actions of the command structure were not attributable jointly and severally to the member States. This joint and several responsibility was justified both in legal principle and by the conduct of the member States".[121]

The Court did not decide on any of these claims. It is not without interest, however, that, as noted by Brownlie, after the destruction of the Chinese Embassy in Belgrade, the British Prime Minister apologised to the Chinese Government, although there had been no suggestion that a British plane had fired the missiles. [122] The Court thus never has expressed itself on questions of responsibility of states acting in concert, and the question whether all such cases can be solved by the principle of independent responsibility remains an open one.

4.3. *Shared Responsibility in Case of Common Organs*

The case concerning *Certain Phosphate Lands in Nauru (Nauru v. Australia)* presented a substantive question of shared responsibility in a slightly different factual scenario. Australia relied on Article 2 of the Trusteeship Agreement to support the argument that it was under no separate obligation:

> the trusteeship obligations rest on the Administering Authority. The three Governments together constituted that 'Administering Authority', as a form of 'Partnership' [...] Accordingly, any breach of the obligations of the Administering Authority would be, *prima facie*, the joint responsibility of the Governments of Australia, New Zealand and the United Kingdom.[123]

---

[118] *Treatment in Hungary of Aircraft and Crew of United States of America (USA v. Hungarian People's Republic and Union of Soviet Socialist Republics)* (Orders and removal from list) (July 12th, 1954), ICJ Reports 1954, p. 99–101 and p. 103–105.

[119] Dominicé, supra n. 24, p. 282.

[120] *Legality of Use of Force* case *(Serbia and Montenegro v. UK)* (Oral Proceedings) supra n. 91.

[121] *Legality of Use of Force (Serbia and Montenegro v. UK)* (Oral Proceedings) (Public Sitting 12 May 1999), *Compte Rendu* 1999/25, p. 16.

[122] Ibid.

[123] *Nauru* case (Preliminary Objections of the Government of Australia), supra n. 82, par. 321.

Australia argued that in so far as Nauru's claims are based on the conduct of Australia as one of the three states making up the Administering Authority under the Trusteeship Agreement, the nature of the responsibility in that respect is such that a claim may only be brought against the three states jointly, and not against one of them individually. This appears to be a claim of joint responsibility, at least in the particular meaning where joint would be opposite of individual, and not necessarily imply several. In effect Australia denied that international law recognised a concept of joint and several liability as known to municipal systems; thus the Court could only determine their potential liability jointly.[124]

In what probably is the most relevant contribution of the case to the law of shared responsibility, the Court noted that no reason had been shown

> why a claim brought against only one of the three States should be declared inadmissible in *limine litis* merely because that claim raises questions of the administration of the Territory, which was shared with two other States. It cannot be denied that Australia had obligations under the Trusteeship Agreement, in its capacity as one of the three States forming the Administering Authority, and there is nothing in the character of that Agreement which debars the Court from considering a claim of a breach of those obligations by Australia.[125]

The Court thus suggested that even though the obligations may have been shared, they were also individual obligations, for which each state individually could be held responsible.[126] Judge Shahabuddeen noted in this respect that "the obligations of the three Governments under the Trusteeship Agreement were joint and several", and that this conclusion disposed of Australia's contention that proceedings will not lie against one only of the three governments.[127] While the use of the term 'joint and several' to refer to primary obligations is not common, it indicates well the nature of such obligations: the obligations were at the same time shared between the states, and continued to rest on them individually. Crawford refers to the Trusteeship Agreement as an example of a situation where "one 'party' to a treaty may be defined to consist of a number of legal persons acting as a collective,"[128] but "the use of a collective designation for one of the 'parties' to a treaty does not prevent that treaty being multilateral in character, if the collective designation does not correspond to a single legal person".[129]

---

[124] Ibid., par. 342, and *Nauru* case, par. 48.
[125] *Nauru* case, par. 48.
[126] Talmon, supra n. 23, p. 209.
[127] Separate opinion of Judge Shahabuddeen in the *Nauru* case, ICJ Reports 1992, p. 270–300, par. 4.
[128] James Crawford, 'Multilateral Rights and Obligations in International Law', (2006) 319 *Recueil des Cours de l'Académie de Droit International*, p. 336.
[129] Ibid., p. 336–338.

4.4. *Distribution of Responsibility under Multilateral Obligations*

Several of the cases in which questions of shared responsibility were raised concerned situations where two or more states are both bound by a common (multilateral) obligation and both states act in breach of that obligation. This was the situation in the *East Timor* case, where Portugal had contended that the right breached (the right of self-determination) was accepted by the Court to be a right *erga omnes*. The implication was that both Australia and Indonesia were obliged to refrain from interfering with this right – *erga omnes* rights are by definition the corollary of multilateral obligations.[130] And in *Certain Phosphate Lands in Nauru*, Australia, New Zealand and the United Kingdom were bound to, and possibly all breached, the same obligation. In such cases, the question may arise how responsibility is to be allocated between multiple responsible states. This is a matter of primary rather than of secondary obligations, but it is one that will have direct consequences for questions of shared responsibility as defined in section 2 above. This is illustrated by the Court's judgment in the *Bosnian Genocide* case. The Court concluded that the basis of Serbia's responsibility was its failure to prevent genocide.[131] If a state that does not directly commit genocide can be responsible for its failure to prevent, there is no *a priori* reason to limit that responsibility to Serbia. Indeed, the obligation under Article 1 of the Genocide Convention is an example of a collective responsibility (used here in the sense of primary obligations) where the collective failure of states to comply with their obligations results in shared responsibility.

While in some respects this is a hypothetical question, as no proceedings were initiated against other states, it is to be recalled that in the ILC's conception of international responsibility, such responsibility does not depend on any claims by injured parties.[132] Moreover, the question of responsibility of other states or entities may come up in different proceedings, whether before an international or a national court.[133] The question then is how responsibility and liability are to be allocated between multiple responsible states. The Court suggested that the obligation varied depending on each state's influence over the authors of the genocide.[134] It said that:

---

[130] See. par. 3.1. The opposite of course is not true, as not all multilateral obligations give rise to *erga omnes* obligations.

[131] *Application of the Convention on the Prevention and Punishment of the Crime of Genocide (Bosnia and Herzegovina v Serbia and Montenegro)* (Merits), ICJ Reports 2007, p. 2 (hereinafter: *Genocide* case), par. 450.

[132] Commentaries to the Articles on State Responsibility, p. 116, Part III.

[133] See *H. Nuhanovic v Kingdom of the Netherlands*, District Court of the Hague, Rechtbank 's-Gravenhage, (10 September 2008), LJN: BF0184, 265615 / HA ZA 06-1671, in which plaintiffs argued that even if responsibility would lie with the UN, such responsibility would not necessarily be exclusive.

[134] Monica Hakimi, 'State Bystander Responsibility', (2010) 21 *European Journal of International Law*, p. 364–65.

> Various parameters operate when assessing whether a State has duly discharged the obligation concerned. The first, which varies greatly from one State to another, is clearly the capacity to influence effectively the action of persons likely to commit, or already committing genocide.[135]

The case raises many questions. One is whether, given that responsibility can arise independently from invocation, all states that did not act were responsible, with capacity only functioning to allocate degrees of responsibility, or liability, or that only those states that actually had capacity to influence Serbia were required to act, and the others did not even breach the obligation. The Court suggested that it opted for the latter interpretation, as it asserted that "[t]he obligation to prevent the commission of the crime of genocide is imposed by the Genocide Convention on any State party which, in a given situation, has it in its power to contribute to restraining in any degree the commission of genocide".[136] This suggests that, while in the abstract all states may have been obliged to act (comparable to a situation that in the abstract everyone may be obliged to act to save a drowning person), only those in the actual situation to do so would act in violation of that obligation if they would not act. Indeed, it has been suggested that the responsibility based on failure to prevent cannot be seen apart from the fact that "Serbia was not a disconnected bystander with only the capacity to influence the Bosnian Serbs".[137] Even though political and military support of Bosnian Serbs did not result in attribution, it may well be that that relationship was relevant, because it meant that Serbia was especially capable of restraining the Bosnian Serbs.[138] This construction may be supported by the Court's statement that a state's capacity must "be assessed by legal criteria" that limit whether the state may act in a particular situation and that define the state's "legal position vis-à-vis the situations and persons facing the danger".[139] These criteria thus would distinguish the position of Serbia from that of other states, unconnected to the conflict, even though they may have had the power to influence the Bosnian Serbs.

The more general point here is that in determining whether breach of multilateral obligations of conduct, in a situation where multiple states have refrained from the required conduct, results in shared responsibility will depend on a careful analysis of the contents and scope of such obligations. Questions of shared responsibility more often than not will turn on an analysis of primary rather than secondary rules.

---

[135] *Genocide* case, par. 430.

[136] Ibid., par. 461.

[137] Hakimi, supra n. 134, p. 364–65.

[138] Ibid., p. 365, noting that "[i]ts causal connection to the abuse provides the normative justification for assigning it an obligation to protect".

[139] *Genocide* case, par. 430.

5. *Principles of Shared Reparation in the Case Law of the Court*

Quite distinct from the question of whether a state can be held responsible in a situation where the wrong, or the injury, was committed also by one or more other states, is the question how in such cases obligations of reparation should be implemented. The question how compensation is to be allocated between two or more states is particularly relevant; much of the doctrine on joint (and joint and several) liability in national law sees precisely to this question.[140]

The case law of the Court relevant to this question obviously is very limited, as the Court rarely pronounces on questions of compensation at all. But, we can infer from the *Corfu Channel* case that the responsibility of an independently responsible state entails an obligation of full reparation of the damage suffered by the injured state to the extent that it was caused by that responsible state, without that obligation being limited in view of the damage caused by the other wrongdoing state.[141] All that the Court had to determine is whether, and to what degree, the respondent in a legal sense caused the damage complained of. Each state is responsible for its own actions and the consequences that follow therefrom, and a finding on the degree of causation by Albania as such would not have had legal consequences for the position of Yugoslavia. In somewhat different factual circumstances, the United States relied on the same principle in its pleadings in the *Aerial Incident of 27 July 1955* case when it said, referring to Article 38, paragraph 1 (c) and (d), of the ICJ Statute, that "in all civilized countries the rule is substantially the same. An aggrieved plaintiff may sue any or all joint tortfeasors, jointly or severally, although he may collect from them, or any one or more of them, only the full amount of his damage".[142] The argument, and indeed the case as such, was not decided upon by the Court.

The ILC relied on both these cases to conclude that, in cases where the injury was effectively caused by a combination of factors and only one of such factors can be linked to the responsible state, "international practice and the decisions of international tribunals do not support the reduction or attenuation of reparation for concurrent causes, except in cases of contributory

[140] See e.g. The European Group on Tort Law, *Principles of European Tort Law. Text and Commentary*, Vienna: Springer 2005, available at <http://www.egtl.org/principles/text.htm>, article 9:101 (2): "Where persons are subject to solidary liability, the victim may claim full compensation from any one or more of them, provided that the victim may not recover more than the full amount of the damage suffered by him."

[141] *Corfu Channel (UK v. Albania)* (Judgment on Compensation), ICJ Reports 1949, p. 250. See also Dominicé, supra n. 24, p. 283; John E. Noyes and Brian D. Smith, 'State Responsibility and the Principle of Joint and Several Liability', (1988) 13 *Yale Journal of International Law*, p. 225, p. 246 and p. 248.

[142] *Aerial Incident of 27 July 1955 (USA v. Bulgaria)* (Merits – Memorial submitted by the United States Government) (2 December 1958), Part I, p. 229.

fault".[143] This would only be different if "some part of the injury can be shown to be severable in causal terms from that attributed to the responsible State, the latter is held responsible for all the consequences, not being too remote, of its wrongful conduct".[144] Special Rapporteur Arangio-Ruiz had taken a different position; he had argued that in cases of concurrent causation, the state's liability should be proportionally reduced.[145] It has been suggested that the language in the commentary on Article 31 of the ILC Articles on State Responsibility ("cases can occur where an identifiable element of injury can properly be allocated to one of several concurrently operating causes alone") would allow for such reduction,[146] but that it also should be observed that this language has not found its way in the commentary on article 47 dealing with the question of a 'plurality of responsible states' in relation to the same internationally wrongful act.[147]

Because in the *Corfu Channel* case the Court did not consider the possible contribution by Yugoslavia, the judgment also does not help us for developing the principles governing allocation of liability between multiple responsible states. In the scenario where both Albania and Yugoslavia would have been found responsible, the question may have arisen how the compensation was to be allocated between the two states. One can speculate on the factors that should be relevant in that scenario. It has been suggested that in such cases of multiple wrongdoing states, the principal burden of the reparation ought to fall on the author of the principal breach.[148] In this respect it can be noted that some authors have interpreted the judgment as saying that the duty on the side of Albania was not an absolute one; Albania was only under a duty to take steps that were actually open to it.[149] On that reading, it may well be that Yugoslavia had more possibilities to prevent, and on that account (quite separate from who was the initial author) it may be argued that Yugoslavia should bear the principal burden of the reparation. In his dissenting opinion in the damages award, Judge Ečer had said that the degree of *culpa* would be relevant for the degree of compensation.[150] However, because the Court based itself on

[143] Commentaries to the Articles on State Responsibility, Commentary to article 31, par. 12.
[144] Ibid., par. 13.
[145] Arangio-Ruiz, 'Second Report on State Responsibility', in: *Yearbook of the ILC 1989*, Vol. II (A/CN.4/SER.A/1989/Add.1) (Part 1), p. 14, par. 44. See also *Yearbook of the ILC 1990*, Vol. I (A/CN.4/SER.A/1990), p. 175, par. 60.
[146] Gattini, supra n. 105, p. 710–11.
[147] Ibid.
[148] Dominicé, supra n. 24, p. 283.
[149] Gerald G. Fitzmaurice, 'Law and Procedure of the International Court of Justice: The General Principles and Substantive Law', (1950) 27 *British Yearbook of International Law*, p. 1, or Malgosia Fitzmaurice, 'The Corfu Channel Case and the Development of International Law', in: Nisuke Ando, Edward McWhinney and Rüdiger Wolfrum (eds.), *Liber Amicorum Judge Shigeru Oda*, The Hague: Kluwer Law International 2002, p. 136.
[150] Dissenting opinion by Judge ad hoc Ečer in the *Corfu Channel* case (Judgment on Compensation), ICJ Reports 1949, p. 252–56, par. 7.

full causation, there is nothing in the judgment that supports consideration of such factors one way or the other.

Finally, because the Court did not consider the possible contribution by Yugoslavia, the judgment also does not help us to construe the legal relationship between Albania and Yugoslavia. In the hypothetical scenario where the United Kingdom subsequently would have pressed charges against Yugoslavia, and a determination would have been made that Yugoslavia was to provide reparation, the scope of such reparation would have to be limited by the principle that the injured state should not obtain compensation greater than the injury sustained.[151] From the perspective of Albania, it may then seem unfair if it would have to shoulder the full compensation – certainly in the suggested scenario where Albania and Yugoslavia in fact had acted in collusion.[152] Hypothetically, Albania might have tried to recover part of the money from Yugoslavia. But the question is what would be the legal basis of such a claim. It also might face procedural barriers: if the two states had not consented to the jurisdictional basis of an international court, the possibility to recover part of the damages may well remain a theoretical one. The point here is that both the substantive and procedural principles governing shared responsibility are underdeveloped, certainly if compared to the comparable principles as they operate in national legal systems.[153]

None of the other cases in which questions of shared responsibility arose contain express pronouncements on the consequences of shared responsibility for the obligation to provide compensation. In the merits stage of the *Nicaragua* case, the possible wrongfulness of acts of Honduras[154] did not play any role. Conceivably, it might have been relevant at the stage of reparation, if the Court would have been asked to determine shares of liability for specific injury in Nicaragua. The second stage that the Court envisaged[155] never materialised. The Court did note, however, that in such a subsequent phase Nicaragua should have been afforded the possibility to demonstrate "exactly what injury was suffered as a result of each action of the United States which the Court had found contrary to international law".[156] While it emphasised the importance of allowing the United States to present argument,[157] it did not refer to any possible role of other states. This suggests that the Court treated this case as one of individual responsibility and individual liability, to be determined on the basis of a causal connection between breach and damage.

---

[151] Article 47 (1) (a) of the Articles on State Responsibility prohibits 'double dipping'.
[152] *Corfu Channel* case, par. 36.
[153] See generally Kees van Dam, *European Tort Law*, Oxford: Oxford University Press 2006.
[154] See section 3.2
[155] *Nicaragua* case, par. 284.
[156] Ibid.
[157] Ibid.

The question of reparation was hinted at in the *Nauru* case. Australia had raised the question "whether the liability of the three States would be 'joint and several' (*solidaire*), so that any one of the three would be liable to make full reparation for damage flowing from any breach of the obligations of the Administering Authority, and not merely a one-third or some other proportionate share".[158] However, as the case was settled before judgment, the Court did not get to a discussion of this question. From the fact that the Court accepted jurisdiction, it cannot be inferred that the Court would have upheld the existence of the principle of joint and several liability in international law, or whether responsibility in these instances should instead be grounded on individual causal contribution.[159]

The possible responsibility of other states for the determination of compensation was also relevant to the Court's holdings on the reparation to be provided by Serbia in the *Bosnian Genocide* case. The Court found that Serbia was not required to provide compensation because it could not be determined that if Serbia had acted, the genocide committed at Srebrenica would not have occurred.[160] This may be taken to imply that the Bosnian Serbs would have done what they did anyway.[161] But it also may be taken to imply that Serbia was on its own not in a position to bring enough power to persuade the Bosnian Serbs to refrain from their plans, and that in that respect there was no full causation. In the latter interpretation, the judgment is difficult to square with the Court's earlier observation that

> it is irrelevant whether the State whose responsibility is in issue claims, or even proves, that even if it had employed all means reasonably at its disposal, they would not have sufficed to prevent the commission of genocide. As well as being generally difficult to prove, this is irrelevant to the breach of the obligation of conduct in question, the more so since the possibility remains that the combined efforts of several States, each complying with its obligation to prevent, might have achieved the result – averting the commission of genocide – which the efforts of only one State were insufficient to produce.[162]

It would have been consistent with this recognition that the combined efforts of states might have been able to produce what Serbia could not do alone, if the Court would have recognised the possibility of alternative causes, leading to a relative share of liability of Serbia, proportionate to its own (causal) contribution to the genocide – however difficult it would have been to calculate this.[163] The Court did not choose this path, however, and did not use what

[158] *Nauru* case, par. 48.
[159] Okowa, supra n. 3, p. 196–97 and p. 200.
[160] *Genocide* case, par. 160.
[161] See section 6.
[162] *Genocide* case, par. 430.
[163] See for critique on the Court's treatment of the question of causation Gattini, supra n. 105, p. 708–9.

perhaps was the best chance to explain the law concerning reparation in situations of shared responsibility.

6. *Shared Responsibility between States and Non-State Actors*

Quite a different set of questions is raised in cases where states and non-state actors share responsibility for a particular wrongful act and/or for a particular injury. Of course, the Court is not well positioned to consider such cases, as non-state entities are not a party in proceedings. However, it would seem that while the Court cannot and will not make determinations of the legal responsibility of non-state entities, such entities may play a role as a concurrent cause in determining shared liability.

6.1. *International Organisations*

Apart from the jurisdictional aspect discussed above, the *Legality of the Use of Force* cases brought by Serbia and Montenegro also raised substantive questions of shared responsibility. Serbia and Montenegro argued that if two or more states together take joint action to the detriment of a third state, they are co-authors of any internationally wrongful act derived from their joint action, and that each of the states would be responsible for that action.[164] The applicant contended that the respondent states were jointly and severally responsible for the actions of the NATO military command structure, which constitutes an instrumentality of the respondent states.[165] While not disputing that NATO had legal personality, it was argued that such legal personality did not preclude the responsibility of the individual members.[166] Relevant considerations in this regard were the fact that under Article 5 of the NATO (Washington) Treaty states shall take action "individually and in concert with others", that the ultimate decision to use force rests with individual states and this remains a sovereign prerogative of NATO Members, that the NATO Handbook stated that "[e]ach nation represented at the Council table or on any of its subordinate committees retains complete sovereignty and responsibility for its own decisions" and that national authorities did have the power to approve or veto the targets, which power would be pertinent to their international responsibility.[167]

---

164 Dominicé, supra n. 24, p. 282.

165 *Legality of Use of Force case (Serbia and Montenegro v. UK)* (Oral Proceedings), supra n. 91, p. 40.

166 *Legality of Use of Force (Serbia and Montenegro v. UK)* (Oral Proceedings) (Public Sitting 21 April 2004), *Compte Rendu* 2004/14, p. 54, par. 28. It can be added that the question whether or not the NATO indeed has legal personality is not entirely beyond dispute: see d'Aspremont, supra n. 95, p. 93, footnote 6.

167 *Legality of Use of Force (Serbia and Montenegro v. UK)* (Oral Proceedings), supra n. 166, p. 49, par. 7.

The argument raised important questions on the command and control over the operations, and the implications thereof for the allocation of responsibility. Arguments by respondent states focused on the alleged absence of any basis in international law for finding that Member States would have concurrent or secondary responsibility if NATO's acts were unlawful,[168] on a possible parallel with UN peacekeeping operations (which Portugal saw as a reason to allocate responsibility to NATO rather than to individual states),[169] and on the question whether individual state responsibility was to be ruled out because the states did not act individually and autonomously ("All the acts in which it took part for those purposes were carried out under the guidance and control of international organizations – and principally NATO"[170]). The position of these states is not insignificant, and may cast doubt on the proposition that even when an organisation would be responsible, this would not necessarily exclude responsibility of member states, in particular those states that were actively engaged in the planning or carrying out of the operation.[171] However, not all participating states relied on the arguments used by France, Portugal and Italy, and it may be inferred that at least some of them actually accepted that by virtue of their control over the operation or on other grounds, they, rather than NATO, remained responsible for the acts. But one should be careful in drawing such conclusions – an alternative explanation may be that some states took the position that NATO could not be responsible because it was not a legal person.

As the Court never reached the merits, it did not consider questions of shared liability – but clearly questions of multiple or concurrent causes might have arisen. The applicant noted that, as the choice and approval of targets was controlled by the highest national authorities, individual states could be held responsible, and added that "[t]he question of whether some Respondents exercised fuller control than the others' would be 'of relevance for the allocation of responsibility at the merits stage".[172] All of this remains undecided by the Court and, partly as a result, the state of the law in this respect remains rather undeveloped and unclear.

6.2. *Other Non-State Actors*

It is of course quite common that a state is being held responsible in conjunction with acts of non-state actors. It then can be said that two actors combine

---

[168] *Legality of Use of Force (Serbia and Montenegro v. Portugal)* (Oral Proceedings) (Public Sitting 19 April 2004), *Compte Rendu* 2004/9, p. 22, par. 4.8 (Portugal - Galvão Teles).

[169] Ibid., par. 4.4 (Portugal - Galvão Teles).

[170] *Legality of Use of Force (Serbia and Montenegro v. France)* (Oral Proceedings) (Public sitting 20 April 2004), *Compte Rendu* 2004/12, p. 19, par. 50.

[171] Orakhelashvili, supra n. 7.

[172] *Legality of Use of Force (Serbia and Montenegro v. Belgium)* (Oral Proceedings) (Public sitting 23 April 2004), *Compte Rendu* 2004/23, p. 32, par. 12.

to cause damage. The *United States Diplomatic and Consular Staff in Tehran* case is an example. The initial seizure of the hostages by militant students (not at that time acting as organs or agents of the state) was attributable to the combination of the students' own independent action and the failure of the Iranian authorities to take necessary steps to protect the embassy.[173] The judgment does not suggest that the fact that the injury in question was caused by a combination of factors, only one of which is to be ascribed to the responsible state, in any way reduced the responsibility, or the obligation to provide reparation by Iran. Indeed, the ILC relied on this case in support of the same principle that it derived from the *Corfu channel case:* "International practice and the decisions of international tribunals do not support the reduction or attenuation of reparation for concurrent causes, except in cases of contributory fault".[174]

In the *Nicaragua* case, Nicaragua had argued that the contras were bands of mercenaries recruited, organised, paid and commanded by the government of the United States who would have no real autonomy in relation to that government. Consequently, any offenses which they have committed would be imputable to the government of the United States.[175] The Court then found that the act of the contras could not be treated as acts conducted by the United States.[176] The Court did note that "the *contras* remain responsible for their acts".[177] It also noted that "[t]he lawfulness or otherwise of such acts of the United States is a question different from the violations of humanitarian law of *which the contras may or may not have been guilty*".[178] What these latter statements mean as a matter of international law is somewhat uncertain, but the use of the term 'responsible' probably should not be qualified in terms of international law. In principle, the Court was not tasked to determine any responsibility or 'guilt' of the contras, and it indeed said that it "does not have to determine whether the violations of humanitarian law attributed to the contras were in fact committed by them".[179] There is nothing in the case that considers whether such responsibility or guilt of the contras would be relevant to the (degree of) responsibility of the US, other than that knowledge of such responsibility or guilt might be relevant for the (performance of) the obligations of the US.[180] The US was responsible for its own acts, notably the

[173] *Consular Staff in Tehran* case; see also Commentaries to the Articles on State Responsibility, Commentary to article 31, par. 12.
[174] Ibid.
[175] *Nicaragua* case, supra n. 11, par. 15.
[176] Ibid. par. 109 and 115.
[177] Ibid. par. 116.
[178] Ibid. (emphasis added)
[179] Ibid.
[180] Ibid.

violation of the prohibition of intervention, and not for the specific violations of human rights law and humanitarian law.

The question may be raised whether, if the Court would have come to a liability phase, any responsibility of the contras for their own act would, as concurrent causes be relevant in that they might limit the degree in which the US could have been held liable to compensate for specific injuries committed by the contras. Such a determination would have to be based on causation between the violations attributed to the US on the one hand, and specific harm on the other hand. In that causal relationship, the responsibility of the contras at least as a factual matter seems an intervening variable. Even though the Court could not determine responsibility of the contras as a matter of international law, their acts may be relevant as a concurrent cause for the sake of mitigating the obligation to compensate. It may be recalled that according to the ILC international law may require a reduction of reparation for concurrent causes, when "an identifiable element of injury can properly be allocated to one of several concurrently operating causes alone".[181]

The possibility that a state commits a wrongful act in conjunction with another entity (not being a state or international organisation) also was raised in the *Bosnian Genocide* case. Here, the Court did in fact make a judgment on a substantive principle of shared responsibility in relation to non-state actors. The Court, first having determined that the acts of genocide were not attributable to Serbia and Montenegro, accepted the possibility that acts which could be characterised as 'complicity in genocide', within the meaning of Article III (e) of the Genocide Convention, could be attributed to the respondent.[182] Significantly for our purposes, it noted that this notion of 'complicity' is similar to the prohibition of aid or assistance in terms of Article 16 of the ILC Articles, thus raising the spectrum of issues of shared responsibility. On the facts of the case, the Court concluded that the international responsibility of Serbia and Montenegro was not engaged for acts of complicity in genocide mentioned in Article III (e), of the Convention.[183] But an interesting, if somewhat speculative question is what would have been the situation if the Court would have found that Serbia and Montenegro would have been responsible for aiding and assisting in the crimes committed by individuals. Of course, the issue before the Court was not the responsibility of individuals or of the Bosnian Serb Republic. But as a factual matter the question of concurrent causes might well be relevant in this type of scenario.

Questions of concurrent causes were also raised by the Court's conclusion that it could not order Serbia and Montenegro to provide compensation because it could not determine that the genocide would not have been

181 Commentaries to the Articles on State Responsibility, Commentary to article 31.
182 *Genocide* case, par. 418.
183 Ibid., par. 424.

committed if Serbia and Montenegro would have attempted to prevent the genocide. The Court said that in order to rule on the claim for reparation, it must ascertain whether, and to what extent, the injury asserted by the Applicant is the consequence of wrongful conduct by the Respondent with the consequence that the Respondent should be required to make reparation for it.[184] The question was whether there is a sufficiently direct and certain causal nexus between the wrongful act, Serbia and Montenegro's breach of the obligation to prevent genocide, and the injury suffered by the applicant.[185] The Court found that it could not "regard as proven a causal nexus between the Respondent's violation of its obligation of prevention" and the genocidal acts of the Bosnian Serb authorities. As a result, it did not consider financial compensation "the appropriate form of reparation for the breach of the obligation to prevent genocide".[186]

The fact that the Court did not find that preventative action by Serbia and Montenegro would have prevented the genocide suggests a degree of autonomy of the perpetrators, who may only to a limited extent be open to influence by Serbia and Montenegro. A more decisive stance on the part of Serbia and Montenegro in preventing the commission of the genocide in Srebrenica would, in the view of the Court, not have made a difference: the genocide would most probably have been committed anyway by the organs of the Republika Srpska. However, as in *Corfu Channel*, the Court did not consider the question of the consequences of 'concomitant causation' – the possibility that the same loss can be linked to more than one cause. The black and white approach of the Court is difficult to understand, and it might well have approached the question in terms of concurrent causes. It then could have attributed to the acts of the Bosnian Serb authorities a weight that would have reduced, rather than excluded, the liability of Serbia and Montenegro.[187] The Court phrased the question as whether there was "a sufficiently direct and certain causal nexus between the wrongful act and the injury suffered by the Applicant, consisting of all damage of any type, material or moral, caused by the acts of genocide". Gattini observes:

> Put in these extreme terms, the answer cannot but be negative. But the point was exactly to determine which part of the damage, be it material or moral, had been caused by the omissions of a state which, to use the same words of the Court, although aware of the grave risk of a genocide and having the means whereby it could at least have tried to prevent it, 'manifestly refrained from employing them'.[188]

---

[184] Ibid., par. 462.
[185] Gattini, supra n. 105.
[186] *Genocide* case, par. 462.
[187] See also section 5.
[188] Gattini, supra n. 105, p. 710.

Whereas in *Corfu Channel*, the possibility of a concurrent cause did not prevent the Court from finding an obligation to provide full compensation for Albania, in this case the presence of a concurrent cause led the Court to find that there was no obligation to provide compensation at all. It is true that the applicant had not asked for compensation for breaches of article 1 of the Convention,[189] but that was not the ground on which the Court rejected compensation, and the absence of any reasoning on this point is indicative of the poor state of development of principles of shared responsibility.

7. *Conclusion*

Although the Court has been confronted with questions of shared responsibility in quite a few cases, its contribution to the principles governing such shared responsibility has been limited. In part, this is explained by the *Monetary Gold* rule that precluded exercise of jurisdiction in the *East Timor* Case. It would seem that the *Monetary Gold* rule should be narrowly construed, and generally should not preclude the exercise of jurisdiction in cases of shared responsibility. More relevant is that in several potentially important 'shared responsibility cases' jurisdiction was declined on other grounds, or the case was settled out of the Court (notably the *Nauru* case). As a result, several important shared responsibility questions have not been adjudicated by the Court, notably the application of the principle to situations of aid and assistance and responsibility of states in connection with the responsibility of international organisations.

Several cases, including *Nauru* and *Nicaragua* have illustrated the tension between the bilateral nature of dispute settlement before the Court and the more collective, multilateral nature of some of the substantive principles (whether *de lege lata* or *de lege feranda*) of shared responsibility. As many authorities will look to the Court as a first port of call for guidance, the procedural aspects of the Court's jurisdiction indeed have hampered the development of the law.

Of the substantive principles of shared responsibility stipulated by the Court, perhaps the two most important are, first, the reaffirmation of the principle of independent state responsibility and the applicability thereof in situations of concurrent responsibility (as in the *Corfu Channel* case) and, second, the principle that in case of acts of a joint organ, each state can individually be held responsible (*Nauru* case). Also of some importance is the rejection of the generic counterclaim in the *Oil Platforms* case, suggesting that in that type of scenario of shared responsibility, where it cannot be demonstrated which state caused what part of the injury, the Court will not apply a principle of joint and

[189] As noted by Gattini, ibid.

several responsibility, but simply reject the claim for lack of evidence of individual causation.

Otherwise, much of the substantive law pertaining to shared responsibility has not been decided by the Court, including questions of responsibility arising out of concerted action (as allegedly at issue in the *Legality of the Use of Force* cases), the possible relevance of the notion of joint enterprise in such a context (as suggested by Brownlie as counsel for the applicant),[190] the conditions and consequences of shared responsibility arising out of aid and assistance, and the questions arising out of shared responsibility between states and organisations (again an issue in the *Legality of the Use of Force* cases).

The Court has had even less opportunity to address questions of reparation arising out of situations of shared responsibility. A major question in this regard was put to the Court by Australia in the *Nauru* case, where it raised the question whether the liability of the three States would be joint and several, "so that any one of the three would be liable to make full reparation for damage flowing from any breach of the obligations of the Administering Authority, and not merely a one-third or some other proportionate share".[191] As the case was settled the Court did not get to a discussion of this question, and this remains a fundamental open question of shared responsibility. On the important question of the influence of concurrent causes in situations of shared responsibility, the Court suggested in *Corfu Channel* that there was no reduction in such cases. But while the conclusion in that case appears unproblematic, the treatment of the issue in the *Bosnian Genocide* case is highly unsatisfactory.

In conclusion, while the Court has laid some important building blocks for principles that can be applied to situations of shared responsibility, major issues have not been examined let alone decided. The increasing degree of cooperation (with resulting risks of multiple state responsibility) makes it likely that the questions will come back before the Court. However, its bilateralist procedure militates against a full consideration of relevant issues. For a fuller understanding, the case law of other courts should also be considered, which, due to a different procedural context, may be better positioned to express themselves on questions of shared responsibility.[192] The whole issue is undertheorised and underexplored, and such case law may, together with the contribution of the Court, help to provide a better understanding and explanation of the law of shared responsibility.

[190] See supra n. 121.
[191] See section 5.
[192] See e.g. *M.S.S. v. Belgium and Greece* (Merits and Just Satisfaction) (Grand Chamber), Application No. 30696/09, 21 January 2011.

CHAPTER TWELVE

BOUNDARY TREATIES AND THEIR INTERPRETATION

*Malcolm N. Shaw QC**

1. *The Special Nature of Boundary Treaties*

Boundary treaties are treaties, but are distinctive. They constitute a special category of treaties. Boundary treaties may constitute a root of title to territory and, as such, will have widespread effect within the international community going far beyond the confines of the treaty itself. Boundary treaties additionally can affect the critical date at which territorial rights are crystallised as between the particular parties. A boundary treaty may shift the pertinent date of crystallisation of territorial rights from the date of independence of the elevant parties to the date of the treaty itself.[1]

Treaties generally bind only those states that have signed and ratified (or acceded to) them. They do not constitute obligations for third states. Further, provisions of a treaty as a matter of general principle exist within the framework of that instrument, so that once ceasing to be a valid agreement for whatever reason, the obligations created thereby naturally fall away.[2] However, boundary treaties are different. They may establish an objective territorial regime which is valid *erga omnes* and thus applicable to third parties. The Tribunal in the *Eritrea/Yemen* case, for example, stated in referring to boundary agreements that "this special category of treaties also represents a legal reality which necessarily impinges upon third states, because they have effect *erga omnes*".[3] Further, such a regime once created by the treaty will take on an existence separate and distinct from it, which is thus capable of continuing irrespective of the treaty, even if the treaty in question itself ceases to apply. The International Court made this point in the *Libya/Chad* case, noting that the boundary between Libya and *inter alia* Chad (as a French colony at the

---

* It should be noted that the author was counsel for Cameroon in the *Cameroon v. Nigeria* litigation. The views expressed in this article, however, are those of the author alone.

[1] See *El Salvador/Honduras*, ICJ Reports 1992, p. 401.

[2] See generally A.D. McNair, *The Law of Treaties*, Oxford: Oxford University Press 1961; Jan Klabbers, *The Concept of Treaty in International Law*, Dordrecht: Martinus Nijhoff 1996; Anthony Aust, *Modern Treaty Law and Practice*, Cambridge: Cambridge University Press 2007; Olivier Corten and Pierre Klein (eds.), *Les Conventions de Vienne de 1969 et de 1986 sur le Droit des Traités: Commentaire Article par Article*, Brussels: Bruylant 2006.

[3] *Eritrea/Yemen* case, 114 *International Law Reports*, p. 48.

time) entrenched in the relevant Treaty of 1955 had not been intended to be provisional or temporary, and concluding that:

> The establishment of this boundary is a fact which, from the outset, has had a legal life of its own, independently of the fate of the 1955 Treaty. (…) A boundary established by treaty thus achieves a permanence which the treaty itself does not necessarily enjoy. The treaty can cease to be in force without in any way affecting the continuance of the boundary. In this instance the Parties have not exercised their option to terminate the Treaty, but whether or not the option be exercised, the boundary remains. This is not to say that two States may not by mutual agreement vary the border between them; such a result can of course be achieved by mutual consent, but when a boundary has been the subject of agreement, the continued existence of that boundary is not dependent upon the continuing life of the treaty under which the boundary is agreed.[4]

This has been re-emphasised by the International Court in two recent cases. In *Nicaragua v. Colombia*, the Court declared that: "[I]t is a principle of international law that a territorial régime established by treaty 'achieves a permanence which the treaty itself does not necessarily enjoy' and the continued existence of that régime is not dependent upon the continuing life of the treaty under which the régime is agreed".[5] This was cited in *Costa Rica v. Nicaragua* in the judgment of 16 July 2009.[6]

This objectivisation of boundaries is reinforced by two further doctrines. First, a boundary established by treaty is unaffected by any succession of states. Waldock, in his first Report on Succession of States and Governments in Respect of Treaties in 1968, declared that:

> the weight both of opinion and practice seems clearly to be in favour of the view that boundaries established by treaties remain untouched by the mere fact of a succession. The opinion of jurists seems, indeed, to be unanimous on the point … [and] State practice in favour of the continuance in force of boundaries established by treaty appears to be such as to justify the conclusion that a general rule of international law exists to that effect.[7]

Bedjaoui noted, for example, that, "in principle the territory devolves upon the successor State on the basis of the pre-existing boundaries".[8] Article 11 of the Vienna Convention on Succession of States in Respect of Treaties (1978), albeit in rather cautious and negative terms, specifies that:

> A succession of States does not as such affect:
>
> (a) a boundary established by treaty; or
> (b) obligations and rights established by a treaty and relating to the regime of a boundary.

---

[4] *Libya/Chad*, ICJ Reports 1994, p. 37.
[5] *Nicaragua v. Colombia, Preliminary Objections*, ICJ Reports 2007, p. 861.
[6] *Costa Rica v. Nicaragua*, ICJ Reports 2009, par. 68.
[7] *Yearbook of the International Law Commission* 1968, volume II, p. 92–3.
[8] Ibid., p. 112.

This rule may be seen as reflective of customary law.[9] Related to this principle is the doctrine of *uti possidetis*. The Latin American version of this concept, whereby the administrative divisions of the former Spanish empire were to constitute the boundaries of the newly independent states in South America in the first third of the last century was the first internationally accepted expression of this approach.[10] It was echoed in US practice[11] and explicitly laid down in resolution 16 of the meeting of Heads of State and Government of the Organisation of African Unity 1964, by which all member states pledged themselves to respect colonial borders.[12] The principle of succession to colonial borders was underlined by the International Court in the *Burkina Faso/ Mali* case.[13] The extension of the principle of *uti possidetis* from decolonisation to the creation of new states out of existing independent states is supported by international practice, taking effect as the transformation of administrative boundaries into international boundaries generally.[14] For example, the Arbitration Commission on Yugoslavia noted in Opinion No. 3 with respect to the status of the former internal boundaries between Serbia on the one hand and Croatia and Bosnia and Herzegovina on the other, that

> except where otherwise agreed, the former boundaries become frontiers protected by international law. This conclusion follows from the principle of respect for the territorial status quo and in particular, from the principle of *uti possidetis*. *Uti possidetis* (...) is today recognised as a general principle.[15]

[9] See e.g. *Tunisia/Libya Continental Shelf* case, ICJ Reports 1982, p. 66, and *Gabčíkovo-Nagymaros*, ICJ Reports 1997, p. 72.

[10] See, for example, the *Colombia–Venezuela* arbitral award, (1922) 1 *Reports of International Arbitral Awards*, p. 228, and the *Beagle Channel* award, 52 *International Law Reports*, p. 93. See also Anthony Cukwurah, *The Settlement of Boundary Disputes in International Law*, Manchester: Manchester University Press 1967 p. 114; D.P. O'Connell, *State Succession in Municipal Law and in International Law*, Cambridge: Cambridge University Press 1967, volume II, p. 273 ff., and Paul de La Pradelle, *La Frontière* (unpublished thesis), Paris 1928, p. 86–7.

[11] See the view of the US Secretary of State in 1856 that the US regarded it "as an established principle of the public law and of international right that when a European colony in America becomes independent it succeeds to the territorial limits of the colony as it stood in the hands of the present country", Manning's *Diplomatic Correspondence*, volume III (Great Britain), doc. 2767, cited in Cukwurah, supra n. 10, p. 106.

[12] See, for example, Malcolm N. Shaw, *Title to Territory in Africa: International Legal Issues*, Oxford: Clarendon Press 1986, p. 185–7, and Malcolm N. Shaw, 'The Heritage of States: The Principle of Uti Possidetis Today', (1996) 67 *British Year Book of International Law*, p. 75

[13] ICJ Reports, 1986, p. 554, p. 565, and *Nicaragua v. Honduras*, ICJ Reports 2007, p. 706.

[14] See e.g. article 5 of the Minsk Agreement establishing the Commonwealth of Independent States of 8 December 1991, and the Alma Ata Declaration of 21 December 1991 which reaffirmed the territorial integrity of the former Republics of the USSR. Note also that under the Treaty on the General Delimitation of the Common State Frontiers of 29 October 1992, the boundary between the two new states of the Czech Republic and Slovakia, emerging out of Czechoslovakia on 1 January 1993, was to be that of the administrative border existing between the Czech and Slovak parts of the former state.

[15] Badinter Arbitration Commission (European Community Arbitration Commission of the Peace Conference on Yugoslavia), 11 January 1992, 31 *International Legal Materials*, p. 1499, and 92 *International Law Reports*, p. 171.

Secondly, the principle of the objectivisation of boundaries is supported by the provision enshrined in article 62 (2) of the Vienna Convention on the Law of Treaties (1969), which stipulates that a fundamental change in circumstances (*rebus sic stantibus*) may not be invoked as a ground for terminating or withdrawing from a treaty that establishes a boundary.[16] This provision has also been accepted as being part of customary law.[17] Accordingly, neither a replacement of sovereignty over the state concerned nor a fundamental change in relevant circumstances will as a matter of law change in any way the territorial regime laid down in the treaty or treaties in question.

The reason for this exceptional approach is to be found in the need for the stability of boundaries,[18] for as Jennings has written, the problem of the legal ordering of territorial stability and territorial change lies at the heart of the whole problem of the legal ordering of international society.[19] This principle of the stability of boundaries constitutes an overarching postulate of the international legal system and one that both explains and generates associated legal norms. It enshrines and reflects the need felt within the international legal and political system for a significant element of permanence and continuity with regard to the spatial configuration of the state in order to prevent as far as possible constant disruption based upon challenges to the territorial integrity of states.

The easiest and most logical method for states to establish a boundary is by virtue of a formal agreement enshrined in a treaty. This may be done either by re-confirming an existing boundary line or by deciding to recognise a particular line whatever its previous status as a boundary line. In this case, the agreement so to recognise it "invests it with a legal force which it had previously lacked".[20] As the Arbitration Tribunal in the *Guinea-Bissau v. Senegal* case noted, "in all cases, the purpose of the relevant [delimitation] treaties is the same: to determine in a stable and permanent manner the area of validity in space of the legal norms of States".[21]

---

[16] See e.g. Shaw (1986), supra n. 12, p. 230 ff., and Malcolm N. Shaw and Caroline Fournet, 'Article 62', in: Olivier Corten and Pierre Klein (eds.), *Les Conventions de Vienne de 1969 et de 1986 sur le droit des traités: Commentaire article par article*, Brussels: Bruylant 2006, p. 2229.

[17] See *Gabčíkovo-Nagymaros,* ICJ Reports 1997, p. 38 and p. 62.

[18] See in particular Kayan Kaikobad, 'Some Observations on the Doctrine of Continuity and Finality of Boundaries', (1983) 54 *British Yearbook of International Law* 1983, p. 119; Daniel Bardonnet, 'Les frontières terrestres et la relativité de leur tracé', (1976) 153 *Receuil des Cours* (volume V), p. 9; Shaw (1996), supra n. 12, p. 81 ff, and Marcelo Kohen, 'Le Règlement des Différends Territoriaux à la Lumière de l'Arrêt de la C.I.J. dans l'Affaire Libye/Tchad', (1995) 99 *Revue Générale de Droit International Public*, p. 320 ff. See also the *Temple* case, ICJ Reports 1962, p. 34 and *Guinea-Bissau v. Sénégal,* (1990) 94 *Revue Générale de Droit International Public*, p. 253.

[19] Robert Y. Jennings, *The Acquisition of Territory in International Law*, Manchester: Manchester University Press 1963, p. 81 ff.

[20] *Libya/Chad,* ICJ Reports 1994, p. 23.

[21] *Guinea-Bissau v. Senegal*, 83 *International Law Reports*, p. 36.

Once created in accordance with international law, a boundary is protected and assumes finality and permanence. What is established on the basis of the consent of the states concerned can only be undone or modified by the exercise, once more, of such consent. As the International Court declared in the *Preah Vihar Temple* case,

> when two countries establish a frontier between them, one of the primary objects is to achieve stability and finality. This is impossible if the line so established can, at any moment, and on the basis of a continuously available process, be called in question, and its rectification claimed, whenever any inaccuracy by reference to a clause in the parent treaty is discovered. Such a process could continue indefinitely, and finality would never be reached so long as possible errors still remained to be discovered. Such a frontier, so far from being stable, would be completely precarious.[22]

The point was repeated in the *Beagle Channel* case, where the Arbitration Tribunal noted that, "a limit, a boundary, across which the jurisdictions of the respective bordering States may not pass, implies definitiveness and permanence".[23] As Jennings has emphasised, "some other kinds of legal ordering need to be capable of constant change to meet new needs of a developing society; but in a properly ordered society, territorial boundaries will be among the most stable of all institutions".[24] Indeed, one may observe that a properly ordered society can hardly be instituted without the requirement of territorial stability. Not that change cannot happen, but it can only take place in a clear, secure and regulated manner. In addition, it is important that such change cannot be too easily accomplished even within the aforementioned guidelines, for territorial change tends to bring with it political disruption which one should be loath to accept too glibly or in too facile a manner. As pointed out by the Court of Arbitration in the *Dubai/Sharjah* case, "the re-opening of the legal status of the boundaries of a State may give rise to very grave consequences, which may endanger the life of the State itself".[25] The approach has recently been reaffirmed in the *Malaysia/Singapore* case, where the International Court declared that:

> Critical for the Court's assessment of the conduct of the Parties is the central importance in international law and relations of State sovereignty over territory

[22] *Case concerning the Temple of Preah Vihear (Cambodia v. Thailand),* ICJ Reports 1962, p. 34. See also Kaikobad's comment that "a continuously available process which allows States to question an established and respected alignment should be denied them in the interests of stability" (Kaikobad, supra n. 18, p. 122).

[23] *Dispute between Argentina and Chile concerning the Beagle Channel*, 18 February 1977, (1977) 21 *Reports of International Arbitral Awards*, p. 88–9. See also the *Aegean Sea Continental Shelf* case, ICJ Reports 1978, p. 35–6 and the *Tunisia/Libya* case, ICJ Reports 1982, p. 66.

[24] Jennings, supra n. 19, p. 70.

[25] *Dubai/Sharjah* Border Arbitration, 13 February 2009, 91 *International Law Reports,* p. 543, p. 578. See also D. Bowett, 'The Dubai/Sharjah Boundary Arbitration of 1981', (1994) 65 *British Yearbook of International Law,* p. 103.

> and of the stability and certainty of that sovereignty. Because of that, any passing of sovereignty over territory on the basis of the conduct of the Parties, as set out above, must be manifested clearly and without any doubt by that conduct and the relevant facts. That is especially so if what may be involved, in the case of one of the Parties, is in effect the abandonment of sovereignty over part of its territory.[26]

2. *Treaty-Based Title to Territory and Other Sources of Title to Territory*

Any boundary query or disagreement will commence in legal terms with a consideration of relevant boundary treaties. If there be any such pertinent treaty or treaties, the dispute in question will revolve thereafter upon the validity, application and interpretation of such instruments.[27] However, there is another source of territorial title and that is the sovereign exercise of effective authority (or *effectivités*). As Huber noted in the *Island of Palmas* case, "the actual continuous and peaceful display of state functions is in case of dispute the sound and natural criterion of territorial sovereignty".[28] In the *Eritrea-Ethiopia* arbitration, the Boundary Commission defined *effectivités* as "activity on the ground tending to show the exercise of sovereign authority by the party engaging in that activity".[29] Examples of *effectivités* submitted by the parties in that case included the establishment of telephone and telegraph facilities, the holding of elections and a referendum on independence, the conduct of a census, the maintenance of local records of such matters as births and death, the payment of taxes and financial tribute, the issue of trading licenses, the establishment of a customs office, the administration of fuel supplies, the structure of local administration, the regulation of religious and social institutions, the stationing of military and police posts and the conduct of military and police patrols, the regulation of land use, provincial administration, the administration of educational facilities, public health administration, steps for the eradication of malaria, the grant of a mineral concession, various local acts carried

---

[26] *Malaysia/Singapore*, ICJ Reports 2008, p. 52.

[27] Note that the International Court in *Sovereignty over Pedra Branca/Pulau Batu Puteh, Middle Rocks and South Ledge* (*Malaysia/Singapore*), ICJ Reports 2008, p. 50, declared that "[a]ny passing of sovereignty might be by way of agreement between the two States in question. Such an agreement might take the form of a treaty (…). The agreement might instead be tacit and arise from the conduct of the Parties. International law does not, in this matter, impose any particular form. Rather it places its emphasis on the parties' intentions (cf. e.g. *Temple of Preah Vihear (Cambodia v. Thailand)* (Preliminary Objections), ICJ Reports 1961, p. 17, p. 31".

[28] *Island of Palmas* case (Netherlands, United States), (1928) 2 *Reports of International Arbitral Awards*, p. 840.

[29] Eritrea-Ethiopia Boundary Commission, Decision of 13 April 2002, 130 *International Law Reports*, p. 25, par. 3.16. See generally Malcolm N. Shaw, 'Title, Control and Closure? The Experience of the Eritrea-Ethiopia Boundary Commission', (2007) 56 *The International and Comparative Law Quarterly*, p. 755.

out by the British Military Administration during the relevant period and the appointment and payment of local officials.[30]

The level, nature and intensity of activities required in the particular case would vary widely and would depend upon the circumstances, including, especially the existence and strength of any competing claims and the nature of the territory itself and its geographical position. Title depending upon *effectivités* is thus relative.[31] However, where title is founded upon a treaty, the role played by *effectivités* changes. The International Court analysed this in *Burkina Faso/Mali* and emphasised that where there is a valid treaty-based title, this will have pre-eminence and *effectivités* may play a confirmatory role. However, where the *effectivités* were in contradiction to such title, the latter will have pre-eminence. In the absence of any legal title, *effectivités* must invariably be taken into consideration. Where the legal title was not capable of exactly defining the relevant territorial limits, *effectivités* would then play an essential role in showing how the title was to be interpreted in practice.[32] Accordingly, examples of state practice may confirm or complete but not contradict legal title established by boundary treaties.[33] In the absence of any clear legal title to any area, state practice comes into its own as a law-establishing mechanism. But its importance is always contextual in that it relates to the nature of the territory and the nature of competing state claims.[34] The conditions under which subsequent *effectivités* may modify an existing boundary treaty will be discussed below.

3. *The Role of the International Court of Justice: the Example of* Cameroon v. Nigeria

What precisely is demanded of the International Court may vary from case to case. One significant example is provided by the *Cameroon v. Nigeria* litigation. In order to examine this, the relevant agreements need first to be noted. The boundary between Cameroon and Nigeria from Lake Chad to the Gulf of Guinea had been the subject of a number of treaties between colonial powers.

[30] *Eritrea-Ethiopia* case, 130 *International Law Reports*, p. 1, 67–8, p. 69, p. 71, p. 73–4, p. 103–4 and p. 110–12.

[31] See e.g. the *Eastern Greenland* case, PCIJ Reports 1933, Series A/B, No. 53, p. 46; the *Clipperton Island* case, (1932) 26 *American Journal of International Law* (Supplement), p. 390; the *Minquiers and Ecrehos* case (*France/United Kingdom*), 17 November 1953, ICJ Reports 1953, p. 47; *Qatar v. Bahrain*, ICJ Reports 2001, p. 100, and *Indonesia/ Malaysia*, ICJ Reports 2002, p. 682.

[32] ICJ Reports 1986, p. 586–7, and the *El Salvador/Honduras* case, where the Chamber also noted that these principles applied both to colonial and post-colonial *effectivités*, ICJ Reports 1992, p. 398. See also *Benin/Niger*, ICJ Reports 2005, p. 127 and p. 149.

[33] See *Cameroon v. Nigeria*, ICJ Reports 2002, p. 353–5.

[34] See also the general statement of principle in *Eritrea/Ethiopia*, 130 *International Law Reports*, p. 42.

The frontiers between the French, German and British possessions prior to the First World War, respectively French Cameroon, German Kamerun and British Nigeria, were delimited in a series of agreements between 1894 and 1913. At the end of the First World War, German Kamerun was divided between Britain and France and placed under the League of Nations' mandate system. The boundary between British Cameroons and French Cameroon was subsequently defined by the Milner-Simon Declaration of 1919 and further clarified and detailed in the Thomson-Marchand Declaration of 1929–31, incorporated in an Exchange of Notes in January 1931.

After the Second World War, the mandated territories became trust territories. By an Order in Council in August 1946, British Cameroons was divided into the two administrative regions of the Northern and Southern Cameroons and the boundary between the two was defined. French Cameroon became independent on 1 January 1960 and Nigeria became independent on 1 October 1960. As a result of plebiscites held under UN authority in 1961, Northern Cameroons joined Nigeria and Southern Cameroons joined Cameroon. Thus the line drawn in the 1946 Order in Council became part of the international boundary between Nigeria and Cameroon. Accordingly, the boundary between Cameroon and Nigeria was defined from Lake Chad to the Order in Council line by the British-French Thomson-Marchand Declaration, then by the Order in Council provisions and thence by the British-German treaties of 11 March and 12 April 1913. This was agreed by the parties, subject only to disagreement as to the application of the 11 March 1913 treaty to the Bakassi peninsula.[35]

Since both parties accepted the validity and applicability of the four instruments noted, with the exception of Nigeria's claims as to the Bakassi Peninsula, the status and scope of these instruments was not an issue. However there was a difference in approach as to how the Court's role was envisaged. Cameroon asked the Court to "specify definitively" the course of the boundary as fixed by the relevant instruments of delimitation. It wanted simple confirmation of the applicability of the instruments and not a delimitation by the Court. While it accepted that there were "some ambiguities and uncertainties" in the delimitation instruments and that there "may be certain difficulties in demarcating the line", Cameroon argued that "the Court cannot, on the pretext of interpreting them, modify the applicable texts" as it suggested Nigeria was requesting the Court to do.[36]

Nigeria argued that mere confirmation of the delimitation instruments would be insufficient since it would not resolve the differences between the

[35] ICJ, *Land and Maritime Boundary between Cameroon and Nigeria* (*Cameroon v. Nigeria*), 22 October 2002, ICJ Reports 2002, p. 358–9.

[36] Ibid., p. 357–80.

parties with regard to the course of the boundary. It therefore asked the Court to "clarify" the delimitation in the areas "in which the delimitation instruments are defective" and to "correct the boundary line claimed by Cameroon in the areas where Nigeria claimed Cameroon was "not observing the clear terms of these instruments". Nigeria also claimed that, while purely technical matters could be settled at the demarcation stage, the "points of difficulty it has identified represent substantive delimitation issues" and believed that "a detailed specification of the land boundary is necessary if future border problems are to be avoided and any eventual demarcation is to take place on a sound basis".[37]

The Court noted that the parties agreed both that the land boundary from Lake Chad to Bakassi had already been delimited and that demarcation was not requested.[38] It concluded that its task was thus "neither to effect a delimitation *de novo* of the boundary nor to demarcate it". The Court concluded that the boundary between Lake Chad and Bakassi was "in reality simply a dispute over the interpretation or application of particular provisions of the instruments delimiting that boundary".[39] However, the Court declared that this meant going beyond simply confirming that the instruments in question were binding on the parties and applicable and required a close examination, a process expressed at one point in terms of "clarification".[40]

4. *Treaty Interpretation*

i) *Delimitation and Demarcation in Boundary Treaties*

Although in principle the difference between the two concepts of delimitation and demarcation in the context of boundaries is clear, in practice some confusion has from time to time been evident. Brownlie notes that delimitation "denotes description of the alignment in a treaty or other written source, or by means of a line marked on a map or chart", while demarcation "denotes the means by which the described alignment is marked, or evidenced on the ground by means of cairns of stones, concrete pillars, beacons of various kinds, cleared roads in scrub, and so on".[41] *Oppenheim's International Law* provides that: "The common practice for land boundaries is, in a boundary treaty or award, to describe the boundary line in words, i.e. to 'delimit' it; and then to

---

[37] Ibid., p. 357–8.
[38] Ibid., p. 358–9, par. 82 and par. 84.
[39] Ibid., p. 358–9, par. 84.
[40] Ibid., p. 371.
[41] Ian Brownlie, *African Boundaries. A Legal and Diplomatic Encyclopedia*, London: Hurst 1979, p. 4.

appoint boundary commissions, usually joint, to apply the delimitation to the ground and if necessary to mark it with boundary posts or the like, i.e. to 'demarcate' it".[42] Cukwurah has concluded that: "This distinction between 'delimitation' and 'demarcation' is now generally accepted",[43] noting, with some exaggeration, that demarcation was the crux of boundary making. The key point is that it is delimitation which determines the frontier line juridically, while demarcation concretises that line on the ground. It is the difference between establishing the law and applying it in the particular circumstances. As the Arbitral Tribunal in the *Laguna del Desierto* case noted, "[a] decision on a boundary issue and the demarcation of the boundary are two distinct acts, each of which has its own legal force".[44]

The Tribunal in the *Taba* case noted that:

> [i]f a boundary line is once demarcated jointly by the parties concerned, the demarcation is considered as an authentic interpretation of the boundary agreement even if deviations may have occurred or if there are some inconsistencies with maps. This has been confirmed in practice and legal doctrine, especially for the case that a long time has elapsed since demarcation.[45]

The Tribunal added that: "The principle of the stability of boundaries (...) requires that boundary markers, long accepted as such by the states concerned, should be respected and not open to challenge indefinitely on the basis of error".[46] However, in practice the relationship between delimitation and demarcation can be unclear and the Court's judgment in *Cameroon v. Nigeria* is of some help in this regard. Both Cameroon and Nigeria agreed that the land boundary between them was delimited, but they disagreed as to what that meant. For Cameroon, the role of the Court was simply to confirm the delimitation of the land boundary authoritatively, while in principle any problems in applying that delimitation on the ground constituted demarcation matters to be resolved bilaterally at a later stage. Nigeria, while accepting the application of the delimitation instruments "in principle", asked the Court to "clarify" the delimitation in the areas in which the instruments were defective.[47] The Court essentially accepted this position.

---

[42] Robert Y. Jennings and Arthur D. Watts (eds.), *Oppenheim's International Law*, London: Longman 1992, p. 662. See also Charles Rousseau, *Droit international public* (volume III), p. 269, par. 184.

[43] Cukwurah, supra n. 10, p. 27.

[44] *Case concerning a boundary dispute between Argentina and Chile concerning the delimitation of the frontier line between boundary post 62 and Mount Fitzroy (Laguna del Desierto* case), 29 October 1994, (2006) 20 *Reports of International Arbitral Awards*, p. 24, par. 67, and 113 *International Law Reports*, p. 43.

[45] *Case concerning the location of boundary markers in Taba between Egypt and Israel*, 29 September 1988, (2006) 22 *Reports of International Arbitral Awards*, p. 56, par. 210, and 80 *International Law Reports*, p. 297.

[46] Ibid., p. 64, par. 235, and 80 *International Law Reports*, p. 306.

[47] *Cameroon v. Nigeria*, ICJ Reports 2002, p. 357.

A number of interesting points were made. First, the fact that an instrument provides for modification by mutual agreement of its terms does not detract from the fact that a fully delimited frontier line has been established. Secondly, the fact that an instrument anticipates detailed demarcation by an agreed method "presupposes a frontier already regarded as essentially delimited". Thirdly, the fact that the term 'delimitation' is used does not necessarily preclude the conclusion that a demarcation is in mind.[48] It all depends on the actual meaning of the term in the light of the intentions of the parties and in particular the nature of the work involved.[49] Fourthly, the fact that a demarcation has yet to take place does not render the delimitation contained in an instrument from being understood as merely 'programmatic' in nature (as Nigeria claimed at one point).[50] Fifthly, the fact that a delimitation instrument contains some technical imperfections and that certain details remain to be specified does not prevent that instrument from constituting a valid delimitation sufficient in general for demarcation.[51]

The line between a delimitation and a demarcation issue still remains elusive however. Many of the issues regarded as purely demarcation matters by Cameroon were examined and clarified by the Court.[52] For example, at one point of the frontier reference was made in the Declaration to "a fairly prominent peak". Despite Cameroon's view that this was simply a demarcation matter, the Court noted that a problem of interpretation was involved, not least because the parties held differing views as to the location of the peak.[53] At one point, the Court held it was not necessary to deal with the frontier line since Cameroon's claim that a mere demarcation was at issue was not challenged by Nigeria.[54] The importance of a particular provision together with the views taken by the parties will clearly play a significant role in deciding whether a delimitation rather than a demarcation matter is involved, but ambiguity still remains and will often need to be considered by the court or tribunal in question.

ii) *The Process of Interpretation*

The International Court made a number of interesting general comments in *Cameroon v. Nigeria* with regard to the bounds of the process of boundary treaty interpretation in the context of litigation. These are worth exploring. The Court noted that where there was no dispute on a particular point between

48 Ibid., p. 339–40.
49 Ibid., p. 343–4.
50 Ibid., p. 340–1.
51 Ibid., p. 340–1 and p. 344.
52 Ibid., p. 392 and p. 396–6.
53 Ibid., p. 389.
54 Ibid., p. 388.

the parties as to the delimitation line, there was no need to address the point. This applied where one party eventually accepted the line proposed by the other[55] or where one party did not oppose the line as proposed by the other[56] or where after some considerable dispute the parties agreed that the description of the line contained in the delimitation instrument was clear even if demarcation issues remained[57] or where an issue raised in the Counter-Memorial but not in the Rejoinder nor at the hearings was accepted by the party concerned as being a demarcation and not a delimitation question.[58]

Where the parties made no submissions on disputed points mentioned briefly during either the hearings or in the written responses to questions put by Members of the Court, there was no requirement to adjudicate upon them.[59] However, the Court was not required to choose between the respective claims of the parties with regard to any particular point. It was at liberty to find its own solution within the framework of the delimitation provisions.[60]

The Court emphasised on several occasions that it could not change the course of the boundary line laid down in the delimitation instruments. With respect to one particular area, but it is a point of general principle, the Court stated that "while it may interpret the provisions of delimitation instruments where their language requires this, it may not modify the course of the boundary as established by those instruments".[61] At another point, it was noted that "[s]ince the authors of the [Thomson-Marchand] Declaration prescribed a clear course for the boundary, the Court cannot deviate from that course".[62] This meant paying close attention to the provision. For example, where the delimitation instrument provided that the boundary followed the line of a particular watershed, a line proposed by Cameroon which would have crossed certain watercourses could not be accepted nor could a line which followed the watershed where the instrument called for a boundary along a line bounded by cultivated land lying to the east of the watershed line. Similarly, where it was provided that a particular village had to be on the Cameroonian side, the Nigerian proposal which would have had the effect of splitting the village could not be accepted.[63] This was so even where the consequences of adhering strictly to the delimitation line clearly impacted upon the local population as a result of natural developments. The Court emphasised with regard

[55] Ibid., p. 384–7.
[56] Ibid., p. 371 and p. 385.
[57] Ibid., p. 384–7.
[58] Ibid., p. 387–8.
[59] Ibid., p. 399.
[60] Ibid., p. 394.
[61] Ibid., p. 370.
[62] Ibid., p. 372.
[63] Ibid., p. 370–81.

to two villages (one Cameroonian and one Nigerian) that a delimitation line could not be modified even where the consequences involved the division of a village, which had over time spread across the boundary. All that could be done in this situation was to point to the responsibility of the parties to "find a solution to any resultant problems, with a view to respecting the rights and interests of the local population".[64] This is probably the correct approach, but it does rely upon the state concerned to pay careful attention to the needs of the inhabitants in the expanded village in question who find themselves on the other side of the boundary line.

iii) *The Framework of Treaty Interpretation*

As treaties, boundary treaties operate generally within the framework of the provisions recognised or contained in the Vienna Convention on the Law of Treaties (1969). In particular, they are to be interpreted in the light of Articles 31 and 32 of this Convention, "in good faith, in accordance with the ordinary meaning to be given to its terms in their context and in the light of its object and purpose".[65] Since many of the boundary treaties that need to be interpreted long pre-date the coming into force of the Vienna Convention,[66] the problem of the applicability of its provisions has arisen, but the view has been taken that the Convention in this respect at least represents customary international law thus apparently obviating the problem.[67]

The Eritrea-Ethiopia Boundary Commission, however, emphasised that the elements laid down in the Vienna Convention were a means of guiding the interpreter in establishing what the parties actually intended or their 'common intention' or 'common will'.[68] To put it another way, the text of the treaties read in the light of their object and purpose, context and negotiating history and the subsequent course of conduct of the parties were to be seen as "tools for

[64] Ibid., p. 370 and p. 373–4. See also Malcom N. Shaw, 'Self-Determination, Human Rights and the Attribution of Territory', in: Daniel-Erasmus Khan (ed.), *From Bilateralism to Community Interest. Essays in Honour of Bruno Simma*, Oxford: Oxford University Press 2011, p. 590.

[65] *Libya/Chad*, ICJ Reports 1994, p. 21–22.

[66] See Article 4 of the Convention, providing that the Convention applies only to treaties concluded after its coming into force (27 January 1980).

[67] See e.g. *Libya/Chad* ICJ Reports 1994, p. 6, 21–22; the *Beagle Channel* case, 52 *International Law Reports*, p. 124, and the *Botswana/Namibia* case, ICJ Reports 1999, p. 1059–60; but cf. the Separate Opinion of Judge Oda, ibid., p. 1118. See also recently the *Genocide Convention* case *(Bosnia and Herzegovina v. Serbia and Montenegro)*, ICJ Reports 2007, par. 160, and *Costa Rica v. Nicaragua*, ICJ Reports 2009, par. 47. See also Doris W. Greig, *Intertemporality and the Law of Treaties*, London: British Institute of International and Comparative Law 2001, p. 108 ff.

[68] *Eritrea-Ethiopia* case, 130 *International Law Reports*, p. 34, quoting the 1966 *Argentina/Chile Frontier* case, 38 *International Law Reports*, p. 89. See also *Costa Rica v. Nicaragua*, ICJ Reports 2009, par. 63.

determining 'the common will' of the parties".[69] This has implications as a methodology in terms both of seeking the meaning of particular terms and in resorting to prior and subsequent materials. The following sections will examine these points.

iv) *The Doctrine of Contemporaneity and Its Limits; The Concept of Evolution*

In the *Eritrea-Ethiopia* case, the Boundary Commission accepted that in interpreting the treaties in question, it should apply the doctrine of 'contemporaneity'. This was understood to mean that, "a treaty should be interpreted by reference to the circumstances prevailing when the treaty was concluded". Further, it was noted that this involved giving expressions used in the treaties (including names), the meaning that they would have possessed at that time.[70] The Commission stated the general principles as follows: "The determination of the meaning and effect of a geographical name used in a treaty, whether of a place or of a river, depends upon the contemporary understanding of the location to what that name related at the time of the treaty".[71]

The problem arose particularly in relation to rivers in the Eritrea-Ethiopia situation. In this regard the Commission emphasised that: "What matters most is the identification of what the parties intended in referring to a watercourse as a feature in the landscape, rather than its name. If the name used is incorrect, then it is the parties' intentions with respect to the reality on the ground rather than the name which is decisive".[72] In seeking to elucidate the intentions of the parties, the Commission declared that, "the principal evidence is what they said in the treaty".[73]

This approach was indeed reflected later that year (2002) by the International Court in *Cameroon v. Nigeria*, where it was emphasised that in seeking to determine the location of the mouth of the River Ebeji under the terms of the relevant international agreement, "the Court must seek to ascertain the intention of the parties at the time".[74] For example, in dealing with the question of the source of the Tsikakiri River, the Court, noting that there existed no definition in geographical theory enabling the principal source of a river to be identified with full certainty where that river has several sources, emphasised that "the task of the Court is not to identify the 'geographical' source of the Tsikakri, but to identify the source through which the drafters of the Thomson-Marchand Declaration intended that the boundary should pass". Noting that

[69] *Eritrea-Ethiopia* case, 130 *International Law Reports*, p. 79.
[70] *Eritrea-Ethiopia* case, 130 *International Law Reports*, p. 34.
[71] Ibid., p. 79.
[72] Ibid., p. 47–50.
[73] Ibid., p. 56–7.
[74] *Cameroon v. Nigeria*, ICJ Reports 2002, p. 346.

the Declaration delimited the boundary in general by means of a physical description of the terrain, the Court stated that "it may reasonably be assumed that the drafters of the Declaration, in referring to the source of the Tsikakiri, intended to designate a point which could be readily identified, both on maps and on the ground" (par. 128).[75] The Court returned to this point in discussing the boundary line on the Sama River, declaring that "just as with the Thomson-Marchand Declaration, the Order in Council describes the course of the boundary by reference to the area's physical characteristics. Here again, the text of this description must have been drafted in such a way as to render the course of the boundary as readily identifiable as possible".[76]

However, the Eritrea-Ethiopia Boundary Commission made reference to the role of modern knowledge in the process of determining the intention of the parties. It noted that the map annexed to the 1900 treaty concerning the Central Sector "may be followed so long as it is not shown to be so at variance with modern knowledge as to render it valueless as an indicator of what the parties could have intended on the ground".[77] This perhaps reflects the view of Judge Higgins in *Botswana/Namibia* that, "our task is to decide what general idea the parties had in mind, and then to make reality of that general idea through the use of contemporary knowledge".[78]

This is not the end of the matter since as already noted, the key element to treaty interpretation in this and other areas is to find the common intention of the parties. Where the meaning of a word or geographical expression has altered over the period since the adoption of the treaty in question, the relevant court or tribunal will have to face the question as to how to deal with the evolving term. There are two possibilities. First, the court may simply seek to determine the meaning as at the date of the treaty itself and apply that or, secondly, the court may seek to determine the meaning as at the date of determination. The question as to which approach to adopt will depend upon an understanding of what the parties actually intended at the date of the treaty, and this may involve the court in some difficult interpretation decisions. The International Court analysed this problem with some care in the *Costa Rica v. Nicaragua* case. The Court began by noting that:

> It is true that the terms used in a treaty must be interpreted in light of what is determined to have been the parties' common intention, which is, by definition, contemporaneous with the treaty's conclusion. That may lead a court seised of a dispute, or the parties themselves, when they seek to determine the meaning of a treaty for purposes of good-faith compliance with it, to ascertain the meaning a

[75] Ibid., p. 375–5. See also with regard to the identification of the river Kohom, ibid., p. 366–7.

[76] Ibid., p. 398.

[77] *Eritrea-Ethiopia*, 130 *International Law Reports*, p. 57.

[78] *Botswana/Namibia*, ICJ Reports 1999, p. 1114.

> term had when the treaty was drafted, since doing so can shed light on the parties' common intention. The Court has so proceeded in certain cases requiring it to interpret a term whose meaning had evolved since the conclusion of the treaty at issue, and in those cases the Court adhered to the original meaning (to this effect, see, for example, the Judgment of 27 August 1952 in the case concerning *Rights of Nationals of the United States of America in Morocco (France* v. *United States of America) (I.C.J. Reports 1952*, p. 176), on the question of the meaning of "dispute" in the context of a treaty concluded in 1836, the Court having determined the meaning of this term in Morocco when the treaty was concluded; the Judgment of 13 December 1999 in the case concerning *Kasikili/Sedudu Island (Botswana/Namibia) (I.C.J. Reports 1999 (II)*, p. 1062, para. 25) in respect of the meaning of "centre of the main channel" and "thalweg" when the Anglo-German Agreement of 1890 was concluded).[79]

The Court then declared that, leaving aside the question of subsequent practice (discussed below), there were situations in which the parties' intent upon conclusion of the treaty was, or may be presumed to have been, to give some or all of the terms used a meaning or content

> capable of evolving, not one fixed once and for all, so as to make allowance for, among other things, developments in international law. In such instances it is indeed in order to respect the parties' common intention at the time the treaty was concluded, not to depart from it, that account should be taken of the meaning acquired by the terms in question upon each occasion on which the treaty is to be applied.[80]

The example given was that of the *Aegean Sea Continental Shelf* case, where it was concluded that the expression "the territorial status of Greece" as used in Greece's instrument of accession to the General Act of 1928 was intended as a generic term denoting any matters comprised within the concept of territorial status under general international law, so that it could be interpreted as including the continental shelf, an expression unknown to international law at the date of Greece's reservation. The Court concluded that in such cases, a presumption necessarily arose that the meaning of the term in question was intended to "follow the evolution of the law and to correspond with the meaning attached to the expression by the law in force at any given time".[81] In the *Costa Rica* case, the Court declared that

> where the parties have used generic terms in a treaty, the parties necessarily having been aware that the meaning of the terms was likely to evolve over time, and where the treaty has been entered into for a very long period or is "of continuing duration", the parties must be presumed, as a general rule, to have intended those terms to have an evolving meaning.[82]

---

[79] *Costa Rica v. Nicaragua*, ICJ Reports 2009, par. 63.
[80] Ibid., par. 64.
[81] *Aegean Sea Continental Shelf* case, ICJ Reports 1978, p. 32.
[82] *Costa Rica-Nicaragua*, ICJ Reports 2009, par. 66.

The Court concluded that

> the terms by which the extent of Costa Rica's right of free navigation has been defined, including in particular the term 'comercio', must be understood to have the meaning they bear on each occasion on which the Treaty is to be applied, and not necessarily their original meaning. Thus, even assuming that the notion of "commerce" does not have the same meaning today as it did in the mid-nineteenth century, it is the present meaning which must be accepted for purposes of applying the Treaty.[83]

By this process, it may be seen that the Court has adopted a rather more flexible approach to the interpretation of boundary treaties than had hitherto been accepted. Only time will tell how far this approach may be taken in future litigation.

v) *Recourse to Other Materials*

The Arbitral Tribunal in the *Argentina/Chile Frontier* case noted that the process of interpretation, which focuses on seeking the 'common will' of the parties, may be aided by recourse to preparatory documents or subsequent action of the parties.[84] Accordingly, as part of the process of interpreting boundary treaties, reference to prior and/or subsequent materials may be permissible.

a. *Prior Materials*

In seeking to resolve an ambiguity in a provision in a boundary treaty, a Court may turn to prior agreements. Several examples may be noted.

In the *Cameroon v. Nigeria* case, the Court needed to determine the boundary in one particular area defined by the relevant Thomson-Marchand Declaration as "starting from Beacon 6, passing Beacon 7, finishing at the old Beacon 8". Nigeria argued that beacons 6 and 8 had not been found. Cameroon noted the matter was one of demarcation and thus for later resolution. In determining the boundary, the Court utilised the provisions of Annex I of the 1906 Anglo-German Agreement concerning the area from Yola to Lake Chad, which had described the method used to determine the locations of the beacons.[85]

Similarly, in the area of Jimbare and Sapeo, the Court noted that the relevant provisions in the Thomson-Marchand Declaration posed problems since the description of the boundary contained a series of material errors and in parts contradicted the representation of that boundary on the 1931 map appended to the Declaration.[86] Reference was made to the Logan-LeBrun *procès-verbal*, which incorporated proposals made by Mair and Pition in 1920.

[83] Ibid., par. 70.
[84] *Argentina/Chile Frontier* case, 38 *International Law Reports*, p. 89.
[85] *Cameroon v. Nigeria*, ICJ Reports 2002, p. 375–8.
[86] Ibid., p. 382–3.

The *procès-verbal* was drawn up in 1930 after the Declaration had been prepared but before it was signed. Under the terms of the *procès-verbal*, a series of proposals was made including attributing the areas of Jimbare to France and Sapeo to Britain. While some of the Logan-LeBrun proposals were incorporated in the Declaration, those concerning Jimbare and Sapeo were not. However, as far as Sapeo was concerned, the Logan-LeBrun proposals were shown on the map attached to the Declaration. The Court also took account of the fact that Sapeo had in practice been regarded by the parties as lying within Nigeria, for example, in the plebiscites of 1959 and 1961 and accordingly held that the Declaration should be interpreted "in accordance with the intention of its authors, as manifested on the map appended thereto and on the ground, namely so as to make the boundary follow the course described in the Logan-LeBrun *procès-verbal*".[87]

By way of contrast, in the Jimbare area the Logan-LeBrun proposals had not been transposed onto the Declaration map. Nevertheless, the Court took the view that the boundary as described in the Logan-LeBrun *procès-verbal* should prevail over the line contained in the Declaration and map since this was held to correspond to the intention of the authors of the Declaration. While this may seem rather surprising, it is highly significant that the line declared by the Court was favourable to Cameroon and unopposed by Nigeria.[88] The Court also took account of the procès-verbal in the Noumberou-Banglang area, where the Declaration contained fundamental errors of a material nature. The Logan-LeBrun document was far more detailed than the relevant paragraph in the Declaration, which as the Court pointed out "contained scant information enabling it to determine the precise course of the boundary in this sector". Accordingly, and since the terms of the procès-verbal clearly "corresponded to the intentions of the authors of the Declaration", the Court applied it to the boundary in the area.[89]

In seeking to clarify the boundary along the Kohom River, the Court noted that the relevant paragraphs of the Declaration failed to provide a decisive answer, while none of the villages mentioned appeared on any of the maps provided by the parties. However, the Court turned to a sketch-map prepared in March 1926 by the French and British officials which served as a basis for the drafting of the relevant paragraphs of the Declaration. The sketch-map was found to show the intentions of the drafters of the Declaration and was "particularly helpful" concerning the relief of the area and the direction of the river.[90]

---

[87] Ibid., p. 383.
[88] Ibid.
[89] Ibid., p. 385.
[90] Ibid., p. 336–7.

However, where reliance upon prior materials or practice is sought, the Court will require a requisite level of evidence and authority. In the case of the boundary in the area from the Hambere Range to the Mburi River (Lip and Yang), Nigeria pointed to a survey conducted by a British colonial official, Dr Jeffreys in 1941 which resulted in a line, to the west of a cairn placed on a particular track, being drawn which differed from that contained in the Order in Council. Cameroon challenged the existence and validity of the 'Jeffreys Boundary'. The Court concluded that it "cannot interpret the Order in Council on the basis of a decision alleged to have been taken unilaterally by a British official in 1941, five years before the adoption of the Order, whose terms were not incorporated in the Order and which Nigeria itself recognises that it has been impossible to locate".[91]

In addition to questions of evidence authority, the Court will only take account such prior materials in the context of the other relevant factors and will weigh its probative value accordingly. For example, in determining which of several channels should be regarded as the river passing close to the village of Limani, the Court noted Nigeria's view that the southern channel should be so regarded since it accorded with a line shown on a sketch-map signed in 1921 by French and British officials fixing the provisional boundary some 300 miles north of Limani. However, the Court concluded that this particular channel did not appear on any map and stereoscopic examination of the aerial photographs of the area demonstrated that this watercourse petered out before the Agzabame marshes, which was incompatible with the terms of the relevant paragraph in the Declaration. The Court identified another channel as constituting the required river.[92]

With regard to the *Eritrea-Ethiopia* case, the Boundary Commission took into account a number of pre-treaty materials in seeking to ascertain the meaning of particular treaty provisions, both materials used in the negotiating process leading to the adoption of the particular treaty provision in question and earlier relevant materials that were not part of the negotiation process. The fact that circumstances might dictate when pre-treaty materials could be pertinent was emphasised by the Commission when it decided not to look at the conduct of the parties prior to the conclusion of the relevant 1908 treaty (concerning the eastern sector of the boundary) where "the terms of the treaty make it clear that the parties intended that the effect of such activities should not be taken into account".[93] There was no such provision in the 1900 (concerning the central sector of the boundary) and 1902 (concerning the western sector of the boundary) treaties (the other relevant treaties).

---

[91] Ibid., p. 391–2 and p. 393.
[92] Ibid., p. 362–3.
[93] *Eritrea-Ethiopia*, 130 *International Law Reports*, p. 110. See further Shaw, supra n. 29.

The Commission discussed the so-called de Chaurand Map of 1894 in the context both of the 1900 and 1902 treaties. In the former case, a map was annexed to the treaty. This treaty map stated that it was based upon de Chaurand's map of the relevant area and the Commission noted that "it is apparent that the Treaty map was in fact a tracing or other direct copy of the relevant part of the de Chaurand map, omitting certain features so as to give prominence to the features most relevant to the 1900 Treaty line". The Commission thus concluded that: "Depictions on de Chaurand's map are therefore directly relevant to an understanding of the Treaty map".[94] The Commission also had recourse to the pre-existing Mai Daro map mentioned in two reports by a major Ciccodicola (the Italian negotiator), dated 16 May 1902 and 28 June 1902 respectively, in interpreting a provision in the treaty of 15 May 1902.[95] Further, in the *Costa Rica* case, the International Court took into account a prior signed but unratified treaty (of 8 December 1857) in interpreting a term used in the relevant 1858 Treaty of Limits.[96]

b) *Subsequent Practice*

The aim to establish the 'common will' of the parties may also include consideration of the subsequent conduct of the parties[97] and the International Court has emphasised that, "when called upon to interpret the provisions of a treaty, the Court has itself frequently examined the subsequent practice of the parties in the application of that treaty".[98]

The subsequent conduct of the parties may be relevant in a number of ways; first, as a method of determining the true interpretation of the relevant boundary instrument in the sense of the 'common will' of the parties, secondly, as a method of resolving an uncertain disposition or situation, for example, whether a particular area did or did not fall within colonial territory for the purposes of determining the *uti possidetis* line[99] or thirdly, as a method of modifying a boundary treaty itself in certain circumstances.

With regard to the third possibility, the Arbitration Tribunal in the *Taba* case[100] accepted that "a clear treaty provision may be varied by the conduct of

[94] Ibid., p. 46. The map was used with regard to a number of locations, see e.g. p. 50–1 and p. 61.

[95] Ibid., p. 80–1.

[96] *Costa Rica-Nicaragua*, ICJ Reports 2009, par. 55.

[97] See e.g. *Argentina/Chile*, 38 *International Law Reports*, p. 89 and the *Eritrea/Ethiopia* case, 130 *International Law Reports*, p. 1. See also article 31 (3) of the Vienna Convention on the Law of Treaties 1969.

[98] *Botswana/Namibia*, ICJ Reports 1999, p. 1076.

[99] See for example the *El Salvador/Honduras (Nicaragua Intervening)* case, ICJ Reports 1992, p. 401, p. 558 ff.

[100] *Taba* case, 80 *International Law Reports*, p. 306–7.

the Parties",[101] and the Eritrea-Ethiopia Boundary Commission declared that "the effect of subsequent conduct may be so clear in relation to matters that appear to be the subject of a given treaty that the application of an otherwise pertinent treaty provision may be varied, or may even cease to control the situation, regardless of its original meaning".[102] The use of the phrase "so clear" needs to be particularly noted.[103] What is critical here is the question of proof, both the onus and the standard of proof. A treaty title is determinative, subject to evidence to the contrary, so that the party alleging a modification of a clear treaty line must prove that the parties directly involved have indeed by their conduct agreed to such modification. Unilateral modification is not possible. The presumption must be that a clear treaty provision stands and undoubted evidence will be required in order to upset the necessary primacy of boundary treaties.

Subsequent conduct may be defined or discussed in terms of a number of different contexts and concepts, including for example, recognition, estoppel, preclusion, acquiescence or implied agreement, where the essential elements were identical.[104] The Commission identified and examined three relevant categories of subsequent conduct: maps, *effectivités* and diplomatic and other similar exchanges and records constituting assertions of sovereignty, or acquiescence in or opposition to such assertions, by the other party.[105] The Commission did accept that the legal title as laid down in the appropriate treaty had been modified in several cases where the parties had, impliedly or explicitly, so agreed. The Commission found this with regard to Zalambessa, Fort Cadorna, Tserona and Bure. In the case of the town of Zalambessa, for example, which had not existed in 1900 (the date of the relevant boundary treaty), the Commission noted the establishment of a customs post agreed by both parties to be 2 kilometres north of the town and held that the location of such a post on one side of the town strongly suggested that the boundary was

[101] As cited by the Eritrea-Ethiopia Boundary Commission, 130 *International Law Reports*, p. 36.

[102] Ibid., p. 34–5, citing the *Serbian Loans* case, PCIJ Reports 1929, Series A, Nos. 20/21, p. 38, and the *Namibia* case, ICJ Reports 1971, p. 22.

[103] But cf. Marcelo Kohen, 'La Relation Titres/Effectivités dans le Contentieux Territorial à la Lumière de la Jurisprudence Récente', (2004) 108 *Revue Générale de Droit International Public*, p. 567.

[104] The Commission noted that "in each case the ingredients are the same: an act, course of conduct or omission by or under the authority of one party indicative of its view of the content of the applicable legal rule – whether or treaty or customary origin; the knowledge, actual or reasonably to be inferred of the other party, of such conduct or omission; and a failure by the latter party within a reasonable time to reject, or dissociate itself from, the position taken by the first. Likewise, these concepts apply to the attitude of a party to its own conduct: it cannot subsequently act in a manner inconsistent with the legal position reflected in such conduct", ibid., p. 35–6. This passage ends with a footnote reference to the *Nuclear Tests* cases, ICJ Reports 1974, p. 267–8.

[105] Ibid., p. 38.

on the same side of the town "since to have a population centre *between* a boundary and a border customs post would be unusual". Ethiopia had also submitted evidence showing that that the customs authorities of Eritrea regularly had dealings with the nearby Ethiopian customs post in such a way as to accept Zalambessa as part of Ethiopia. In addition, in an exchange in 1996, Eritrea had referred to an Ethiopian request to allow a survey team into its territory as being incidental to the task of "rechecking border delineating points in Zalambessa [sic] area (Tigray region)". Accordingly, the Commission adjusted the 1900 boundary line so as to place Zalambessa in Ethiopian territory. The basic reason for this appeared to have been the "considerable number of significant administrative activities by Ethiopian authorities" there coupled with Eritrean acknowledgment that the town fell within Ethiopia.[106]

With regard to Fort Cadorna and Tserona, the Commission noted Ethiopian statements in its Reply noting that these points were "mostly (…) undisputed Eritrean places". The Commission interpreted this statement, made formally in a written pleading, as an "admission of which the Commission must take full account". Accordingly, the 1900 treaty line was adjusted so as to include Fort Cadorna and Tserona in Eritrean territory.[107]

With regard to Bure, located on the Ethiopian side of the relevant line, the Commission noted that both states had accepted, notwithstanding that the border was placed at this point, by virtue of an agreement signed by both parties on 7 November 1994, incorporating a report of 12 July 1994. Part of the report noted that the main checkpoints along the Addis-Assab corridor included "Bure Ethiopian border" and "Bure Eritrean border". This was reinforced by an internal Eritrean memorandum of 30 April 1994 (copied to the Ethiopian Embassy in Asmara) that referred to Ethiopian trucks "entering Eritrea through the checkpoints both in Zalambessa and Burre". The Commission thus concluded that both parties had agreed that their common border was placed at Bure and accordingly held that the boundary "passes equidistantly the checkpoints of the two parties".[108]

The International Court of Justice has on a number of occasions referred to subsequent practice as an aid to interpretation. For example, in *Cameroon v. Nigeria*, the Court analysed the starting point of the boundary. This was the tripoint in Lake Chad, the longitudinal reading of which was defined in the Thomson-Marchand Declaration as "approximately 14 degrees 05 minutes east" of Greenwich. Nigeria argued that this left the delimitation in the area "undetermined". The Court referred to the work of the Lake Chad Basin Commission (LCBC) established in 1964, whose functions included that of demarcation. The LCBC sought to reach a designation of the tripoint in more

[106] Ibid., p. 70–1 (emphasis in original).
[107] Ibid., par. 4.69–4.71.
[108] Ibid., p. 111–3.

specific terms than contained in the Declaration and in 1994 approved the demarcation report produced by the Institut Géographique National – France International. The Court noted that the Marking Out of the Boundary Report was not binding on Nigeria, but concluded that this did not "preclude the Court, when called upon to specify the frontier, from finding work that has been done by others to be useful". After an examination of the Moisel map attached to the 1919 Milner-Simon Declaration and of the map attached to the Henderson-Fleuriau Exchange of Notes of 1931 incorporating the Thomson-Marchand Declaration, the Court reached the same conclusions as the LCBC and determined the tripoint to be at 14 degrees 04 minutes and 59.9999 seconds longitude east.[109]

Similarly, in seeking to determine the location of the "mouth of the Ebeji" River as the next point on the boundary from the tripoint in Lake Chad, the Court referred to the work of the LCBC. The problem was that significant geographical changes had taken place. Lake Chad had markedly reduced in size since 1931, while the Ebeji River

> today has no single mouth through which it discharges its waters into the Lake. Rather, it divides into two channels as it approaches the Lake. On the basis of information the Parties have made available to the Court, it appears that the eastern channel terminates in water that is short of the present Lake Chad. The western channel seems to terminate in a muddy area close to the present water line.[110]

The Court, as it had done with regard to the tripoint, rejected the claim by Cameroon that work of the LCBC, specifying coordinates for the mouth of the Ebeji, constituted an "authentic interpretation" of the Declaration and 1931 Exchange of Notes. Cameroon produced an alternative, which relied upon the western channel, citing the tests adduced by the Court in the *Botswana/Namibia* case[111] for identifying the main channel of a river. Reference was made in particular to the greater flow and depth of the western channel. Nigeria argued for the eastern channel, basing the claim on factors such as length, size of drainage area and discharge, noted in *Argentina/Chile*.[112] The Court emphasised that it needed to define the mouth of the river and not the main channel (as in *Botswana/Namibia*), and that in order to define the former "the Court must seek to ascertain the intention of the parties at the time". Such intention as demonstrated by the 1919 and 1931 instruments necessitated one mouth only. The Court noted that the coordinates as calculated on the maps appended to the 1919 and 1931 instruments were "strikingly similar" and moreover identical with those used by the LCBC even though to the north of the 'mouth' suggested by the parties for the western and eastern

[109] *Cameroon v. Nigeria*, ICJ Reports 2002, p. 341–5.
[110] Ibid., p. 345.
[111] *Botswana/Namibia*, ICJ Reports 1999, p. 1064–1071.
[112] *Argentina/Chile*, 38 *International Law Reports*, p. 93–5.

channels respectively. Accordingly, the coordinates as used by the LCBC were taken as the mouth of the Ebeji as noted in the instruments.[113]

In determining the boundary in the Sapeo area, as noted above, the Court, while relying upon the Logan-LeBrun procès-verbal, noted in addition that the area had always been regarded as lying within Nigerian territory and cited the practice in the 1959 and 1961 plebiscites, coupled with Cameroon's failure to exercise any form of administration over the village and knowledge of Nigeria's administration.[114]

As in the case with prior materials, the Court will require evidence before it will consider subsequent materials or practice in relation to the interpretation of a provision of an agreement, particularly where it is claimed the provision has been modified. While determining the boundary with regard to the Sama River, the Court noted, in referring to Cameroon's claim that the parties had in practice always taken the northern rather than the southern tributary of the river as marking the course of the line, that "Cameroon had produced no evidence of this practice".[115]

The issue of the interpretation of treaties concerning territorial regimes arose also in *Costa Rica v. Nicaragua,* where the central issue concerned the meaning of terms appearing in article VI of the relevant 1858 treaty between the two states. The treaty laid down the boundary in relation to the San Juan River and provided for the "perpetual right" of Costa Rica along a certain portion of the river "of free navigation 'con objetos de comercio'". The Court noted that while limitations of the sovereignty of a state over its territory were not to be presumed, this did not mean that treaty provisions establishing such limitations should for this reason be interpreted *a priori* in a restrictive way. It was emphasised that

> [a] treaty provision which has the purpose of limiting the sovereign powers of a state must be interpreted like any other provision of a treaty, i.e. in accordance with the intentions of its authors as reflected by the text of the treaty and the other relevant factors in terms of interpretation.[116]

The Court proceeded to analyse the phrase in question in the light of the ordinary meaning of the words and taking into account other provisions of the treaty using the same terminology. However, the Court took into account in interpreting the key article VI of the 1858 treaty, the Arbitral Award made by US President Cleveland on 22 March 1888 and the decision rendered, on the application of Costa Rica, by the Central American Court of Justice on

---

[113] *Cameroon v. Nigeria*, ICJ Reports 2002, p. 345–6.
[114] Ibid., p. 383.
[115] Ibid., p. 398.
[116] *Costa Rica v. Nicaragua*, ICJ Reports 2009, par. 48.

30 September 1916.[117] In particular, the Court considered it a "significant indication" that in 1887 when the two parties each submitted an English translation of the 1858 Treaty to President Cleveland for use in the arbitration proceedings he was asked to conduct, even though their translations were not identical on all points, "they did use the same phrase to render the original 'con objetos de comercio': 'for the purposes of commerce' ".[118]

5. *Conclusion*

The following points may be briefly made in conclusion. First, boundary treaties are a distinctive form of treaties. The general community interest in stability, predictability and certainty with regard to inter-state relations concerning territorial issues requires this to be so. Secondly, within the law of territory, boundary treaties retain the position of hierarchical supremacy. If a relevant treaty exists, it will take precedence over other sources of territorial title and this is why boundary treaties are so important. Thirdly, the process of judicial determination of disputed boundaries has evolved so that delimited lines may be subject to 'clarification', although the room for such manoeuvres is necessarily constrained, while such process may encompass the consideration and/or resolution of demarcation questions. Fourthly, with regard to the critical question of interpretation of boundary treaties, the key is to determine the 'common will' of the parties utilising the text of the instrument itself together with any pertinent prior and subsequent materials. In so doing, the courts or tribunals would pay attention to the doctrine of contemporaneity whereby the original intention of the parties at the date of conclusion of the instrument would be determined. However, this doctrine may be modified where it can be shown that the parties intended to take into account any evolving meaning of the term in question or where the nature of the provision itself (particularly a generic term) is such that the parties may be presumed to be aware that the meaning of such provision may vary over time. This latter possibility appears to herald a rather more flexible approach to key aspects of boundary treaty interpretation.

[117] Ibid., par. 41.
[118] Ibid., par. 56.

CHAPTER THIRTEEN

THE AMBIT AND LIMITS OF THE ADVISORY FUNCTION OF THE INTERNATIONAL COURT OF JUSTICE

Photini Pazartzis

1. *Introduction*

It is a pleasure to contribute an essay to this volume dedicated to Professor Karel Wellens on an aspect of the international judicial function, particularly in the light of his work in the field of international dispute settlement.

Apart from its contentious jurisdiction, the International Court of Justice is also vested with an advisory jurisdiction on legal questions at the request of authorised UN organs. In comparison to the increased recourse by states to the Court's contentious jurisdiction witnessed in recent years, its advisory function appears to have been under-utilised.[1] Indeed, there have at times been calls for a greater use of the advisory jurisdiction of the Court, and proposals have been advanced for the extension of this function to more organisations.[2]

At the same time, recent advisory opinions have called to attention the evolving nature of the Court's judicial function in the exercise of its advisory jurisdiction. Beyond the potential of the advisory jurisdiction of the Court in the clarification of points of international law as well as in the formation of a coherent jurisprudence,[3] lies the question of the proper role of the advisory function of the 'principal judicial organ of the United Nations', and its

---

[1] It has been observed that the renewed interest in the advisory function of the ICJ is due to concerns of its 'parsimonious' use, rather than to fears of its proliferation; see Marie-Clotilde Runavot, 'La fonction consultative de la Cour internationale de justice', in: Alain Ondoua and David Szymczak (eds.), *La fonction consultative des juridictions internationales*, Paris: Pedone 2009, p. 21–45.

[2] See Speech by H.E. Judge Shi Jiuyong, President of the International Court of Justice, to the Sixth Committee of the General Assembly of the United Nations (on the advisory function of the ICJ), on November 5, 2004 (available on the website of the ICJ: <www.icj-cij.org>). Further, Rosalyn Higgins, 'A Comment on the Current Health of Advisory Opinions', in: Vaughan Lowe and Malgosia Fitzmaurice (eds.), *Fifty Years of the International Court of Justice. Essays in Honour of Sir Robert Jennings*, Cambridge: Cambridge University Press 1996, p. 567–581; Robert Jennings, 'Advisory Opinions of the International Court of Justice', in: *Boutros Boutros-Ghali Amicorum Disciplinorumque Liber. Peace, Development, Democracy*, Bruxelles: Bruylant 1998, p. 531–537.

[3] Charles de Visscher, *Aspects récents du droit procédural de la Cour international de justice*, Paris: Pedone, 1966, p. 195 ff.

contribution towards the settlement of international disputes.[4] Recent advisory opinions, and in particular the much commented opinions on *Nuclear Weapons*[5] and the *Wall*,[6] apart from addressing contentious substantive issues of international law, brought to the fore equally interesting questions on the ambit of the advisory jurisdiction of the Court and discretion and judicial propriety in the exercise of this jurisdiction.

In this regard, the advisory opinion issued by the Court on *Kosovo*[7] presents another opportunity to reflect on the advisory function of the Court and its current potentiality. The request and the ensuing advisory opinion attracted much attention and stirred debate across the international community.[8] While it is true that the International Court, on previous occasions – through the exercise of its advisory jurisdiction – had the opportunity to address issues involving the right to self-determination in a post-colonial context,[9] this was a first case regarding an act of secession outside this context to be brought before the International Court. It was therefore natural that an authoritative interpretation of the law emanating from the 'principal judicial organ' of the United Nations would be awaited with much interest.[10] This interest was reflected in the participation of a large number of states in the different phases of the proceedings, including all the permanent members of the Security Council, as well as the authors of the unilateral declaration of independence, and the procedure was described as "truly global".[11] In the light of the

---

[4] On the 'effets pacificateurs' of the Court's advisory function, see Mohammed Bedjaoui, 'Les ressources offertes par la fonction consultative de la Cour internationale de justice: bilan et perspectives', in: United Nations, *International Law as a Language for International Relations*, The Hague-London-Boston: Kluwer Law International 1996, p. 117–143.

[5] *Legality of the Threat or Use of Nuclear Weapons*, Advisory Opinion, ICJ Reports 1996, p. 226.

[6] *Legal Consequences of the Construction of a Wall in the Occupied Palestinian Territory*, Advisory Opinion, ICJ Reports 2004, p. 136.

[7] *Accordance with International Law of the Unilateral Declaration of Independence in Respect of Kosovo*, Advisory Opinion of 22 July 2010 (hereafter *Kosovo* opinion).

[8] For some commentaries, see the contributions in 11 *German Law Journal*, 2010/8 (*Kosovo in the International Court of Justice: The Case*), 24 *Leiden Journal of International Law*, 2011/1, p. 71–161 (*Kosovo Symposium*), *Hague Justice Portal* (*The International Court of Justice on Kosovo: Opinion or Non-Opinion?*), 28 September 2010 (available on <www.haguejusticeportal .net>).

[9] Notably, *International Status of South West Africa*, Advisory Opinion of 11 July 1950, ICJ Reports 1950, p. 128; *Legal Consequences for States of the Continued Presence of South Africa in Namibia (South West Africa) notwithstanding Security Council Resolution 276 (1970)*, Advisory Opinion of 21 June 1971, ICJ Reports 1971, p. 16; *Western Sahara*, Advisory Opinion of 16 October 1975, ICJ Reports 1975, p. 12. See James Crawford, 'The General Assembly, the International Court and Self-Determination', in: Vaughan Lowe and Malgosia Fitzmaurice (eds.), *Fifty Years of the International Court of Justice. Essays in Honour of Sir Robert Jennings*, Cambridge: Cambridge University Press 1996, p. 585–605.

[10] For commentaries before the proceedings, see *Agora: Kosovo*, 8 *Chinese Journal of International Law*, 2009/1, pp. 1–61.

[11] See Statement by H.E. Judge Hishashi Owada, President of the International Court of Justice, to the Security Council, 27 October 2010, p. 3 (available on the website of the ICJ: <www.icj-cij.org>). Thirty-six member states of the United Nations filed written statements, in

opportunity presented to the Court to address a question which had polarised the international community, most reactions to the 'minimalistic' approach adopted by the Court were characterised by disappointment.[12]

In this procedure, the Court was once again confronted with the ambit and limits of its advisory function and the underlying themes of judicial economy and judicial restraint, both on a substantive as on a jurisdictional level. Notwithstanding the interesting substantive issues addressed in the Opinion, the present contribution will focus on some aspects of the role of the advisory function of the International Court of Justice, in the light of this Opinion.

2. *The Advisory Jurisdiction of the ICJ: Past and Present Trends*

The advisory jurisdiction of the Court was an 'invention' of the drafters of the League of Nations Covenant, introduced in article 14, which provided for the establishment of the Permanent Court of International Justice, and subsequently fleshed out through the judicial practice of the Court.[13] The Covenant provided that the Permanent Court "may also give an advisory opinion upon any dispute or question referred to it by the Council or by the Assembly". The main intention in giving this jurisdiction to the Court was to offer assistance to the Council and the Assembly on the discharge of their duties in the settlement of disputes, by giving authoritative opinions on points of law.[14] The advisory jurisdiction of the Permanent Court became particularly important, and the Court rendered 27 advisory opinions between 1922 and 1940.

---

addition to the authors of the unilateral declaration of independence who filed a written contribution; fourteen states also submitted written comments on statements by other states and the written contribution of the authors of the declaration of independence.

[12] For example, Robert Howse and Ruti Teitel, 'Delphic Dictum: How Has the International Court of Justice Contributed to the Global Rule of Law?', (2010) 11 *German Law Journal*, p. 841–845; Thomas Burri, 'The Kosovo Opinion and Secession: The Sounds of Silence and the Missing Links', (2010) 11 *German Law Journal*, p. 881–889; Mindia Vashakmadze and Matthias Lippold, '"Nothing but a Road towards Secession"? The International Court of Justice's Advisory Opinion on Accordance with International Law of the Unilateral Declaration of Independence in Respect of Kosovo', (2010) 2 *Göttingen Journal of International Law*, p. 619–647; Theodore Christakis, 'The ICJ Advisory Opinion on Kosovo: Has International Law Something to Say about Secession?', (2011) 24 *Leiden Journal of International Law*, p. 73–86. For a more mitigated view, Jean d'Aspremont, 'The Creation of States before the International Court of Justice: which (Il)Legality?', *Hague Justice Portal* (supra, n. 8); Marc Weller, 'Modesty Can be a Virtue: Judicial Economy in the ICJ *Kosovo* Opinion?', (2011) 24 *Leiden Journal of International Law*, p. 127–147.

[13] Manley O. Hudson, 'Les avis consultatifs de la CPJI', (1925) 8 *Recueil des Cours de l'Academie de Droit International*, p. 341–412, Dharma Pratap, *The Advisory Jurisdiction of the International Court*, Oxford: Clarendon Press, 1972; Michla Pomerance, 'The Advisory Role of the ICJ and its "Judicial" Character: Past and Future Prisms', in: Sam Muller et al. (eds.), *The International Court of Justice*, The Hague-Boston-London: Martinus Nijhoff Publishers 1997, p. 271–323.

[14] Pratap, supra n. 13, p. 5.

In practice, it was primarily the Council of the League which requested opinions for its own purposes and also for other international bodies, while in a number of cases requests for advisory opinions were instigated by two or more states wishing to use this method as a way of settling (some or all of the) legal aspects of a dispute through a non-binding procedure, thus paving the way for future discussion and resolution. It has been noted that the kinds of questions the Permanent Court had to deal with in its advisory capacity were not very different from those which it addressed in its contentious jurisdiction.[15]

However, controversies as to the precise ambit of the advisory jurisdiction, its discretionary nature, or the boundaries between contentious and advisory proceedings continued to remain of concern.[16] Some of these issues became evident in the *Eastern Carelia* case,[17] where the Permanent Court declined jurisdiction for the only time in its history, on the basis of the lack of consent between the parties of the underlying dispute. In this case, the Council of the League, at the instigation of Finland, requested an advisory opinion on a dispute between Finland and Russia over the status of Eastern Carelia. The Court refused to give the requested opinion because Russia, who was not a member state of the League nor a party to the Statute of the Permanent Court of International Justice, had not agreed to have the Council handle its dispute, thus, this body was in fact incompetent to refer the matter to the Court.

Despite initial concerns that the advisory function might be incompatible with the role of a court of law, the dual function of the Court, assigned with both contentious and advisory jurisdiction, became a permanent characteristic of this institution.[18] With the creation of the United Nations and the International Court of Justice as its principal judicial organ, the advisory jurisdiction was maintained and widened. The scope and subject matter of advisory opinions also evolved with time. Most of the advisory opinions concerned institutional aspects of the functioning of international organisations, such as, for example, the legal status of international organisations, the admission of states to membership in the United Nations, the expenses of the United

[15] See Pomerance, supra n. 13, p. 288, who also notes that "broad, abstract formulations which might entail policy-setting more than dispute settlement were notably absent from League Council requests".

[16] Charles de Visscher, 'Les avis consultatifs de la CPJI', (1929) 26 *Recueil des Cours de l'Academie de Droit International*, p. 1–76, p. 58 ff.

[17] *Status of Eastern Carelia*, Advisory Opinion, PCIJ Reports 1923, Series B no. 5.

[18] Runavot, supra n. 1, p. 22. On the advisory jurisdiction of the International Court of Justice, see Pratap, supra n. 13; Kenneth J. Keith, *The Extent of the Advisory Jurisdiction of the International Court of Justice*, Leiden: Sijthoff 1971; Mahasen M. Aljaghoub, *The Advisory Function of the International Court of Justice 1946–2005*, Berlin-Heidelberg-New York: Springer 2006; Anthony Aust, 'Advisory Opinions', (2010) 1 *Journal of International Dispute Settlement*, p. 123–151.

Nations, privileges and immunities of human rights rapporteurs.[19] Others relate to questions of general international law pertaining to activities carried out by the United Nations, but with a broader relevance, such as the use of nuclear weapons,[20] or to legal aspects of an on-going dispute, such as the *Wall* case and the most recent *Kosovo* case. While the case-load of the Court has not been too heavy in terms of its advisory jurisdiction (the Court has issued 26 advisory opinions from 1945 to 2010), there is an accumulated jurisprudence through which the Court has developed its judicial practice regarding the exercise of this jurisdiction.

According to article 65 (1) of the ICJ Statute, "[t]he Court may give an advisory opinion on any legal question at the request of whatever body may be authorised in accordance with the Charter of the United Nations to make such a request". This provision is to be read in connection with article 96, which provides that such requests may be addressed by the General Assembly or the Security Council as well as by other organs and specialised agencies so authorised by the General Assembly.[21]

When the Court is requested to give an advisory opinion, it must first determine whether the request falls within its jurisdiction, both *ratione personae* and *ratione materiae* and, if it establishes jurisdiction, whether it should exercise its discretionary authority to decline to give an advisory opinion. The Court has developed a generally consistent jurisprudence with regard to its jurisdiction and discretionary authority. It has only once declined to give an advisory opinion due to lack of jurisdiction, because the request did not relate to a question within the scope of the activities of the requesting organisation.[22]

Even when the Court has jurisdiction to render an advisory opinion, it is not compelled to do so. The Court has discretion in exercising its advisory jurisdiction, which means that is has a right to refuse to give an opinion if it

---

[19] Laurence Boisson de Chazournes, 'La procédure consultative de la Cour internationale de Justice et la promotion de la règle de droit: remarques sur les conditions d'accès et de participation', in: Pierre-Marie Dupuy, Bardo Fassbender, Malcolm Shaw and Karl-Peter Sommermann (eds.), *Common Values in International Law, Essays in Honour of Christian Tomuschat*, Kehl-Strasbourg-Arlington: Engel Verlag 2006, p. 479–492; such issues have been qualified as 'house-keeping', see Aust, supra n. 18, p. 131.

[20] As has been noted, the decision of the Court in the *Nuclear Weapons* opinion "is significant because it is the first advisory opinion of the Court to deal with a question not relating to institutional matters before the requesting organ or to a particular factual situation constituting the subject of dispute in the relevant organ", Dapo Akande, 'The Competence of International Organizations and the Advisory Jurisdiction of the International Court of Justice', (1998) 9 *European Journal of International Law*, p. 440.

[21] In this last case, requests for opinions can only concern 'legal questions arising within the scope of their activities' (article 96 (2)).

[22] *Legality of the Use by a State of Nuclear Weapons in Armed Conflict*, ICJ Reports 1996, p. 66, where the Court refused to accede to a request made by the World Health Organization on the basis that the request was not within the competences of the WHO.

considers that there are reasons which make it improper to accede to a request.[23] The Court has consistently held that according to article 65 of the Statute, it has "the power to examine whether the circumstances of the case are of such a character as should lead it to decline to answer the request".[24] At the same time, the Court has considered that, as a matter of principle, it will not refuse to answer a request for an advisory opinion, since the Court's advisory jurisdiction represents its participation in the activities of the United Nations, of which it is an organ.[25] The position of the Court has been summarised in the *Nuclear Weapons* Opinion:

> Article 65, paragraph 1, of the Statute provides: 'The Court *may* give an advisory opinion... (Emphasis added.) This is more than an enabling provision. As the Court has repeatedly emphasized, the Statute leaves a discretion as to whether or not it will give an advisory opinion that has been requested of it, once it has established its competence to do so...The Court has constantly been mindful of its responsibilities as 'the principal judicial organ of the United Nations' (Charter, Article 92). When considering each request, it is mindful that it should not, in principle, refuse to give an advisory opinion. In accordance with the consistent jurisprudence of the Court, only 'compelling reasons' could lead it to such a refusal (...).[26]

In the light of the Court's jurisprudence, the prevailing opinion seems to be that the discretionary authority of the Court is in fact very much limited to exceptional situations where it has to safeguard its judicial integrity.[27] In the words of Judge Cançado Trinidade,

> [i]n the more distant past, there was a trend of opinion that favored wide discretion on the part of the Hague Court to deliver an Advisory Opinion or not; it was

---

[23] See further e.g. Pratap, supra n. 13, p. 142.

[24] *Western Sahara*, Advisory Opinion, paragraph 23.

[25] See *Interpretation of Peace Treaties with Bulgaria, Hungary and Romania*, Advisory Opinion, ICJ Reports 1950, p. 71, where the Court stated that "the reply of the Court, itself an 'organ of the United Nations', represents its participation in the activities of the Organization and, in principle, should not be refused" (p. 71).

[26] *Legality of the Threat or Use of Nuclear Weapons*, Advisory Opinion, ICJ Reports 1996, p. 226, at paragraph 14 (references to case law omitted). In the *Wall* opinion, the Court recalled that "[t]he present Court has never, in the exercise of this discretionary power, declined to respond to a request for an advisory opinion...Only in one occasion did the Court's predecessor, the Permanent Court of International Justice, take the view that it should not reply to a question put to it (*Status of Eastern Carelia, Advisory Opinion, 1923, PCIJ, Series B, No. 5*) (...).", *Legal Consequences of the Construction of a Wall in the Occupied Palestinian Territory*, Advisory Opinion, ICJ Reports 2004, paragraph 44.

[27] Georges Abi-Saab, 'On Discretion. Reflexions on the Nature of the Consultative Function of the International Court of Justice', in: Laurence Boisson de Chazournes and Philippe Sands (eds.), *International Law, the International Court of Justice and Nuclear Weapons*, Cambridge: Cambridge University Press 1999, p. 36–50; Robert Kolb, 'De la prétendue discretion de la Cour internationale de justice de refuser de donner un avis consultatif', in: Laurence Boisson de Chazournes and Vera Gowlland-Debbas (eds.), *The International Legal System in Quest of Equity and Universality, Liber Amicorum Georges Abi-Saab*, Leiden-Boston: Martinus Nijhoff Publishers 2001, p. 609–627; Runavot, supra n. 1, p. 28–29.

> followed by another trend of opinion which accepted that discretion, but only exceptionally and in face of 'compelling reasons' (*raisons décisives*). A more enlightened trend of opinion discards discretion, accepting only admissibility to protect judicial integrity.[28]

Indeed, the Court has shown itself very reluctant to refuse an opinion, or to find that it has no jurisdiction to give one.

Concerns about the propriety of the Court's exercise of its advisory function have arisen when the subject-matter of a request has been connected in some way with an actual dispute between states.[29] The Court has recognised that the lack of consent of an interested state may render the giving of an advisory opinion incompatible with the Court's judicial character.[30] An instance would be when the circumstances disclose that to give a reply would have the effect of circumventing the principle that a state is not obliged to allow its disputes to be submitted to judicial settlement without its consent.[31] However, the Court has never declined to give an opinion due to a connection between a dispute involving states and the subject of the request. It has clarified that the question of consent is not as such relevant in establishing its jurisdiction in advisory proceedings:

> [t]he consent of States, parties to a dispute, is the basis of the Court's jurisdiction in contentious cases. The situation is different in regard to advisory proceedings even where the request for an opinion relates to a legal question actually pending between States. The Court's reply is only of an advisory character: as such, it has no binding force. It follows that no State, whether a Member of the United Nations or not, can prevent the giving of an advisory opinion which the United Nations considers to be desirable in order to obtain enlightenment as to the course of action it should take. The Court's opinion is given not to States, but to the organ which is entitled to request it (…)."[32]

The Court has noted that by becoming a member of the United Nations, states accept, and give consent to the exercise of the Court of its advisory jurisdiction in accordance with the UN Charter and the Statute.[33] Furthermore, the Court has stressed the 'organisational' aspects of requests, and correspondingly

[28] *Kosovo* Opinion, Separate Opinion of Judge Cançado Trinidade, paragraph 25 (footnote omitted).

[29] See D.W. Greig, 'The Advisory Jurisdiction of the International Court and the Settlement of Disputes between States', (1966) 15 *The International and Comparative Law Quarterly*, p. 825–868.

[30] *Western Sahara*, Advisory Opinion, ICJ Reports 1975, paragraph 33.

[31] Ibid.

[32] *Interpretation of Peace Treaties with Bulgaria, Hungary and Romania*, ICJ Reports 1950, p. 71. See also, the Western Sahara Opinion, where the Court noted that: "the consent of an interested State continues to be relevant, not for the Court's competence, but for the appreciation of the propriety of giving an opinion", ICJ Reports 1975, paragraph 32.

[33] Ibid., paragraph 30.

minimised their 'quasi-contentious' aspects:[34] it has construed the question before it as relating to the exercise of functions of the requesting organ rather than to an ongoing dispute, and has perceived its role as giving its advice to this organ to assist it in fulfilling its task. The Court followed this reasoning in the recent *Wall* opinion. After observing the radically different views expressed by Israel and Palestine on the legal consequences of the construction of the wall, and the objections raised by Israel as to the Court's jurisdiction, the Court held nonetheless that the request could not be regarded as only a bilateral matter between Israel and Palestine, but that "the opinion is requested on a question which is of particularly acute concern to the United Nations, and one which is located in a much broader frame of reference than a bilateral dispute".[35] However, as it has been noted, this approach taken by the Court results in a broadening of the field of questions on which an advisory opinion could be requested.[36] Judge Higgins, in her separate opinion in the *Wall* case, raised this issue, pointing out that the request actually concerned a dispute between Israel and its Arab neighbours, and in recent years between Israel and the Palestine authority, "thus a dispute between two international actors".[37] In contrast to *Western Sahara*, where the request was sought to secure advice on the General Assembly's decolonisation duties, in the *Wall* case the request was in order to exercise powers over the dispute or controversy.[38] It remains that "the relationship between advisory opinions and existing disputes has been one of the most problematic areas for the Court".[39] Indeed, the question was again raised in the *Kosovo* case, which has been considered as another instance in which there was a factual situation which referred to an actual dispute, between Serbia and a non-state entity.[40]

---

[34] Pomerance, supra n. 13, p. 299.

[35] *Legal Consequences of the Construction of a Wall in the Occupied Palestinian Territory*, Advisory Opinion, ICJ Reports 2004, p. 136, paragraph 50.

[36] See Jochen Abr. Frowein and Karin Oellers-Frahm, 'Commentary on Article 65', in: Andreas Zimmerman, Christian Tomuschat and Karin Oellers-Frahm (eds.), *The Statute of the International Court of Justice. A Commentary*, Oxford: Oxford University Press 2006, p. 1401–1426, at p. 1412; Hugh Thirlway, 'Advisory Opinions', in: *Max Planck Encyclopedia of Public International Law*, <www.mpepil.com>, paragraph 16 (noting that "this approach (…) would be a striking innovation, considerably extending the powers of the majority in the General Assembly and curtailing the freedom of choice belonging to States in the field of settlement of disputes").

[37] *Legal Consequences of the Construction of a Wall in the Occupied Palestinian Territory*, Advisory Opinion, ICJ Reports 2004, Separate Opinion of Judge Higgins, paragraph 7.

[38] Ibid., paragraph 12. Thus, according to Judge Higgins, "the Court, by its very silence essentially revises, rather than applies the existing law" (par. 13).

[39] Higgins, supra n. 2, p. 570.

[40] See Eric de Brabandere, 'The *Kosovo* Advisory Proceedings and the Court's Advisory Jurisdiction as a Method of Dispute Settlement', *The Hague Justice Portal* <www.haguejustice-portal.net>, who argues that the Court's advisory function is not the best way to settle disputes between states or states and non-state entities. On the other hand, the advisory route is the only way by which non-state actors can participate in the working of the Court.

3. *The Exercise of the Court's Advisory Jurisdiction in the* Kosovo *Case*

On 10 June 1999, after NATO's military intervention in the conflict between Kosovo and Serbia, the United Nations Security Council adopted Resolution 1244, which placed Kosovo under an interim international administration (UNMIK). The mandate of UNMIK was to "facilitate the desired negotiated solution for Kosovo's future status, without prejudging the final outcome of the negotiating process".[41] However, negotiations failed to determine Kosovo's final status, and the Provisional Institutions of Self-Government declared independence on 17 February 2008. This act was rejected by Serbia, while by the time of the publication of the Advisory Opinion in July 2010 some 69 states had proceeded to recognise Kosovo's independence.

On October 8, 2008, following an initiative of Serbia, the General Assembly adopted a resolution requesting the Court to give an advisory opinion on the question: "Is the unilateral declaration of independence by the Provisional Institutions of Self-Government of Kosovo in accordance with international law?"[42] The final conclusion of the Court, in its advisory opinion issued on July 22, 2010, was that the declaration was not prohibited by general international law nor by any specific sources of international law.[43] The proactive approach taken by the Court in deciding to exercise its advisory function in the case contrasts with the economy of its approach to the issues of substance raised.

As with previous advisory opinions, the Court first turned to the question of jurisdiction and discretion, to conclude on this point that it had jurisdiction to deal with the request.[44] While the Court's jurisdiction was mostly uncontested, the issue of the Court's discretionary authority to refuse a request was evident in a number of written and oral statements by some participants, and was addressed extensively in the declarations, separate and dissenting opinions by some of the judges, whose views were reflected in the final vote on the question of jurisdiction.[45] The Court adopted the majority view in

---

[41] *Kosovo* Opinion, paragraph 99; for an account of the factual background; Sienho Yee, 'Notes on the International Court of Justice (Part 4): The *Kosovo* Advisory Opinion', (2010) 9 *Chinese Journal of International Law*, p. 764–766.

[42] UN doc. A/RES/63/3, 8 October 2008. The resolution was adopted with 77 votes in favour, 6 votes against and 74 abstentions.

[43] The Court found, by ten votes to four, "that the adoption of the declaration of independence of 17 February 2008 did not violate general international law, Security Council resolution 1244 (1999) or the Constitutional Framework" and concluded that "[c]onsequently the adoption of that declaration did not violate any applicable rule of international law".

[44] "When seized of a request for an advisory opinion, the Court must first consider whether it has jurisdiction to give the opinion requested and whether, should the answer be in the affirmative, there is any reason why the Court, in its discretion, should decline to exercise any such jurisdiction in the case before it", *Kosovo* opinion, paragraph 14.

[45] While the Court found unanimously that it had jurisdiction to give the opinion, the decision to respond to the request was taken by nine votes to five (Vice-President Tomka and Judges Koroma, Keith, Bennouna and Slotnikov voted against).

disposing of the arguments put forth, in consonance with its previous judicial practice.

The first issue that the Court dispensed with rather laconically was the question whether it possessed jurisdiction to give the advisory opinion requested by the General Assembly. The Court's jurisdiction *ratione personae* and *rationae materiae* was mostly unchallenged, given the text of article 96 of the UN Charter and article 65 (1) of the ICJ Statute. Regarding its jurisdiction *ratione personae*, the Court considered that the fact that the Security Council is seized of the Kosovo issue precludes neither the General Assembly from requesting an advisory opinion nor the Court from delivering it. The Court observed that "[a] request for an advisory opinion is not in itself a 'recommendation' by the General Assembly with regard to [a] dispute or situation within the meaning of article 12 (1) of the UN Charter".[46] Accordingly, while article 12 may limit the scope of the action which the General Assembly may take subsequent to its receipt of the Court's opinion, it does not in itself limit the authorisation to request an advisory opinion which is conferred upon the General Assembly by article 96 (1).[47]

On the question of the Court's jurisdiction *ratione materiae*, some participants argued that the question posed by the request was political rather than legal and that the act of making a declaration of independence was a political act of an 'internal' nature that could only be regulated by domestic law.[48] Unsurprisingly, the Court refuted these arguments relying on its well-established jurisprudence whereby it has rejected challenges of its jurisdiction on the basis of political considerations. It found that a question "which expressly asks the Court whether or not a particular action is compatible with international law certainly appears to be a legal question".[49] The Court recalled that it has repeatedly stated that the fact that a question has political aspects does not suffice to deprive it of its character as a legal question, while it also made clear that, in determining the jurisdictional issue of whether it is confronted with a legal question, it is not concerned with the motives which may have inspired the request or the political implications which its opinion might have.[50]

---

[46] *Kosovo* opinion, paragraph 24.

[47] The Court returned to this question more extensively when examining the question of its discretionary authority; see infra.

[48] See Written Statements of Albania, France, United Kingdom, United States. For some, the Court should have declined its jurisdiction on the basis that the conduct of non-state actors falls beyond its natural jurisdiction; see Dov, see Dov Jacobs, 'The *Kosovo* Advisory Opinion: A Voyage by the ICJ into the Twilight Zone of International Law', available at <www.haguejusticeportal.net>.

[49] *Kosovo* Opinion, paragraph 25.

[50] Ibid., paragraph 27. On the political/legal dichotomy, see Takane Sugihara, 'The Judicial Function of the International Court of Justice with Respect to Disputes Involving Highly Political Issues', in: Sam Muller et al. (eds.), *The International Court of Justice. Its Future Role after Fifty Years*, The Hague-Boston-London: Martinus Nijhoff Publishers, p. 117–138.

Its jurisdiction established, the Court devoted more comprehensive considerations to the issue of its discretionary authority. Several participants had called upon the Court to exercise its discretion in order to decline the exercise of jurisdiction. Judicial restraint was advocated on various grounds, namely that the request did not relate to any substantive item on the General Assembly's agenda and was used primarily to further the interests of individual states rather than those of the requesting organ; that the Court's opinion would lack any useful purpose; that the opinion could potentially have adverse effects on peace and security in the region and that it was inappropriate for the General Assembly to request an opinion regarding a matter upon which the Security Council was seized.[51] As with previous advisory opinions, the Court gave consideration to the issue of whether there were compelling reasons for it to refuse to respond to the request from the General Assembly. While the Court came to the conclusion that it should not use its discretion to refuse the request, this was not undisputed. Five judges raised concerns similar to those voiced by several states.[52]

Again the Court addressed most of the arguments in line with its previous jurisprudence. It noted that:

> [t]he advisory jurisdiction is not a form of judicial recourse for States but the means by which the General Assembly and the Security Council, as well as other organs of the United Nations and bodies specifically empowered to do so by the General Assembly in accordance with Article 96, paragraph 2 of the Charter may obtain the Court's opinion in order to assist them in their activities. The Court's opinion is given not to States but to the organ which has requested it.[53]

The Court further considered that the motives behind a request for an advisory opinion, or the motives of individual states which sponsor a resolution, are not relevant to the Court's exercise of its discretion whether or not to respond. It also held that it should not examine any "adverse political consequences" to which its advisory opinion might lead, particularly in the absence of any basis on which to make such an assessment.[54]

An objection that was discussed in more detail concerned the respective roles of the General Assembly and the Security Council in relation to the situation in Kosovo. The fact that the Security Council was the organ primarily

---

For a critique, Michla Pomerance, 'The ICJ's Advisory Jurisdiction and the Crumbling Wall Between The Political and the Judicial', (2005) 99 *American Journal of International Law*, p. 26–42; Aust, supra n. 18 (who argues that the Court should refuse a request when the underlying problem is politically controversial).

[51] See Written Statements by Albania, Czech Republic, France, Maldives, United States. Further, the adoption of the decision to request an advisory opinion, by a relative majority and with many abstentions, could have commended some prudence.

[52] Judges Tomka, Koroma, Keith, Bennouna and Slotnikov.

[53] *Kosovo* opinion, paragraph 33.

[54] Ibid., paragraph 35.

involved in the situation could be considered as a compelling reason which could have induced the Court to decline the request. Such a refusal to answer was advocated by a number of judges in their declarations and opinions. In particular, Judge Bennouna, in his dissenting opinion, summed up this issue in the following terms:

> It is the first time that the General Assembly has sought an advisory opinion on a question which was not, as such, on its agenda and which it had until then dealt with essentially in terms of authorizing the expenditure of the United Nations Mission in Kosovo (…) if it had declined to respond to the request, the Court could have put a stop to any "frivolous" requests which political organs might be tempted to submit to it in future, and thereby protect the integrity of its judicial function.[55]

Echoing these concerns, Judges Tomka and Keith expressed the opinion that, under the given circumstances, the Court should provide its advice only if it were asked by the Security Council, which was actively seized of the situation in Kosovo.[56]

These objections are based on the institutional structure of the United Nations, in particular the system of collective security which is regarded as falling primarily within the competence of the Security Council. It can be observed that article 24 of the UN Charter refers to a primary, but not exclusive, competence of the Security Council. On the other hand, the UN Charter seeks to exclude any contact between the activities of the Security Council and those of the General Assembly when it attributes, in article 12, preference to the Security Council. The question was particularly relevant in the Kosovo situation since this situation was still on the agenda of the Security Council, while the General Assembly had not substantially dealt with it since 1999.[57] The Court observed that article 12 does not bar all action in respect of threats to international peace and security which are before the Security Council, and that the limit placed on the General Assembly restricts the power of the General Assembly to 'make any recommendation' regarding a situation with respect to which the Security Council is exercising jurisdiction, but not its power to engage in a discussion.[58] The Court has seen this approach as a

---

[55] Dissenting Opinion of Judge Bennouna, paragraph 2.

[56] Declaration of Vice-President Tomka, paragraphs 5–9; Separate Opinion of Judge Keith, paragraphs 6–14.

[57] See *Kosovo* opinion, paragraph 38, for a list of relevant General Assembly resolutions. For a discussion, see Raphaël van Steenberghe, 'The General Assembly Resolution requesting the *Kosovo* opinion and the *ultra vires* issue', available at <www.haguejusticeportal.net>.

[58] *Kosovo* opinion, paragraph 40. In its Advisory Opinion on the *Wall*, the Court discerned an evolution according to which the prerogatives of the Security Council have been reduced: "[T]he Court notes that there has been an increased tendency over time for the General Assembly and the Security Council to deal in parallel with the same matter concerning the maintenance of peace and security. (…) It is thus the case that, while the Security Council has tended to focus on aspects of such matters related to international peace and security, the

special expression of the development which started with the *Uniting for Peace* Resolution of 1950, which the Court referred to in the present advisory opinion.[59] The General Assembly may therefore have recourse to the Court's advisory jurisdiction to discuss legal aspects of the situation in Kosovo provided that it does not interfere with the powers of the Security Council, within the conditions set out in the *Uniting for Peace* Resolution.[60] Against this background, the Court found no compelling reasons to decline the request. It appears that the General Assembly may, whenever it has a 'legitimate interest', consult the Court on any legal question, and that the Court will accede to the request, absent compelling reasons (which in fact are greatly reduced in scope).

In establishing jurisdiction and rejecting arguments advocating an exercise of discretion in declining to exercise its jurisdiction, the Court once again seems "to tread on known ground, relying on previous jurisprudence and widely accepted views of the institutional role of the ICJ within the United Nations system".[61]

While a majority decided to reply to the request by the General Assembly, the Court provided its answer only after having 'adjusted' the question. Claiming that it did not need to reformulate the question, despite having the authority to do so,[62] the Court actually interpreted the question in a different way, thus setting up the framework for its response. On the one hand, the Court stripped the question from the reference to the 'Provisional Institutions of Self-Government of Kosovo', in order to keep its autonomy concerning the 'authors' of the declaration. This adjustment was in fact

General Assembly has taken a broader view, considering also their humanitarian, social and economic aspects" (ICJ Reports 2004, paragraph 27). For a discussion, see Geoffrey Watson, 'The "Wall" Decisions in Legal and Political Context', (2005) 99 *American Journal of International Law*, p. 8–9.

[59] *Kosovo* opinion, paragraph 42.

[60] For a critique of the applicability of the *Uniting for Peace* Resolution to the particular case at hand, see Peter Hilpold, 'The ICJ Advisory Opinion on Kosovo: Different Perspectives of a Delicate Question', available at <http://ssrn/com/abstract=1734443>. The author notes that the situation of Kosovo was incomparable to other situations, in that it was regulated in detail by the Security Council which, moreover, established an international administration in the disputed territory; to apply this Resolution would "extremely amplify its reach and change its very meaning. The functions of the General Assembly and the Security Council become, to a vast extent, interchangeable, a development that was surely not intended by the drafters of the UN Charter and which is hardly reconcilable with the structure of this constitutional order", pp. 22–23.

[61] See the comments by Richard Falk on the *Wall* case, who adds that the *Wall* opinion "encourages the discharge of General Assembly responsibilities in a manner that accords with the most authoritative interpretation of the relevance of international law, and more generally clarifies the bearing of international law issues (…).", 'Towards Authoritativeness: The ICJ Ruling on Israel's Security Wall', (2005) 99 *American Journal of International Law*, p. 43.

[62] *Kosovo* opinion, paragraph 50. See Jörg Kammerhofer, 'Begging the Question? The *Kosovo* Opinion and the Reformulation of Advisory Requests', available at <http://ssrn.com/abstract=1684539>.

'outcome determinative'.[63] On the other hand, the Court read the question whether the declaration was 'in accordance with international law' as 'whether or not the declaration of independence was adopted in violation of international law'. In other words, the Court adopted a narrow view of the question by framing it in terms of a rule of prohibition. It followed, in the Court's words, that:

> The Court is not required by the question it has been asked to take a position on whether international law conferred a positive entitlement on Kosovo unilaterally to declare its independence, or, a fortiori, whether international law generally confers an entitlement on entities situated within a state unilaterally to break away from it. Indeed, it is entirely possible for a particular act -such as a unilateral declaration of independence- not to be in violation of international law without necessarily constituting the exercise of a right conferred by it. The Court has been asked for an opinion on the first point, not the second.[64]

In adopting such a narrow approach, the Court thus eschewed more general issues underlying the request which remain disputed. In so doing, the Court departed from its previous – broader – approach as to the way in which it ascertains the question submitted to it.[65] In his declaration, Judge Simma expressed his concerns about the opinion's "unnecessarily limited – and potentially misguiding – analysis". For him, the phrase 'in accordance with' should not only be interpreted as a question of whether or not there was a prohibition, but in a broader sense, which would include addressing the question in terms of the existence of a positive entitlement to declare independence under certain conditions.[66]

The Court ultimately concluded that the unilateral declaration of independence was not in violation of international law, without determining other issues, such as the question of self-determination of the population of Kosovo, the existence of a right to remedial secession, or the issue of recognition.

The opinion of the Court has been criticised as being an exercise of 'mechanical jurisprudence', or of judicial economy. In fact, if the Court's advisory function is to clarify the law and to render an opinion which could assist the organs of the United Nations, it can be doubted whether the Court fulfilled this function in the present case. Keeping in mind that the jurisdiction of the Court was shaped by the narrow focus of the request, it is not surprising

[63] Declaration of Vice-President Tomka, paragraph 1.

[64] *Kosovo* opinion, paragraph 56.

[65] *Interpretation of the Agreement of 25 March 1951 between the WHO and Egypt*, Advisory Opinion, ICJ Reports 1980, p. 73. In this case, the Court reformulated the question submitted to it, in order to identify 'the true legal question' under consideration, since, in its opinion, "a reply to questions of the kind posed in the present request may, if incomplete, be not only ineffectual but actually misleading as to the legal rules applicable in the matter under consideration by the requesting Organization". (par. 35).

[66] Declaration of Judge Simma. In his Separate Opinion, Judge Yusuf also observed that the restriction of the scope of the question voids it of much of its substance (at paragraph 2).

that the Court would chose to abide by a principle of judicial economy and not venture into a development of broader legal issues that did not necessarily need to be considered in answering the question before it.[67] However, it can also be argued that the question as such did not necessarily limit the Court's range of action.[68] The advisory function of the Court, which consists in clarifying points of law when addressing 'legal questions', can provide an occasion for more ample elaborations on issues of international law, which in fact are of interest 'to the international community as a whole'.[69]

However, taking into consideration the Court's jurisprudence in respect of its discretionary authority, as well as its cautious approach to highly charged political questions, the final outcome of the proceedings should not come as a surprise. It appears that the Court adopts a proactive approach in not refusing a request, while exercising judicial restraint in replying to the request.

It has been pointed out that, in the *Kosovo* case, the Court was called upon to act as an arbitrator of a universal multilateral political dispute that the international community had not been able to settle itself.[70] In this context, the Court could have exercised its discretion to decline the request. Its refusal – once again – to exercise its discretionary authority shows that the Court perceives it has a role to play as the principle judicial organ of the United Nations, in view of its duty to cooperate, albeit that this role might be limited. In light of the charged political circumstances surrounding the *Kosovo* issue and its potential ramifications, it may well be that the Court could not have done otherwise than adopt a cautious stance. Ultimately, given this conservative approach, the significance of the Opinion remains limited as to the future status of Kosovo.[71]

4. *Conclusion*

Despite its relatively limited use, in contrast to the League of Nations era, the advisory jurisdiction of the International Court of Justice provides the Court

[67] Weller, supra n. 12, p. 132–134, who also notes that the opinion does contain certain important findings of general relevance to issues of statehood and secession (p. 130).

[68] As Judge Lauterpacht has observed: "Clearly, in order to reply to [the] question, the Court is bound in the course of its reasoning to consider and to answer a variety of legal questions. This is the very essence of its judicial function which makes it possible for it to render Judgments and Opinions which carry conviction and clarify the law" (*Voting Procedure in Questions Relating to Rights and Petitions concerning the Territory of South West Africa*, Advisory Opinion, ICJ Reports 1955, Separate Opinion of Judge Lauterpacht, p. 92).

[69] See Jean Salmon, 'Quels sont les destinataires des avis?', in: Laurence Boisson de Chazournes and Philippe Sands (eds.), *International Law, the International Court of Justice and Nuclear Weapons*, Cambridge: Cambridge University Press 1999, pp. 28–35.

[70] d'Aspremont, supra n. 12, p. 2; de Brabandere, supra n. 40, p. 1.

[71] Hurst Hannum, 'The Advisory Opinion on Kosovo: An Opportunity Lost, or a Poisoned Chalice Refused?', (2011) 24 *Leiden Journal of International Law*, p. 159.

with an opportunity to contribute to the development of international law. While advisory opinions are not binding,[72] they can constitute an authoritative pronouncement on issues of international law and thus may serve to promote the rule of law in international relations, a leitmotif which is currently predominant in the work of the United Nations. As has been shown, recent advisory opinions have also brought to the fore questions concerning the ambit and limits of the Court's advisory function. Opinions, such as the one on *Kosovo*, also present an occasion for reconsidering whether the advisory jurisdiction of the Court is the best-suited forum for settling international disputes. However, a proper use of the Court's advisory function may well be of assistance in reducing tensions and controversies and in improving the 'modalities' of peaceful settlement of disputes in the long run.

[72] See further on their status Karel Wellens, 'L'autorité des prononcés de la Cour internationale de justice', in: Nicolas Angelet et al. (eds.), *Droit du pouvoir, pouvoir du droit. Mélanges offerts à Jean Salmon*, Bruxelles: Bruylant 2007, p. 734–735.

CHAPTER FOURTEEN

L'AVIS DE LA COUR INTERNATIONALE DE JUSTICE CONCERNANT LA DÉCLARATION UNILATÉRALE D'INDÉPENDANCE RELATIVE AU KOSOVO: UNE NOUVELLE FLEUR DE LOTUS?

Pierre Michel Eisemann

1. *Avant-propos*

Parmi ses nombreux centres d'intérêt, le professeur Karel Wellens est notamment bien connu pour ses travaux portant sur le Conseil de sécurité, d'une part, et sur la jurisprudence de la Cour de La Haye, d'autre part. Il nous a donc semblé parfaitement opportun d'apporter à ces mélanges rassemblés en son honneur cette modeste contribution qui traite d'une question où l'un et l'autre sont réunis. Mais, avant toute chose, il nous semble indispensable de rendre au professeur Wellens l'hommage personnel qu'il mérite si bien. Participer à des mélanges – mieux vaut d'ailleurs employer la traditionnelle appellation latine, *liber amicorum* –, c'est avoir été reconnu comme un ami du dédicataire. C'est avec un profond plaisir personnel que j'ai répondu à l'invitation qui m'a été faite de participer à cet hommage rendu par ses collègues et amis à un homme dont la discrétion n'a d'égale que la fidélité.

Il y a fort longtemps, j'ai fait la connaissance de Karel Wellens à l'occasion d'un colloque de la Société française pour le droit international (dont il est un membre assidu) et c'est toujours avec le même bonheur que je l'ai retrouvé par la suite, profitant de son infinie gentillesse tout comme de la finesse de son esprit. Plus d'une fois, je l'ai sollicité pour participer à des jurys de thèse et il s'est toujours acquitté avec grâce de cette charge, marquant ainsi la soutenance par ses judicieuses observations tout en témoignant d'une sincère générosité à l'égard du doctorant. Bienveillance envers le jeune chercheur qui n'exclut cependant aucunement une perspicacité sans faille et de vastes connaissances, telle est sans doute l'image du maître. Qu'il me soit donc permis de rendre ici un hommage à la personne de Karel Wellens, véritable savant et homme de cœur, que je suis honoré de compter au nombre de mes amis.

2. *Introduction*

Le 22 juillet 2010, la Cour internationale de Justice rendit son avis consultatif concernant la conformité au droit international de la déclaration unilatérale d'indépendance relative au Kosovo. Près de deux ans auparavant, le 8 octobre

2008, l'Assemblée générale avait adopté sa résolution 63/3 par laquelle elle invitait la Cour à donner son avis sur la question suivante:

> La déclaration unilatérale d'indépendance des institutions provisoires d'administration autonome du Kosovo est-elle conforme au droit international ?

Comme on le sait, l'Assemblée générale s'était contentée d'adopter un projet de résolution présenté par la Serbie, projet dont les termes furent soigneusement choisis tant pour orienter la réponse de la Cour que pour éviter les nombreux écueils sur lesquels aurait pu s'échouer cette manœuvre essentiellement politique. Il ne fallait aucunement évoquer la création même d'un État kosovar au risque d'embarrasser tous ceux qui avaient procédé à sa reconnaissance, mais bien plutôt tenter de circonscrire le débat au droit spécial et transitoire que constitue la résolution 1244 (1999) que le Conseil de sécurité adopta le 10 juin 1999. Même si l'on ne peut dire avec certitude quelles furent les intentions des États membres en adoptant cette résolution, il n'est pas interdit de relever le manque d'enthousiasme de l'Assemblée générale où il ne se trouva que 77 États pour voter en faveur de ce texte, alors que 6 votèrent contre et que 74 s'abstinrent.[1] Reste que la machine infernale était lancée et qu'elle plaçait la Cour face à une question biaisée dont la teneur politique était bien plus forte que le contenu juridique.

Conformément à la procédure en la matière, la Cour a décidé que l'Organisation des Nations Unies et ses États membres pourraient présenter des exposés écrits et des observations écrites, de même que les « auteurs de la déclaration unilatérale d'indépendance ». Sans compter ces derniers (qui se désignent sous le nom de République du Kosovo), 35 états présentèrent ainsi des exposés écrits et 14 d'entre eux ajoutèrent des observations après avoir eu connaissance de l'ensemble des exposés. Ce sont quelque deux mille pages qui furent soumises à la Cour. Si certains états se contentèrent de commentaires particulièrement laconiques, d'autres[2] présentèrent de longs documents soigneusement étayés. Bien entendu, les écritures de la Serbie tout comme celles des « auteurs de la déclaration unilatérale d'indépendance » furent les plus prolixes, représentant en nombre de pages presque la moitié de l'ensemble des pièces produites au cours de cette phase. Pour compléter l'information de la Cour – si besoin en était! –, cette dernière organisa plusieurs audiences publiques, du 1er au 11 décembre 2009, au cours desquelles elle entendit la Serbie, les « auteurs de la déclaration unilatérale d'indépendance » ainsi que 27 États membres des Nations Unies.

On devine que tous les arguments possibles et imaginables ont pu être avancés à loisir dans le cours de cette longue et lourde procédure. En fait, deux

---

[1] Voir A/63/PV.22, 8 octobre 2008.

[2] Comme l'Allemagne, Chypre, l'Espagne, les États-Unis, la France ou encore le Royaume-Uni.

camps émergent clairement. D'un côté, le camp de ceux qui estiment que la question n'est pas juridique et que la Cour devrait s'abstenir de répondre à la demande d'avis ou, à tout le moins déclarer que la déclaration d'indépendance du Kosovo ne contrevient pas au droit international. De l'autre, le camp de ceux qui privilégient l'intégrité territoriale des états constitués, s'appuyant souvent pour ce faire sur la violation de la *lex specialis* constituée par la résolution 1244 (1999). Il n'est pas difficile de discerner derrière ces positions, pour les premiers le souhait de ne pas voir indirectement mise en cause leur reconnaissance du Kosovo, et pour les seconds la volonté de lutter contre toute tentative sécessionniste pouvant menacer leur propre intégrité territoriale.

Beaucoup de bruit (et d'efforts) pour peu de chose? Il est à craindre que l'avis rendu par la Cour ne satisfasse pas grand monde.[3] Il est vrai que sa lecture laisse une impression mitigée tant sa structure est parfois curieuse, laissant imaginer les trésors d'adresse diplomatique ayant été nécessaires pour parvenir à une décision majoritaire. Les juges ayant exprimé une opinion personnelle sont les premiers à adresser de vives critiques à l'avis ainsi rendu, critiques où l'on sent percer des préoccupations qui peuvent ne pas être totalement dénuées de lien avec la situation prévalant dans leur pays d'origine.

3. *Le cheminement de l'avis*

3.1. *Introduction*

Quel est donc le cheminement de l'avis consultatif?

3.2. *Compétence et pouvoir discrétionnaire*

On ne reviendra pas sur la motivation de l'avis portant sur la compétence de la Cour car elle se situe dans la droite ligne de la jurisprudence entendant d'une manière très large ladite compétence. Ainsi, l'article 12 de la Charte ne fait pas obstacle à ce que l'Assemblée générale sollicite un avis consultatif alors même que la situation au Kosovo est sous examen par le Conseil de sécurité. De même, la notion de « question juridique » est entendue de manière large et le fait qu'une question revête des aspects politiques ne lui fait pas perdre pour autant son caractère juridique, alors que par ailleurs la Cour ne doit pas tenir compte de la nature politique des motifs pouvant avoir inspiré la demande, ni des conséquences politiques que pourrait avoir son avis.

---

[3] Il est symptomatique que l'un des premiers commentaires parus évoque une « occasion manquée ». Voir Thomas Margueritte, 'L'avis consultatif de la Cour internationale de Justice sur le Kosovo: une occasion manquée ?', (2010) 28 *L'observateur des Nations Unies*, p. 257–276.

S'agissant de son pouvoir discrétionnaire d'exercer sa compétence, la Cour reste également fidèle au principe selon lequel elle doit satisfaire la demande dont elle a été saisie, sauf raisons décisives. Ne constitue pas de telles raisons le fait que la demande servirait les intérêts d'un seul État, que l'avis n'aurait pas d'effet juridique utile ou qu'il risquerait d'avoir des conséquences politiques négatives, ou encore que la demande provienne de l'Assemblée générale et non du Conseil de sécurité alors même que la Cour pourrait être ainsi amenée à interpréter des résolutions de ce dernier. Rappelant sa jurisprudence, la Cour balaye les arguments de ceux qui l'invitaient à exercer sa discrétion et donne, au contraire, suite à la demande de l'Assemblée générale.

3.3. *La question posée*

Passant à l'examen de la portée et du sens de la question posée, la Cour procède de manière quelque peu contournée. Elle rappelle que, par le passé, elle s'est déjà écartée du libellé de la question qui lui était posée lorsque celle-ci n'était pas « correctement » formulée ou qu'elle ne mettait pas en évidence les points de droit véritablement en jeu. Rien de tel en l'espèce:

> la question posée par l'Assemblée générale est clairement formulée. C'est une question circonscrite et précise, visant à obtenir l'avis de la Cour sur la conformité ou la non-conformité de la déclaration d'indépendance du Kosovo au droit international.[4]

Et la Cour d'en profiter pour bien délimiter ce qui lui est demandé. Elle

> n'est pas priée de dire si le Kosovo a ou non accédé à la qualité d'État, ni de se prononcer sur la validité ou les effets juridiques de la reconnaissance du Kosovo comme État indépendant par certains États.[5]

Reste que la question n'est peut-être pas aussi bien posée que cela puisque la Cour annonce qu'elle ne se sent pas liée par la désignation de l'auteur de la déclaration unilatérale d'indépendance telle qu'elle figure dans la résolution de l'Assemblée générale, à savoir les « institutions provisoires d'administration autonome du Kosovo ». Invoquant une raison assez contestable – le fait que l'intitulé du point de l'ordre du jour de l'Assemblée sous lequel ce qui deviendra la résolution 63/3 a été examiné ne mentionne pas les auteurs de la déclaration d'indépendance –, la Cour affirme qu'elle ne considère pas que l'Assemblée ait entendu poser des limites à sa liberté de trancher elle-même ce point. L'Assemblée générale ne peut avoir entendu lier ou gêner la Cour dans l'exercice de ses fonctions judiciaires, or

[4] CIJ *Conformité au droit international de la déclaration unilatérale d'indépendance relative au Kosovo*, Avis consultatif de 22 juillet 2010, par. 51.
[5] Ibid.

> [a]ux fins d'apprécier la conformité au droit international de la déclaration d'indépendance, la Cour doit être libre d'examiner le dossier dans son ensemble et de déterminer elle-même si cette déclaration a été prononcée par les institutions provisoires d'administration autonome ou par une autre entité.[6]

Enfin, mentionnant le fait que de nombreux participants à la procédure ont fait référence à l'avis donné par la Cour suprême du Canada dans l'affaire du *Renvoi par le Gouverneur en conseil au sujet de certaines questions ayant trait à la sécession du Québec du reste du Canada*[7], la Cour procède à une distinction entre les deux affaires pour bien insister sur le fait qu'il ne lui est pas demandé de dire si le droit international confère au Kosovo un « droit positif de déclarer unilatéralement son indépendance, ni, *a fortiori*, [...] si le droit international confère en général à des entités situées à l'intérieur d'un État existant le droit de s'en séparer unilatéralement »[8]. Ce faisant, elle insiste sur le fait qu'elle doit se prononcer sur la « conformité au droit international » de la déclaration unilatérale d'indépendance, question distincte de celle de l'existence d'un éventuel droit à la sécession.

3.4. *Conformité au droit international général*

Ces préalables posés et après avoir évoqué le contexte factuel de la situation, la Cour en vient à la question qui lui est soumise, celle de la conformité de la déclaration d'indépendance au droit international. Pour ce faire, elle analyse le droit international général avant de s'attacher au droit spécial constitué par la résolution 1244 (1999) et le cadre constitutionnel de la MINUK établi en vertu de cette résolution.

L'évocation du droit international général est pour le moins rapide. Sans véritable démonstration, la Cour, se référant aux nombreuses déclarations d'indépendance intervenues entre le XVIIIe siècle le début du XXe, affirme que

> la pratique des États ne semble pas indiquer que la déclaration de l'indépendance ait jamais été considérée comme une transgression du droit international[9]

et que

> [a]u contraire, il ressort clairement de la pratique étatique au cours de cette période que le droit international n'interdisait nullement les déclarations d'indépendance.[10]

Puis, faisant un inutile détour par l'émergence d'un droit à l'indépendance au bénéfice des peuples des territoires non autonomes et de ceux qui étaient

---

[6] Avis, par. 54.
[7] (1998) 115 *International Law Reports*, p. 536.
[8] Avis, par. 56.
[9] Avis, par. 79.
[10] Ibid.

soumis à la subjugation, à la domination ou à l'exploitation étrangères, la Cour affirme que la pratique de la seconde moitié du XXe siècle ne révèle pas l'apparition d'une nouvelle règle interdisant que ne soient faites des déclarations d'indépendance hors de ces cas particuliers.

Ce constat réalisé, la Cour répond à deux arguments avancés par divers participants à la procédure. Selon le premier, l'interdiction des déclarations unilatérales d'indépendance serait implicitement contenue dans le principe de l'intégrité territoriale. Mais la Cour, s'appuyant sur la Charte des Nations Unies, la résolution 2625 (XXV) adoptée en 1970 par l'Assemblée générale et l'Acte final d'Helsinki, confine – comme il se doit – ce principe « à la sphère des relations interétatiques »[11]. Le second argument repose sur la condamnation de certaines déclarations d'indépendance par le Conseil de sécurité (Rhodésie du Sud, nord de Chypre, Republika Srpska). Ici la Cour rappelle justement que le Conseil s'était prononcé sur des situations concrètes et que

> l'illicéité de ces déclarations découlait (…) non de leur caractère unilatéral, mais du fait que celles-ci allaient ou seraient allées de pair avec un recours illicite à la force ou avec d'autres violations graves de normes de droit international général, en particulier de nature impérative (*jus cogens*),[12]

une situation qui n'a rien à voir avec celle du Kosovo. Tirant même du caractère exceptionnel des résolutions sus-évoquées un argument supplémentaire, la Cour voit confirmée par la pratique du Conseil de sécurité l'absence d'interdiction générale des déclarations unilatérales d'indépendance[13].

A ce stade, la Cour ne peut donc que relever que « le droit international ne comporte aucune interdiction applicable des déclarations d'indépendance » et elle en conclut que « la déclaration d'indépendance du 17 février 2008 n'a pas violé le droit international général. »[14]

3.5. *Conformité à la résolution 1244*

Pour ce qui est du droit spécial, la Cour s'en tient à la résolution 1244 (1999) dont, souligne-t-elle, nul n'a contesté qu'elle fasse partie du droit pertinent au regard du Kosovo. Elle précise néanmoins que le cadre constitutionnel – qui tient sa force obligatoire du caractère contraignant de la résolution 1244 (1999) – revêt de ce fait un caractère juridique international et qu'il fait

---

[11] Avis, par. 80.
[12] Avis, par. 81.
[13] Bien qu'elle ait insisté sur le fait qu'elle n'avait pas à rechercher s'il existait un droit à la sécession, la Cour fait encore curieusement référence aux arguments selon lesquels la population du Kosovo aurait eu le droit de créer un État indépendant au nom d'un droit à l'autodétermination ou encore en vertu d'un droit de « sécession-remède » (avis, par. 82–83), mais elle se contente de déclarer qu'elle ne juge pas nécessaire de trancher ces questions en l'espèce.
[14] Avis, par. 84.

également partie du droit international qu'il convient de considérer pour répondre à la question posée par l'Assemblée générale.

Analysant et interprétant la résolution 1244 (1999), la Cour conclut que son objet et son but étaient « d'établir un régime juridique temporaire de caractère exceptionnel qui s'est substitué, sauf lorsqu'il l'a expressément conservé, à l'ordre juridique serbe et visait à stabiliser le Kosovo »[15]. La question est donc de savoir si cette résolution contenait une interdiction spécifique de toute déclaration d'indépendance. Pour répondre à cette question la Cour commence par rechercher l'identité des auteurs de la déclaration d'indépendance: s'agissait-il de l'« Assemblée du Kosovo » en tant qu'institution provisoire d'administration autonome établie conformément au « cadre constitutionnel » ou d'une autre entité? Se fondant sur divers indices dont le caractère probant peut laisser à désirer (par ex. terminologie adoptée, procédure d'adoption, silence du représentant spécial du Secrétaire général), la Cour déduit que la déclaration d'indépendance

> n'est pas le fait de l'Assemblée du Kosovo en tant qu'institution provisoire d'administration autonome agissant dans les limites du cadre constitutionnel, mais est celui de personnes ayant agi de concert en leur qualité de représentants du peuple du Kosovo, en dehors du cadre de l'administration intérimaire.[16]

Ce déplacement de l'acteur principal conduit à une conséquence particulièrement importante. Il n'y aura plus lieu de savoir si la déclaration d'indépendance est simplement contraire au cadre constitutionnel établi[17] mais plutôt si le droit spécial impose une obligation spécifique (i.e. une interdiction) aux auteurs de la déclaration. La Cour insiste sur le caractère intérimaire du régime institué par la résolution 1244 (1999) pour en déduire que cette dernière n'excluait pas la déclaration d'indépendance qui, elle, constitue une tentative de déterminer définitivement le statut du Kosovo et elle ajoute que les auteurs de la déclaration ne sont pas destinataires de la résolution, c'est-à-dire qu'ils ne font pas partie de ceux à l'égard desquels le Conseil de sécurité a voulu créer des obligations juridiques contraignantes. Ainsi ne peut-on trouver dans la résolution 1244 (1999) une interdiction de procéder à une déclaration d'indépendance qui pèserait sur les auteurs de cette dernière, pas plus que l'on ne pourrait inférer une telle interdiction du texte de la résolution, lu dans son contexte et à la lumière de son objet et de son but. Ces derniers consistent « à mettre en place une administration intérimaire au Kosovo, sans prendre aucune décision définitive quant aux questions relatives au statut final ».[18]

---

[15] Avis, par. 100.

[16] Avis, par. 109.

[17] Si la Cour n'avait pas changé l'identité des auteurs de la déclaration, elle aurait sans doute été obligée de constater un dépassement de ses pouvoirs par l'Assemblée du Kosovo, et par suite de conclure à l'illicéité de ladite déclaration.

[18] Avis, par. 118.

Même si la Cour concède que le libellé de la résolution laisse place à une certaine ambiguïté, elle n'en affirme pas moins que celle-là « ne faisait pas obstacle à ce que les auteurs de la déclaration du 17 février 2008 proclament l'indépendance du Kosovo vis-à-vis de la République de Serbie ».[19]

Ne voyant d'interdiction ni dans le droit international général, ni dans la *lex specialis*, la Cour se déclare d'avis, par dix voix contre quatre[20] que la déclaration d'indépendance du Kosovo n'a pas violé le droit international.

5. *Quelques reflections*

Que penser de cet avis et du raisonnement quelque peu laborieux de la Cour? Plusieurs critiques ont été exprimées en son sein même: la Cour aurait dû exercer sa discrétion et refuser de répondre à la demande de l'Assemblée générale, elle aurait indûment modifié le sens de la question posée par l'Assemblée, elle aurait méconnu la portée de la résolution 1244 (1999) et, enfin, elle aurait laissé passer l'occasion de clarifier les règles relatives à l'exercice de l'autodétermination post-coloniale. Ces critiques, émanant de près du tiers des juges, sont sévères et elles reflètent les difficultés politiques masquées derrière la question juridique soumise à la Cour.

Même si l'avis reste très discret sur cet aspect des choses, il ne faut pas oublier que la question du Kosovo s'inscrit dans le contexte douloureux de la dissolution de l'ex-Yougoslavie, marqué par de patentes et graves violations des droits de l'homme.[21] L'action des autorités serbes est à l'origine de la situation et l'Organisation des Nations Unies avait, elle-même, construit des institutions destinées à protéger la population kosovare. Un passé tragique encore présent dans toutes les mémoires explique donc que cette population ne veuille plus se trouver sous l'autorité de la Serbie, quand bien même cette dernière se refuserait à toute idée de sécession. Cet antagonisme et ces revendications contradictoires des deux parties en présence expliquent que, malgré tous les efforts entrepris dans le cadre des Nations Unies, une solution consensuelle n'ait pu être trouvée entre Serbes et Kosovars, laissant perdurer un régime transitoire reposant sur une résolution du Conseil de sécurité dont les termes sont loin d'être dépourvus d'ambiguïté. L'une des questions sous-jacentes est celle de la sortie de ce régime transitoire: la résolution 1244 (1999) peut-elle obliger Serbes et Kosovars à demeurer indéfiniment sous l'empire du régime

---

19 Avis, par. 119.

20 Il s'agit du vice-président Tomka et des juges Koroma, Bennouna et Skotnikov.

21 A la différence de l'avis, l'opinion individuelle du juge Cançado Trindade insiste longuement – et non sans lyrisme – sur l'aspect humanitaire de la situation ayant prévalu au Kosovo et sur la réponse que devrait apporter en de tels cas ce qu'il désigne sous le nom de « droit des gens ». De manière plus discrète, mais sans doute pas moins efficace, le juge Yusuf se réfère également à la spécificité de la situation en cause.

transitoire qu'elle institue au seul motif que les acteurs n'arrivent pas à trouver une solution de compromis ou que le Conseil de sécurité ne parvient pas à s'accorder sur une autre formule? Mise à part toute argutie juridique relative à l'interprétation même de la résolution, celle-ci conserve-t-elle une légitimité suffisante dix ans après son adoption pour paralyser l'avènement d'une solution finale extérieure à la voie qu'elle avait tracée ? On comprend bien que les opposants à la sécession du Kosovo aient entendu enfermer toute issue dans le processus prévu par la résolution 1244 (1999)[22] – celui-ci impliquant un accord avec la Serbie –, mais il est également compréhensible que d'autres aient pu souhaiter, après tous les efforts infructueux en direction d'une solution consensuelle, priver la Serbie de son pouvoir de blocage et privilégier l'avènement d'une solution définitive, quitte à contourner la résolution 1244 (1999). Au moment où la Cour est saisie de la demande, des États membres de l'ONU – et non des moindres – ont déjà pris position en reconnaissant le nouvel État kosovar au lendemain de la déclaration d'indépendance, créant, si ce n'est une effectivité, à tout le moins une situation de fait accompli. Il est clair que la réponse à la question relative à la conformité au droit international de la déclaration d'indépendance ne serait pas sans effet sur l'appréciation des reconnaissances déjà intervenues, plaçant ainsi la Cour dans une situation « politique » particulièrement inconfortable. On peut imaginer que les juges ont été extrêmement attentifs à ce contexte lorsqu'ils ont examiné la question à eux transmise par l'Assemblée générale.[23]

La compétence de la Cour ne faisant pas de doute, on aurait pu imaginer qu'elle exerce sa discrétion pour refuser de donner suite à la demande d'avis consultatif. Cinq juges[24] inclinaient en ce sens pour des raisons différentes quoique convergentes. Le point commun de leurs positions tenait aux rôles respectifs de l'Assemblée générale et du Conseil de sécurité dans l'examen de la question kosovare qui ne justifiaient pas la démarche de l'Assemblée. Ainsi, l'un (M. Keith) met en avant le rôle ténu de l'Assemblée, tandis qu'un autre (M. Skotnikov) insiste sur la nécessité de protéger l'action du Conseil de sécurité. De son côté, le juge Bennouna invoque la nécessité de défendre la crédibilité de la Cour à laquelle il serait « demandé finalement de s'ériger en décideur politique, au lieu et place du Conseil de sécurité »[25]. Sans doute faut-il comprendre que, aux yeux de ces juges, l'Assemblée générale a été instrumentalisée

---

[22] A cet égard, il est intéressant de relever que le juge Skotnikov a estimé que la Cour aurait dû s'appuyer exclusivement sur la résolution 1244 (1999) pour répondre à la question posée par l'Assemblée générale (voir son opinion dissidente, par. 17). Voir également l'opinion dissidente du juge Koroma.

[23] Il est symptomatique que le vice-président Tomka ait reproché à la majorité d'avoir préféré prendre en considération l'évolution de la situation et des réalités politiques au détriment de la stricte légalité, dépassant ainsi les limites du « *judicial restraint* » (voir sa déclaration, par. 35).

[24] Le vice-président Tomka et les juges Koroma, Keith, Bennouna et Skotnikov.

[25] Opinion dissidente du juge Bennouna, par. 7.

par la Serbie qui l'a conduite à demander un avis à la Cour alors même qu'elle n'est pas directement concernée par la recherche d'un règlement de la situation. Reste que, même si ce n'est pas totalement inexact, on ne saurait reprocher à la Cour d'avoir suivi sa jurisprudence constante privilégiant l'exercice de sa compétence consultative. L'utilisation qui pourrait être faite d'un avis n'est pas la même chose que l'avis lui-même et la Cour a pu très légitimement décider de ne pas voir dans les circonstances propres à la présente affaire de raisons décisives l'amenant à refuser de répondre à la demande de l'Assemblée générale.

S'agissant du fond, les critiques faites à la majorité sur la reformulation de la question et sur la lecture du droit applicable se conjuguent. Non sans paradoxe, alors que l'avis déclare que la question posée par l'Assemblée générale est « clairement formulée »,[26] il lui est reproché non seulement de l'avoir reformulée,[27] mais même de l'avoir fait « au point d'en bouleverser le sens et la portée ».[28] Ces critiques visent évidemment l'identification des auteurs de la déclaration d'indépendance comme autres que les « institutions provisoires d'administration autonome ». Par ailleurs, là où la Cour s'attache à la lettre même de la question et se concentre sur la « déclaration unilatérale d'indépendance », il lui est fait grief de l'avoir entendue trop étroitement et de ne pas s'être attachée au « scope and legal content of the right of self-determination, in its post-colonial conception, and its applicability to the specific case of Kosovo ».[29]

Comme on l'a vu, la Cour écarte astucieusement la *lex specialis* en faisant des « représentants du peuple du Kosovo » les véritables auteurs de la déclaration d'indépendance. Ceci posé, il était relativement aisé de ne pas trouver dans la résolution 1244 (1999) de prohibition s'adressant directement aux dits auteurs,[30] permettant ainsi de s'en tenir à une réponse tirée du droit international général. Accessoirement, cette mise à l'écart de la résolution permettait de laisser dans l'ombre des questions extrêmement délicates comme celle de la détermination de sa portée exacte au regard de la recherche d'une solution finale compte tenu de l'effet du temps ou celle de la nature juridique du cadre constitutionnel.[31] On peut rester sceptique face à cette « substitution » visant

---

26 Avis, par. 51

27 Voir la déclaration du vice-président Tomka, l'opinion dissidente du juge Koroma et l'opinion individuelle du juge Sepúlveda-Amor.

28 Opinion dissidente du juge Bennouna, par. 27.

29 Opinion individuelle du juge Yusuf, par. 5.

30 Comme le relève, de manière critique, le juge Bennouna, « il suffirait, en quelque sorte, de se mettre hors de la loi pour ne plus avoir à respecter la loi » (opinion dissidente, par. 46).

31 Alors que l'avis déclare que « [l]e cadre constitutionnel tient sa force obligatoire du caractère contraignant de la résolution 1244 (1999) et, partant, du droit international » (par. 88), le juge Yusuf estime, pour ce qui le concerne, que cette affirmation procède d'une confusion entre la source de l'autorité pour la promulgation des règlements au Kosovo et la nature même de ces derniers. Selon lui, il s'agit d'éléments du système juridique local et non d'éléments relevant du droit international (voir son opinion individuelle, par. 18 à 21).

l'auteur de la déclaration tant les arguments avancés par la Cour sont faibles, contradictoires et peu convaincants. Pour reprendre les mots du vice-président Tomka, la redéfinition de l'auteur de la déclaration «*has no sound basis in the facts relating to the adoption of the declaration and is nothing more than a* post hoc *intellectual construct*».[32] Toutefois, plutôt que de faire purement et simplement reproche à la Cour d'avoir procédé à une fausse analyse des faits et d'avoir reconstruit une réalité imaginaire, on peut se demander, comme on le verra ci-après, si elle n'a pas entendu, en requalifiant l'auteur de la déclaration, adresser aux États un message particulier.

Puisque la Cour s'en est tenue à une lecture restrictive de la question posée par l'Assemblée générale, elle ne peut donner qu'une réponse très laconique qui, bien que peu étayée n'est pas véritablement contestable: le droit international n'interdit pas les déclarations d'indépendance. Ce qui n'est pas interdit est-il permis? On voit apparaître l'ombre du *Lotus*, ce qui fait dire au juge Simma que le raisonnement de la Cour est obsolète et que sa réponse pêche par le cadre d'analyse trop étroit qu'elle s'est imposée; en s'appuyant sur le principe du *Lotus*, «*the Court fails to seize a chance to move beyond this anachronistic, extremely consensualist vision of international law*»[33] alors qu'une recherche plus complète du droit applicable aurait conduit à «*a more intellectually satisfying Opinion*».[34] D'autres membres de la Cour auraient souhaité que l'avis aille plus loin dans l'identification du droit gouvernant la question. Ainsi, insistant sur la primauté de la protection de l'intégrité territoriale des États sur le droit à l'autodétermination, le juge Koroma redoute-t-il que l'avis serve de «*guide and instruction manual for secessionist groups the world over*»[35]. Plus nuancé, le juge Yusuf refuse aux groupes raciaux et ethniques le droit de faire sécession librement,[36] privilégiant la préservation des États constitués, mais il reconnaît dans le même temps qu'il existe des exceptions, regrettant que la Cour ait raté l'occasion de clarifier le droit.

On peut sans doute regretter que la Cour n'ait pas pris soin de définir plus attentivement ce qu'elle entend par «déclaration d'indépendance» et qu'elle ne se soit pas interrogée sur le point de savoir pour quelle raison un tel acte – émanant d'un auteur intra-étatique – devrait relever du droit international. Mais il reste qu'une déclaration d'indépendance n'est que la manifestation

---

[32] Déclaration du vice-président Tomka, par. 12.
[33] Déclaration du juge Simma, par. 3.
[34] Ibid., par. 7.
[35] Opinion dissidente, par. 4.
[36] «[A] racially or ethnically distinct group within a State, even if it qualifies as a people for the purposes of self-determination, does not have the right to unilateral secession simply because it wishes to create its own separate State, though this might be the wish of the entire group. The availability of such a general right in international law would reduce to naught the territorial sovereignty and integrity of States and would lead to interminable conflicts and chaos in international relations» (opinion individuelle, par. 10).

d'une volonté de sécession sans pour autant suffire à constituer la sécession par elle-même. En s'engageant dans la voie d'une clarification des règles du droit international applicable à l'autodétermination ou à la sécession, la Cour n'aurait-elle pas franchement débordé le cadre de la question à elle posée par l'Assemblée générale au double risque de ne pas s'accorder sur le contenu de ces règles et de se placer en porte-à-faux par rapport aux États ayant déjà reconnu l'État kosovar ? On peut penser que telle fut la crainte des juges majoritaires qui refusèrent de s'aventurer sur ce chemin périlleux.

6. *Conclusion*

Alors, l'avis consultatif constitue-t-il une occasion perdue? Sans doute est-ce l'opinion de ceux qui avaient espéré que la Cour en profite pour poser les règles relatives à la sécession. Ce ne sera pas celle de ceux qui pensent qu'il lui appartenait de s'en tenir à la question qui lui avait été soumise. Ces derniers pourront même apprécier la façon dont, en fin de compte, la Cour s'est acquittée de la mission délicate que lui avait confiée l'Assemblée générale.

Quant à savoir si l'avis n'est qu'une simple résurgence de la jurisprudence *Lotus*, on se permettra de proposer une interprétation allant un peu plus loin. Non seulement la Cour a entendu affirmer que le droit international n'interdit pas les déclarations d'indépendance, mais en déclarant que l'auteur de la déclaration d'indépendance n'était pas l'Assemblée du Kosovo (en tant qu'institution provisoire d'administration autonome agissant dans les limites du cadre constitutionnel), mais des personnes ayant agi de concert en leur qualité de représentants du peuple du Kosovo (en dehors du cadre de l'administration intérimaire), elle a sans doute voulu signifier que, nonobstant les structures politiques et les limitations établies – dans un cadre national ou international –, le peuple concerné conservait toujours le pouvoir originaire de manifester sa volonté d'autodétermination, sans être entravé par le droit international. Reste que la concrétisation de cette volonté, sous la forme d'une sécession, demeure, quant à elle, certainement soumise à des règles de droit international que l'avis consultatif n'avait pas pour objet de préciser.

CHAPTER FIFTEEN

CONCLUSION: EVOLVING INTERNATIONAL LAW – CONNECTING UNDERLYING TRENDS AND PRINCIPLES

Eva Rieter and Henri de Waele

1. *Purpose of this Chapter*

This book has dealt with several important contemporary issues and portrayed some general patterns in the development of international law. The authors of the various chapters discussed various trends, principles and rules through different thematic lenses. The purpose of these concluding remarks is not to devise a theory based on the use by international adjudicators and international law scholars of the terms 'principle' and 'rule'. After all, they often use these interchangeably. It is nevertheless possible to identify a number of structural trends, and clarify whether certain principles form an expression of these trends, or otherwise help explain them. This chapter briefly refers to fundamental values of the international community and the role of principles in the evolution of international law. It then singles out specific principles and identifies their bearing on the humanisation of international law.

2. *Trends in International Law*

Several trends already observed for many years have in the meantime been consolidated. Obviously, over the last decades there has been a spectacular increase in substantive rules coupled with a dramatic decrease of matters falling within the exclusive domestic jurisdiction. The obligations of the international community to serve the general interest,[1] including human security,[2] have become more and more important, bringing to the fore the 'publicness' of public international law and the importance in this respect of the international rule of law.[3]

[1] See e.g. Teruo Komori and Karel Wellens (eds.), *Public Interest Rules of International Law: Towards Effective Implementation*, Farnham: Ashgate 2009.

[2] See Theo van Boven (chapter 8).

[3] See Teruo Komori (chapter 7), as well as Mariano Aznar-Gómez (chapter 3). Komori links in with Kingsbury's argument that public order in international law should be constructed as inter-public law, law among public entities other than states, instead of as inter-state law, where

One predominant notion in international discourse is that of the Responsibility to Protect (RtoP).[4] It is the primary duty of the state itself to protect those under its jurisdiction.[5] Yet, in situations where national authorities are manifestly failing to protect populations from genocide, war crimes, ethnic cleansing and other crimes against humanity, the international community should step in to take collective action, in a timely and decisive manner, through the Security Council, in accordance with the UN Charter.[6] However, RtoP involves more than just humanitarian intervention. RtoP has been referred to in the context of natural disasters and pandemics as well.[7] Moreover, it refers to a full range of obligations: to prevent, to react (including, if necessary, with military intervention) and to rebuild, in other words, all actions required by the international community, including binding resolutions under chapter VII of the UN Charter.[8] At times, this responsibility requires the institution of international administrations.[9] RtoP has a growing impact in international law, and while the Security Council initially only reaffirmed it in the abstract,[10] it has now referred to it in chapter VII resolutions authorising military intervention.[11]

the only relevant entities are states. He contends that the components of publicness are the principles of legality, rationality, the rule of law, and human rights (see Benedict Kingsbury, 'International Law as Inter-Public Law', in: Henry Richardson and Melissa Williams (eds.), *Moral Universalism and Pluralism*, New York: New York University Press 2009, p. 188).

[4] See Theo van Boven (chapter 8) and Mariano Aznar-Gómez (chapter 3).

[5] On 25 March 2011, the African Court on Human and Peoples' Rights (ACtHPR) issued its first ever provisional measures order under Art. 27 (2) of the Protocol establishing the Court, calling on Libya to "immediately refrain from any action that would result in loss of life or violation of physical integrity of persons, which could be a breach of the provisions of the African Charter on Human and Peoples' Rights or of other international human rights instruments to which it is a party". See ACtHPR, *African Commission on Human and Peoples' Rights v. Great Socialist People's Libyan Arab Jamahiriya*, application no. 004/2011, Order for provisional measures of 25 March 2011.

[6] See Theo van Boven (chapter 8).

[7] See e.g. Karel Wellens, 'Solidarity as a (Re-)Emerging Constitutional Principle: Some Further Reflections', in: Rüdiger Wolfrum and Chie Kojima (eds.), *Solidarity: A Structural Principle of International Law*, Berlin-Heidelberg: Springer 2010, p. 12, p. 14.

[8] See the report of the International Commission on Intervention and State Sovereignty (a commission sponsored by the Canadian government), *The Responsibility to Protect* (December 2001), available at <http://iciss.ca/pdf/Commission-Report.pdf>. The principle has not only been embraced by scholars, but also by the UN and individual states, sometimes enthusiastically, sometimes more tepidly. See further e.g. Laurence Boisson de Chazournes and Luigi Condorelli, 'De la "responsabilité de protéger", ou de une nouvelle parure pour une notion déjà bien établie en droit international', (2006) 110 *Revue Générale de Droit International Public*, p. 2, and Laurence Boisson de Chazournes, 'Responsibility to Protect: Reflecting Solidarity?', in: Rüdiger Wolfrum and Chie Kojima (eds.), *Solidarity: A Structural Principle of International Law*, Berlin-Heidelberg: Springer 2010, p. 93–109.

[9] Cf. Mariano Aznar-Gómez (chapter 3), referring to Judge Cançado Trindade's description of a population as the "most precious constitutive element of statehood".

[10] See e.g. S/RES/1674 (2006).

[11] See S/RES/1970 (2011), 26 February 2011 and S/RES/1973 (2011), 17 March 2011 (recalling the Libyan authorities' responsibility to protect its population); and S/RES/1975 of

The role of intergovernmental organisations has increased exponentially, and therefore also the expectations for international governance,[12] as well as the likelihood of wrongful acts committed by these organisations.[13] More and more situations of shared responsibility occur, calling for the development of clear principles.[14] At the same time the question arises what is the relationship between international organisations and their individual member states, for instance with regard to liability for wrongful acts.[15]

Yet, the increasing role of intergovernmental organisations in performing some governmental functions triggers various questions, not just with regard to attribution of responsibility and liability, but also with regard to effectiveness and legitimacy.

In light of the legitimacy question, important trends in thinking about international law, such as that of constitutionalism or the constitutionalisation of international law, cannot be overlooked.[16] The idea of constitutionalisation, it has been put forward, plays a role in public international law as it evolves, together with other guiding principles. These do not replace the principle of state sovereignty but are complementary to it. They include human security,

---

30 March 2011 (involving the situation in Côte d'Ivoire, reaffirming the primary responsibility of each State to protect civilians).

[12] On international public authority, international institutional law or even international administrative law see e.g. the contributions in Tomer Broude and Yuval Shany (eds.), *The Shifting Allocation of Authority in International Law*, Oxford: Hart Publishing 2008, and in Armin von Bogdandy et al. (eds.), *The Exercise of Public Authority by International Institutions. Advancing International Institutional Law*, Berlin-Heidelberg-New York: Springer 2010.

[13] See Laurence Boisson de Chazournes and Pieter Jan Kuijper (chapter 5) and André Nollkaemper (chapter 11).

[14] See André Nollkaemper (chapter 11), showing the need for further research in this area while setting out the few rules that the ICJ did express so far. The Court reaffirmed the principle of independent state responsibility and its applicability in situations of concurrent responsibility, and the principle that in case of acts of a joint organ, each state can individually be held responsible. When it cannot be demonstrated which state caused what part of the injury, the ICJ thus far does not apply a principle of joint and several responsibility, but simply rejects the claim for lack of evidence of individual causation.

[15] See Frans Nelissen (chapter 2).

[16] See Teruo Komori (chapter 7). Diverse ways of approaching constitutionalism have been proposed, see e.g. Jan Klabbers, Anne Peters and Geir Ulfstein (eds.), *The Constitutionalization of International Law*, Oxford: Oxford University Press 2009; Anne Peters, 'Compensatory Constitutionalism: The Function and Potential of Fundamental International Norms and Structures', (2006) 19 *Leiden Journal of International Law*, p. 579; Christine E.J. Schwöbel, *Global Constitutionalism in International Legal Perspective* (Queen Mary Studies in International Law: 4), Leiden-Boston: Martinus Nijhoff Publishers 2011; Erica de Wet 'The Emergence of International and Regional Value System as a Manifestation of the Emerging international Constitutional Order', (2006) 19 *Leiden Journal of International Law*, p. 611; Ronald St.J. MacDonald and Douglas M. Johnston (eds.), *Towards World Constitutionalism: Issues in the Legal Ordering of The World Community*, Leiden-Boston: Martinus Nijhoff Publishers 2005; Christian Tomuschat, 'Obligations Arising for States Without or Against their Will', (1993) 241 *Recueil des Cours*, p. 194. See also Eric Suy 'The Constitutional Character of Constituent Treaties of International Organizations and the Hierarchy of Norms', in: Ulrich Beyerlin, Michael Bothe and Rainer Hofmann (eds.), *Recht Zwischen Umbruch und Bewahrung. Festschrift für Rudolf Bernhardt*, Berlin-Heidelberg-New York: Springer 1995, p. 267–277.

the respect for human rights, the 'global common interest' and the rule of law.[17] It is noteworthy that several contributions to this volume refer to legitimacy aspects of Security Council resolutions adopted under chapter VII of the UN Charter.[18]

The protective function of the international judiciary is equally relevant. If one can speak at all of three branches of international governance, it is clear that the international judiciary cannot be equated to the 'third branch' of the domestic constitutional system. There are significant differences in the possibility of balancing between the 'branches'. In addition, the non-domestic situation in itself and the (initial) principle of state consent to the jurisdiction of international adjudicators make the comparison problematic. Moreover, as discussed by Laurence Boisson de Chazournes and Pieter Jan Kuijper, "[t]he articulation of a framework for judicial review of Security Council action (even if only indirectly by review of regional implementation measures) meets obstacles of a systemic character, having to do with the shaping of the international judicial space".[19]

A clearly related issue is the legitimacy of the case law developed by international adjudicators. What, for instance, is – or should be – the approach by the ICJ towards the assessment of evidence, how does it motivate its decisions, what is its approach to judicial economy and how does it perceive its legal function?[20]

Another important trend, already indicated above in the development of RtoP, is that of the humanisation of international law.[21] The principle of effective protection of persons and groups '(also relevant in light of the protective function of the international judiciary) is increasingly gaining priority over the principle of state consent. To a large extent, this appears to be due to the

[17] Peters, supra n. 16, p. 586.

[18] See e.g. the contributions by Laurence Boisson de Chazournes and Pieter Jan Kuijper (chapter 5), Eric Myjer (chapter 4), Frans Nelissen (chapter 3), Eric Suy (chapter 6) and André de Hoogh (chapter 10).

[19] See chapter 5. See also Karel Wellens, 'L'autorité des prononcés de la Cour internationale de justice', in: Nicolas Angelet et al. (eds.), *Droit du pouvoir, pouvoir du droit. Mélanges offerts à Jean Salmon*, Bruxelles: Bruylant 2007, p. 729–781.

[20] See e.g. Photini Pazartzis (chapter 13), referring to Judge Lauterpacht's statement that it is the "very essence" of the Court's legal function to consider and answer a variety of legal questions in order to reply to the main question. This makes it possible for the Court "to render Judgments and Opinions which carry conviction and clarify the law" (ICJ, *Voting Procedure in Questions Relating to Rights and Petitions concerning the Territory of South West Africa*, Separate Opinion of Judge Lauterpacht, ICJ Reports 1955, p. 92). Discussing the ICJ's pronouncement on *Kosovo*, Pierre Michel Eisemann (chapter 14) points out that with its approach to the identity of the authors of the declaration of independence, the Court did acknowledge that the people living in the territory under discussion always maintain their original power to express their wish towards self-determination.

[21] See in particular the contributions by Theo van Boven (chapter 8), Laurence Boisson de Chazournes and Pieter Jan Kuijper (chapter 5), Mariano Aznar-Gómez (chapter 3) and Teruo Komori (chapter 7).

ever-increasing activities and visibility of civil society and, more recently, also the social media. The trend of humanisation has become so entrenched that it would be difficult to reverse altogether. Nevertheless, there is certainly no reason for complacency. After all, state consent and traditional approaches to sovereignty are often still predominant.[22]

Yet, even in inter-state proceedings not directly dealing with human rights, state sovereignty is not the only relevant principle. Other relevant principles may be effective protection of the environment, the preservation of peace, or preventing irreparable harm to persons. Several of these general interest principles reflect the trend towards humanisation and towards protection of other interests beyond those of individual states.

3. *Fundamental Values of the International Community*

The humanisation of international law is not just a trend, but in itself also a value, a criterion against which to judge the law as it is developing. The same applies to legitimacy.[23] The latter includes a range of criteria such as transparency, accountability, and participation. Participation, in turn, is also important to humanisation. Other criteria, particularly relevant in assessing case law, are consistency, coherence and the careful balancing of flexibility and predictability. These criteria may also be referred to as principles used to assess the state of the law.

The principles of *liberté*, *égalité* and *fraternité* are fundamental values that originated in the French Revolution, but have been argued to apply in different times and places as well, adapted to the specific context, but ideally all three of them in harmony.[24] Equally, values such as democracy, underlying principles like the principle of solidarity[25] and 'umbrella rights', such as the

---

[22] See e.g. André de Hoogh (chapter 10). Nevertheless, as Mariano Aznar-Gómez stresses (chapter 3), such state sovereignty should not be fictitious. Sometimes the international community must step in, while respecting the ultimate sovereignty and human rights of the population concerned. See also Pierre Michel Eisemann (chapter 14), pointing out that the Court's *Kosovo* opinion is not just a matter of a "simple résurgence de la jurisprudence *Lotus*", because, as noted above, it did mean that "nonobstant les structures politiques et les limitations établies – dans un cadre national ou international –, le peuple concerné conservait toujours le pouvoir originaire de manifester sa volonté d'autodétermination, sans être entravé par le droit international". See also Samantha Besson, 'The Authority of international Law – Lifting the State Veil', (2009) 31 *Sydney Law Review*, p. 343.

[23] E.g. in order to uphold internal legitimacy of decisions, it is vital to adhere to principles of procedural fairness.

[24] See Rein Müllerson (chapter 9). See also e.g. Antonio Cassese, 'The Diffusion of Revolutionary Ideas and the Evolution of International Law', in: Antonio Cassese, *The Human Dimension of International Law*, Oxford: Oxford University Press 2008, p. 70–98.

[25] The General Assembly has referred to the principle of solidarity as a fundamental value: see the resolution *Promotion of a Just and Equitable International Order*, A/RES/59/193, 18 March 2005.

right to development, the right to self-determination and the developing right to peace, are clearly interrelated.[26] These are all values of the 'international community'.[27]

Another important fundamental value, on which RtoP appears to be premised, is that of human security. This human security, in turn, is related to the freedom from want and from fear.[28] One non-derogable rule expressing the freedom from fear is the prohibition of torture and cruel treatment. Indeed, the notions of human security underlying RtoP are the opposite of the sort of dehumanised 'security' invoked by those behind the policies of extraordinary rendition, legal black holes and 'waterboarding'. These policymakers make up facts (such as that waterboarding led to discovery of the whereabouts of Osama Bin Laden) to assist in suggestive arguments accusing their opponents of not wishing to protect people against terrorism. Those policymakers (and the media repeating their messages) do not appear to care about what the use of this kind of method does to society, and how it dehumanises everyone involved, and therefore also the law itself.

4. *The Role of Principles in the Evolution of International Law*

Scholars of international law cannot ignore the role of principles when assessing or explaining international legal developments. Of course, principles may take various forms. Moral principles underlie legal principles. Legal principles underlie the development, interpretation and application of rules. Some of these underlying principles may be recognised as general principles of law in the sense of article 38 (1) ICJ Statute.[29]

---

[26] See e.g. the contributions by Mariano Aznar-Gómez (chapter 3) and by Theo van Boven (chapter 8), the latter connecting the principle of solidarity – as expounded by Karel Wellens – with the developing 'right to peace'.

[27] On the distinction between international society and international community, see e.g. Wellens, supra n. 7, p. 7–9. Wellens quotes Pierre-Marie Dupuy's argument that the "international community as a whole" is "la fiction d'une solidarité universelle affirmée a priori, pour inciter les états à agir comme si elle existait vraiment" (i.e. Pierre-Marie Dupuy, 'La communauté internationale. Une fiction?', in: Nicolas Angelet et al. (eds.), *Droit du pouvoir, pouvoir du droit. Mélanges offerts à Jean Salmon*, Bruxelles: Bruylant 2007, p. 396).

[28] See e.g. Theo van Boven (chapter 8).

[29] As already noted in our introduction, general principles of law are often derived from domestic systems, although not always based on a comprehensive examination of the full range of domestic systems worldwide. They can also be "derived from the specific nature of the international community" (e.g. *pacta sunt servanda* and the examples referred to in chapter 1 of this book) and even be "intrinsic to the idea of law and basic to all legal systems" (e.g. the principles of reciprocity and of equality of parties before a tribunal). See Oscar Schachter, *International Law in Theory and Practice*, Dordrecht: Martinus Nijhoff Publishers 1991, chapter IV ('General Principles and Equity'), p. 85. See further e.g. Bruno Simma and Philip Alston, 'The Sources of Human Rights Law: Custom, Jus Cogens and General Principles', (1992) 12 *Australian Yearbook of International Law*, p. 82.

The fact that some general principles of law are based on the 'general conception of law' was famously expressed by the Permanent Court of International Justice: "[I]t is a principle of international law, and even a general conception of law, that any breach of an engagement involves an obligation to make reparation."[30] Other principles assist in legal reasoning and the interpretation of concrete legal norms without themselves constituting such norms. They are nevertheless substantive legal principles applied in treaty interpretation. They can be applied not just with regard to decisions on the merits, but also with regard to procedural decisions. Even if they are referred to as 'procedural principles', their function is nevertheless normative.

Moreover, as mentioned before, courts, scholars and litigants often refer to judicial precedents by invoking 'the principle' or 'the rule'. Quite often, the rulings invoked are rather specific and might be labelled 'rules'. Regularly, a more abstract underlying principle can be discerned that helps explain the rule involved, as the principle of state consent does for the *Monetary Gold* rule.

In addition, there are obviously moral principles that play a role in assessing developments in the law. A case in point is the use of the principle of legitimacy in the assessment of international decision-making. Certain phenomena or trends may be based on, and explained by, underlying moral values, as is the case with the humanisation of international law. The conviction that the fate of human beings should be a central concern in stages of judicial decision-making, also in inter-state cases, is a moral principle that may explain a trend. At the same time it is a moral principle that could be used to *assess* developments in judicial interpretation.'

While international law is never static,[31] the question arises whether the underlying principles themselves are evolving, or whether it is the law that is evolving, in part because of a (renewed) focus on certain firm legal principles. A case in point is RtoP. On the one hand, as noted in the introductory chapter, some might see reason to qualify it as a strikingly new principle of contemporary international law. Yet, it is at the same time a concept that reflects pre-existing principles and propels those to greater prominence.[32]

As was also observed earlier, principles often contain a 'hard core' (e.g. a general principle of law such as *audiatur et altera pars*). However, principles are applied in contexts that change over time, whereby the application of the principle may change, as well as the choice of principle. In fact, this often

---

[30] PCIJ, *Chorzów Factory* (*Germany v. Poland*), Indemnity, PCIJ Reports 1928, Series A, No. 17, p. 29.

[31] Shaw (chapter 12) points out that even international law concerning territory appears to be evolving to some extent. He observes that in *Dispute regarding Navigational and Related Rights (Costa Rica v. Nicaragua)*, Judgment of 13 July 2009, the ICJ "has adopted a rather more flexible approach to the interpretation of boundary treaties than had hitherto been accepted". See also section 6 below.

[32] See e.g. Boisson de Chazournes and Condorelli, supra n. 8.

means that the rules evolve, rather than the underlying principles themselves. Nevertheless, this does not rule out that principles are evolving too; for example, a principle may start out rather diffuse and 'soft', and gradually become more defined.

5. *The Application of Specific Principles and their Bearing on the Humanisation of International Law*

When interpreting international law, inevitably principles are applied, either explicitly or implicitly, and sometimes even unconsciously. These principles express values of the international community. They may play a role in the application, interpretation and development of the law. Obviously they should match the situation.

The function of 'general principles of law' as referred to in article 38 ICJ Statute is to fill gaps in the law. As noted in the introduction to this book, the function of 'principles' in international law is more diverse. Their function is not just to fill gaps in the law itself, but to serve in its interpretation and application.[33]

Equity

One predominant underlying principle is that of equity. Equity surfaces in many contexts, from an equitable international order[34] to equitable representation in the Security Council.[35] The principle of equity might be referred to as an inherent feature of law. Judge Weeramantry discussed several functions of equity. Among others, he related it to general principles of law, as "traced" from positive law universally applied at the domestic level, "through the general feeling of mankind for the requirements of equity and to equity itself". He referred to 'objective justice' or 'equity' as evidenced by the legal conscience worldwide.[36]

It has been pointed out that "[w]e need to distinguish equity as a factor to be taken into account by judicial or arbitral tribunals in particular cases from the use of ideas of equity for the development of principles and rules".[37]

---

[33] See e.g. Malgosia Fitzmaurice, Olufemi Elias and Panos Merkouris (eds.), *Treaty Interpretation and the Vienna Convention on the Law of Treaties: 30 Years On* (Queen Mary Studies in International Law: 1), Leiden-Boston: Martinus Nijhoff Publishers 2010.

[34] Theo van Boven (chapter 8).

[35] Eric Suy (chapter 6).

[36] ICJ, *Maritime Delimitation in the Area between Greenland and Jan Mayen* (*Denmark v. Norway*), 14 June 1993, Separate Opinion of Judge Weeramantry, par. 84.

[37] Oscar Schachter, 'The Nature and Process of Legal Development in International Society', in: Ronald St.J. MacDonald and Douglas M. Johnston (eds.), *The Structure and Process of International Law*, Dordrecht: Martinus Nijhoff Publishers 1989, p. 95.

Procedural and substantive principles are perceived as equitable because they are justified on grounds of fairness and reasonableness.[38]

Stability of boundaries

In his contribution to his volume, Malcolm Shaw speaks of the principle of the 'objectivisation of boundaries'.[39] In turn, this principle is based on the principle of the stability of boundaries. The latter principle "constitutes an overarching postulate of the international legal system". Shaw adds that the principle of objectivisation of boundaries is reinforced by the rule, in treaty[40] and customary law, that a fundamental change of circumstances (*rebus sic stantibus*) may not be invoked as a ground for terminating or withdrawing from a treaty that establishes a boundary. He notes that in practice, the consequence of the application of the principle of the 'objectivisation of boundaries' could be the division of a village. In such case, he notes, one must rely upon the state concerned to pay careful attention to the needs of the inhabitants in the expanded village in question who find themselves on the other side of the boundary line.

Self-determination

In his chapter on the extinction of states, Mariano Aznar-Gómez discusses how states could be considered displaced in their exercise of authority over territory and population to the extent that they no longer control events within their territory. Yet, it is clear from his discussion that such extinction does not diminish the ultimate sovereignty of the population in question. He stresses the right of self-determination, invoking the ICJ's reference to self-determination as "one of the essential principles of contemporary international law". He also points out that the extinction of states does not diminish the applicability of the principle of stability of boundaries either. In addition, he refers to the principle that denies any 'effectiveness' to land occupation by force (*ex iniuria non oritur ius*).

---

[38] Ibid., p. 96.

[39] Shaw (chapter 12). Referring to case law, he gives three examples of rules explained by this overall principle: (1) boundaries agreed on by treaties receive a permanence that the treaty itself does not necessarily enjoy; (2) boundaries are not affected by state succession and (3) the principle of succession to colonial borders, referred to as the general principle of *uti possidetis,* has now been extended beyond the decolonisation context to adopt the internal administrative boundaries as the international boundaries of new states created out of pre-existing independent states. The latter is argued by reference to the Badinter Arbitration Commission (European Community Arbitration Commission of the Peace Conference on Yugoslavia), 11 January 1992, 31 *International Legal Materials*, p. 1499, and 92 *International Law Reports*, p. 171.

[40] See article 62 (2) VCLT.

Solidarity

Another important principle of the international community is the principle of solidarity. Karel Wellens has referred to it as a structural and constitutional principle of international law, because of the function it performs.[41] He describes solidarity as "one of the multifunctional, constituent elements of the concept of justice in public international law".[42] He points out that while the law of coexistence and the law of cooperation still exist and will continue to do so for a long time to come, it must be recognised that "the law of solidarity is here to stay as well and that it is becoming operational".[43]

With regard to solidarity, the General Assembly has pointed out that "global challenges must be managed in a way that distributes costs and burdens fairly, in accordance with basic principles of equity and social justice".[44] The UN Independent Expert on International Solidarity, referring to a questionnaire sent to states, observes that "[i]nternational solidarity is perceived by virtually all respondents as a principle, and by several as a right in international law".[45] He notes that the "integral concept" of sustainable development is particularly relevant when examining the principle of solidarity. It includes "the right to development, common but differentiated responsibilities, inter- and intra-generational equity and constituent principles, such as the precautionary principle".[46]

Boisson de Chazournes has pointed out that RtoP reflects the notion of solidarity and gives legal expression to it.[47] Van Boven has suggested that basic principles of equity and social justice are not just at the root of the fundamental value of solidarity, but also of composite rights such as the right to development and the right to peace.[48] The UN Human Rights Council has approached the development of the right to peace as an emerging right from a perspective of international collective and individual solidarity. Van Boven concludes that "[i]n final analysis, the right to peace not only symbolises but also strengthens solidarity among nations, peoples and human beings. It is universalist and inclusive; it is based on the premise that human rights, security and development must go hand in hand".

[41] Wellens, supra n. 7, and id., 'Solidarity as a Constitutional Principle: Its Expanding Role and Inherent Limitations', in: Ronald St.J. MacDonald and Douglas M. Johnston (eds.), *Towards World Constitutionalism: Issues in the Legal Ordering of The World Community*, Leiden-Boston: Martinus Nijhoff Publishers 2005, p. 775 ff.

[42] Wellens, supra n. 7, p. 7.

[43] Wellens, supra n. 7, p. 42.

[44] United Nations Millennium Declaration, 8 September 2000, par. 6.

[45] *Report to the Human Rights Council of the Independent Expert on Human Rights and International Solidarity, Rudi Muhammad Rizki*, 5 July 2010, A/HRC/15/32, p. 3, par. 6.

[46] Ibid., p. 15, par. 47.

[47] Boisson de Chazournes, supra n. 8, p. 109

[48] Van Boven (chapter 8).

Protecting the environment

Principles protecting values of the international community also include environmental law notions such as sustainable development and precaution, as well as the principle of common but differentiated responsibilities.[49] In *Pulp Mills*, the ICJ accepted the requirement of environmental impact assessment in the context of preventing transboundary environmental damage.[50] Moreover, the Court in fact confirmed Judge Weeramantry's position in *Gabčíkovo* that monitoring should be continuous.[51] The ICJ considered "that an environmental impact assessment must be conducted prior to the implementation of a project. Moreover, once operations have started and, where necessary, throughout the life of the project, continuous monitoring of its effects on the environment shall be undertaken".[52] While the Court did refer to sustainable development, it did not require social impact assessment. In that sense the case does not reflect humanisation.[53] Moreover, strictly speaking, it does not require environmental impact assessment for domestic projects without a third state protesting. Nevertheless, it is clear that the underlying principles do involve the protection of interests beyond those of the state.[54]

Pacta sunt servanda

The fundamental principle of *pacta sunt servanda*[55] plays a crucial role in understanding the obligations of state parties to human rights treaties. As part

---

[49] See e.g. Wellens, supra n. 7, p. 13. See also e.g. Malgosia Fitzmaurice, *Contemporary Issues in International Environmental Law*, Cheltenham: Edward Elgar Publishing 2009.

[50] ICJ, *Pulp Mills on the River Uruguay* (*Argentina v. Uruguay*), Judgment of 20 May 2010.

[51] ICJ, *Gabčíkovo-Nagymaros Project (Hungary/Slovakia)*, Separate Opinion of Judge Weeramantry, ICJ Reports 1997, p. 111–113.

[52] ICJ, *Pulp Mills on the River Uruguay* (*Argentina* v. *Uruguay*), Judgment of 20 May 2010, par. 205.

[53] Clearly, environmental degradation has human rights implications (e.g. with regard to culture, health, livelihood), and the right to be informed, as well as consultation and participation rights, are obviously relevant (and litigated) in the field of human rights. Yet, we would not go as far as to state, as Judge Weeramantry does, that "environmental rights are human rights" (*Gabčíkovo-Nagymaros Project (Hungary/Slovakia)*, Separate Opinion of Judge Weeramantry, ICJ Reports 1997, p. 114). If one takes an eco-centric rather than an anthropocentric approach, a dynamic interpretation can be warranted as well. This is not reserved to the application of human rights obligations alone.

[54] See further Komori (chapter 7). See also ICJ, *Certain Activities Carried out by Nicaragua in the Border Area* (*Costa Rica v. Nicaragua*), Order for provisional measures of 8 March 2011, where, despite the fact that the Court ordered that the personnel of both states should stay clear of the disputed territory, it also allowed Costa Rica to "dispatch civilian personnel charged with the protection of the environment to the disputed territory, including the caño, but only in so far as it is necessary to avoid irreparable prejudice being caused to the part of the wetland where that territory is situated; Costa Rica shall consult with the Secretariat of the Ramsar Convention in regard to these actions, give Nicaragua prior notice of them and use its best endeavours to find common solutions with Nicaragua in this respect".

[55] See also article 26 VCLT.

of their good faith observance of the treaty they committed to, they must recognise the authority of the supervisory body to this treaty, such as the Human Rights Committee (HRC), supervising the International Covenant on Civil and Political Rights (ICCPR). In light of this Committee's function, its decisions have acquired legal authority.[56]

The ICJ has indeed acknowledged the role of treaty bodies made up of independent experts interpreting and applying the provisions of the treaty. It recognised, for instance, the extraterritorial application of the International Covenant on Civil and Political Rights by reference to the case law of the supervisory body to this treaty.[57]

State parties to the Optional Protocol have voluntarily accepted the right of individual complaint of everyone under their jurisdiction claiming to be a victim of acts or omissions by the state, upon exhaustion of domestic remedies. Such an individual complaint procedure, as recognised by the State, must indeed serve a function. Despite the misguiding name ("Views") given to its decisions at the time, in practice they concern judicial decisions determining a legal conflict, by a competent and independent body of experts.[58] Considering the Committee's Views as mere exhortatory remarks would deprive the right of individual complaint of any meaning. Instead, a state party must comply in good faith with its obligations under the Optional Protocol and under the ICCPR itself and respect the Committee's decisions. Indeed, the practice of the HRC indicates that it considers states legally bound to respect and implement its Views.[59] The obligation of good faith compliance with this procedure

---

[56] In its General Comment on Article 2, the HRC pointed out that states parties are required to give effect to the obligations under the ICCPR in good faith, pursuant to "the principle articulated in" article 26 VCLT (HRC, *General Comment No. 31: Nature of the General Legal Obligation Imposed on States Parties to the Covenant* (Article 2), 29 March 2004, par. 3–4). When domestic courts of States that have ratified the ICCPR are dealing with provisions of this treaty, either because the domestic legal system gives them direct effect or because they inform the meaning of domestic legal concepts, they must take into account the decisions and comments of the HRC as the most authoritative interpretation of ICCPR law. See also e.g. HRC, *General Comment No. 33: The Obligations of States Parties under the Optional Protocol to the International Covenant on Civil and Political Rights*, CCPR/C/GC/33, 5 November 2008, par. 12.

[57] ICJ, *Legal Consequences of the Construction of a Wall in the Occupied Palestinian Territory*, Advisory Opinion of 9 July 2004, par. 109–112, as confirmed in *Armed Activities on the Territory of the Congo* (*Congo* v. *Uganda*), judgment of 19 December 2005, par. 180 and 216.

[58] See also Joanna Harrington, 'Punting Terrorists, Assassins and other Undesirables: Canada, the Human Rights Committee and Requests for Interim Measures of Protection', (2003) 48 *McGill Law Journal*, p. 65.

[59] Since 1990, it points out, as part of its Views finding violations, that pursuant to article 2 ICCPR, the state party has undertaken to ensure to all individuals within its territory or subject to its jurisdiction the rights recognised in the Covenant. The state has undertaken as well to provide an effective and enforceable remedy in case a violation has been established. The HRC also wishes to receive from the state party, within 90 days, information about the measures taken to give effect to the Committee's Views. In addition, the Committee requests the state to publish its Views. See e.g. HRC, *Rawle Kennedy v. Trinidad and Tobago*, 26 March 2002; *Silbert Daley v. Jamaica*, 31 July 1998, and *Anthony McLeod v. Jamaica*, 31 March 1998. The HRC has stressed that its monitoring role is an "essential element in the design of the Covenant,

implies that the state is internationally bound to respect the contents of the View. State parties have the legal obligation to implement these Views and to redress the violations found by the Committee.[60] Thus, it is submitted that the obligation to prevent (further) violations, as determined by the Committee, must be respected at minimum. Without this one cannot speak of good faith compliance with the treaty.[61]

Equality before the law

In human rights proceedings involving a state and (groups of) individuals, the principle of equality before the law requires taking into account the factual inequality between the parties, which could be seen as a more concrete principle. It has, for instance, been argued that with regard to the use of provisional measures, the due process principle of taking into account the *de facto* inequality between the parties has also influenced the assessment of jurisdiction, admissibility and immediacy.[62]

Effective protection against irreparable harm to persons

The *Bosnia Genocide* case could be seen as an early recognition of the Responsibility to Protect. Within the confines of its jurisdiction in the case, the ICJ only pronounced itself on the obligation to prevent genocide. Yet, its

which is also directed to securing the enjoyment of the rights". See *General Comment 24 on reservations to the ICCPR or the Optional Protocols*, 4 November 1994, par. 11. It was in 1990 that the HRC created the mandate of a Special Rapporteur for follow-up on Views to monitor the compliance of states parties with its Views. See A/45/40, Vol. II, Annex XI. The HRC further amended its guidelines for the preparation of state party reports under article 40 ICCPR. In these reports, states should provide information on follow-up as well. This information should be provided in addition to the responses as part of the follow-up procedure itself. See *Consolidated Guidelines for State Reports under the ICCPR*, adopted July 1999 and amended October 2000, CCPR/C/66/GUI/Rev.2, 26 February 2001, Guideline F1.

[60] Under international law, such redress includes the obligation to provide the victim of the violation with an effective remedy. This is also an explicit obligation under the ICCPR, where article 2 (3) (a) provides that each state party undertakes to ensure that any person whose rights or freedoms are violated shall have an effective remedy. See *General Comment 31 on the Nature of the General Legal Obligation Imposed on States Parties to the Covenant* (Article 2), 29 March 2004. Moreover, the state party to the Optional Protocol is under an obligation to ensure that similar violations do not occur in the future. In other words, this is the obligation, under international law, of non-repetition of an act declared to have been in violation of an international rule.

[61] See e.g. HRC, *Glenn Ashby v. Trinidad and Tobago*, 21 March 2002: "[H]aving regard to the fact that the representative of the Attorney-General informed the Privy Council that Mr. Ashby would not be executed until all possibilities of obtaining a stay of execution had been exhausted, the carrying out of Mr. Ashby's sentence notwithstanding that assurance constituted a breach of the principle of good faith which governs all States in their discharge of obligations under international treaties, including the Covenant. The carrying out of the execution of Mr. Ashby when the execution of the sentence was still under challenge constituted a violation of article 6, paragraphs 1 and 2, of the Covenant."

[62] See Eva Rieter, *Preventing Irreparable Harm. Provisional Measures in International Human Rights Adjudication*, Antwerp: Intersentia 2010, p. 1097–1103.

treaty interpretation with regard to this obligation does fit within a general trend to interpret treaties involving public interest rules in a manner that is most protective to human beings.[63]

In most inter-state proceedings not involving human rights, the principle of state sovereignty (and in particular state consent) is still important. Yet in human rights adjudication (mostly between an individual and a state, but also inter-state), the principle of effective protection against irreparable harm to persons is predominant. This principle involves protection of the very existence of persons and groups. Indeed, human rights adjudicators (and even the ICJ), alleged victims, NGOs and states appear to have assumed this principle, even if implicitly.[64]

In practice international adjudicators have given 'special treatment' to core human rights, those rights involving the protection of personal integrity and life. The underlying principle is that of protection against irreparable harm. In this context, the principle of effectiveness (the *effet utile* of the human rights treaty) plays a role as well. Moreover, in light of the consistent practice of all adjudicators, it could be argued that the prevention of irreparable harm is not just an underlying principle used in treaty interpretation, but has developed into a general principle of law, which is, as such, binding on states (article 38 (1) (c) ICJ Statute).

One of the current trends in scholarship is to ignore the separate existence of general principles as binding norms and to require the same method of proving their existence as is required for customary international law.[65] However, general principles are mentioned as a separate source of international law not just in the ICJ Statute. They have also been used by other international adjudicators in order to fill gaps that would exist in the law if one would rely on treaty and customary law alone. States are predominant in the development, identification and application of customary rules, while international adjudicators have a much more prominent role in identifying and applying general principles of law. In this respect it is noteworthy that one can now speak of an 'acquis humanitaire' based on the standards of protection that all human rights adjudicators – regional courts and international treaty bodies – have in common.[66]

[63] This observation does not apply to other aspects of the judgment, such as the criteria for complicity in genocide and for choosing forms of reparation.

[64] Rieter, supra n. 62, p. 697–726.

[65] For an elaborate criticism of this trend, see e.g. ICJ, *Pulp Mills on the River Uruguay (Argentina v. Uruguay)*, Separate Opinion by Judge Cançado Trindade, available on <http://www.icj-cij.org/docket/files/135/15885.pdf>.

[66] The term 'acquis humanitaire' was also used by Bruno Simma, 'International Human Rights and General International Law: A Comparative Analysis', in: *Collected Courses of the Academy of European Law*, Dordrecht: Kluwer Law International 1993, p. 173.

6. *Principles Regarding Coherence of International Law*

This section reviews those principles that specifically deal with the question what rules to apply in order to achieve coherence in the various manifestations of public international law. This aim of achieving coherence is partially expressed in article 31 (3) (c) VCLT.[67] The principle of systemic integration refers to "any relevant rules of international law applicable in the relations between the parties" as an element that must be taken into account together with the context when interpreting a treaty provision. A presumption exists of consistency of the text to be interpreted with general international law, unless this would undermine the object and purpose of the system. The aim of increasing coherence in the law is particularly relevant when dealing with public interest rules, to the extent that coherence enhances legitimacy and effectiveness.

The following refers to principles dealing with the question what rules to apply in light of the underlying aim of achieving coherence. This includes taking into account other relevant (case) law; applying by approximation important rules that cannot be applied in full; applying treaties in light of new situations and new legal developments. In addition, this section deals with the relevance of methods of treaty interpretation and with the importance of the overall narrative.

Boisson de Chazournes and Kuijper have referred to the principles of subsidiarity[68] and complementarity that are applied in order to ensure coherence, as well as to legal techniques, such as that of the national margin of appreciation or that of formal equivalence.[69] Moreover, international treaties should cross-reference and adjudicators should take into account other applicable law. This has been referred to as the principle of "soutien mutuel" (mutual supportiveness).[70]

It is to be noted that the supervisory bodies to UN human rights treaties, in particular the Human Rights Committee, have come to be included in the inevitable international judicial cross-referencing, and sometimes indeed in an international judicial dialogue.[71] Their authority with regard to the

---

[67] See generally Teruo Komori (chapter 7).

[68] While the legal principle of subsidiarity is predominant in the ECHR system, the idea, or even the underlying principle, of subsidiarity appears to be more universal and underlies, for instance, the rule on exhaustion of domestic remedies. On a related note, subsidiarity serves as an important legal and political yardstick in the exercise of (non-exclusive) competences in the European Union; cf. article 5 (3) TEU.

[69] Boisson de Chazournes and Kuijper (chapter 5).

[70] Laurence Boisson de Chazournes and Makane Moise Mbengue, 'A Propos de Principe du Soutien Mutuel – Les relations entre le Protocole de Cartagena et les Accords de 'OMC'', (2007) 111 *Revue Générale de Droit International Public*, p. 829–862.

[71] See e.g. Anne-Marie Slaughter, 'A Typology of Transjudicial Communication', (1994) 29 *University of Richmond Law Review* 99, p. 99–135; id., 'A Global Community of Courts', (2003)

interpretation and application of the treaties they supervise can no longer be ignored, as acknowledged also by the International Court of Justice.[72]

Approximate treaty application

In 1956, Hersch Lauterpacht referred to the principle of approximate treaty application as central to public international law: "It is a sound principle of law that whenever a legal instrument of continuing validity cannot be applied literally owing to the conduct of one of the parties, it must, without allowing that party to take advantage of its own conduct, be applied in a way approximating most closely to its primary object. To do that is to interpret and to give effect to the instrument – not to change it."[73]

The Dutch government's Advisory Committee on Issues of Public International Law and its Advisory Council on International Affairs agreed on the application of this principle in order to deal with a humanitarian disaster, when the Security Council becomes deadlocked because of the veto by one of the permanent members.[74] Advisory Committee members Eric Myjer and Karel Wellens argued, moreover, that this principle could only appropriately be applied to justify humanitarian intervention if this intervention were sanctioned by the General Assembly instead. In his contribution to this volume, Myjer suggests another situation of Security Council failure that the General Assembly could help remedy through the principle of approximate treaty application. This is the situation of a state maintaining its continued right of self-defence for several years because the Security Council fails to determine, under article 51 UN Charter, that it has taken the 'necessary measures' to maintain international peace and security. If the Security Council is unable to declare an end to the right of self-defence, could not the General Assembly do so based on this principle?[75]

---

44 *Harvard International Law Journal*, p. 191–219; Irit Weiser, 'Undressing the Window: Treating International Human Rights Law Meaningfully in the Canadian Commonwealth System', (2004) 37 *University of British Columbia Law Review*, p. 1–34.

[72] ICJ, *Legal Consequences of the Construction of a Wall in the Occupied Palestinian Territory*, Advisory Opinion of 9 July 2004, par. 109–112, as confirmed in *Armed Activities on the Territory of the Congo* (*Congo* v. *Uganda*), judgment of 19 December 2005, par. 180 and par. 216. More recently, see ICJ, *Case concerning Ahmadou Sadio Diallo* (*Republic of Guinea v. Democratic Republic of the Congo*), Judgment of 30 November 2010, par. 66 and par. 77.

[73] ICJ, *Admissibility of Hearings of Petitioners by the Committee on South West Africa*, Advisory Opinion of 1 June 1956, Separate Opinion of Sir Hersch Lauterpacht, ICJ Reports 1956, p. 46.

[74] In ICJ *Gabčíkovo-Nagymaros Project (Hungary/Slovakia)*, Judgment of 25 September 1997, ICJ Reports 1997, p. 7, par. 75 the ICJ pointed out that 'if such a principle existed, it could by definition only be employed within the limits of the treaty in question'.

[75] Myjer (chapter 4). It could even hold an emergency special session under its 'Uniting for Peace' resolution to request the International Court of Justice to give an advisory opinion on a point of law, for instance, regarding the issue of the 'necessary measures' criterion. Myjer notes that the ICJ would thereby "perform its creative supervisory function". On the cautious approach of the ICJ, see Photini Pazartzis (chapter 13).

Inter-temporal law

When examining older treaties, but also acts that took place a long time ago, questions arise as to what law to apply: the law contemporaneous to these treaties and acts or the law as it has evolved. The principle of contemporaneity calls for an appreciation of facts in light of the meaning attached to the terms used at the time of conclusion of the treaty and in light of international law as applicable at that time. What then about the evolution of the law?

In the approach of arbitrator Max Huber in the famous *Island of Palmas* Arbitration (1928), involving title to land, a distinction is made between the creation of rights and the continued existence of these rights. In other words, his doctrine of inter-temporal law is not just based on contemporaneity, but also on the evolution of the law: a "juridical fact must be appreciated in the light of the law contemporary with it", but the existence of the right, its continued manifestation "shall follow the conditions required by the evolution of the law".[76]

The issue of inter-temporal law is most commonly associated with boundary treaties. Shaw discusses how boundary treaty interpretation is markedly different from the interpretation of other treaties because of the great importance attached to the stability of boundaries. This means a greater attachment to contemporaneity, to what the states wanted at the time of conclusion. What it comes down to is that international adjudicators are more likely to take an 'original intent' of the drafters approach when they interpret such treaties. At the same time, Shaw points out, again in the context of boundary dispute cases, that there are situations in which the common intention of the parties, upon conclusion of a treaty, may be presumed to have been to give its terms a meaning capable of making allowance for such things as developments in international law.[77] He refers to the 2009 judgment in *Dispute regarding Navigational and Related Rights* (*Costa Rica v. Nicaragua*), in which the ICJ declared that "where the parties have used generic terms in a treaty, the parties necessarily having been aware that the meaning of the terms was likely to evolve over time, and where the treaty has been entered into for a very long period or is 'of continuing duration', the parties must be presumed, as a general rule, to have intended those terms to have an evolving meaning".[78]

Views differ as to the extent of the doctrine of inter-temporal law and its applicability to human rights law.[79] It is clear, however, that human rights

[76] Arbitrator Max Huber, *Island of Palmas* case (Netherlands, United States), (1928) 2 *Reports of International Arbitral Awards*, p. 845.

[77] See chapter 12.

[78] ICJ, *Dispute regarding Navigational and Related Rights (Costa Rica* v. *Nicaragua)*, Judgment of 13 July 2009, par. 66. See also ICJ, *Gabčíkovo-Nagymaros Project (Hungary/Slovakia)*, Judgment of 25 September 1997, Separate Opinion of Judge Weeramantry, p. 113–115.

[79] See e.g. Paul Tavernier, 'Relevance of the Inter-temporal Law', in: James Crawford, Alain Pellet and Simon Olleson (eds.), *The Law of International Responsibility*, Oxford: Oxford

adjudicators generally deal with claims of (on-going) human rights violations by applying their treaty as a 'living instrument' in light of 'present-day conditions'.[80] Moreover, the ICJ has equally taken an evolutionary approach to applying certain rules, as can been seen, among others, in its Advisory Opinion regarding Namibia.[81]

Methods of treaty interpretation

Legal principles assisting in the interpretation of international law should be distinguished from the 'canons' of treaty interpretation; grammatical/textual; contextual; purposive; dynamic; historical, etc. At the same time, there is an obvious relation between applying legal principles and choosing a certain method of treaty interpretation. The predominance of certain substantive principles in the minds of the members of the adjudicatory body may result in the emphasis on certain methods of interpretation.

A purposive method of treaty interpretation appears to be warranted when interpreting substantive and procedural law with regard to human rights or the protection of other general interests of the international community. Precisely the principle of effective protection would lead to a dynamic approach rather than one reflecting the original intent of the drafters as derived from the *travaux*.[82] Nonetheless, an approach that is so dynamic that it ignores the intention of the parties as derived from the text, in its context, will fail to meet other principles of international law, such as the principle that states are only bound to rules to which they previously consented. While a trend can be perceived in international law to give priority to the principle of effective protection over the principle of state consent, this does not mean that the principle of consent can be ignored altogether. Importantly, when assessed based on the moral principle of legitimacy, judicial decisions that ignore the principle of consent altogether and do so in a manner that is too sudden and unexpected, are likely to fail. The requirements of internal legitimacy will not be met, because the adjudicator will not be able to show an existing foundation for its decision, indicating a lack of motivation. Moreover, the decision will lack predictability for states. External legitimacy will likely be undermined as well, because states will insist on the principle of consent and now

University Press 2010, p. 397–403, and Rosalyn Higgins, 'Time and the Law: International Perspectives on an Old Problem', in: Rosalyn Higgins, *Themes and Theories, Selected Essays, Speeches, and Writings in International law*, Oxford: Oxford University Press 2009, p. 875–892.

[80] For the obvious reference to the European Court of Human Rights, see *Tyrer v. UK*, judgment of 25 April 1979, par. 31.

[81] ICJ, *Legal Consequences for States of the Continued Presence of South Africa in Namibia (South West Africa) notwithstanding Security Council Resolution 276, Advisory Opinion*, ICJ Reports 1971, p. 31, par. 53.

[82] See also article 32 VCLT.

have an easy argument, as they will be able to dispute internal legitimacy. In the end, this may undermine the effective protection of the rights included in the human rights treaty. Clearly, adjudicators sometimes have to be bold, precisely in order to ensure effective protection, but then they should pay particular attention to careful motivation.

Gaps and cautionary tales

Ultimately, what is central to the application of international law is the choice of underlying principles, on the one hand, and the manner in which the facts are presented, on the other. Indeed, next to principles, stories of actual conflict, and how they are told, determine how rules are applied.

In addition, there will be a continued need for allegoric stories as well, triggering reflections on principles and their application in practice. Egbert Myjer and Peter Kempees, for instance, wrote a 'cautionary tale' on maintaining the achievements of the European human rights system: 'Jack and the Solemn Promise'.[83]

"Once upon a time there was a gap…", Roger O'Keefe opened his speech at the 2010 Biennual Conference of the European Society of International Law. The "Comptroller-General for the Complete System was performing his quarterly 'stress test' on the normative integrity of the international legal system" when he discovered this existential gap in the law. This resulted in "fevered speculation" in the international legal community. The ILC appointed a Special Rapporteur on Gaps and Silences in the Law. In his 32nd report, he provisionally concluded that "while there may or may not be gaps in international law, there are never silences".[84] Obviously, we need more stories such as these to put all the principles in perspective.[85]

7. *In Conclusion*

In conclusion, one might wonder whether the application of the above principles reflects the overall trend of humanisation or not. *Pacta sunt servanda* and principles of equity, as predominant principles of international law, appear to be neutral to humanisation. Moreover, principles of environmental law do not, as such, have a bearing on humanisation, but their application does display an awareness of the importance of the protection of interests beyond those of the state.

---

[83] Egbert Myjer and Peter Kempees, *Jack and the Solemn Promise. A Cautionary Tale*, Nijmegen: Wolf Legal Publishers 2010.

[84] Roger O'Keefe, 'Once upon a time there was a gap …', Speech at the 2010 Biennual Conference of the European Society of International Law (available on <http://www.ejiltalk.org/author/rokeefe>), p. 6.

[85] As with most stories, it is recommended to read them in full.

Would it be possible to perceive the trend of humanisation in the application of the principle of the objectivisation of boundaries? Just pointing out to the states concerned that they should take into account the needs of the inhabitants[86] is not exactly a true sign of humanisation. Nevertheless, the underlying principle of the stability of boundaries could itself be seen as necessary to prevent constant disruption and challenges that could lead to armed conflict. Maintaining stability could in that sense be seen as contributing to ensuring peace. Moreover, in its use of provisional measures in border conflict cases, the ICJ has taken into account the risk to the lives of people living in border areas, even if this was not the main concern of the parties themselves.[87] This indicates a measure of humanisation in international adjudication.

The application of the principle of solidarity is an obvious example of humanisation. The same applies to the application of the principle of self-determination, which has by now become an explicit rule of *ius cogens*. The fact that human rights adjudicators have applied the due process principle of equality before the law by taking into account the *de facto* inequality is also an obvious sign of humanisation. Finally, the principle of effective protection against irreparable harm to persons clearly underlies the decisions by a range of international adjudicators, including, to some extent, the ICJ.

Overall then, it is clear that several of the principles discussed in this volume reflect the humanisation of international law Karel Wellens so often refers to in his teachings. In addition, the principles determining what the relevant rules of public international law are in a given situation indeed contribute to the aim of achieving coherence in international law. The question remains nonetheless how the international community can translate these principles into practice in a manner that truly serves humanity, as well as the planet. This requires further analysis with regard to the legitimacy of the actions (and omissions) of states and international organisations, as well as of the international 'judiciary'. The research agendas of scholars in this area, including Karel Wellens and the contributors to the volume published in his honour, undoubtedly remain full for years to come.

---

[86] As Shaw noted (chapter 12), in its judgment in the case *Land and Maritime Boundary Between Cameroon and Nigeria* (*Cameroon v. Nigeria*), Judgment of 10 October 2002, p. 370 (par. 107) and p. 373–4 (par. 173), all that could be done by the ICJ in its judgment on the merits was to point out the responsibility of the parties to "find a solution to any resultant problems, with a view to respecting the rights and interests of the local population".

[87] See ICJ, *Frontier Dispute* case (*Burkina Faso v. Mali*), Order of 10 January 1986, and *Land and Maritime Boundary Between Cameroon and Nigeria* (*Cameroon v. Nigeria*), Order of 15 March 1996. See Rosalyn Higgins,'Interim Measures for the Protection of Human Rights', (1997) 36 *Columbia Journal of Transnational Law*, p. 91–108. See also e.g. ICJ, *Request for Interpretation of the Judgment of 15 June 1962 in the case concerning the Temple of Preah Vihear (Cambodia* v. *Thailand*), Order of 18 July 2011.

INDEX